The ALCHEMICAL TRADITION
in the Late Twentieth Century

The ALCHEMICAL TRADITION
in the Late Twentieth Century

edited by
RICHARD GROSSINGER

Io
31

North Atlantic Books
Berkeley, California

The Alchemical Tradition in the Late Twentieth Century

Copyright © 1979, 1991 by Richard Grossinger
Copyrights of individual pieces to their respective authors
ISBN 1-55643-133-3
All rights reserved

Published by
North Atlantic Books
2800 Woolsey Street
Berkeley, California 94705

This is issue #31 in the *Io* series

Front Cover Art: Solonius, Siren, 18th century
Back Cover Art: Anonymous, King and Queen in Solution, 14th Century
Cover Design by Paula Morrison
Printed in the United States of America

A previous edition, including several of the works republished here, was issued under the title: *Alchemy: Pre-Egyptian Legacy, Millennial Promise* in 1979.

The Alchemical Tradition in the Late Twentieth Century is sponsored by the Society for the Study of Native Arts and Sciences, a nonprofit educational corporation whose goals are to develop an educational and crosscultural perspective linking various scientific, social, and artistic fields; to nurture a holistic view of arts, sciences, humanities, and healing; and to publish and distribute literature on the relationship of mind, body, and nature.

Library of Congress Cataloging in Publication Data
Main entry under title:

Alchemy: pre-Egyptian legacy, millennial promise
    (Io, 31)
    1. Alchemy—Addresses, essays, lectures.
I. Grossinger, Richard, 1944-   . II. Series.
QD26, A57 1983   540'.1'12   82-22399
ISBN 1-55643-133-3

CONTENTS

Zosimos: On Divine Virtue 7
Paracelsus: The Philosophy of Theophrastus Concerning
    the Generation of the Elements 11
Paracelsus: The Philosophy Addressed to the Athenians 18
Paracelsus: The Economy of Minerals 22
Diane di Prima: Paracelsus: An Appreciation 26
Basilius Valentinus: The Triumphal Chariot of Antimony 34
Charles Stein: Reading Basil Valentine in a Mountain Cabin 48
Thomas Vaughan: Lumen de Lumine 51
Edward Kelly: The Theatre of Terrestrial Astronomy 56
Janus Lacinius: A Form and Method of Perfecting
    Base Metals 69
Archibald Cockren: Alchemy Rediscovered and Restored 75
Rudolf Hauschka: The Vital Properties of the Metals 79
Robert Kelly: An Alchemical Journal 90
Diane di Prima: 14° Sagittarius
    Minnesota Morning Ode 120
Harvey Bialy: Poem 122
Charles Stein: Three Notes on a Magnetic Sense 124
Helen Ruggieri: The Alchemists Wedding
        Ischua
        Shadow
        Stone Birth 127
Robert Kelly: The Alchemist 130
Gerrit Lansing: The Heavenly Tree Grows Downward
    In Northern Earth 134
Jed Rasula: The Bath 135
Diane Furtney: Pairs 136
Charles Poncé: The Alchemical Light 172
Edward Whitmont: Non-Causality as a Unifying Principle
    of Psychosomatics—Sulphur 183
Jacques de Langre: Seasalt and Alchemy 194
Robert Duncan: The H.D. Book: Chapter 5 of Part I 203
                              Chapter 6 of Part I 223
Richard Grossinger: Alchemy: pre-Egyptian Legacy,
    Millennial Promise 240

Illustrations

Robert Fludd: Creation (17th Century) 139-143
Sapientia veterum philosophorum sive doctrina eorundum
      de summe et universali medicina (18th Century) 144-153
Charles Stein (20th Century) 154
Ruth Terrill: Self Portrait (20th Century) 155
Philip Terry Borden: Male and Female Principles;
      cover of original |Io| Alchemy Issue (20th Century) 156
Charles Stein: Qabbalistic Creation (20th Century) 157
Robert Fludd: Tetragrammaton (17th Century) 158
Anonymous, Bibleoteca Mediceo-Laurenziana, Florence:
      King and Queen in Solution *[see also back cover]*
      (14th Century) 159
Aurora Consurgens: Androgyne (14th Century)......................... 160
Rosarium philosophorum: Green Lion (16th Century).................... 161
Theodoros Pelecanos: Ouroboros (15th Century) 162
Carole Sivin: Chinese Charms and Seals (20th Century) 163-167
Ruth Terrill: Kundalini (20th Century)................................... 168
Pretiosissimum Donum Dei: Solution, Nigredo
      (17th Century) 169-170
Ruth Terrill: Over the Edge (20th Century) 171

Zosimos

ON DIVINE VIRTUE

PRAXIS A

1/ The composition of the waters, and the movement, and the growth, and the removal and restitution of bodily nature, and the splitting off of the spirit from the body, and the fixation of the spirit on the body are not operations with natures alien one from the other, but, like the hard bodies of metals and the moist fluids of plants, are One Thing, of One Nature, acting upon itself. And in this system, of one kind but many colors, is preserved a research of all things, multiple and various, subject to lunar influence and measure of time, which regulates the cessation and growth by which the One Nature transforms itself.

2/ And saying these things, I slept, and I saw a certain sacrificing priest standing before me and over an altar which had the form of a bowl. And that altar had fifteen steps going up to it. Then the priest stood up and I heard from above a voice say to me, "I have completed the descent of the fifteen steps and the ascent of the steps of light. And it is the sacrificing priest who renews me, casting off the body's coarseness, and, consecrated by necessity, I have become a spirit." And when I had heard the voice of him who stood in the altar formed like a bowl, I questioned him, desiring to understand who he was. He answered me in a weak voice saying, "I am Ion, Priest of the Adytum, and I have borne an intolerable force. For someone came at me headlong in the morning and dismembered me with a sword and tore me apart, according to the rigor of harmony. And, having cut my head off with the sword, he mashed my flesh with my bones and burned them in the fire of the treatment, until, my body transformed, I should learn to become a spirit. And I sustained the same intolerable force." And even as he said these things to me and I forced him to speak, it was as if his eyes turned to blood and he vomited up all his flesh. And I saw him as a mutilated image of a little man and he was tearing at his flesh and falling away.

3/ And being afraid I woke and considered, "Is this not the composition of the waters?" I thought that I was right and fell asleep again. And I saw the same altar in the shape of a bowl and water bubbled at the top of it, and in it were many people endlessly. And there was no one whom I might question outside of the bowl. And I went up to the altar to view the spectacle. And I saw a little man, a barber, whitened with age, and he said to me, "What are you looking at?" I answered that I wondered at the boiling water and the men who were burning but remained alive. And he answered me saying, "The spectacle which you see is at once the entrance and the exit and the process." I questioned him further. "What is the nature of the process?" And he answered saying, "It is the place of the practice called the embalming. Men wishing to obtain virtue enter here and, fleeing the body, become spirits." I said to him, "And are you a spirit?" And he answered, saying, "Both a spirit and a guardian of spirits." As he was saying these things to me and the boiling increased and the people wailed, I saw a copper man holding a lead tablet in his hand. He spoke aloud, looking at the tablet, "I counsel all those in mortification to become calm and that each take in his hand a lead tablet and write with his own hand and that each bear his eyes upward and open his mouth until his grapes be grown." The act followed the word and the master of the house said to me, "Have you stretched your neck up and have you seen what is done?" And I said that I had and he said to me, "This man of copper whom you have seen is the sacrificial priest and the sacrifice and he who vomited out his own flesh. To him was given authority over the water and over those men in mortification."

4/ And when I had seen these visions, I woke again and said to myself, "What is the cause of this vision? Is this not the white and yellow water, boiling, sulphurous, divine?" And I found that I understood well. And I said that it was good to speak and good to hear and good to give and good to receive and good to be poor and good to be rich. And how does the Nature learn to give and to receive? The copper man gives and the water-stone receives; the thunder gives the fire that flashed from it. For all things are woven together and all things are taken apart and all things are mingled and all things combined and all things mixed and all things separated and all things are moistened and all things are dried and all things bud and all things blossom in the altar shaped like a bowl. For each, by method and by weight of the four elements, the interlacing and separation of the whole is accomplished for no bond can be made without method. The method is natural, breathing in and breathing out, keeping the orders of the method, increasing and decreasing. And all things by division and union come together in a harmony, the method not being neglected, the Nature is transformed. For the Nature, turning on itself, is changed. And the Nature is both the nature of the virtue and the bond of the world.

5/ And, so that I need not write to you of many things, friend, build a temple of one stone, like ceruse, like alabaster, like marble of Proconnesus in appearance, having neither beginning nor end in its building. Let it have within, a pure stream of water glittering like sunlight. Notice on what side the entry to the temple is and take your sword in hand and seek the entry. For thin-mouthed is the place where the opening is and a serpent lies by it guarding the temple. First seize him in your hands and make a sacrifice of him. And having skinned him, cut his flesh from his bones, divide him, member from member, and having brought together again the members and the bones, make them a stepping stone at the entry to the temple and mount upon them and go in, and there you will find what you seek. For the priest whom you see seated in the stream gathering his color, is not a man of copper. For he has changed the color of his nature, and become a man of silver whom, if you wish, after a little time, you will have as a man of gold.

PRAXIS B

1/ Then, again wishing to ascend the seven steps and to behold the seven mortifications and, as it happened, one day only did I ascend the way. Retracing my steps, I thereupon ascended the way many times. And on returning, I could not find the way, and becoming discouraged, not seeing how to get out, I fell asleep. And I saw in my sleep a certain little man, a barber, wearing a red robe and royal garments, and he stood outside of the place of the mortifications and said, "What are you doing, Man?" I said to him, "I stand here because I have missed every road and am lost." He said, "Follow me." And going out, I followed him. And being near to the place of the mortifications, I saw the little barber man leading me and he cast into the place of the mortifications and his whole body was consumed by fire.

2/ Seeing this, I fled and trembled from the fear and I woke and said to myself, "What is this that I have seen?" And again I took thought and determined that this barber man is the man of copper. It is necessary for the first step to throw him into the place of the mortifications. My soul again desired to ascend—the third step also. And again, alone, I went along the way, and as I drew near the place of the mortifications, again I got lost, losing sight of the path, and stood, out of my mind.

3/ And again I saw an old man of hair so white my eyes were blinded by the whiteness. His name was Agathodaemon. And the white old man, turning, looked on me for a whole hour. And I asked him, "Show me the right way." He did not turn toward me but hastened to go on the right way. And going and coming in this manner he quickly effected the altar. As I went up to the altar I saw the white old man. He was cast into the mortifications. O Creator-gods of celestial natures—straightway the flames took him up entire, which is a terrible story, my brother. For from the great energy of the mortifications his eyes became full with blood. And I questioned him saying, "Why do you lie there?" And he opened his mouth and said, "I am the man of lead and I am withstanding an intolerable force." And then I woke out of fear and sought in myself the cause of this fact. And again I reflected and said to myself, "I understand well that thus must one cast out the lead—truly the vision is concerning the combination of liquids.

PRAXIS G

And again I knew the theophany and again the sacred altar and I saw a certain priest clothed in white celebrating those same terrible mysteries and I said, "Who is this?" And answering he said to me, "This is the priest of the Adytum. He wishes to put blood into the bodies, to make the eyes clear, and to raise up the dead. And again I fell asleep for a while and while I was mounting the fourth step I saw one with a sword in his hand coming out of the east. And I saw another behind him, holding a disk, white and shining and beautiful to behold. And it was called the meridian of the Sun and I approached the place of the mortifications and the one who held the sword said to me, "Cut off his head and sacrifice his meat and muscles part by part so that first the flesh may be boiled according to the method and that he might then suffer the mortifications." And waking, I said, "I understand well that these matters concern the liquids of the art of the metals." And the one who held the sword said "You have fulfilled the seven steps beneath." And the other said at the same time as the casting out of the lead by all the liquids, "The Work is completed."

Paracelsus

THE PHILOSOPHY OF THEOPHRASTUS CONCERNING THE GENERATIONS OF THE ELEMENTS

BOOK THE FIRST

Concerning the Element of Air

TEXT I.

In the beginning, Iliaster, which is nothing, was divided, thus giving and arranging the four elements. It was even as the seed from which springs the stem. What the seed gives forth does not receive in the same form into itself again. But this Iliaster again attracts to itself the four elements. Thus, that is dissolved and becomes what it was before the four elements were produced, provided only one year of the world has elapsed. The four elements are the growth produced from the Iliaster. And the seed does not give those very things from which the infant is produced after this year of the world; but the four elements are both mothers and daughters. Of this family nothing is found surviving after death; but its end is the same as its origin; and so whatever is in it perishes at the same time. Although another world follows after, which is the daughter of this one in name, still, it is not so in form, in essence, or the like. For this will not pass away, but will remain like the soul, which is indeed made and created but not mortal. Such is also the lot of this world.

TEXT II.

Now, it is quite certain that the Eternal Father, who is not only the father of His own Son, but also of all things, mortal and immortal, permanent and transitory, blessed and damned together, created *Domor*, that is, heaven and earth, the firmament and the water, to which He also gave His own Divine will. We will not further discuss this subject here, but the same things can be read in the Paramira. He formed the natural from the non-natural. From that which had never perceived any nature, He produced another nature, and following that nature He willed that yet another nature should be produced, whilst a year revolves, wherein His majesty Himself carries on the Divine rule, which man now moderates and possesses. Yet these primal natures differ, so that from the earth springs the pear-tree, from the sand the thistle, from the water cachimiae, from the sky chaos, and from the fire snow. But seeing how wonderful these things are, and how unlike they seem to the first source from which they sprang, we ought to make it a matter of knowledge and of philosophy, that the element of water is not water only, but a mineral as well; that the element of earth is not earth only, but a grape as well, and so with the rest. For that philosophy in vain which gives it out that the earth is an element, indeed, but not a nut, or that fire is an element, but not snow. So, too, those who say that the four elements exist in all and everything, advance mere nonsense.

TEXT III.

The earth is an element, and whatever is produced from it. So is the water and all produced therefrom. So then that is an element which produces. And an element is a mother, and there are four of them, air, fire, water, earth. From these four matrices everything in the whole world is produced. And the speech is inconsiderate of those who assert that an element is simply endowed with a complexion, warm, dry, cold, moist, or a compound of these. All these things are in all these four elements. You can understand it thus: the earth is cold and dry, cold and moist, warm and dry, warm and moist. This is how matters stand. Whatever thing which is warm and dry grows out of the earth, grows out of that which in the earth is warm and dry. Whatever is or is produced cold and moist, is produced from that in the earth which is of a similar nature. So also from fire four complexions proceed. Snow, for example, from that in the fire which is cold and dry; and lightning from that in the fire which is warm and dry. It is the same with the other two elements. I would have you then, at this point, before all to be advised not to determine the elements according to their complexions, but according to their forms, that is, what are the four matrices which they have within them. The earth is material, clayey, conglutinous. Such it is whether it be warm, dry, cold, or moist. The water is humid, sensible, tangible, but not corporeally, not materially. And such is the element, whether it be cold or warm. The fire is a firmament, and is the element of fire, though it be in one place warm, in another cold. The air is a heaven which comprises all things, and is moist, warm, cold, or dry, as shall hereafter be set forth.

TEXT IV.

Now, in order to advance towards the established principle with regard to the elements, understand this. The Iliaster was originally distributed into four parts—the air, which is a heaven embracing all things; fire, which is a firmament producing day and night, cold and heat; earth, which affords fruits of all kinds and a solid foundation for our feet; and water from whence are given forth all minerals and half the means of nutriment for living things.

These nutriments are twofold, one found in air and fire, the other in earth and water. The two former nourish us as if spiritually and invisibly; the two latter materially and corporeally. These four elements are divided into two classes. One is constituted of air and fire; the other of earth and water. The air sustains fire, the earth water. Air and fire hold water and earth; while these two hold air and fire. So then all things were created in due order, that the one might support, seek for, and nourish the other. Thus the Iliaster was divided into one *domor,* of which there are two globules, an outer and an inner, each enclosed with two elements.

Beyond is nothing, so far as we know. Within is what we see, and touch, and what the light of nature suggests to us. He who created these things is not among us, but dwells without us. But He who was begotten of Him is amongst us. Still we must not philosophise further concerning the four elements than Nature teaches and points the way for us.

TEXT V.

In the beginning the body of the four elements was founded with that form and amplitude in which the heaven lies extended; and it was made corruptible or perishible so far as the air surrounds it. There was the throne of God and the centre of His Kingdom, from which centre the world was created, but so that it should be something mortal and perishable created by God. To rightly understand this you must know that from that centre the world arose and was made material. On this seat Christ hung from the cross; on this seat sat the prophets; it is the footstool of God. Here, therefore, material and corporeal things are made God, and His work, the centre of His Kingdom, and His throne.

It should be known, then, at the outset, and before the philosophy itself is unfolded, that God has made the centre of His heaven, and even Himself, perishable. For as corporeally He is called the Son, so the world is His house. But although it be thus made and created, still we must believe that it will not perish as it was produced. Of man the heart will endure: of the world the flower will be permanent.

TEXT VI.

As to the manner in which God created the world, take the following account. He originally reduced it to one body, while the elements were developing. This body He made up of three ingredients, Mercury, Sulphur, and Salt, so that these three should constitute one body. Of these three are composed all the things which are, or are produced, in the four elements. These three have in themselves the force and the power of all perishable things. In them lie hidden the mineral, day, night, heat, cold, the stone, the fruit, and everything else, even while not yet formed. It is even as with wood which is thrown away and is only wood, yet in it are hidden all forms of animals, of plants, of instruments, which any one who can carve what else would be useless, invents and produces. So the body of Iliaster was a mere trunk, but in it lay hidden all herbs, waters, gems, minerals, stones, and chaos itself, which things the supreme Creator alone carved and fashioned most subtly, having removed and cast away all that was extraneous. First of all He produced and separated the air. This being formed, from the remainder issues forth the other three elements, fire, water, earth. From these He afterwards took away the fire, while the other two remained, and so on in due succession.

TEXT VII.

The four fields, therefore, having been in this way set apart and separated, there remained also four storehouses for keeping the four elements, namely, the hot, the cold, the moist, the dry. Each of these was far from being unimportant. First the air was arranged; afterwards the fire; then the earth; and, lastly, the water, in the following way: From the air proceeded chaos, the throne, the chain, the foundation. From the fire, night and day, the sun and the moon. From the earth, trees and herbs, grasses and fruits. From the water, minerals and stones. Of these the succession was so arranged that from the superfluity was continually produced something else. For instance, from the Iliaster of the earth beech wood was extracted and the wood of apples removed. Each was disposed in its own place; nothing being corrupted or intermixed. In water gold was separated from the rest of the metals, and afterwards the others also were removed in turn. In the fire, the cold withdrew from the heat, the light from the darkness. In the air, chaos was set in order for preserving all things, and for separating earth from heaven. These four Iliastri having been created and arranged according to elements, that is, according to the matrices of their fruits, the air was prepared before all else; then afterwards the fire. These two were linked together in union. Afterwards the earth, too, and the water, being separated from the two former, were joined in one. These are now conjoined Iliastri. The air is by itself, and the fire. In like manner, also, the earth and the water.

Thus it was that God made the material centre of His throne, and afterwards sundered it in three primal elements, from which constantly emerges everything that is born. Without these three, nothing in the four Iliastri can grow. But while they grow they are elements, and so, moreover, they lose their name of Iliastri and are called elements.

TEXT VIII.

These four elements were sundered into their own places and seats, so that none of them should be mixed. All these were removed, just as a sculptor when making a statue throws away what does not suit the intended image. So there are four elements, but only three primary ones; three in the air, three in the fire, three in the earth, and three in the water. Everywhere there is only a single triad of the primaries, that is, one Mercury in all, one Sulphur in all, one Salt in all. Yet they differ in their properties. Whatever is growing, herb, leaf, grass, or the like, was relegated to the earth. Whatever is mineral withdrew into the water. Whatever is warm, cold, day, night, betook itself to the fire. Whatever is air spread itself out over chaos. And all these three are one, each in itself. It is just as when a stone is divided into four parts, and out of one is made a statue, out of another a pitcher, out of a third some other kind of a vessel, and out of the fourth a milestone; yet all are stones, nay, all one stone, though divided into four portions.

Of these Iliastri there are four, and no more; these being sufficient. So God disposed the world in a quaternary. He was satisfied with this number, though He could have made eight parts. One portion of nutriment He conferred on the air, a second on the fire, a third on the earth, a fourth on the water. Nowhere was there any deficiency.

And now it is further necessary that in the course of our philosophising we should go on to treat of these four under the name of elements, to tell of their possibilities and performances, and to state in what they excel. We will begin with the air, and conclude our philosophy with the water, adding such explanations as the nature of insensible things requires.

TEXT IX.

The element of the air was appointed for no other purpose than to be the abode of the other three, each to be conserved, as it were, within its close in the following way. The air encloses in itself every mortal thing, and shuts it off from what is immortal, as a wall divides a city from the fields. It strengthens the world and keeps it together, as a dam does a marsh. And just as there is nothing in an egg to one who looks at it from without, or outside the egg, which agrees with what is inside, so the sky is a shell dividing heaven and earth, just as the egg-shell separates the egg from what is outside it. The air, again, is like a skin in which is stored up a body, the whole world, to wit, and wherein the earth is contained and preserved. The air, then, is this sky, a skin, or egg-shell, or wall, or mound, beyond which nothing can burst through, and within which nothing can break in. Moreover the air is breath, from which all draw their life. This is truly air itself, and puts forth the air which nourishes the four elements, and at the same time sustains the life of man. Without it none could live. Without this no element could advance, no wind could blow, no rain or snow could fall, no sun could shine, no summer could flourish, no water could flow, no earth could sustain. All this force proceeds from the air, and is attracted by the four elements. For as the lungs every moment inhale air, so does the earth, while the water and the fire each do the very same thing. That is a palpable error which lays it down that winds are caused by the air. They burst in upon us like poison, not as a means of life. The first element brings air, but fire gives the winds.

TEXT X.

From this same element, too, flows forth a power by which fire is joined to the air, so that it may not fall down. Thus it is like a chain which, without materiality or visibility, holds together and binds. This is does by means of its chaos, which it inserts between the pellicle and the earth. There is also a middle space extending from heaven to earth, in which are balanced the fire, the earth, and the water. And as the chicken is sustained in the egg by its albumen without touching the shell, so chaos sustains the globe and prevents it from tottering. This chaos is invisible, though it appears of a slight green tint. It is an intangible albumen, having the power and property of sustaining, so that the earth shall not fall from its position. As the chick in its albumen, so this globe of earth and water is balanced in the air. As a ship is borne up by the ocean, so is this globe by the air. It is one vast and marvellous albumen which invisibly supports the globe of earth and water. It bears up even the firmament itself, which is placed in it as the seed of the cucumber is placed in its mucilage. And as every morsel of flesh lies in its own liquid, or the generating seed in the sperm, so the stars lie in this albumen, and move therein like a bird in its flight. In no other way are they borne up than in what is clear from the illustrations which are named. There is at least only this difference: that the chaos is unlike the albumen or the sperm, in that it is impalpable and extremely subtle. Otherwise, in all its powers and energies it corresponds exactly to those things which have been enumerated.

TEXT XI.

While discussing the powers of this element, it should, moreover, be pointed out that the air and its chaos and the sky exist in a round form which is inherent in them. No one can point out or distinguish what is above or what is below. Let us give an example. If it could be brought about that one should be shut up within an egg, it would be impossible to know which part looked towards the sky and which towards the earth. The rotundity prevents there being any "up" or "down." So we are prisoned within a shell, and do not know which is up and which is down. Walking over the whole world, we look up to the sky, and everywhere there is height, whilst at the same time everywhere there is depth. The cause lies in the rotundity of the globe and of the sky, and thus it is natural to every mortal body that all things grow in a threefold line, and not only man walks, but also trees, veins of metal, and springs take this course. As God created the circle of the globe and the sky, so he founded also the semicircle, the diameter and the meridian—a threefold line—and other similar ones. For in heaven and earth, in fire and water, are found all lines and all circles. Here, too, are the true Geography, Cosmography, and Geometry. By the elementary geography of the air are conserved the structures of the air, that is, the sun and moon, all the stars, the trees of the earth, and other things, as the minerals of the water and the rest. Here, too, beyond a doubt, is found the true basis of all geometry, where man stands like the straight line looking up to heaven. Of this geometry God alone is the artificer, the mason, the geometrician. From this line nothing falls away or emerges, be it water, fire, earth, tree, man, beast. All things tend towards this aërial geometry, which God made and graved as a mason does the statues on a tower.

TEXT XII.

Now, as to the philosophy of the three prime elements, it must be seen how these flourish in the element of air. Mercury, Sulphur, and Salt are so prepared as the element of air that they constitute the air, and make up that element. Originally the sky is nothing but white Sulphur coagulated with the spirit of Salt and clarified by Mercury, and the hardness of this element is in this pellicle and shell thus formed from it. Then, secondly, from the three primal parts it is changed into two—one part being air and the other chaos—in the following way. The Sulphur resolves itself by the spirit of Salt in the liquor of Mercury, which of itself is a liquid distributed from heaven to earth, and is the albumen of the heaven, and the mid space. It is clear, a chaos, subtle, and diaphanous. All density, dryness, and all its subtle nature, are resolved, nor is it any longer the same as it was before. Such is the air. The third remnant of the three primals has passed into air, thus: If wood is burnt it passes into smoke. So this passes into air, remains in its air to the end of its elements, and becomes Sulphur, Mercury, and Salt, which are substantially consumed and turned into air, just as the wood which becomes smoke. It is, in fact, nothing but the smoke of the three primal elements of the air. So, then, nothing further arises from the element of air beyond what has been mentioned. Many of the ancients and later writers, nay, even some now living, ascribe wind to the air, making out its cause to be the mobility of the sky. That is all nothing. It never reaches the sky; and the air is by itself, coming forth from its element as smoke from wood. Whoever wishes to understand more clearly about it, and what its motion is, let him read about the properties of fire, where more is set down than can be here comprised.

Paracelsus

THE PHILOSOPHY ADDRESSED TO THE ATHENIANS

BOOK THE THIRD

TEXT I.

Everything in existence necessarily has a body. The mode and manner may be understood as being like a smoky spirit, which indeed has substance, but is not a body, nor is it tangible. But, though this be the case, still both bodies and substances can be produced from it. This may be understood from fuming arsenic; since after the generation of a body, nothing more is seen of the fume of the spirit, just as if it had been all reduced to a body. But this is not so. Something of a most subtle nature still remains in that place of generation. Thus by the process of separation there are produced something visible and something invisible. By this method and in this mode all things are propagated. Wood has still surviving the spirit from which it has been separated. So have stones, and so all things, without any exception. Their essence still survives just as it was separated from it. Man, in like manner, is nothing else than a relic and a survival from the separated fume. But mark this, that a certain spirit existed, and from that man is made up, and is most subtle in spirit. This spirit is the index of a twofold eternity, one being the caleruthum, and the other the meritorium. The caleruthum is the indication in the first eternity. It seeks or makes for the other, that is, God. That is a natural cause because all things affect or tend towards that from which they proceeded, or those natures which have been in contact with it; for whatever anything when building up used in the process, that the thing when it is built up desires after and pursues. And this should be understood, that a thing which has been built up does, by Nature, or by natural instinct, tend not towards its builder, but towards that from which it has proceeded. So the human body longs for the matter from which it has been separated, and not for God, since it was not taken out of Him. And that matter is the life and the habitation in which the eternal meritorium abides. So everything returns to its essence.

TEXT II.

Since, then, everything has an appetency for its source, that is, for the mystery whence it sprang, it must now be further understood that this is eternal life, and that what comes forth from thence is mortal. None the less, however, there remains in the mortal something eternal, that is, the soul, as may be learnt elsewhere. And if a perishable thing is to return to its pristine condition, that can only be done by a conjunction of what is permanent; then at length there is a collocation and a union of things. The form and substance, however, both of transitory and of non-transitory things, proceeds from that spirit of fume, just as hail or lightning emerges from a cloud. These are corporeal, and that matter from which they have proceeded remains invisible. So, then, it may be laid down that all things spring from the invisible, yet, without its suffering loss, for the matter has always the power of regenerating and recuperating that loss. Hence, also, it happens that the whole world will pass away like snow and return to the same essence of the spirit of smoke, and then will come together or coalesce apart from all tangible essence. In this way, it can be again re-born as at first. Hence, also, it is known that no created thing exists which has been born, but only as it has been built up or created. So, the chief good is constituted in the beginning of all things that anything shall thus proceed from the invisible and become corporeal, and then shall afterwards be separated again from its body, and once more become invisible. Then all things are again joined together and united and reduced to their primal matter. And although, indeed, they may be united, yet still they involve some distinction and difference one from the other. One is the abode of the other; that other is the inmate of the abode. For that is the habitation of all things; sensible and insensible alike must all return to that condition and to that place. For, whether rational or irrational, nothing is free from this change, but will return to its habitation, from which it has been separated, and there appear.

TEXT III.

So, too, every body, or every tangible substance, is nothing else but coagulated smoke. Hence it may be assumed that such coagulation is manifold. One kind refers to wood, another to stone, a third to metal. But the body itself is none other than smoke, breathing forth from the matter or the matrix in which it is present. What grows from the ground is a smoke brought forth from the liquid of Mercury, which is various, and emits a manifold smoke for herbs, trees, and the like. But that smoke, if it issues forth from its primal, or as soon as it expires from the matrix touches foreign air, is thereupon coagulated. So this smoke constantly and persistently evaporates. As long, therefore, as it is driven and disturbed, so long the thing grows, but when the ebullition ceases the smoking also ceases. This terminates, too, both the coagulation and the growth. Wood is the smoke from Derses. Therein is latent a specific from which wood is produced. Nor is it only produced from this smoke; it may be produced also from other dersic matter. In like manner, leffas is boiling matter, from the smoke of which all herbs are gendered. For the only predestination of herbs is leffa; there is no other. God is more wonderful in specifics than in all other natures. Stannar is the mother of metals, furnishing the first matter for metals by its fume. Metals, in fact, are nothing but the coagulated fume from stannar. Enur is the fume of stones. In fine, whatever is corporeal is nothing but coagulated smoke, in which there is latent a specific predestination. All things, too, will ultimately be resolved like smoke; for the specific which coagulates has no power save for a definite time. The same may also be said of coagulation. All bodies will at last pass away and vanish in smoke, and will be terminated only in smoke. This is the consumption of everything corporeal, both living and dead.

TEXT IV.

Man is coagulated smoke. Only from the boiling vapours and spermatic members of the body is the coagulation of spermatic matter produced. Man, too, will be resolved into a vapour of this kind; so that death may be like birth. Moreover, we see in ourselves nothing else than that man is coagulated smoke formed by human predestination. Whatsoever, too, is taken or given forth is merely the coagulated fume from liquids. And so whatever is injected is consumed by the life on the same principle, so that the coagulation may be again dissolved and liquefied, as ice is liquefied by the sun, that it may afterwards vanish into the air like smoke. Life consumes everything; for it is the spirit of consumption in all corporeities and substances. Here, too, attention must be given to the preparation of the digested mystery; for if everything is due to return to that state from which it originated, and so anything is given forth, then it is consumed together with the life. This, however, happens only in those things which are not transmuted. Transmutation is not driven back or repressed; and some transmutation is produced by means of life. Thus, then is transmutation altered into the frailty of the body; but, nevertheless, it is again separated from the body. For in its putrefaction, transmutation has no further power, and in putrefaction the digested mystery ensues as a consequence. In the meantime, there are mutually separated all the properties which man had in himself from herbs and other things, each returning to its own essence. Separation is, in fact, like that process by which, if ten or twelve things are mixed they are again dissevered, so that each regains its own special essence. Thus, eating is nothing else than a dissolution of bodies. Hence the materials of bodies are separated in vomitings and dejections from the bowels, which are simply foetid smoke mixed with good. Nature, indeed, seeks only the subtle, avoiding what is dense. Stones, metals, and earths—in a word, all things—are dissolved by life; nor is there any other dissolution of them by the body than that which is brought about by its life.

TEXT V.

Moreover, it is equally necessary to understand the process by which each separate thing regains its own essence. This cannot be more fitly compared to anything than to fire, which is elicited from a hard flint, flaming and burning beyond all natural knowledge. For, as that hidden fire takes its origin and proceeds to work its effects, in the same form and appearance also is the essence led to its nature. And here reflect that in the beginning there existed only one thing, without any inclination or speciality, and from this afterwards all things issued forth. This origin exactly resembles some well-tempered colour, purple for instance, having in itself no inclination to any other colour, but conspicuous in its just temperature. Yet, notwithstanding, in that colour all colours are existent. For the other colours cannot be separated from it—red, green, blue, clay colour, white, black. Each of these colours, again, brings forth other blind colours, while yet each one is by itself entirely and properly tinted. And although many and various colours are latent in them, still, nevertheless, they are all hidden under one colour. In the same manner, too, everything had its essence in the Great Mystery, which the Supreme

Architect afterwards separated. The crystal emits fire, not from a fiery nature, but on account of its hardness and solidity. It also hides in itself other elements, not essentially, but materially, ardent fire, blowing air, moistening water, and earth which is black and dry. Besides all these things it possesses in the composition of its qualities all colours, but hidden within itself, as the fire lies hid in the steel, betraying its presence neither by burning, nor by shining, nor by casting a colour. In this respect, all colours and all elements are present in everything. But how all things arrive at and penetrate to all other things, if anyone cares to know, let him believe that all these matters are brought about and cared for by Him alone, who is the Maker and Architect of all things.

TEXT VI.

Although, as has been said, Nature lies invisibly in bodies and in substances; nevertheless, that invisibility is led to visibility by means of those bodies themselves. According as the essence of each is situated, so is it seen visibly in its virtues and in its colours. Invisible bodies, however, have no other method than this corporeal one. So mark, then, that the invisibles contain within themselves all the elements, and operate in every element. They can send forth from themselves fire and the virtue of its element; and so, too, do they send forth air, as a man sends forth his breath, or water, as a man sends forth urine. They are also of the nature of earth, and sprung from the earth. Know this, too, that the liquid of the earth always boils, and sends forth on high, beyond itself, the subtle spirit which it contains in itself. From this are nourished the invisibles and the firmament itself, and this could not be done without vapour. Incorporeal as well as corporeal things need food and drink. For this reason stones come forth from the earth from a like spirit of their nature. Each one attracts its own to itself. From the same source come spectres, fiery dragons, and the like. If, therefore, invisible as well as visible are each in its own essence, this is due to the nature of the Great Mystery, as wood acquires ignition from a light or a taper, though this suffers no loss. And though, indeed, it be not corporeal, still it needs something corporeal in order to escape death, which is produced by the wood. In the same way, all invisibles need to be sustained, nourished, and increased by some visible thing. With these, indeed, they will at length perish and come to an end, still, however, having their activity in them without any waste or loss to other things, that is to say, to the corporeal and the visible, although this is brought about by the invisible, and apprehended by the visible.

Paracelsus

THE ECONOMY OF MINERALS

Concerning the Field, the Roots, and the Trees of Minerals

The Most High created the element of water to be, as it were, a field in which the roots of mineral trees, springing forth from their seeds, should be fixed, and thence the trunk and the branches should be thrust forth over the earth. He separated it, therefore, from the other three, so that neither in the air, nor in the earth, nor in heaven, but placed on the lower globe, it should exist by itself as a free body, to be on the earth and to have its centre there where it was founded, created after such an admirable order that it should bear man upon it like the earth; so that man borne in a ship should speed over the water and get possession of it. What is more marvellous still is that though it surrounds our globe in every direction, the water does not fall down from its own limits, though the part at our antipodes seems to hang downwards, just as our part seems to them, and yet each remains spread out a plane surface on its own sphere, wherever you look at it, as if some pit should be imagined which, descending perpendicularly to the abyss, should find no bottom nor be sustained by the earth. It is even more wonderful than the egg in its shell, provided with all that it requires. The generations of minerals, then, from the element of water are protruded into the earth, just as from the element of earth all fruits are pushed forward into the air, so that nothing but the root remains in the earth. Exactly so, all metals, salt, gems, stones, talc, marcasites, sulphurs, and every similar substance, pass from their mother, the water, to another mother, namely, the earth, in which the operation of their trees is perfected, while their roots are fixed in the water. For as those things which grow from roots in the earth are finished in the air, in like manner, those which derive their origin from the water are altogether completed by Nature in the earth, so that they reach, as the others did, their ultimate matter. The ancients, led astray by this opinion, because they saw that metals were found in the earth, were so little advanced that they did not see their error when, on the subject of minerals, they wrote that out of the earth grew nothing but wood, leaves, flowers, fruits, and herbs, and that everything else was produced from water. No less mythical was the saying of that man who asserted that all things which were produced on the earth had their origin from the air, because they are in the air and are perfected there, though he saw their roots in the earth. Because he did not see the roots of minerals with his bodily eyes he would even feign that they are fixed in the earth. Such is the physical science of the Greeks, deduced only from what is seen, recognising nothing occult by mental experiment. It is just a fiction of lazy men who presume to chatter about natural science from eyesight alone; and who do not experiment so as to observe those occult things which underlie the things which are manifest, the one over against the other.

Concerning the Fruits and the Harvest of Minerals

Just as all the fruits of the earth have their harvest and autumn on the earth and in the air, according to the predestined time in their generation, so the fruits of the water, that is to say, minerals, are gathered at their own time of maturity. When the mineral root first germinates they rise to their own trunk and tree, that is, into the body from which minerals or metals are subsequently produced; just as a nut or a cherry is not immediately produced from the earth, but first of all a tree, from which at length the fruit is generated. In like manner, Nature puts forth a mineral tree, that is, an aqueous body, in the element of water. This tree is produced in the earth so far as it fills the pores thereof, just in the same way as the earth itself fills the air. From this are eventually produced fruits according to the nature and property of its species, at the extremities of its branches, just as occurs in trees which we see on the surface of the earth. We must seek, then, first of all, for the aqueous tree, and by-and-by for its fruits, by a method not inaptly borrowed from agriculture, and in the following manner. Some of the visible trees produce their fruits covered up; for instance, chestnuts under a prickly bark, walnuts under one that is green and bitter, under that a wooden covering, and under this again a bitter membrane, and then at last the kernel. So it happens in minerals, the kernels of which, that is to say, the metals, are separated just like those others by barks. Other trees produce their fruits naked, such as plums, cherries, pears, apples, grapes, etc., where there is no such separation as that just described. So also some aqueous trees produce their gold, silver, corals, and other metals of that kind, free and naked, according to the condition and nature of the water. As we know by the rind what fruit lies concealed within it, and as the spirit is known by its body, just so, in the case of minerals, the spirit of the metal is recognised, though hidden, beneath its corporeal or mineral bark. The spirit of the aqueous element produces the body, of one kind in the mineral, of a different kind in the fruit. Although, then, gold may be in a mineral body, nevertheless that body is of no moment; it has to be separated from the gold as impure, while the gold itself is pure. There are, therefore, in a mineral two bodies, of which one is the fruit, the pure body of gold, wherewith its spirit is inseparably incorporated. So the fruits are first introduced from the element into the tree, as the spirit into an impure body, and with that at last into the earth, as something noble and pure. The same thing is seen in man, to whom have been given two bodies, one corrupt, but the other incorrupt, which will be eternally united with him, since it is the image of God, and by its possession especially man differs from all other creatures.

Concerning the Death of the Elements, especially of Water

Elements die, as men die, on account of the corruption in them. As water at its death, as it were, consumes and devours its own fruit, so does the earth its own fruits. Whatever is born from it returns to it again, is swallowed up and lost, just as the time past is swallowed up by yesterday's days and nights, the light or darkness of which we shall never see again. It is no weightier today than yesterday, not even by a single grain, and will after a thousand years be of the same weight still. As it gives forth, so, in the same degree, it consumes.

The death of the water, however, is in its own proper element, in that great terminus and centre of water, the sea, wherein the rivers, and whatever else flows into it, die and are consumed as wood in the fire. Rivers, indeed, are not the element of water, but the fruit of that element, which is the sea; from this they derive their origin, and in this they receive both their life and their death.

Concerning the Death of the Tree of Minerals

After Nature has planted the mineral root of a tree in the centre of its matrix, whether to produce a metal, a stone, a gem, salt, alum, vitriol, a saline or sweet, cold or hot spring, a coral, or a marcasite, and after it has thrust forth the trunk to the earth, this trunk spreads abroad in different branches, the liquid of whose substance—both of branches and stalk—is formally neither a water, nor an oil, nor a lute, nor a mucilage; in fact, it can only be conceived as wood growing out of the earth, which is, nevertheless, not earth, though sprung therefrom. They are spread in such a manner that one branch is separated from another by an interval of two or three climates and as many regions: sometimes from Germany to Hungary, and even beyond. The branches of the different trees of the same kind are extended over the whole sphere of the earth, just as the veins in the human body are extended into various limbs far apart from each other. But the fruits put forth by the extremities of the twigs, by the nature of the ultimate matter, soon fall to the earth. There is a momentary coagulation of them, and then at length, when all its fruit is shed, this tree dies and is utterly consumed by dryness, its offspring being left in the earth. Afterwards, according to its state of nature, a new tree appears. So, then, the first matter of minerals consists of water; and it comprises only Sulphur, Salt, and Mercury. These minerals are that element's spirit and soul, containing in themselves all minerals, metals, gems, salts, and other things of that kind, like different seeds in a bag. These being poured into water, Nature then directs every seed to its peculiar and final fruit, incessantly disposing them according to their species and genera. These and like things proceed from that true physical science, and those fountains of sound philosophy from which, through meditative contemplation of the works of God, arises the most intimate knowledge of the Supreme Creator and of His virtues. To the minds and mental sight of true philosophers, no less than to their carnal eyes, the clear light appears. To them the occult becomes manifest. But that Greek Satan has sown in the philosophic field of true wisdom, tares and his own false seed, to wit, Aristoteles, Albertus, Avicenna, Rhasis, and that kind of men, enemies of the light of God and of Nature, who have perverted the whole of physical science, since the time when they transmuted the name of Sophia into Philosophy.

Concerning the Variation of the Primal Matter of Minerals,
in proportion to the different species and individuals thereof:
also concerning the various colours, etc.

We have before said that the primal matter exists in its mother, just as if in a bag, and that it is composed of three ingredients meeting in one. But there are as many varieties of Mercury, Salt, and Sulphur as there are different fruits in minerals. For a different Sulphur is found in lead, iron, gold; in sapphire, and other gems; in stones, marcasites, and salts; likewise a different Salt in metals, salts, etc. So, too, is it with Mercury: one kind exists in gems, another in metals. Besides, in respect of the composition of these, different individuals are found under the same species. Gold is sometimes found, one specimen heavier or more deeply coloured than another: and so of the rest. Moreover, there are as many Sulphurs of gold, Salts, and diversities of Mercury of gold, and of the others, as there are greater and lesser degrees. Nevertheless, all which among them receives particularity from the subject always is comprised under the universality of one and the same Sulphur, Salt and Mercury, mysteriously comprehended in universal Nature. In this respect Nature may be compared parabolically to a painter, who from some few colours paints an infinite number of pictures, no one exactly like another. The only difference is, that Nature produces living pictures, but the artist only imitates these. He represents the same things to the eye; but they are dead things. Now, all natural colours proceed from the Salt of Nature, in which they exist together with the balsam of things and coagulation. Sulphur exhibits the substance of bodies and their building up; Mercury, their virtues and arcana. God alone assigns life to all, so that from every one should be produced that which He, from all eternity, had predestinated to be thence produced, as He determined and willed that all should be. Whoever, therefore, wishes to understand the bodies of natural things, let him learn from natural Sulphur that which he may first of all have well understood, if he seeks natural colours as the foundation from Salt. But if he wishes to know the virtues of things, he must scrutinise the arcana belonging to the Mercury of that thing whose virtues he wishes to learn. All these matters does that one and the same Nature at once embrace in one, and separate; at the same time distributing, removing, or completely blotting out the colours from such. Consider, I beseech you, this tiny grain of seed, black or brown in colour, out of which grows a vast tree, producing such wonderful greenness in its leaves, such variegated colours in its flowers, and flavours in its fruits of such infinite variety; see this repeated by Nature in all her products, and you will find her so marvellous, so rich, in her mysteries that you will have enough to last you all your life in this book of Nature without referring to paper books. If God, then, shews Himself to our discernment in Nature so powerful and so wise, how much more glorious will He reveal Himself by His Holy Spirit to our mind if we only seek Him? This is the way of safety which leads from below to above. This is to walk in the ways of the Lord, to be occupied in admiring His works, and to carry out His will, so far as is in us, or as it should and can be in us. This has been my Academia, not Athens, Paris or Toulouse. After I had read many deceitful books of wise men I betook myself to this one alone, from which I learnt all that I write, which also I know to be true. Still, I confess, there are many more things which I do not know, but which will surge up to the surface in God's own time. There is nothing so occult which shall not be revealed when the Almighty wills it so to be.

This, however, I know, that after me will come a disciple of this school, one who does not yet live, but who will disclose many things.

Diane di Prima
PARACELSUS: AN APPRECIATION

Paracelsus—one of the greatest of western mystics and adepts, a man who brought to its highest point the science of alchemy, physician, philosopher, vagabond, who hurled invective at the doctors of his day, found himself sleeping by the wayside in the company of gypsies, bandits, and pilgrims, learning from them, poor homeless, hunted, writing his best works only when his career was in ruins, when he had been expelled from the University of Basel for incensing the Medical Association of the time against himself. A name out of a myth, scholar, drinker, traveller—a man who some say gave rise to the Faust legend, beloved to this day, but rarely read, and almost never understood.

We have, perhaps, lost the key to the alchemical texts, as is to often stated, but they stand as one of the great documents of a great and high science. For alchemy was not, as we have been told in school, merely the "forerunner of modern chemistry," but a complete and highly developed discipline, a western equivalent of the great spiritual disciplines of the East.

Examine the tables of elements—how many are there now? Ninety-six? One hundred and eight? Well, for Paracelsus there were the four elements; fire, water, earth, and air; and the three substances: mercury, sulphur, and salt. What have we gained by the change? Aside from the inconveniences of nuclear fission, poisoned food, and fluoridated water, we are supporting the dead weight of a huge number of inane technicians, engaged day and night in inventing new entities to bolster their crumbling systems: fermions, bions, ergons, etc., *ad nauseam*.

Listen to this description of "ultimate matter": "I call the ultimate matter of anything that state in which the substance has reached its highest grade of exaltation and perfection." "Exaltation?" "Perfection?"—applied to matter? It is a kind of pantheism: spirit pervades even the densest substance. It has a *virtù*, gives forth a force. Gold "rejoices in its lucidity and transparency." There is a give and take going on between the substance and the mind of the observer, which we are today slowly coming to discover again.

The alchemists of Paracelsus' day saw unity (a single substance, or principle, under many disguises) where we spend years cataloguing differences: they felt the world as organic. Read, for example, his wonderful description of the mineral tree, which has its roots in the water and its branches in the earth, where the minerals, like chestnuts, were "enclosed in their rinds and their chief excellence lay concealed in their nucleus." They saw all nature in a state of flux, all substances deriving from the *materia prima* (the first matter), one growing out of another. (How unlike our concept of the elements, separate and distinguishable, static and unchanging!) We are reminded at once of eastern thought, of the void, the "sea of consciousness" out of which everything grows spontaneously.

The world into which Paracelsus was born was at least as complicated as ours. In the year before his birth Columbus had reached the New World. The previous century had seen a schism within the Church: a Pope at Rome and a Pope at Avignon. The old order, which had for so many centuries seemed unshakable, the feudal society, the Catholic Church, was threatening at any moment to come crashing down. Joan of Arc had been burned at the stake, Constantinople had fallen to the Turks, who were threatening all Europe. The Renaissance was well-launched, and the best of the Italian work already done. The new humanism was spreading north from Florence and Sienna, Padua and Bologna, into Germany and England. Savanarola had made his desperate attempt to reform the Church from within, and had died for it by the time Paracelsus was six.

In Paracelsus' lifetime, small but fiercely fought and desperate revolts of the serfs broke out time and time again in Germany under the banner of the *Bundschuh*. They culminated finally in 1525 in the Peasants War, in which perhaps 100,000 peasants were slaughtered by the nobles, who had finally become desperate enough to sink their differences and band together. On an international scale, war was flaring up all over Europe. France and Spain fought over the Two Sicilies. The German army sacked Rome in 1527, leaving it almost a ruin, in a state equalled only by that it had seen a thousand years before at the hands of the Huns. Modern nations were emerging from the feudal provinces, at the cost of great bloodshed. Paracelsus, we may be sure, did not remain aloof from all this turmoil in his wanterings. There would have been almost no way that he could. One story has it that he was forced to leave Salzburg for Basel in order to avoid the repercussions of the Peasants War, in which he is said to have taken part. Almost all accounts of his life agree that he was an army doctor in the Venetian wars, some accounts adding Denmark, Russia, and Austria.

Printing was in its heyday. The great presses of medieval Europe were established, and busy grinding out the classics of antiquity, and the new treatises and speculations on man and his nature and the course of the cosmos that sprang into being by the thousands. Basel, where Paracelsus taught in 1526-28, was the home of Froben, a printer famous for his publication of Erasmus and other humanists. His press was the center of serious intellectual activity at the University. The exchange of ideas was effected at a rate, and in a volume, that was unprecedented in the history of western man. Theology, philosophy, science, literature, all that rightly belongs to the world of books and ideas, was in a ferment. And these ideas, once exclusively circulated among the learned, were now filtering down to the masses of the people. In 1522 Luther translated the Bible into German. Paracelsus lectured in German at Basel, to the disgust of the academicians, and wrote in a mixture of German and bad Latin which his translators complain of to this day.

The great universities of Europe were in a uproar. They were the centers of the political and religious upheaval that was brewing. The students, under the protection of Rome, exempt from punishment by secular law, and from taxation, bored by bad teachers, driven by poverty, were completely out of hand. The Latin War—a pitched battle between the burghers and the students in the streets of Vienna—lasted several days. In the course of his travels, Paracelsus is to be found at many of the leading universities of Europe. Vienna, Paris, Oxford, Cologne, Padua, Bologna, and Ferrara, are mentioned by various sources. We may be sure that he left his mark wherever he went, studying and teaching, and influencing, by his life and his words, as much as by his writings, the course that was taken by the thought of his time.

Dürer and Lucas Cranach were his contemporaries, as was Erasmus, that gentle, fence-sitting humanist. Luther's lifetime emcompassed Paracelsus'—he was born ten years earlier and died five years later. Luther burned Leo X's Bull of Excommunication in 1520; in 1526 Paracelsus burned the works of Avicenna and Galen on Midsummer Night at the University of Basel, and soon thereafter found himself expelled from the university. He was even dubbed "Luther medicorum"—the Luther of the doctors.

Europe in 1541, when Paracelsus died, bore little resemblance to the continent where he had been born, less than half a century earlier. The Reformation had effectively claimed England, Denmark, Sweden and northern Germany. The nations of Europe had pretty much taken the form that they have to this day. The Hapsburgs were a rising family. Copernicus and Galileo were preparing to change the shape of the universe. "I see no end of it," Erasmus had written, "but the turning upside down of the whole world." The long, slow process of the dissolution of European society had begun.

But chaotic as the world was, it had not yet been fragmented as it is today. The unity of the microcosm and the macrocosm, the harmony between the courses of the stars, the cycles of the seasons, and the spiritual life of man, was not in question. "All things are concealed in all." It was possible, by looking into the heart of matter to study the matter of the heart. The alchemist's laboratory was the place where the secrets of man's essential nature surfaced, and were explored. And as the outer and the inner were one, there could be no basic antagonism between faith and reason, between experimental truth and the truth of intuition. Paracelsus was to this extent untouched by the Reformation. He is a bridge between the old order and the new. It may seem strange to us to find, in the midst of a highly technical treatise, a reference to the subtle and glorious workings of God, but to him there was no strangeness in this, for how could there be one without the other? The human race was fortunately in a wholer state than it has been in since. To live one's life in harmony with the cosmos, to understand its laws and workings, was not only an ideal of philosophy, but practical commonsense. It was at once the root of the art of medicine, and a high expression of religion (reverence).

This doctrine of the correspondence, indeed the identity, of the outer and inner worlds, of the events in the life of man and the changes of the seasons, or the motions of the stars, the axiom that man, in his most basic sense *must* be in harmony with the universe, reaches its highest expression in *I Ching, The Book of Changes* of ancient China. It is the theory of what Jung calls "synchronicity," presupposing "a peculiar interdependence of objective events among themselves as well as with the subjective state of the observer" at any given moment. It is, of course, the axiom on which astrology, as well as alchemy in this higher sense—and all magic—is predicated. It seems to be a world view that was at one time common to all men. (The linear time of past, present, and future, in which causality manifests itself is a rather late, and western, concept.) It finds voice in the Upanishads: "Orange, blue, yellow, red are not less in man's arteries than in the sun. As a long highway passes between two villages, one at either end, so the sun's rays pass between this world and the world beyond. They flow from the sun, enter into the arteries, flow back from the arteries, enter into the sun."

But Paracelsus was a Renaissance man. As in Masaccio's paintings more than half a century earlier the horizon line was on a level with the heads of the human figures, so for Paracelsus, the human mind was not simply one expression of the universal "force" manifesting itself at that point in time (parallel to the reactions of the substances in the crucible), but somehow it controlled that universal impulse. "So high and so lofty is human wisdom that it hath in its power all the stars, the firmament itself, and universal heaven. And as the power thereof pervades all the earth, so it extends over heaven. The Sun and Moon are its subjects. Even as the hand changes and compels the soil, so also the inner microcosmus compels the zenith to obedience."

Legend has it that Paracelsus traveled and studied in the East, that he was captured by the Tartars while in Russia and brought back to India as a doctor or tutor to the Khan's son. Some would have it that he even went to China. These tales of his eastern travels have been dismissed as fantasy in modern times. We tend to feel that we are the only ones who have possessed the secret of mobility; that the early Chinese could not possibly have gotten to Mexico, nor the Vikings to New England, nor Paracelsus to India. And yet, the fact remains that there is Teutonic amber to be found in Korea, that the Mayan carvings hark back to the Shang bronzes, and that throughout the alchemical writings of Paracelsus there runs a strong vein of eastern thought. Too sure we are, that we are the first really mobile, and yet we may land on Mars only to find another Stonehenge there!

If Paracelsus did not actually go to China, he made that trip in one sense, at least, for recent discoveries show that alchemy was practiced there around 400 B.C., and passed from there to Alexandria around the first century of our era. It was in the East that alchemy took on what were to be two of the basic axioms of its thought: the *materia prima*, and the polarity of the masculine and feminine principles.

The *materia prima* is the single substance of which all matter is composed, as "all pots are of clay." "The ultimate and also the primal matter of everything is fire," says Paracelsus, though elsewhere he agrees with the bulk of his contemporaries in calling it water. He also calls it "increatum," the uncreated, and says that it is immaterial and cannot be described. He is the first to claim that it fills the entire cosmos, and is eternal, "the one unique mother of all mortal things...a mother to all the elements and in them likewise a grandmother to all stars, trees, and creatures of the flesh."

The opposition of Sol and Luna (gold and silver) as the masculine and feminine or yang and yin elements, viz.:

YANG	YIN
Male	**Female**
Right	**Left**
Light	**Dark**
Fire	**Water**
Red	**White**
Sun	**Moon**
Sol	**Luna**
Gold	**Silver**
"The King"	**"The Queen"**
"Red Lion"	**"White Eagle"**
Sulphur	**Mercury**

recalls not only the yang and yin of Chinese philosophy, but also the red and white veins, male and female respectively, on the right and left side of the spinal column, and *also called the Sun and the Moon,* which form the nervous system in Tantric philosophy.

(We would note in passing that in Chinese alchemy the Philosopher's Stone first makes its appearance, as a simple "pill of immortality.")

It is true that much of what Paracelsus writes is obscure to us. It is more obscure than it need be. For what is required to penetrate the secrets of these books is an attribute most difficult of accomplishment by the modern reader: faith. When Paracelsus declares that, having burned a flower, he can again raise its *eidolon,* or phantom, from the ashes, or that he has grown an homonunculus out of human sperm incubated in horse dung, and educated it, he is not, as we would fain believe, speaking figuratively. He means exactly and literally what he says. The whole of modern criticism has as its aim the softening of the statements of poets, alchemists, philosophers, into something symbolical and therefore twice removed and digestible without effort and without faith. It is a conspiracy to render harmless the words of those who would not be silenced. Do you but bring the blind faith of a child to the works of Paracelsus or of any other great mystic, and you will find new universes opening before you.

But if you cannot bring such faith to the alien world and unfamiliar pursuits of this man, it is very exciting to read him as a puzzle, a conumdrum, each section of which will give you clues to the others, so that as you go on more and more of his work lies open before you. The field is wide open. The Rosetta stone of Hermetic alchemy has yet to be discovered, though Carl Jung in his great works on this subject has given us the key. Here, for example, is a table of the names of the planets, and the metals that they stand for:

Sol	**Gold**
Luna	**Silver**
Saturn	**Lead**
Venus	**Copper**
Mars	**Iron**
Jupiter	**Tin**
Mercury	**Mercury**

But remember that Sol was not only gold, gold was the sun:

"But that gold is not burned in the element of terrestrial fire, nor is even corrupted, is effected by the firmness of Sol. For one fire cannot burn another, or even consume it; but rather if fire be added to fire it is increased and becomes more powerful in its operations. The celestial fire which flows to us on the earth from the Sun is not such a fire as there is in heaven, neither is it like that which exists upon the earth, but that celestial fire with us is cold and congealed, and it is the body of the Sun. Whereof the Sun can in no way be overcome by our fire. This only happens, that it is liquefied, like snow on ice, by that same celestial Sun. Fire therefore has not the power of burning fire, because the Sun is fire, which dissolved in heaven, is coagulated with us."

"Aurum nostra non est aurum vulgi"—our gold is not the gold of the crowd. For the *Magnum Opus*—the making of gold from base metals—was merely a discipline designed to make perfect an imperfect man, in other words, to lead to enlightenment. The metallic transmutation could not be accomplished without the spiritual transformation. It was a coincident and parallel process.

As it was with Sol and gold, so it was also with the other metals and their planets. The metals had, somehow, the same *virtù* as the planet, or rather, a single spirit infused both planet and metal, one a celestial and one a terrestrial manifestation of the same force. This was not symbolism, but something much closer to literal speech, a fine line between the two which has been lost to us, and to our language.

Paracelsus has been celebrated by our age as the first "modern chemist," which is rather as if the anteater should condescendingly praise the elephant for the length of his nose. His work abounds in that iconoclasm, the will to rely on nothing but experience and the "light of nature," which led him to burn the works of Avicenna and Galen: "Paying little heed to the method of the ancients, we will follow experience as our guide, and those prescriptions which experience proves to be of no use we will omit." It is filled with a steady and attentive awareness, close to the Zen "mindfulness," which it kindles in us too as we read. "Everywhere there is presented to us earth, or dust, or sand, which often contains much gold or silver, and this you will mark." Or, "There is, indeed, diffused through all things a Balsam created by God, without which putrefaction would immediately supervene."

Precise and lucid definitions are his forte. Embedded in an obscure paragraph, they leap out of it to delight mind and spirit. "To conjure is nothing else than to observe anything rightly, to know and to understand what it is." They often bring with them distinctions so fine as to anticipate Kant or Hume: "...death brings with it no disease, nor is it the cause of any. On the other hand, no disease causes death. And although the two coexist together, they are still no more to be compared one with the other than fire and water. They are no more akin one to another, nor do they agree better together. Natural sickness abhors death, and every member of the body avoids it. Death, then, is something distinct from disease."

Relying as he does on experience, it is not surprising to find somewhat unorthodox and highly delightful reinterpretations of the Scriptures (the vogue and new excitement of the age) scattered throughout his work. "He who created man also created science. What has man in any place without labor? When the mandate went forth: Thou shalt live by the sweat of thy brow, there was, as it were, a new creation. When God uttered his fiat the world was made. Art, however, was not then made, nor was the light of nature. But when Adam was expelled from Paradise, God created for him the light of Nature when he bade him live by the work of his hands."

You may read Paracelsus for his wonderful prose, as rich as the *Anatomy of Melancholy,* or for the marvelous universe he pictures, the images he calls up. I remember especially his description of the waters surrounding the earth, containing, like an eggshell, all that is needed within them, and the discussion of the generation of monsters through the imagination of a pregnant woman. Or, listen to this paragraph "Concerning the Death of the Elements, especially of water:"

> "Elements die, as men die, on account of the corruption in them. As water at its death, as it were, consumes and devours its own fruit, so does the earth its own fruits. Whatever is born from it returns to it again, is swallowed up and lost, just as time past is swallowed up by yesterday's days and nights, the light or darkness of which we shall never see again."

Or you may search out his prophecies, some of which may come to pass in our own day. "At present the palm is given to debauchery, until one third part of mankind or of the population of the world shall be killed, another shall be finished off by disease, and the remaining third only shall be saved and survive." It is a description of the inevitable, the events of the Kaliyuga. But he holds out a hope for the time that comes after: "By this arcanum the last age shall be illuminated clearly and compensated for all its losses by the gift of grace and the reward of the spirit of truth, so that since the beginning of the world no similar germination of the intelligence and of wisdom shall ever have been heard of."

No matter what your starting point, you will find yourself at last reading these volumes simply for the man that they reveal. He is surely one of the most fascinating figures of the Renaissance. Arrogant before his enemies, humble before his art, full of a childlike faith, investigating everything by the "light of nature," bombastic, despairing, hopeful, infinitely curious, a man who saw deeply into the secrets of matter, and into the souls of men, who at the end called a truce to anger, to restlessness and doubt and came to terms with the "uncreated," receiving the sacraments of the church and dividing his pittance among the poor. He stands neither in the medieval world, nor in the modern one, but bridges the two for us, making his era more accessible by his immediacy, his closeness to our own.

Today we stand again at the brink of a new age. Science has failed us, as the Church failed the man of Paracelsus' day. In five or ten years the "science bubble will burst," as a good friend of mine who specializes in the Philosophy of Science expressed it recently. To be born again, to make the world anew, will be no easy task. We shall have increasingly to have recourse to the wisdom of other times, to the philosophies of the East, to the mystics and masters of the "occult," to those adepts for whom there was no dualism, for whom spirit and matter, man and cosmos, were one. Paracelsus stands at the gateway of the old knowledge. He beckons to us, he leads us in by the hand.

"The eternal position of all things, independent of time, without beginning or end, operates everywhere. It works essentially where otherwise there is no hope. It accomplishes that which is deemed impossible. What appears beyond belief or hope emerges into truth after a wonderful fashion."

December 16, 1965
Ananda Ashram
Monroe, New York

Basilius Valentinus

THE TRIUMPHAL CHARIOT OF ANTIMONY

Hence I would thus advise men of all ranks, who are anxious to obtain knowledge: Demand first of your masters true teaching, which consists in preparation and the proportion of ingredients; then you will hold your title with honour, and give real help to your fellow-men; you will also have good reason to return thanks to the Creator out of an unfeigned heart.

Let every one seriously consider in his own mind what he should do, what he should leave undone, and whether his title belongs to him of right, or not. Whoever assumes a title should know its meaning, and whether he is justified in claiming it. A rational man must be able to assign a reason for everything, and when he smells a dung-heap of a very penetrating odour, he should be able to say why he calls it good dung, and also why a certain person who has partaken of fragrant and sweet-smelling food, gives it out in the shape of highly malodorous excrement. The answer is to be found in the conditions of natural putrefaction and corruption. The same thing is observable in the transmutations of all fragrant substances. Hence the Sage should enquire what an odour is, whence it derives its properties, and how those properties can be turned to good account. For the earth is nourished with stinking dung, and precious fruits are produced thereby. To account for this phenomenon there is a multiplicity of causes which it would take a whole book to explain, if we attempted to describe, even briefly, all natural mutations and generations. But digestion and putrefaction are the Master Keys of the process. Fire and air produce a kind of maturity, by which a change can take place out of water and earth. This is the kind of transmutation by which fragrant balsam becomes stinking dung, and stinking dung fragrant balsam. But you will ask me why I quote such simple and absurd examples. The example, I confess, smacks of the stables rather than of the drawing-room; but the careful student of Nature will understand me all the better for that reason. He will see that the highest things become the lowest, and the lowest are changed into the highest—*i.e.,* a medicine into a poison, and a poison into a medicine; a sweet thing into a bitter, acid, and corrosive substance; and a common thing, on the other hand, into something useful

But, good God!—how difficult it is for us shortlived men to explore the whole compass of Nature. Thou hast reserved to Thyself many things in Creation which are objects of maravel rather than of knowledge. Therefore permit me to the end of my life to keep Thee in my heart, that in addition to the temporal health and wealth, which Thou givest freely, I may also obtain the salvation of my soul, and spiritual riches. Of this I dare not doubt, for Thou has shed the balm and sulphur of my soul on the bitter cross—a balm which to the Devil is deadly poison, but to sinners the most potent medicine. I strive to heal the souls of my brethren with prayer, and their bodies with suitable remedies. May God grant that we may all dwell together in His mansions on high!

But to return to the science of Antimony. You should know that all things contain operative and vital spirits, which derive their substance and nourishment from their bodies; nor are the elements themselves without these spirits whether good or evil. Men and animals have within them an operative and vitalizing spirit, and if it forsakes them, nothing but a dead body is left. Herbs and trees have spirits of health, else no Art could turn them to medicinal uses. In the same way, minerals and metals possess vitalizing spirits, which constitute their whole strength and goodness: for what has no spirit has no life, or vitalizing power. Know that in Antimony also there is a spirit which is its strength, which also pervades it invisibly, and the magnetic property pervades the magnet.

Now, there are different kinds of spirits, which are partly visible, and yet cannot be touched as the natural body of a man can be touched. Such are especially those spirits which have fixed their domicile in the elements, spirits of fire, light, and other light-dispensing objects. Such are the aërial spirits which dwell in the air; watery spirits in the water; terrestrial spirits, or "earth men" in the earth, especially where there are rich veins of ore. These spirits have reason and sensation, are skilled in the different Arts, and can assume a variety of shapes, until the time of the judgment, which perhaps even now God has pronounced against them.

Other spirits which cannot speak, nor exhibit themselves by their own power, are those which dwell in men and animals, in plants and minerals. They have an occult, operative life, and manifest themselves by the efficacy of their working; when separated from bodies by our Art they have a most marvellous sanative virtue.

In this way the operative spirit and virtue of Antimony bestows its gifts, and imparts them to men, when it has been separated from its body so as to penetrate other bodies with its sanative virtue. In this process the Artist and Vulcan (fire) must be of one mind. The fire causes the separation, the Artist forms the substance. So the smith uses one fire and one material, vis., iron; and yet produces out of them a great variety of different instruments, a spit, spurs, an axe, or some other tool. In the same way Antimony can be put to a great many different uses, wherein the smith is the skilled Artist, while the fire is, as it were, the key which opens, and practical experiment results in experience and a useful conclusion.

Alas, if men only had eyes to see, and ears to hear not merely what I say, but to understand the secret meaning, they would no longer drink those turbid and unwholesome potions, but would hasten hither, and receive the limpid water of the well of life!

It is my design to shew that those great doctors, who think themselves wise, are very fools, while my book may make many foolish and unlearned persons the depositaries of true wisdom.

All men who are real lovers of knowledge, and humbly seek after it by day and by night, are herewith cordially invited to listen to my teaching, to pore over my book with the greatest care, and thereby to obtain the desire of their hearts. Their gratitude will, after my death, raise me from the grave, and render my name immortal. If any one be opposed to my opinions, he will find a crushing reply in this work. Nor am I fearful that my disciples who, through my teaching, obtain the empire over Nature, will ever suffer my name to sink into oblivion, or to be bespattered with vile calumnies.

Know then, benevolent and sincere observer of art, that there are two kinds of Antimony, which differ widely from each other. One is beautiful, pure, and of a golden quality, containing a considerable amount of Mercury. The other has much Sulphur, is not so friendly to goad as the first, and is known by its beautiful, long, brilliantly white streaks. Now, one Antimony is more useful than the other, both for Alchemistic and Medicinal purposes. There are many different kinds of flesh, the flesh of fishes and the flesh of animals; and as both are flesh, so two widely different substances may be called Antimony.

Many have written about the inward virtue of Antimony, but few know either the true foundation of its power, of the origin thereof. Their knowledge is verbal erudition only; it is devoid of a solid grounding, and bears no fruit.

To write on Antimony, there is needed profound meditation, a large mind, a wide knowledge of its preparation, and of its true soul, in which consists all its usefulness. If you are familiar with these, you can truly tell what is good and medicinal, what is bad and poisonous, in it. It is surely worth while to enquire into the essential and fundamental nature of Antimony, and to discover how its venomous quality against which so loud an outcry is raised, may be removed, and itself prepared, changed, and transmuted into a pure Medicine, containing not a single trace of poison.

Many Anatomists have subjected Antimony to all manner of singular torments and excruciating processes, which it is difficult either to believe or to describe. Their studies have led to no result, because they did not seek the true soul of Antimony, and, therefore, did not soon find that fictitious soul of which they were in search their path being obscured with black colours which rendered invisible what they desired to see. Antimony, like Mercury, is comparable to a circle, without beginning or end, composed of all colours; and the more is always found in it, the more diligent and prudent the search which is made. One man's life is too short to discover all these mysteries. It is a most potent poison; then, again, it is free from poison, and a most excellent Medicine, both for external and internal application. This is hidden from many through their blindness, and they judge it to be a foolish, incredible, and vain thing. We must excuse them on account of their ignorance, and permit them to plead their stupidity in extenuation of their folly. The worst of it is that they will not be taught.

Antimony has the four first qualities; it is frigid and humid, and yet hot and dry; it accomodates itself to the four seasons of the year, and is both volatile and fixed. Its volatility is poisonous, its fixed state free from all poison. Hence Antimony is one of the seven wonders of the world, and many have written about it without knowing the meaning of their own words; no one before me, and even at the present time no one besides myself, has any real acquaintance with its potency, virtues, powers, operation, and efficacy. If any such person could be found, he would be worthy to be drawn about in a triumphal car, like great kings and warriors after mighty and heroic achievements in the battlefield. But I am afraid that not many of our Doctors are in danger of being forcibly placed in such a car.

Men of this world, who are at the same time students of our art, are so given up to the desire of gain that they can think only of the riches which Antimony is to bestow upon them; they do not realize that the medicinal virtues of Antimony should be the first object of our search, in order that the name of God shall be glorified, and that our fellowmen may be truly benefitted.

We admit that greater riches are to be found in Antimony than it is possible to imagine, even for me, though I know much more about this matter than you who are so exceedingly wise in your own conceits. But let none be afraid for this reason, or despair of ultimately attaining to this highest felicity of human life; for the loving kindness of God is great in the dispensation of His gifts. But because of the ingratitude of men, He has covered their eyes, as it were, with cobwebs, so that they cannot perceive the mysteries hidden in this mineral form.

All clamour aloud: We want to be rich, rich! Yes, you desire wealth, and say with Epicurus: Let us provide for our bodies, and leave our souls to take care of themselves. Even as Midas in the fable, you desire to change all things into gold. So are there numerous persons who seek this coveted wealth in Antimony, but since they do not care for God, and have cast far away from them the love of their neighbour, they will look at the horses's teeth of Antimony forever without knowing anything about its age or qualities. Like the wedding-guests of Cana, they may behold the miracle by which water is turned into wine; they may know that it was water, and they may taste that now it is wine; yet they can never learn the way in which the change was brought about.

Nevertheless, it is every one's duty to investigate the mysteries and wonderful secrets which the Creator has infused into all things. We may not be able to understand and explain everything. Yet many things are possible to industry and perseverance; and though many an one may be severely handicapped in the struggle for wealth and health, yet, through the grace of God, he may still attain thereto. Therefore he should not think any labour too great which is likely to advance his knowledge of Antimony. Whoever, then, would perfectly understand the Anatomy of Antimony, should, in the first place, become acquainted with the manner of its solution, so that he may be able to seize it in the right place, and proceed in the right way, without entering into devious paths. In the second place, he should learn how to regulate the fire, so that it shall be neither too fierce nor too feeble. Fire is the root of the whole matter. By means of fire the vitalizing spirits are extracted and dissolved for the purposes of our operation. But care must be taken not to mortify and destroy the spirit by means of too much heat.

The third point for consideration is the proportion of the substance, the discovery of the proper measure, as I have already noted, when enumerating the five points which are requisite in Alchemy. It is necessary to enlarge further upon this matter.

The substance is prepared by means of dissolution; it is perfected by means of coction in fire. This is the axe that kills the ox, and divides it into parts. But men cannot partake of the flesh till it has been cooked over the fire, by which means the red colour of the meat is removed, and a white nitritious substance is substituted in its place. If a man, driven by hunger, were to eat the raw, red flesh, it would be a poison to him rather than a medicine, because the stomach has not sufficient natural heat to digest the raw material. In the same way, it will be so much the more dangerous for you to use Antimony before separation, preparation, and coction, as the mineral substance is more gross and poisonous in its raw state than that obtained from the animal body.

Therefore Antimony must be so thoroughly deprived of its poisonous nature that it can never again return to it, just as wine which has once been changed into vinegar by putrefaction and corruption, can never again produce the spirit of wine, but must always remain vinegar. But when, by means of distillation, the spirit alone is removed from the wine, so that the watery part is separated from the spirit, and the spirit is afterwards sublimed, the wine can never thenceforth become vinegar, even though it were kept a hundred years, but would always remain spirit of wine, just as the vinegar always remains vinegar.

This change of wine into vinegar is a wonderful thing, for thereby something is actually produced out of the wine which did not before exist in its vegetable essence. In the distillation of wine the first product is spirit; in the distillation of vinegar the first product is a watery substance, and thus a spirit, as I explained above. Hence the spirit of wine, being itself volatile, renders other things volatile, but the spirit of vinegar fixed and renders solid all medicaments, both mineral and vegetable, so that they attract fixed matter and expel fixed diseases.

Pay diligent attention to this fact, and observe it well, for here lies the master key of our whole Art.

Antimony, which contains within itself its own vinegar, should be so prepared as to entirely remove its poisonous nature, in order that he who drinks it may not swallow with it any venom, but rather drive away and cast out all poison from his body.

The preparation of Antimony, or the Key of Antimony, is that by which it is dissolved, opened, divided, and separated. Such processes are calcination, reverberation, sublimation, as we have previously declared. In extracting its essence, in vitalizing its Mercury, the process is continued, and this Mercury must afterwards be precipitated in the form of a fixed powder. By our Art it can also become an oil, which is a specific against the new disease imported into this country by French soldiers.

The same process may be observed, for instance, in the brewing of beer; barley, wheat, or other grain, must undergo all these processes before it becomes a palatable beverage. It must first be mashed and dissolved in water, as I have observed them do in Belgium and England, when I was a young man. This is Putrefaction, or Corruption. Then the water is poured off, and the moist grain is left in a warm place, till it germinates and sticks together. This is Digestion.

Thereupon the grains are once more separated from each other, and dried, either in the sun or before the fire. This is Reverberation and Coagulation.

The prepared germ is then ground in the mill. This is vegetable Calcination. It is afterwards cooked over the fire, and its nobler spirit is mingled with the water in a way which would not have been possible before it was so prepared. Thus water becomes beer, and this we may call Distillation. If hops are added to the beer they are its vegetable salt, which preserves it from all adverse corrupting influences. This method of converting water into a fermented beverage by the extraction of the spirit of grain is unknown to the Spaniards and Italians, and in my native country of Germany I have only found a few, in the Rhenish districts, who understand such Art.

Afterwards a new separation takes place by means of Clarification. A little yeast is added to the beer, which stirs up its internal heat and motion, and thus, in time, the gross is separated from the subtle, and the pure from the impure. The beer thereby becomes a perfect beverage of great efficacy; before this clarification this would not be, because such operative spirit was clogged and hindered by its own uncleanness from fulfilling its objects. Does not experience teach the same lesson in the case of wine? It is not perfect, nor can it properly fulfil its object, till it has been freed from all impurity. Unclarified beer or wine is not half so intoxicating as beer or wine when it is purified.

After this, we may bring about another separation by means of Vegetable

Sublimation. The spirit of wine, or beer, by this process, and by Distillation, is separated, and prepared in the form of another beverage, or ardent spirits. Here the operative virtue is separated from its body; the spirit is extracted by means of fire, and has deserted its inert and lifeless habitation, in which before it was domiciled.

If such ardent wine, or spirit of wine, be rectified, you have Exaltation. When this is done, the spirit of wine is several times distilled, and so condensed by being purified from all phlegm and wateriness that one measure is more effectual than twenty measures were before; it intoxicates more rapidly, and it volatile, and subtle in penetrating and acting upon substances.

Here I exhort you, who desire through my teaching to secure health and riches as the reward of your study of Antimony, not to suppose that there is so much as a superfluous word or letter in what I have hitherto said. I tell you there are many words sprinked up and down in my writings which may make it well worth your while to turn over the pages again and again, and to ponder very frequently the meaning of sentences in which every word is worth its weight in gold. Know that though the illustrations which I have given have a rustic and simple appearance, they set forth a grand truth of the highest moment. But it is neither desirable nor necessary to praise my own works; they will praise themselves, as soon as the suggestions contained in them are practically tried. I purposely use rude and common illustrations. For it is my business to set forth the hidden virtues of Antimony; and as this is a very profound and abstruse speculation, it is useful to prepare the way by throwing upon my subject all the light which can be gained from common and familiar things; otherwise, you might be in danger of losing your road at the very outset of your journey. Antimony is also likened to a bird which is borne through the air on the wings of the wind, and turns whither it will. The wind, or air, here represents the Artist, who can move and impel Antimony whither it pleases him, and place it wherever he likes. He can colour it red or yellow, white or black, according to the way in which he regulates the fire, since Antimony, like Mercury, contains within itself all colours.

If a book be placed before an illiterate person, he does not know what the letters mean; he stands staring stupidly at the characters, like a cow at a new gate. But if that person were taught to read, were shewn the signification of the letters, and instructed in the meaning of the work, he would no longer be a prey to stupid wonder, but the why and the wherefore of the whole thing would be plain and familiar to him. Such a book is Antimony to those who have not yet learned to read it: hence all such persons should pay the most careful attention to my preliminary instruction, and should not be offended if I offer to teach them the alphabet of Antimony. Let them study this alphabet diligently, in order that they may learn to read the book, and thus advance from class to class in this our school of Alchemy, until they have reched the highest grade of all.

But at this point I remember that there is, from time to time, a great clamour, and cry of "Away with them!" raised against those who prepare medicines out of poisons such as Mercury, Arsenic, and Antimony. It is averred that by means of such medicines many have met with a sudden death, or are dragging on a miserable existence. This clamour is most persistently raised by those Doctors of Medicine (save the mark!) who do not know the difference between a poison and a theriac, nor yet how a poison shall be prepared in order that it may become a salutary medicine, and exchange its malignancy for health-giving qualities. I protest against being numbered amongst the persons who administer to their patients orpiment, arsenic, and mercury, which, in their unprepared state, are, of course, deadly poisons. But after legitimate preparation all venom is removed and expelled, and there remains only a Medicine which resists all internal poisons, and radically removes them. It is also the surest antidote against every unprepared poison, and changes all such into its own wholesome nature.

This assertion will excite a fierce controversy among Doctors, and many will be ready to maintain to the last breath that it is utterly impossible to remove the deadly nature of mineral poisons. I do not wonder at their incredulity, since they are hopelessly ignorant of all similar preparations, and have no conception of the deeper mysteries of science. Yet those who are more reasonable will be ready to admit that it is possible considerably to improve a vile and worthless substance.

But before I attempt to declare the virtue of Antimony, you should know that, although Antimony in its raw state is a deadly poison, yet poison can attract to itself poison more effectually by far than any other heterogeneous substance.

This assertion is proved by the fact that the body of an unicorn, which is entirely free from poison, repels every poisonous thing. Place a live spider inside a circle formed by a strip of the skin of an unicorn, and you will observe that the spider will not be able to pass. But if the circle be composed of some envenomed substance, the spider will have no difficulty in crossing the line, which is homogenous to its own nature.

Any similar experiment would yield the same result. Hollow out a silver coin, and let it float on the water like a boat. Then hold close to it, yet without making actual contact, a particle of a true unicorn. The coin will be as surely repelled and moved backward as the duck which sees the sportsman taking aim at it with his gun.

That homogeneous substances always attract each other you may learn from the fact, that if you place a piece of pure, unadulterated bread in a bowl of water, so that it floats on the surface, and hold, not very far from it, a piece of true unicorn, the bread will float in any direction in which the piece of unicorn is moved. So great is the attraction of like to like in Nature that poison always draws towards it irresistibly all that is poisonous, and substances which are free from venom exert the same influence over substances which enjoy a similar immunity.

Hence poison can be removed in two ways: firstly, by its contrary which repels it, as the unicorn repels the spider; secondly, by its like, which attracts it by magnetic power. The poison which is to cure a homogeneous poison must have been so prepared that it shall have become a medicine instead of a poison, in order that it may attract the other, may take it up into ist own nature and expel it.

A proof of this action of natural affinities may be observed in the effect of soap upon linen. Soap is composed of oil, fat and other greasy substances, which seem much more likely to sully than to cleanse linen. But by means of digestion, and through the action of salt, a certain rectification and separation has taken place, so that the soap now, instead of smirching the linen, attracts to itself all the impurities with which it is defiled, and renders it clean and white. In the same way poison may be so prepared as to become instead a purifying medicine, which attracts to itself all the corruption of the human system, and restores it to perfect soundness and health.

As we have begun to point out to the true student of medicine what is good and what is evil in Nature—a question in regard to which our so-called doctors maintain a supine carelessness—it will be well to set forth the truth, and to make it plain by a few more experiments and illustrations.

Let an egg, which is congealed by the winter's frost, be placed in icy-cold water. The shell will soon be covered with ice, but the frost will be extracted from the egg, and it will be fresh and vital as before.

If any man's hand or foot be frozen, he should at once apply snow or ice-water to it. The cold will thus be extracted and the limb saved.

On the contrary, inflammation is best cured by means of some hot or burning substance. If you have an inflammation in your hand, apply to it spirit of wine (which is pure fire), or quintessence of sulphur; the outward heat will attract to itself the inward fire, and not only will you experience immediate relief, but the limb will become strong as before.

In order still further to confirm this truth, I add yet another illustration. Take the spawn of frogs, which is found in March; dry it on a plate in the sun, place it on a wound inflicted by a viper or other venomous serpent, and the wound will be so prepared as to be healed subsequently by other medicines. Or you may spread the spawn on a linen rag, and then apply it to the wound with the same result.

Similarly, you may take a venomous toad, dry it in the sun, reduce it to ashes in a carefully closed pot, pulverize, and apply the powder to any poisoned wound, whereupon it will attract to itself all the poison of the wound. Why? By the combustion or calcination of the toad, its inward efficacy is called out, and becomes operative. The principle which we have so largely illustrated holds good in all cases. If you are seized with the plague, treat it with *astrum solis,* or spirit of Mercury, for the spirit of Mercury attracts every poisonous matter, and purifies the system of all its morbific particles.

The efficacy of *astrum solis* (Star of the Sun) is infinitely greater. For it concentrates within itself all the quickning power of the Sun, which is the life of Nature. It is the Soul of Gold, and the generative principle of all minerals and metals. I will say more about this wonderful *astrum solis* in its own proper place.

In the same way, we must treat Antimony, which has the like operative qualities as the body of gold. I do not now speak of the Star of the Sun. "For," says Antimony, "I know that I must quake and tremble exceedingly before it, and though I greatly excel it in many principal respects, yet, on the whole, I can effect none of those things, which the Star of the Sun, strengthened by heavenly testimony, is able to accomplish. I do not speak either of the star of Mercury, whose parentage is the same as mine. But as to intense penetrative virtue, I must yield the palm to the Star of the Sun."

My books and sayings are related to each other by experience, like the metals, one of which must be tested and known in its relation to the rest. In like manner, my writings and prescriptions have one common scope or aim. The guide who alone can lead you to the place where Plutus sits enthroned, is Vulcan (the god of fire). If you strike steel with a flint, the violent collision elicits a spark, and calls forth the hidden sulphur, or hidden fire, which is kindled by the air so that it burns truly and effectually. Salt remains in the ashes, and mercury is struck out together with the burning sulphur.

In Antimony, too, the mercury must, by a natural method, be separated from its sulphur and salt. Unless the fire which is latent in the steel becomes visible and tangible, it can be of no use; and so our Medicine will produce no effect, unless it be first separated from its gross elements, rectified, manifested, clarified, and prepared, that all may see how a separation of the pure from the impure has taken place, and that the pure metal is purged of all earthy elements, after which the harvest may be expected. But this cannot take place, until the metal has been opened and dissolved by a carefully regulated fire.

In order that I may comprehend much matter of importance within a small compass, this, shortly, is the sum of the science of Antimony.

Whatever is hidden from common observation is the province of Art; but as soon as the hidden has become manifest and visible, the task of our Art is accomplished, and all that remains to be done is purely mechanical, as I have more than once set forth in my other books.

The bee extracts honey from the flower by the art which God has given to her; but when once the honey is visibly perfect, that sweet and fragrant liquid can be prepared in such a way as to become a most potent and deadly poison. This is a fact which no one will believe who has not seen experimental proof of it. Nevertheless, though a corrosive poison is prepared from honey, no one has any right to say that honey itself is poisonous or harmful. Here is something which may deliver our doctors from Divine vengeance. Honey is indirectly prepared from the excrements of brute beasts, with which the meadows are manured, and whence hundreds and thousands of sweet and fragrant flowers spring up. From these the quintessence is sucked by the bees whereby there takes place an alteration and generation of one thing into another, i.e., into an aliment of different form and taste, resembling its former condition in no particular, and designated honey. This honey may be either a pleasant form of food for man, or there may be prepared from it a poison of the most deadly effect, both on man and beast.

Therefore, gentle reader, whoever and whatever you are, follow me and Nature. I will teach you the whole truth without any admisture of falsehood. I will instruct you how to distinguish truth from error, good from evil, the highest from the lowest. For though Antimony be a deadly poison, there can be prepared from it a medicine which radically destroys all diseases, and penetrates and consumes them, by coction, like fire.

First, Antimony must be prepared so as to become a true Stone, which is its quintessence. And forasmuch as in this operation it is in all things like fire, I call it, after its coagulation, the Fire Stone. When this Fire Stone has been properly prepared, according to the directions given at the end of this treatise, its medicinal virtue is such as to consume all noxious humours, purify the blood to the highest degree, and be in all things equal to the efficacy of potable gold.

Here let me advertise the lover of art that the virtue of Antimony is not one among many precious stones, but it combines the virtues of al other precious stones, as is sufficiently evidenced by its colours. Its red represents carbuncle, pyropus, and coral; its white, diamond and crystal; its blue, sapphire; its green, emerald; its yellow, jacynth; its black, granite. As to the metals, its black corresponds to Saturn, its red to iron, its yellow to gold, its green to copper, its blue to silver, its white to mercury, its mixed colours to tin. And not only does Antimony contain the colours, it also contains the virtues and qualities of all other stones and metals, only human life is too short for any one to learn how to educe all the potencies that lie concealed in the heart of Antimony. You may get from it, by distillation, an acid humour, like pure vinegar. By another way, you may prepare a red pellucid substance, as sweet as refined sugar or honey—or you may obtain a bitter substance, like absynth—or an acid substance, like salt oil. At one time it is red, yellow, or white, and is borne upward like a flying eagle. Then, again, it exhibits various colours, and is driven downwards, and, by reverberation, becomes a metal, like lead. Sometimes it looks like transparent glass of a red, yellow, black, white or variegated colour. All of these it is inadvisable to use in medicines unless they have been subjected to some other test. It may also become a variety of subtle oils, whose medicinal virtue transcends their outward appearance; their use is chiefly for applications to wounds and ulcers. The manifold variations which it undergoes might puzzle the oracle of Delphi.

Out of it we may evolve living mercury, and sulphur which burns like common sulphur; moreover, a grey powder can be prepared from it, with real natural salt and many other things.

We will therefore now speak of its preparations, its magistery, arcanum, and tincture, its elixir, and its special essence, which you will be able to extract when I have told you about the Fire-Stone and its preparation, and many other arcana and secrets, of which the wise man of this world know nothing, and to which too little attention has been paid since the decay of the Egyptians, Arabs, and Chaldeans. These truths are of the greatest importance in the study of the true medicine.

Take care that the different operations shall follow each other in the exact order in which I declare and describe; for if the result is to be perfection, every part of the work must be properly attended to. Now, fixed medicines expel and eradicate fixed diseases; but Antimony, in its crude state, is only a purgative, which does not touch the real root of the disease.

I will therefore declare the preparation of all things which belong to Antimony; I will deliver up the keys thereof, and earnestly ask the student to bear in mind that fire is the sure key by which access is obtained to most of the secrets of our Art. This mineral preparation of Antimony is prepared in various manners by the regimen of fire and by a multiple manual operation, whence its medicinal activity, virtue, potency, and colour flow and emanate.

As Antimony is distinguished by a crude, black colour, variegated with white, I will now speak of the first operation to which the substance is subjected, viz., calcination, or incineration, which is carried out in the following manner:

Take best Hungarian Antimony, or any kind you can get; pulverize it as finely as possible, spread thinly on an earthenware dish (round or square) provided with a low margin; place the dish on a calcinatory furnace over a coal fire, which should at first be moderate. As soon as you see smoke rise from the Antimony, stir it about with an iron spoon, and continue doing so till there is no more smoke, and the Antimony sticks together in the shape of small globules. Remove it from the fire, pulverize again into a fine powder, place it on fire, and calcine, as before, till there is no more smoke. This calcination must be repeated not only till the Antimony gives out no more smoke, but does not conglomerate into globules, and has the appearance of pure white ashes. Then has the calcination of Antimony been successfully completed.

Place this calcined Antimony in a crucible, such as goldsmiths use for melting gold and silver, and set it over a violent fire, either lighted in a wind furnace or increased by means of the bellows, till the Antimony becomes liquid like pure water. To test whether Antimony has acquired its proper glassy transparency, dip in it an oblong piece of cold iron, and examine the Antimony which clings to it carefully. If it be clear, pure, and transparent, it is all right, and has attained its due maturity. The tyro, or beginner, shuld know (these remarks are addressed to beginners who are students of the Spagyric Art) that glass, whether prepared from metals, minerals, or any other substance, must be subjected to heat, till it has attained to maturity, and exhibits a clear and pellucid transparency. Let all and several remember that that maturity and this transparency are performed solely by Vulcan operating on the secret and concealed nature. Otherwise, it is unprofitable for any further medicinal development.

When Antimony has become vitrified in the way described, heat a flat, broad copper dish over the fire, pour into it the Antimony in as clear and thin a state as possible, and you will have pure, yellow, pellucid glass of Antimony. This preparation of what I call the glass of Antimony is the simplest, best, and most efficacious with which I am acquainted.

Glass of Antimony may also be prepared with an admisture of borax, as follows:

Take one part of crude Antimony and two of Venetian borax; pound finely, place in crucible, melt them together in a reverberatory furnace, or by a fire kept up with the bellows, pour into hot copper dish, and prepare as before; you will then have a beautiful, pellucid Antimony like pyropus.

The redness of this Antimony may be extracted by means of spirit of wine.

Transparent white glass of Antimony, after its commixture, is further prepared as follows: Pound, together, one part of Antimony till it becomes a fine powder, and four parts of Venetian borax; melt in crucible till the substances are in flux, when they will become first yellow and then white as glass, for, under the continuous regimen of the fire, the yellow here gives place to the white, and a beautiful glass results. The white colour is matured as before, and is tested, in like manner, by the insertion of a piece of cold iron.

There are many other ways in which Antimony can be vitrified. I only describe the results of my own practical experience, and the first way of preparing Antimony, or glass of Antimony, is the very best that can be conceived for all practical purposes. We thus purge out the black colour, which has evaporated in a volatile form through the chimney. Nevertheless, the Antimony still retains a considerable amount of its poisonous nature, and I will now proceed to declare to you how the poison is separated from the medicine, the pur from the impure, in return for which instruction I expect the everlasting gratitude of all my readers, and the approbation of all discerning men in every part of the world.

The first separation of sulphur from its body and the extraction of the Tincture from its salt, are performed as follows:

Take pure glass of Antimony prepared in the first way, and uncombined with any foreign matter; pound it as fine as the finest flour, and place in a broad-bottomed glass vessel, called Cucurbit.

Pour over the Antimony some highly rectified vinegar, subject to digestive fire, or, in summer, expose to the rays of the sun, shaking it once and again every day.

Let this slow digestion be continued till the vinegar assumes a yellow, or rather a reddish, colour, like that of well purified gold. Then pour off this clear and pure extracted substance, add more vinegar, and repeat the same process till no more gold-coloured Tincture can be extracted. Mix all the extract, filter, place in cucurbit, put on lid, distil the vinegar in S. Mary's Bath, till there remains at the bottom a gold-coloured powder approaching red; pour on this powder the distilled rain water; let it evaporate by distillation, add more rain water, and repeat this till all the acidity is washed out, and there remains a sweet and pleasant powder.

This sweet powder you should pound in a hot marble or glass mortar, place in cucurbit, pour on it best highly rectified spirit of wine till it covers the powder to the height of three inches; expose to gently digestive heat, as above, and there will be extracted a beautiful red Tincture with an earthy sediment at the bottom.

The extract is sweet and pleasant to the taste; the sediment still retains its poisonous character, but the Tincture is a wonderfully potent external Remedy, both for man and beast, passing almost the possibility of belief in any one who is inexperienced in this matter.

Three of four grains of this medicine will cure leprosy, and the new French disease. It purifies the blood, dispels melancholy, resists every poison, removes asthma and all chest complaints, including difficulty of breathing, and relieves the stitch in the side. Moreover, this Remedy cures many other diseases, if it be properly applied.

Our Fire Stone should be prepared and matured, like our food and all other medicines, by the corporal fire which reigns in the little world. Where the solar fire of the great world leaves off, there our corporal fire begins a new generation. Corn grows and ripens by the heat of the great Fire; but a new process of cooking and maturing is brought about by the action of the little fire, in order that men may be able to use it for their bodily sustenance.

The oil of Antimony, from which our Fire Stone is prepared, is exceedingly sweet. It is rendered so brilliant by the removal of its earth, and of all impurities, that it may be compared to a bit of crystal on which the meridian rays of the sunshine fall. The method of its preparation is as follows:

Take, in the name of God, equal parts of the ore of Antimony, obtained after sunrise, and of saltpetre; pulverize finely, mix well, place over a gentle fire, bake dextrously (and the method of this baking is the key of the whole work). (Take care at this point not to scorch the pinions of your bird, which is already winging its flight above the hills.) There will remain a blackish substance. Out of this prepare glass, which pound, extract its red Tincture with strong distilled vinegar (made of the same ore), and remove the vinegar by distillation in the bath. There remains a powder from which you shuld make a second extract with highly rectified spirit of wine. Let the faeces settle. You have then a beautiful, sweet, red extract of great medicinal value. This is the pure Sulphur of Antimony. If you have two pounds of this extract, take four ounces of salt of Antimony (of which I have given the receipt). Pour over these the extract, circulate for at least a month in a well-closed vessel, when the salt will unite with the extract of sulphur; remove sediment, if any, extract spirit of wine in S. Mary's Bath, sublilme the powder which remains, and it will be distilled in the form of a many-coloured, sweet, pellucid, reddish oil. Rectify this oil in S. Mary's Bath, so that the fourth part remains, and it is then prepared.

Then take living Mercury of Antimony, which I have taught you how to compose. That is, the Mercury of the Sages so often alluded to. Whoever tells you the secret of this Mercury will be your Pylades, and you will be his Orestes. I, for my part, shall be glad to make a third in such a company. Pour to it red oil of vitriol, made over iron, and highly rectified: remove by distillation in sand the viscidity of the Mercury, and you will have a precious precipitate of a glorious colour, which is of the greatest medicinal value in chronic diseases and open wounds. For it quickly dries up their symptomatic humours, which represent the radical moisture of the disease.

Take equal parts of this precipitate and of our sweet oil of Antimony; put into a well-closed phial; if exposed to gentle heat, the precipitate will gradually be dissolved and fixed in the oil: for the fire consumes its viscidity, and it becomes a red, dry, fixed, and fluid powder, which does not give out the slightest smoke.

Keep reverent silence: for now the King enters his bridal chamber, where he will delight himself many months with his spouse; and they will only leave the chamber when they have grown together, and produced a son who, if not the King of Kings, is at least a King, and delivers his subjects from disease and want.

When you have reached this point, my friend, you have the Medicine of men and of metals; it is pleasant, sweet, and penetrating, and may be used without any risk. Without being a purgative, it expels all impure and morbid matter from the body. It will restore to you health, and relieve you of want in this life; nor can you ever discharge to God your obligation of gratitude for it. I fear that as a monk and religious man I have transcended the proper bounds of reticence and secrecy, and spoken out too freely. At any rate, I have told you enough; and if after all that has been said you do not discover the secret, it will not be my fault.

I have spoken lucidly and openly, nay, I fear, more openly, than the rules of our brotherhood permit. For it is not lawful for every one to eat of the Tree of Knowledge which stands in the midst of Paradise. I will now proceed to describe the uses of this Elixir.

With reference to its medicinal application to the human body, the dose ought to be regulated and determined by careful observation of individual peculiarities of constitution. Nevertheless, an excessive quantity is not really dangerous, as there is no poison in our Elixir. Three or four grains at a time, given in spirit of wine, are sufficient for the cure of every disease; for this Medicine penetrates every part of the body, and contains within itself the potency of many arcana. It removes dizziness and all pulmonary complaints, as well as cough and all difficulty of breathing. It is a wonderful remedy for leprosy and the French (venereal) disease. It cures the plague, dropsy, and all kinds of fevers, and constitutes a powerful antidote to poison. It invigorates the brain and the whole nervous system, the stomach, the liver, and the kidneys, breaks up the calculus and expels it, restores the vital spirits, promotes the menstrual discharge, removes barrenness both in men and women. Taken internally, and aided by suitable external plasters, it cures cancer, fistula, caries of the bones, and all corroding ulcers. In short, it relieves and finally removes all symptoms which indicate disease in the human body, as you will soon discover, if God has called you to be a physician.

I have now told you all that I know about Antimony; it is my prayer that you may discover the rest, so that the fulness of God's wonderful gifts to men may be made known before the end of the world. I return to my Monastery, where I mean to devote myself to further study, and, if possible, to elucidate the secrets of vitriol, common sulphur and the magnet, their origin, preparation, and virtues.

May the God and Lord of Heaven and Earth vouchsafe unto us health in time here, and hereafter salvation, with eternal rest to our souls, on thrones of joy and gladness, world without end! Amen.

Thus I conclude this Treatise on Antimony. Pay particular attention to what has been said of the red oil of Antimony, which is prepared from highly purified sulphur, and of the spirit which is prepared from its salt; compare these operations with what I have written concerning the Fire Stone, and then put the two together. For in this way you will run down the deer which you have been pursuing for so long.

Charles Stein

READING BASIL VALENTINE IN A MOUNTAIN CABIN

The clogged air.
The mountain rises in it
as if only through the foggy morning
to aither, higher, clearer air
above it,
        clouds only — that simple.

Sewage passes under the cabin, I hear at 5 a.m., earliest
and quietest time I am up
passing it seems from right under the mountain.

The fog-brained alchemist says, sees
this too:

        for the earth is nourished
        with stinking dung
        and precious fruits
        are produced thereby

the pine light starts
breath of the gods collected
over the mountain,
        the wind
and the sun now in it make
the mist by 9 skim
the water
      slide over
the cold surface of it, the sunrise
                burning tips
                   of the water mist

        have seen the bride
        cleansed of all impurity
        in the fiery bath
        which enables her to lie in the bridal bed
        with her chosen spouse

                as honey, he says
                comes indirectly
                from the ordure
                of beasts

but in another place, by "feces" it is clear
he means any

precipitate
        and the light remains
uncertain.
     shit stays shit then.
     or does it?

I am constantly manufactured, constantly changed by
fashioned to

            what hands, the woods

                "our art"

            am I the mage, the doctor, or
            as it seems
                    my body, the patient
                    I am in

                    turning the light
                    in its variety
                    through the branches

The Bride is
the soul and
            she waits in her chamber, the body, the woods
for the spiritual word, her husband
to take her up
            to take veils
off, the mist, say,
from the water

            even the thick of these
            words, these woods
            have 'soul'
                  in them, made right
            for the spirit, something
            from outside
            a light
                appearing
                        a distant character
            infused

                made ready by affinity
                and repulsion of opposite
                natures.
                he offers an experiment:

            Place a live spider

> *inside a circle*
> *formed by the strip of the skin of*
> *an unicorn*
> *and you will observe*
> *that the spider will not be able to pass*

                    gives little
                encouragement—

                        o courageous
                who pass
                into the ring-pass-not

The water, the Bride, then,
the sun, whose warm morning takes
the mist up off of it,   Christ
the husband.

            I still have trouble with the wording and
who exactly these
characters are, what shit's
supposed to be
            why
the flushing of all these mountain toilets
put in since last year
come running it seems from out of the mountain just
when I get up
to breathe—

                my air is stopped
                through which I cannot pass
                but hold to the light
                that invisibly abounds in it

                as any hunter

Thomas Vaughan

LUMEN DE LUMINE

I think it were more plain and to some capacities more pleasing if I express myself in this popular, low dialect. It was about the dawning or daybreak when, tired with a tedious solitude and those pensive thoughts which attend it, after much loss and more labour, I suddenly fell asleep. Here then the day was no sooner born but strangled. I was reduced to a night of a more deep tincture than that which I had formerly spent. My fancy placed me in a region of inexpressible obscurity, and—as I thought—more than natural, but without any terrors. I was in a firm, even temper and, though without encouragements, not only resolute but well pleased. I moved every way for discoveries but was still entertained with darkness and silence; and I thought myself translated to the land of desolation. Being thus troubled to no purpose, and wearied with long endeavours, I resolved to rest myself, and seeing I could find nothing I expected if anything could find me.

I had not long continued in this humour but I could hear the whispers of a soft wind that travelled towards me; and suddenly it was in the leaves of the trees, so that I concluded myself to be in some wood or wilderness. With this gentle breath came a most heavenly, odourous air, much like that of sweet briars, but not so rank and full. This perfume being blown over, there succeeded a pleasant humming of bees amongst flowers; and this did somewhat discompose me, for I judged it not suitable with the complexion of the place, which was dark and like midnight. Now was I somewhat troubled with these unexpected occurrences when a new appearance diverted my apprehensions. Not far off on my right hand I could discover a white, weak light—not so clear as that of a candle, but misty and much resembling an atmosphere. Towards the centre it was of a purple colour, like the Elysian sunshine, but in the dilation of the circumference milky; and if we consider the joint tincture of the parts, it was a painted Vesper, a figure of that splendor which the old Romans called *Sol Mortuorum*. Whiles I was taken up with this strange scene there appeared in the middle purple colours a sudden commotion, and out of their very centre did sprout a certain flowery light, as it were the flame of a taper. Very bright it was, sparking and twinkling like the day-star. The beams of this new planet—issuing forth in small skeins and rivulets—looked like threads of silver, which, being reflected against the trees, discovered a curious green umbrage; and I found myself in a grove of bays. The texture of the branches was so even—the leaves so thick and in that conspiring order—it was not a wood but a building.

I conceived it indeed to be the Temple of Nature, where she had joined discipline to her doctrine. Under this shade and screen did lodge a number of nightingales, which I discovered by their whitish breasts. These, peeping through their leafy cabinets, rejoiced at this strange light, and—having first plumed themselves—stirred the still air with their music. This I thought was very pretty, for the silence of the night, suiting with the solitude of the place, made me judge it heavenly. The ground, both near and far off, presented a pleasing kind of checker, for this new star meeting with some drops of dew made a multitude of bright refractions, as if the earth had been paved with diamonds. These rare and various accidents kept my soul busied, but to interrupt my thoughts, as if it had been unlawful to examine what I had seen, another, more admirable object interposed.

I could see between me and the light a most exquisite, divine beauty—her frame neither long nor short but a mean, decent stature. Attired she was in thin loose silk but so green that I never saw the like, for the colour was not earthly. In some places it was fancied with white and silver ribbons, which looked like lilies in a field of grass. Her head was overcast with a thin, floating tiffany, which she held up with one of her hands and looked as it were from under it. Her eyes were quick, fresh and celestial but had something of a start, as if she had been puzzled with a sudden occurrence. From her black veil did her locks break out, like sunbeams from a mist. They ran dishevelled to her breasts and then returned to her cheeks in curls and rings of gold. Her hair behind her was rolled to a curious glove, with a small short spire, flowered with purple and sky-coloured knots. Her rings were pure, entire emeralds—for she valued no metal—and her pendants of burning carbuncles. To be short, her whole habit was youthful and flowery: it smelt like the East and was thoroughly aired with rich Arabian diapasons. This and no other was her appearance at that time; but whiles I admired her perfections and prepared to make my addresses she prevents me with a voluntary approach. Here indeed I expected some discourse from her; but she, looking very seriously and silently in my face, takes me by the hand and softly whispers I should follow her. This, I confess, sounded strange; but I thought it not amiss to obey so sweet a command, and especially one that promised very much but was able in my opinion to perform more.

The light which I had formerly admired proved now at last to be her attendant, for it moved like an usher before her. This service added much to her glory, and it was my only care to observe her, who though she wandered not yet verily she followed no known path. Her walk was green, being furred with a fine, small grass which felt like plush, for it was very soft, and pearled all the way with daisies and primrose. When we came out of our arbours and court of bays I could perceive a strange clearness in the air, not like that of day, neither can I affirm it was night. The stars indeed perched over us and stood glimmering, as it were, on the tops of high hills; for we were in a most deep bottom and the earth overlooked us, so that I conceived we were near the centre. We had not walked very far when I discovered certain thick, white clouds—for such they seemed to me—which filled all that part of the valley that was before us. This indeed was an error of mine; but it continued not long, for coming nearer I found them to be firm, solid rocks but shining and sparkling like diamonds. This rare and goodly sight did not a little encourage me, and great desire I had to hear my mistress speak—for so I judged her now—that if possible I might receive some information. How to bring this about I did not well know, for she seemed averse from discourse. But having resolved with myself to disturb her, I asked her if she would favour me with her name. To this she replied very familiarly, as if she had known me long before.

"Eugenius"—said she—"I have many names, but my best and dearest is Thalia, for I am always green and shall never wither. Thou dost here behold the Mountains of the Moon, and I will shew thee the original of Nilus; for she springs from these invisible rocks. Look up and peruse the very tops of these pillars and cliffs of salt, for they are the true, philosophical, lunar mountains. Did'st thou ever see such a miraculous, incredible thing?"

This speech made me quickly look up to those glittering turrets of salt, where I could see a stupendous cataract or waterfall. The stream was more large than any river in her full channel; but notwithstanding the height and violence of its fall it descended without any noise. The waters were dashed and their current distracted by those saltish rocks; but for all this they came down with a dead silence—like the still, soft air. Some of this liquor—for it ran by me—I took up, to see what strange woollen substance it was that did thus steal down like snow. When I had it in my hands it was no common water but a certain kind of oil of a watery complexion. A viscous, fat, mineral nature it was, bright like pearls and transparent like crystal. When I had viewed and searched it well, it appeared somewhat spermatic, and in very truth it was obscene to the sight but much more to the touch. Hereupon Thalia told me it was the First Matter and the very natural, true sperm of the great world. "It is"—said she—"invisible and therefore few are they that find it; but many believe it is not to be found. They believe indeed that the world is a dead figure, like a body which hath been sometime made and fashioned by that spirit which dwelt in it, but retains that very shape and fashion for some short time after the spirit hath forsaken it. They should rather consider that every frame, when the soul hath left it, doth decompose and can no longer retain its former figure; for the agent that held and kept the parts together is gone. Most excellent then is that speech which I heard some time from one of my own pupils. 'This world'—saith he—'of such divers and contrary parts, would not have reached unity of form had there not been One who did join together such contrary things. But, being brought together, the very diversity of the natures joined, fighting one with another, had discomposed and separated them, unless there had been One to hold and keep those parts together which He at first did join. Verily the order of Nature could not proceed with such certainty, neither could she move so regularly in several places, times, effects and qualities, unless there were Some One Who disposed and ordered these varieties of motions. This, whatsoever it is, by which the world is preserved and governed, I call by that usual name God.'

"Thou must therefore, Eugenius"—said she—"understand that all compositions are made by an Active, Intelligent Life; for what was done in the composure of the great world in general, the same is performed in the generation of every creature, and its sperm in particular. I suppose thou dost know that water cannot be contained but in some vessel. The natural vessel which God hath appointed for it is the earth. In earth water may be thickened and brought to a figure; but of itself, and without earth, it hath an indefinite flux and is subject to no certain figure whatsoever. Air also is a fleeting and indeterminate substance, but water is his vessel; for water being figured by means of earth the air also is thickened and figured in the water. To ascend higher, the air coagulates the liquid fire, and fire incorporated involves and confines the thin light. These are the means by which God unites and compounds the elements into a sperm, for the earth alters the complexion of the water, and makes it viscous and slimy. Such a water must they seek who would produce any magical, extraordinary effects; for this spermatic water coagulates with the least heat, so that Nature concocts and hardens it into metals. Thou seest the whites of eggs will thicken as soon as they feel the fire; for their moisture is tempered with a pure, subtle earth, and this subtle, animated earth is that which binds their water. Take water then, my Eugenius, from the Mountains of the Moon, which is water and no water. Boil it in the fire of Nature to a twofold earth, white and red; then feed those earths with air of fire and fire of air; and thou hast the two magical luminaries. But because thou hast been a servant of mine for a long time, and that thy patience hath manifested the truth of thy love, I will bring thee to my school, and there will I shew thee what the world is not capable of."

This was no sooner spoken but she passed by those diamond-like, rocky salts and brought me to a rock of adamant, figured to a just, entire cube. It was the basis to a fiery pyramid, a trigon of pure *pyrope,* whose imprisoned flames did stretch and strive for heaven. To the four-square of the frontlet of this rock was annexed a little portal and in that hung a tablet. It was a painted hedgehog, so rolled and wrapt up in his bag he could not easily be discomposed. Over this stood a dog snarling and hard by him this instruction: Softly, or he pricks.

In we went, and having entered the rocks, the interior parts were of a heavenly, smaragdine colour. Somewhere they shined like leaves of pure gold, and then appeared a third inexpressible, purple tincture. We had not gone very far but we came to an ancient, majestic altar. On the offertory, or very top of it, was figured the trunk of an old rotten tree, plucked up by the roots. Out of this crept a snake—of colour white and green—slow of motion like a snail and very weak, having but newly felt the sun that overlooked her. Towards the foot or basis of this altar was an inscription in old Egyptian hieroglyphics which Thalia expounded, and this is it:

TO THE BLESSED GODS
IN THE UNDERWORLD
N. L.
τ.α.v.φ.

From this place we moved straight forward till we came to a cave of earth. It was very obscure and withal dankish, giving a heavy odour—like that of graves. Here we stayed not long, but passing this churchyard we came at last to the Sanctuary, where Thalia turning to me made this her short and last speech.

"Eugenius, this is the place which many have desired to see, but saw it not. The preparatives to their admission here were wanting. They did not love me but mine. They coveted indeed the riches of Nature, but Nature herself they did both neglect and corrupt. Some advantages they had in point of assault, had they but studied their opportunities. I was exposed to their hands but they knew me not. I was subject in some measure to their violence, but He that made me would not suffer me to be rifled. In a word, the ruin of these men was built on their disposition. In their addresses to me they resembled those pitiful things which some call courtiers. These have their antics and raunts, as if they had been trained amongst apes. They scrape—as one hath well expressed it—proportions mathematical, make strange legs and faces, and in that phrase of the same poet

> 'Vary their mouths as 'twere by magic spell
> To figures oval, square and triangle.'

So these impudent sophisters assaulted me with vainglorious humours. When I looked into their hearts there was no room for me. They were full of proud thoughts and dreamed of a certain riotous happiness which must be maintained by my expenses and treasures. In the interim they did not consider that I was plain and simple, one that did not love noise but a private, sweet content. I have, Eugenius, found thee much of my own humour. I have withal found thy expectations patient. Thou canst easily believe where thou has reason to thy faith. Thou hast all this while served without wages: now is the time come to reward thee. My love I freely give thee, and with it these tokens—my key and seal. The one shuts, the other opens: be sure to use both with discretion. As for the mysteries of this my school, thou hast the liberty to peruse them all; there is not anything here but I will gladly reveal it to thee. I have one precept that I shall commend to thee, and this is it: you must be silent. You shall not in your writings exceed my allowances. Remember that I am your love, and you will not make me a prostitute. But because I wish you serviceable to those of your own disposition, I here give you an emblematical type of my Sanctuary, with a full privilege to publish it. This is all, and I am now going to that invisible region where is the abode of the immortals. Let not that proverb take place with you: Out of sight, out of mind. Remember me and be happy."

These were her instructions, which were no sooner delivered but she brought me to a clear, large light; and here I saw those things which I must not speak of. Having thus discovered all the parts of that glorious labyrinth, she did lead me out again with her clue of sunbeams—her light that went shining before us. When we were past the rocks of Nilus she shewed me a secret staircase, by which we ascended from that deep and flowery vale to the face of this our common earth. Here Thalia stopped in a mute ceremony, for I was to be left all alone. She looked upon me in silent smiles, mixed with a pretty kind of sadness, for we were unwilling to part. But her hour of translation was come, and taking—as I thought—our last leave, she passed before my eyes unto the eternal, into the ether of Nature.

Edward Kelly

THE THEATRE OF TERRESTRIAL ASTRONOMY

Many books have been written on the art of Alchemy, which, by the multiplicity of their allegories, riddles, and parables, bewilder and confound all earnest students; and the cause of this confusion is the vast number and variety of names, which all signify and do set forth one and the same thing. For this reason I have resolved in my own mind to loosen and untie all the difficult knots of the ancient Sages. I will speak first of the inventors and restorers of the Art; secondly, of the mutual conversion of elements, and how through the predominance of one element the substance of metals is generated; thirdly, I will shew the affinity and homogeneity of metals, procreated in the bowels of the earth, their sympathies and antipathies, according to the purity and impurity of their Sulphur and Mercury; and that as metals consist of Sulphur and Mercury, they can furnish us with the first matter of the Elixir; 4°, the preparation of Mercurial water; 5°, the conversion of prepared Mercury into Mercurial earth; 6°, the exaltation of Mercurial water; 7°, the solution of gold by Mercurial water; 8°, the preparation of the water or Moon of the Sages; 9°, the conjunction of sun and moon; 10°, the blackness, or Raven's Head, by means of which the solution and copulation of Sun and Moon do both take place; 11°, the peacock's tail; 12°, the white Tincture; 13°, the perfect red Elixir. This Art being given by Divine inspiration, and as a secret revealed from above, we implore God's help for every part of our work, the small as well as the great, for He alone hath the power to give or to withhold this knowledge from whomsoever He will. No one taketh this honour to himself, but God alone can enlighten the eyes and lift the cloud of natural mysteries, so that albeit you cannot understand the plainest things without Him, yet will you apprehend the most difficult arcana if He give you light. I will now speak of the illustrious men who, before and after the Flood, have discovered and established the chemical Art.

Of the Inventors and Restorers of this Art

All Sages agree that the knowledge of this Art was first imparted to Adam by the Holy Spirit, and He prophesied, both before and after the Fall, that the world must be renewed, or, rather, purged with water. Therefore his successors erected two stone tables, on which they engraved a summary of all physical arts, in order that this arcanum might become known to posterity. After the Flood, Noah found one of these tables at the foot of Mount Ararat. Others say that the knowledge of the Art was restored by Hermes Trismegistus, whose mind was a treasury of all arts and sciences; and alchemists are still called sons of Hermes. Bernard of Trevisa states that the said Hermes came to the valley of Hebron, and there found seven stone tables, on which a summary of the seven liberal Arts had been inscribed before the Flood; for this same Hermes flourished both before and after the Flood, and is identified with

Noah. Then this Art found its way into Persia, Egypt, and Chaldaea. The Hebrews called it the Cabbala, the Persians Magia, and the Egyptians Sophia, and it was taught in the schools together with Theology; it was known to Moses, Abraham, Solomon, and the Magi who came to Christ from the East. Magia derived its origin from the doctrine of the Divine Ternary and the Trinity of God. For God has stamped and sealed all created things with this character of Trinity, as a kind of hieroglyphical writing, whereby His own nature might be known. For the number 3 and the magic number 4 make up the perfect number 7, the seat of many mysteries. And seeing that the Quaternary rests in the Ternary, it is a number which stands on the horizon of eternity, and doth exhibit everything bound with God in us, thus including God, men, and all created things, with all their mysterious powers. Adding three, you get ten, which marks the return to unity. In this arcanum is concluded all knowledge of hidden things which God, by His word, has made known to the men of His good pleasure, so that they might have a true conception of Him. And this is the figure which is called the sphere of Heaven. The said sphere consists of a circle, which circle represents the Trinity of the Deity in unity, God with three heads and one crown, surmounted by a triangle, encircled with a rainbow, and above the sun and moon. The

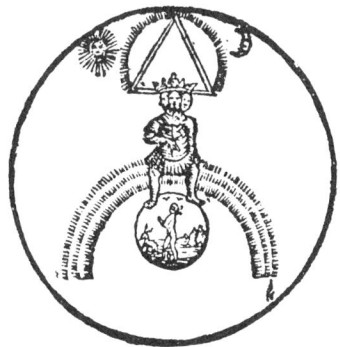

first colour of the rainbow, on which God sits, is black, with the sign of Saturn; the second, dark brown, with the sign of Jupiter; the third, red, with the sign of Mars; the fourth, green and yellow, with the sign of the Sun; the fifth, green, with the sign of Venus; the sixth, yellow, green, white, and red, with the sign of Mercury; the seventh, a silver grey, with the sign of the Moon, and yellow beneath.

His feet are placed on the terrestrial globe, in which are animals and hills, with a white and brown man, whose eyes are bandaged, and an egg is between his feet.

Of the Mutual Conversion of Elements; How One Element Predominates Over Another; Whence the Substance of the Metals is Generated.

Geber, Morienus, and other Sages have pronounced the conversion of one element into another a very necessary process in the composition of the

Stone: convert the elements, and you have what you seek. There are four elements, air, water, fire, earth, with their four qualities, hot, cold, moist, dry. Two are active, air and fire, and two passive, water and earth. Two are light, and two heavy. Contradictory qualities are united only by means of a third. Hot and dry are not contradictory, and therefore form the element of air; cold and dry are not contradictory, and become earth; nor are cold and moist, which constitute water: but hot and cold are united only by means of a medium, viz., dry, as otherwise they would destroy each other. Hence hot and cold are united and separated by dissolving and coagulating the homogeneous quality. Moist and dry, on the other hand, are united and separated by constriction and humectation; simple generation and natural transmutation are by the operation of the elements. For those elements which conquer cold generate that which is hot. It is clear that all things are generated by heat and cold; and all elements must belong to the same genus, or else they could not act on each other. After creating the matter of the metals, namely, living Mercury, Nature added to it an active quality. For Mercury, the substance, could not of itself manifest its effects, and Nature wisely joined to it an active kind of mineral earth, unctuous and fat, thickened by long digestion in the mineral caverns of the earth, which is commonly called Sulphur. This Mercury is, however, not the common metal, but the principle and origin of metals. Mercury is the matter, Sulphur the form of metals, natural heat acting on the matter of Mercury, as upon a fit and well adapted subject.

The picture represents a black rock, on the summit of which stand black Saturn; Jupiter, the white kind; Mars, the red soldier; Sol, with a golden head and ruddy neck; Venus, in a green robe; Mercury, with helmet, and red, green, purple, white, yellow, ochre, black gown, and yellow, red, blue wings; the Moon white and black.

On the black plain stands Mercury of many colours, the Moon with the sign ☽ on her head, and Sulphur on both sides of Mercury is signified by the term Hermaphrodite; the four elements from the four corners blow upon the place where Mercury and the Moon are.

Of the Homogeneous Affinity of Metals generated in the bowels of the Earth; Harmony and Antipathy of Metallic Qualities. Metals consist of Mercury and

Sulphur, and furnish us with the first substance of the Elixir.

The various conversions of the elements which produce the first matter of metals have been now described. We must next treat of the nature of the said metals. It is clearer than daylight that there are seven planets, seven days, seven metals, and seven operations. The metals are called after the planets, because of their influence and their mutual relations. The mineral principles are living Mercury and Sulphur. From these are generated all metals and minerals, of which there are many species, possessing diverse natures, according to the purity and impurity of the Mercury and Sulphur, resulting in the purity or impurity of the generated metal. Gold is a perfect body, of pure, clear, red Mercury, and pure, fixed, red, incombustible Sulphur. Silver is a pure body, nearly approaching perfection, of pure, clear, fixed white Mercury, and Sulphur of the same kind; it is a little wanting in fixation, colour, and weights. Tin is a pure, imperfect body, of pure, fixed and unfixed, clear, white Mercury outside, and red Mercury inside, with Sulphur of the same kind. Lead is an impure, imperfect body, of impure, unfixed, earthy, white, fetid Mercury and Sulphur outside, and red Mercury inside, with Sulphur of the same quality. Copper is an impure and imperfect body, of impure, unfixed, dirty, combustible, red Sulphur and Mercury. It is deficient in fixation, purity, and weight, while it abounds in impure colour and combustible terrestreity. Iron is of impure, imperfect, excessively fixed, earthy, burning, white and red Sulphur and Mercury, is wanting in fusion, purity, and weight, abounding in fixed, impure Sulphur and combustible terrestreity. Nature transmutes the elements into Mercury, just as Sulphur transmutes the first matter. The nature of all metals must be the same, because their first substance is the same, and Nature cannot develop anything out of a substance that is not in it.

The picture represents a black rock, on which stand, hand in hand, the planets: 1, Black Saturn, falling down; 2, Jupiter; 3, Mars; 4, Mercury of many colours; 5, Venus, with green robe, and the Sun and Moon. Lower down, on the black rock, stands an old man with a pick-axe, cutting a piece out of the rock, whence Saturn falls, and near him lie, as if dead, Jupiter and Saturn.

Of the Preparation of Mercurial Earth

Know that out of all metals a perfect Medicine can be made, which can transmute the remaining metals into gold and silver; for out of the perfect metals you get, by proper separation of elements, the Salt of Nature, otherwise Ore of the Philosophers, by some called Philosophical Lili, without which the work of the Sages cannot be accomplished. For Art presupposes a substance created by Nature alone, in which Art assists Nature and Nature assists art.

A vessel like an urinal stands, encircled at its base by a ring of twisted straw; within it are Mercury, Mars, and Saturn, lying on their backs, and an old man is on the point of throwing in Venus and Jupiter. Behind the old man, on the black rock, stand the Sun and Moon.

Of the Conversion of Prepared Mercury into Mercurial earth

Metals, as above stated, contain a salt, out of which fire and the sagacity of the artist can educe a water, which the Sages call Mercurial water, the Virgin's milk, Lunaria, May dew, the Green Lion, the Dragon, the Fire of the Sages. This Mercurial water they have compared to corrosive aqua fortis, because just as those waters which are composed out of atrament, alum, copperas, Armenian salt, etc., corrode metals, and break them up, so this Mercurial spirit, or water, dissolved its body, and separates from it the Tincture.

The picture represents a hill, on which stand many trees; at the foot of the hill is a yellow lion suckling a green lion.

There is a furnace in which is a pumpkin-shaped vessel (cucurbit), from which blue serpents ascend into the alembic, and are collected into a receptacle by an old man who seems on the point of carrying it away.

Of the Exaltation of Mercurial Water

The ancient Sages have spoken of the composition of the Green Lion or Dragon, emanating from the seven Planets, in a style saturated with the darkness of night itself; but instead of vainly endeavouring to untie their Gordian knots, I will try to sketch its composition with a few strokes of my pen. It is generated by the subtle influences descending into the elements; then its substance is scattered abroad in the heavens, its workshop is in the clouds, and again it descends into its earth, with rain water and a white vapour, thus receiving the strength of things above and things below; it is nourished by its own body, eating its wings and tail with its teeth, the whole body being swallowed by the head, and remaining in it for ever. This is the hidden and incomparable treasure of all the Sages, which none can obtain except through the teaching of a Master, or by revelation of God, who, in His goodness makes it known to whom He will.

An old man stands near a vessel, like an urinal, in which a Green Dragon is devouring blue serpents. Above the Dragon is the yellow, green, blue, black, red sign of Mercury. Above the urinal is a Green Dragon biting its tail. Near the urinal a Green Lion bites a piece out of the back of a Red Lion, so that the blood flows down. In the background are forests and hills.

Of The Solution of the Sun with Mercurial Water

It should be noted at this point that the Tincture is not found otherwise than in gold. This may be understood from the parable of Bernard, who says that the Sun, on entering the bath, first of all puts off his golden robe. For what the eagle is among birds, the lion among beasts, the salmon among fishes, the Sun among planets, such gold is among metals. In it are the red and white tincture, because it tinges, transforms, and illumines all bodies. For gold is made out of the substance of the most subtle living Mercury, and out of pure, red, fixed, self-cleansed Sulphur, which tinges, and contains in itself, the soul, which is called the form of gold, and by some Sages the Ferment of Philosophers. This soul of gold with its heat digests and tinges its substance, and imparts to it its form, so that through its mediation the day begins to dawn. To corrupt the gold, to dissolve and volatize it while still preserving its form is our great object, as it is also our grand labour.

The Sun, encircled by a red rainbow, shines among the clouds, and a Green Lion is biting the Sun in the face, so that the blood flows. An old man is holding in his hand an urinal, in which is red water; and in this water a winged man stands up to his navel. Out of the urinal is flying a Green Dragon, which bites the face of the Sun as he stands with the Moon on a rock, so that the blood flows under the dragon into the urinal. Under the black rock is a Green Dragon, whose tail is cut off, and the same is gnawing his wings.

Of the Preparation of the Earth, or Moon of the Sages

When the soul of gold has been separated from its body, or when the body, in other words, has been dissolved, the body of the Moon should be watered with its proper menstruum, and reverberated, the operation being repeated as often as necessary, i.e., until the body becomes subtle, broken up, pure, dissolved, coagulated. This is done, not with common fire, but with that of the Sages, and at last you must see clearly that nothing remains undissolved. For unless the Moon or Earth is properly prepared and entirely emptied of its soul, it will not be fit to receive the Solar Seed; but the more throughly the earth is cleansed of its impurity and earthiness, the more vigorous it will be in the fixation of its ferment. This earth or Moon of the Sages is the trunk upon which the solar branch of the Sages is engrafted. This earth, with its water, putrefies and is cleansed; for heat, acting on a dry substance, causes whiteness. Azot and fire wash Laton, or earth, and remove its opacity.

A fire is laid under the Sun, which is burning, and much smoke is ascending. An old man has in his hands an urinal, in which is the Moon lying on her back in blackish water. Out of the vessel is flying a green Dragon, holding the Moon in its mouth by the navel, and placing its fore feet on a black rock. Beneath the rock a green Dragon lies dead on his back.

The Conjunction of Sun and Moon

The ancient philosophers have enumerated several kinds of conjunction, but to avoid a vain prolixity I will affirm, upon the testimony of Marsilius Ficinus, that conjunction is union of separate qualities, or an equation of principles, viz., Mercury and Sulphur, Sun and Moon, agent and patient, matter and form. When the virgin or feminine, earth is thoroughly purified and purged from all superfluity, you must give it a husband meet for it; for when the male and the female are joined together by means of the sperm, a generation must take place in the menstruum. The substance of Mercury is known to the Sages as the earth and matter in which the Sulphur of Nature is sown, that it may thereby putrefy, the earth being its womb. Here the female seed awaits that of the male, by means of which they are inseparably united, the one being hot and dry, and the other cold and moist; the heat and dryness of the male are tempered with the cold and moisture of the female, and, in due time, the matter will assume a specific form. For all action tends to the production of a form, being, as it is, an efficient principle.

Opposition

A very red Sun is pouring blood into an urinal. An old man is pouring blood out of another urinal, together with a winged child, into a third urinal, which stands on straw and contains the Moon lying on her back in blackish water. Near the Sun a jug is pouring white rays, or drops, into an urinal. On the hill stands a Phoenix, biting its breast, out of which drops blood, the same being drunk by its young. Beneath the rock a husbandman is scattering seed in his field.

Of the Blackness or Raven's Head by means of which the copulation of Sun and Moon takes place

The second conjunction is of three, viz., body, soul, and spirit; and these three we must make one. For as the soul is the bond of the spirit, so the body must also join to itself the soul, which can only be after putrefaction; for nothing can be improved if its form has not previously been utterly destroyed. The signs of this are a black colour and a fetid smell. For heat, acting on moisture, produces blackness, which is the sign of the perfect mingling of the substance with a specific form. For solution and putrefaction begin with a fetid smell, and the process gradually develops, and therefore the Raven's Head is called a deadly poison. The odour is rather intellectually than sensuously perceptible. The blackness must precede whiteness. For putrefaction begins with solution, but does not end with it. The second solution of the more perfect stone is better than the first, because the more it develops, the more the stone is subtilized. Our whole magistery, then, is based on putrefaction; for it can come to nothing, unless it is putrefied.

Conjunction

BLACK SUN   BLACK MOON

An old man with a book in his hand stands by the furnace.
A black Sun in the vessel
Behind the furnace is a field of green barley springing up out of the earth.
The Pavement, on which the furnace stands, is black.

Of the Peacock's Tail

Our substance, according to the Sages, has a red head, white feet, and black eyes. The beginning of our work is the Black Raven, which, like all things that are to grow and receive life, must first putrefy. For putrefaction is a necessary condition of solution, as solution is of birth and regeneration. This putrefaction is not impure, but a commixtion, in their smallest parts, of earth with water, and water with earth, till the whole body becmes one. The red male must be digested in union with his white wife, till both become dry—for otherwise no colours will appear. When the dry principle acts on the moist, flowers of all the colours of a Peacock's Tail begin to spring up in the Sage's vessel. Sometimes the vessel will seem inwardly covered with gold, which is a sign of the action of the male seed, of Sulphur, on the female menstruum, or Mercury, one mingling with the other as the result of their conflict. As the moisture is gradually dried up, these shifting coloure give place to a settled whiteness.

An ole man stands near the furnace, both towers are open, the urinal constantly changes its colour; behind the furnace is barley producing ears.

Of the White Tincture

Having treated of the matter, the mode of procedure, and of the regimen of the fire, I proceed now to the description of the composition of the white and the red Stone. The blackness becomes whiteness very slowly; the operation must be gradual, as a fierce fire would burst the vessel, and mar our work. As the Mercury becomes white, our white Sulphur becomes incombustible, containing the poison, whose whiteness is like the whiteness of alabaster. The whole magistery takes place in one vessel, and with one fire, viz., the dry and moist elementary fire of the matter, till it is all dissolved again and again, and conagulated and thickened into a mass of a clear snow-white colour, which, when cool, becomes like a hard gum. The decoction, however, must be continued till the Eagle is revived (or vitrified), and becomes a crystalline stone which melts, tinges, and coagulates Mercury and other imperfect metals into pure silver. This white tincture, or elixir, is also called the Virgin's milk, the everlasting water, and water of life, because it is as brilliant as white marble; it is also called the White Queen, who by increasing the fire becomes the Mighty King, the white transforming into yellow and saffron, and at last into a deep ruby colour.

A white King sits on the throne, having at his feet the Moon, and the five Planets on their knees. Near at hand is a field, with yellow, ripening ears of

barley. Behind the furnace is an old man inspecting the coals, and in the urinal is the full Moon.

Of the Perfect Red Elixir

Xiphilinus and the rest of the philosophers agree in this, that the white colour must precede the red. As you can have no red colour where the substance has not first been white, so the black cannot become orange unless it first become white. In like manner, the Rosary says that nothing can become gold that has not first been silver. He who knows how to convert gold into silver, also knows how to convert silver into gold. Gold, to become silver, must first be corrupted and made black, and there is no method of becoming yellow except by way of white; in the same way the white must become red by way of yellow. Heat, acting on moisture, causes blackness; acting on dryness, especially if it be continued carefully and unceasingly, there is developed true whiteness; out of white comes yellow, and out of yellow a permanent and tinging ruby colour.

An old man in a tunic stands by a furnace, one tower of which is open, and in the urinal of the other is a purple Sun.

A King, like a Pontiff, in a purple robe, sits on the throne, and at his feet kneel the Sun and Moon, with the five planets; behind the King stands an old man with uncovered head.

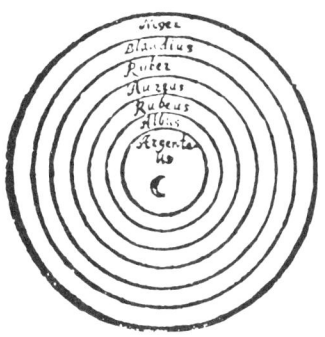

The Circles are: 1, Black; 2, Blue; 3, Red; 4, Golden; 5, Ruddy; 6, White; 7, Argentine, with the sign of the Moon.

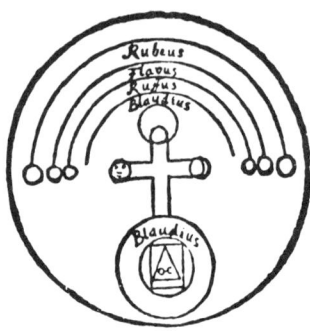

The Circle is black, white, blue, red, yellow, tawny, blue; in the Cross are the Sun and Moon. The lower Circle is blue, and contains a quadrangle of red, blue, black, and white. The triangle is black, blue, and red, and in its centre are the Sun and Moon.

Janus Lacinius Therapus, the Calabrian

A FORM AND METHOD OF PERFECTING BASE METALS
(excerpt) "Exposition of the Typical Figures"

Three measures must be served in our art: the first is to know thoroughly the elements, their many names and traditions, the various paths of their formation and corruption: to provide the experiment with the proper material; the second is to work continuously, allowing each process to flow over into the next: a clear path is corrupted by artificial breaks in the sequence; the third is to cultivate a patience, a faith based on knowledge of the stars and sun and the works of time: the rhythms and cycles of Nature contain the code and root of our handiwork.

Then seek (as the first substance of your work) the highly pure Water of Life, and keep it; but do not presume that the sparkling clarets of Bacchus are the moistures that transmute all things. For while you anxiously look about in out-of-the-way places and long for extraordinary events to come to you, while you are desirous of witch's brews and love potions and instant cures from odd stones, you pass by the clear motions of the blessed stream. While you gather in groups to spot unprecedented lights and colors in the night-time sky, while you await incredible assignations of power on earthly lands, the Stone, the good Heavenly Stone, lies at your feet.

Enter the Palace in which there are fifteen mansions, where the king, his brow encircled with the diadem, is borne on a majestic throne. He holds in his hand the scepter of the whole world: before him, in robes of different colors, kneel his son and five servants; they petition him for a share of his power; they plead and press; he does not even answer them.

The son, spurred and encouraged by the servants, stabs the father while he sits on the throne. (Let an amalgam be made of the purest water, etc.)

In the third picture we see that the son is taking his father's blood upon his robe (this is the second sequence in our art, which has already been explained in our discussion of method).

In the fourth mansion a grave is dug (this is the furnace). Its depth is measured by two hands, its width by four inches.

Now we are in the fifth mansion where the son planned to throw his father into the tomb, and then leave him there; but (through our art) both fell in together.

The sixth mansion is the one in which the son struggles to get free, but another (who arose from the first during the events of the second mansion) steps forth in order to close him back in.

The father and son are in the tomb together; a swift decay sets upon their ashes (or they take a very hot bath).

The eighth mansion includes that which has come about during the seventh; i.e., the residue may be examined now that the vessel has cooled, etc.

We have arrived at the ninth mansion; here the bones are removed from the tomb; they contain the whole body's putrefaction: as the precipitate they undergo a sequence of liquid filters. Now that you have dissolved the mass, store it carefully.

The tenth operation begins with an allotting of the bones to their nine natural divisions. The body's deliquescence is then brought to an oven and left there to cook for nine days. As certain areas blacken they are gently ousted from the pot to be stored in another vessel (whose position might also be called hot). The dilutent body is softly warmed for another nine days, after which again a certain portion has turned black and is removed and placed with the rest. Such is the succession of the work until the water is made clear and pure. I.e., and this highly refined pool, o nomad, is the Water of Life. Now let those successive chars of the last process be returned in a small decanter, and douse them in that glass with the Water of Life, until its wet levels shall rise over them by an inch. Let this puddle stand over a moderate flame for nine days, each day renewing the water as it is necessary. (And so the earth shall become a brilliant white albumen, rich as yolk, as will any precipitate that is continuously corroded and purged by its own juices and salts).

Whereby an angel is sent, who strews the bones on the distilled and whitened field (which is now mingled in its own seed, and let this unit be placed in a tightly-shut jar with its alembic, i.e., by which the percolating spirit is guided and retained; and let the denser mass be driven below the pure liquid by a torrid fire; it will serve as the osseous matter at the bottom).

Now we come to the eleventh mansion where the servants pray to God that he might restore their king. Henceforth the entire work is made pertinent to his restoration.

A second angel arrives at the twelfth mansion; he scatters the additional set of bones upon the earth (till they all congeal and thicken: then a wonderful thing happens).

The angels come now in succession. The first, second, third, and fourth part of the bones are cast upon the earth and they coalesce into clear white bodies, translucent and rich. So the fifth and sixth divisions, when cast out, become yellow; and the seventh, eighth, and ninth are touched at the xanthic harmonic also. The earth of these bones has become as red as blood, as red as ruby-stones.

As the king rises from the tomb, we see that he is full of the grace of God. His body is wholly spiritual and built on heavenly fires; he has the power to make all his servants kings.

Now he executes his dominion upon his servants and his son, laying diadems onto each of their heads, making them kings by his mercy and majesty (for God has given him supernatural power and holy grace).

Let no usurper, let no avaricious or lustful person lay hands upon this miraculous work, for all that he touches must go the way of the damned. Let the man of God, the Christ, the humble bearer of a wise and compassionate heart come forth; let him come hither whose life is a quest, and whose quest is the mystery, and whose mystery is the hidden causes of things on earth.

Archibald Cockren

ALCHEMY REDISCOVERED AND RESTORED

I believe that in this art lies man's salvation from sickness and disease, and the secret of his ultimate perfection, but needless to say in order to utilize to the full the physical benefits of alchemistic research, man must undertake the transmutation of certain baser elements in his emotional and mental make-up. With this process of psychological transmutation I do not propose to deal for the moment, but I am convinced that in this present age of chaos, when new ideas, new values, and, as I believe, new understanding are coming into being, it may be possible that some of these more unorthodox conceptions will meet with less opposition and more sympathy than previously. Since the complete destruction of all those conditions which in the nineteenth century seemed so permanent and immovable, man has been far less inclined to reject out of hand any new idea which may be put before him. For this reason I write down my findings of an age-old truth in the belief that it is a task destiny has set me, and whether my words be accepted or no lies not with me but with those to whom they are addressed.

Come with me, therefore, to my little laboratory with its array of alembics, crucibles, and sandbaths, and hear something of the struggles of the would-be alchemist and of the mysteries he seeks to unravel.

After a careful study of Basil Valentine's 'Triumphal Chariot of Antimony,' I decided to make my first experiments with antimony. I soon found, however, that on arriving at a crucial point, the key had almost invariably been deliberately withheld, and a dissertation on theology inserted in its place. Gradually, however, I came to realize that the theological discourse was not without object, but actually the means of veiling a valuable clue of some kind. After much labour, a fragrant golden liquid was finally obtained from the antimony, although this was merely a beginning. The alkahest of the alchemist, the First Matter, still remained a mystery.

Then followed processes with iron and copper. After purification of the salts or vitriol of these metals, of calcination, and the obtaining of a salt from the calcined metal by a special process, followed by careful distillation and re-distillation in rectified spirits of wine, the oil of these metals was obtained, a few drops of which used singly, or in conjunction, proved very efficacious in cases of anaemia and debility which the ordinary iron medicine failed to touch.

The conjunction of iron and copper proved to be an elixir of a very stimulating and regenerating character, the action being such as to clear the body from toxins, and I well remember on taking a few drops one evening that the prospect of a spell of fairly strenuous mental work, even after a really laborious day, seemed to hold no terrors for me!

But still the alkahest remained an enigma, and so further experiments were made with silver and mercury. For those with silver, fine silver was reduced with nitric acid to the salts of the metal, carefully washed in distilled water, sublimated by special process, finally yielding up a white oil which had a very soothing effect on highly nervous cases.

In the case of mercury, the metal on being reduced to its oil, produced a clear crystalline liquid with great curative properties, but unlike common mercury, no poisonous qualities.

After this I decided to work upon fine gold—gold, that is, without any alloy. This was dissolved in Aqua Regia and reduced to the salts of gold; these were washed in distilled water, which in its turn was evaporated in order to remove its very caustic properties. It was at this point that a very real difficulty arose, for when these salts of gold lose their acidity, they slowly but surely tend to return to their metallic form again. Nevertheless, an elixir was finally produced from them by distillation, although even then a residue of fine metallic gold remained behind in the retort.

Having got so far I realized that without the alkahest of the philosophers the real oil of gold could not be obtained, and so again I went back and forth in the alchemists' writings to obtain the clue. The experiments which I had already made considerably lightened my task, and one day while sitting quietly in deep concentration the solution to the problem was revealed to me in a flash, and at the same time many of the enigmatical utterances of the alchemists were made clear.

Here, then, I entered upon a new course of experiment, with a metal for experimental purposes with which I had had no previous experience. This metal, after being reduced to its salts and undergoing special preparation and distillation, delivered up the Mercury of the Philosophers, the Aqua Benedicta, the Aqua Celestis, the Water of Paradise. The first imtimation I had of this triumph was a violent hissing, jets of vapour pouring from the retort and into the receiver like sharp bursts from a machine-gun, and then a violent explosion, whilst a very potent and subtle odour filled the laboratory and its surroundings. A friend has described this odour as resembling the dewy earth on a June morning, with the hint of growing flowers in the air, the breath of the wind over heather and hill, and the sweet smell of the rain on the parched earth.

Nicholas Flamel, after searching and experimenting from the age of twenty, wrote when he was eighty years old:

> 'Finally I found that which I desired, which I also soon knew by the strong scent and odour thereof.'

Does this not coincide, this voice from the fourteenth century, with my own description of the peculiar subtle odour? Cremer, also writing in the early fourteenth century, says:

> 'When this happy event takes place, the whole house will be filled with a most wonderful sweet fragrance, and then will be the day of the nativity of this most blessed preparation.'

Having arrived at this point my next difficulty was to find a way of storing this subtle gas without danger to property. This I accomplished by coils of glass piping in water joined up with my receiver, together with a perfect government of heat, the result being that the gas gradually condensed into a clear golden-coloured water, very inflammable and very volatile. This water had then to be separated by distillation, the outcome being the white mercurial water described by the Comte St. Germain as his athoeter or primary water of all the metals. I will again quote from Manly Hall's introduction to 'The Most Holy Trinosophia,' the passage in which Casanova describes the athoeter:

'Then he showed me his magistrum which he called *Athoeter.* It was a white liquid contained in a well stopped phial. He told me that this liquid was the universal spirit of Nature and that if the wax of the stopper was pricked ever so slightly, the whole of the contents would disappear. I begged him to make the experiment. He thereupon gave me the phial and the pin and I myself pricked the wax, when, lo, the phial was empty.'

This passage aptly describes this water which is so volatile that it rapidly evaporates if left unstoppered, boils at a very low temperature, and does not so much as wet the fingers. This mercurial water, this athoeter of St. Germain, is absolutely necessary to obtain the oil of gold, which is obtained by its addition to the salts of gold after those salts have been washed with distilled water several times to remove the strong acidity of the Aqua Regia used to reduce the metal to that state. When the Mercurial Water is added to these salts of gold, there is a slight hissing, and increase in heat, and the gold becomes a deep red liquid, from which is obtained, by means of distillation, the oil of gold, a deep amber liquid of an oily consistency. This oil, which is the potable gold of the alchemist, never returns to the metallic form of gold. I can understand now, I think, how it is that some of the patients to whom Salts of Gold injections have been administered have succumbed to gold poisoning. So long as the salts are in an acid solution, they remain soluble, but directly the dissolving medium loses its acidity and becomes neutral or alkaline, the salts tend to form again into metallic gold. This is probably what happens in the case of the injection of gold salts into the alkaline intercellular fluids, which in some cases leads to fatal results.

Do not imagine that chemists know all about metals! They do not, as the following quotation from the report of Professor Charles Gibson's presidential address on 'Recent Investigations in the Chemistry of Gold' would seem to show:

'The address was of a highly technical nature. One of the chief points brought forward was that current text-book views of the constitution of salts of gold are incorrect. These are never of the same nature as normal metallic salts with simple formulae such as $AuCl$ or $AuBr_3$, but always of a complex constitution....'

From the golden water I have described can be obtained this white water, and a deep red tincture which deepens in colour the longer it is kept; these two are the mercury and the sulphur described by the alchemists, Sol the

Father and Lune the Mother, the Male and the Female Principles, the White and Red Mercuries, which two conjoined again form a deep amber liquid. This is the *Philosophic Gold,* which is *not* made from metallic gold, but from another metal, and is a *far more potent* Elixir than the oil of gold. This deep amber liquid literally shines and reflects and intensifies rays of light to an extraordinary degree. It has been described by many alchemists, which fact again corroborates my work in the laboratory. Indeed, every step which I have taken in the laboratory I have found in the work of the various followers of the Spagyric Art.

And now to the final goal, the Philosophers' Stone. Having found my two principles, the Mercury and the Sulphur, my next step was to purify the dead body of the metal, that is, the black dregs of the metal left after the extraction of the golden water. This was calcined to a redness and carefully separated and treated until it became a white salt. The three principles were then conjoined in certain exact quantities in a hermetically sealed flask in a fixed heat neither too hot nor too cold, care as to the exact degree of heat being essential, as any carelessness in its regulation would completely spoil the mixture.

On conjunction the mixture takes on the appearance of a leaden mud, which rises slowly like a dough until it throws up a crystalline formation rather like a coral plant in growth. The 'flowers' of this plant are composed of petals of crystal which are continually changing in colour. As the heat is raised, this formation melts into an amber-coloured liquid which gradually becomes thicker and thicker until it sinks into a black earth on the bottom of the glass. At this point (the Sign of the Crow in alchemical literature) more of the ferment or mercury is added. In this process, which is one of continual sublimation, a long-necked, hermetically sealed flask is used, and one can watch the vapour rising up the neck of the flask and condensing down the sides. This process continues until the state of 'dry blackness' is attained. When more of the mercury is added, the black powder is dissolved, and from this conjunction it seems that a new substance is born, or, as the early alchemists would have expressed it, a Son is born. As the black colour abates, colour after colour comes and goes until the mixture becomes white and shining; the White Elixir. The heat is gradually raised yet more, and from white the colour changes to citrine and finally to red—the Elixir Vitae, the Philosophers' Stone, the medicine of men and metals. From their writings, it appears that may alchemists found it unnecessary to take the Elixir to this very last stage, the citrine coloured solution being adequate for their purpose.

It is of interest to note that an entirely different manifestation comes into being after the separation of the three elements and their re-conjunction under the sealed vase of Hermes. By the deliberate separation and unification of the Mercury, Sulphur, and Salt, the three elements appear as a more perfect manifestation than in the first place.

Rudolf Hauschka

THE VITAL PROPERTIES OF THE METALS

Lead

Lead, which comes first in our list of metals, has the least lustre, a dull resonance and almost no conductivity. Outwardly it is even plainer than tin. It is heavy and dark grey; one might almost call it gloomy, with a moribund gleam. It is completely moistureless, with an even more negative relationship to water than tin has. Though soft, it is brittle and therefore not malleable. Lead ore lacks the slightest moisture content, and the soluble salts of lead crystallize with no water of crystallization. As we have seen that water is the basis of all life, we can see that lead's heavy, gloomy aspect has a relationship to death.

But if we pick up a piece of lead, we are surprised to find it feeling softer and warmer than one would have expected of a metal. It even feels strangely oily. For all its plainness, lead apparently possesses unsuspected qualities. And if one goes on to make a closer study of it, one comes to know another, most important side of lead which has nothing to do with heaviness: the fire that lives hidden in its depths. Some lead ores show it quite externally.

Though the chief lead ore, galenite, has lead's typically gloomy look, there is a whole series of lead ores whose bright colouring betrays the fire within. Yellow, orange and red occur most frequently. Croconite and wulfenite, the red and yellow ores, and several others, sparkle as though fire itself had fashioned them. White lead ore, cerussite, though a colourless white, brings hidden fire to expression in the way it is shaped. It is built of sheaves of needles, or is a network of glittering laminae. It looks amazingly like bone structure. Thus lead unites two very strongly contrasting forces: rigid heaviness and revivifying inner fire.

The fire-nature of lead is beautifully illustrated in an experiment which we will describe in some detail because it is generally so little known. If we want to pulverize lead to a very fine powder, we have to work in a vacuum, for the powder would otherwise ignite and gradually burn down to bright yellow ash.

Although this pulverizing is impossible on account of the sticky consistency of lead, there is another way of achieving the same end and producing pyrophorus lead. The technique is as follows. Lead citrate is put in a glass tube sealed at one end and gently shaken till it settles at the bottom. The open end of the tube is attached to a vacuum pump. The citrate is slowly broken down with the heat of a small flame, while the vapour and carbon monoxide thus generated are drawn off by the vacuum. The end product is metallic lead in the form of a fine powder.

When the tube is sealed with a glass cock, taken off the flame and the pump disconnected, the lead can be kept for weeks or months, provided the seal is tight enough. But the moment air gets in, the lead bursts into flame and is gradually consumed.

The chemistry of lead, like that of tin, is simple and straightforward. Its lack of affinity to the lively chemical activity of water renders it chemically sluggish. This quality makes it excellent pipe material.

Bells made of bronze with a lead alloy ring with a warm depth of tone. But impermeability to rays of energy such as those given off by X-rays and radium is a special characteristic of lead and makes it particularly well-suited to serve as a shield against their destructive action.

Lead's double nature, its dead weight counterposed to living fire, together with its shielding properties, can easily be understood when we consider its cosmic source of origin: Saturn.

This planet has two characteristics which are at once apparent to telescopic observation—its dark core and the bright ring that encircles it. And its distant orbit encloses the whole planetary system, shielding it from cosmic radiation. We forget all too readily that the life of earth and its creatures is made possible and maintained in a carefully attuned balance of forces by the sheaths that surround it. Earth has its hydrosphere, its air and warmth mantles, and its ionized layers, and beyond these the planetary spheres. The last and most important enclosure, which separates the planetary system from the rest of the cosmos and makes it an independent entity, is the Saturn sheath; or, we might say, the lead process. And when forces such as X-rays and radium appear in the earth sphere, it is lead again that protects us from these deadly energies and enables us to live independently of them.

Lead's protective function appears very clearly in the smelting process. Lead ores are always found in conjunction with silver, and the smelting process produces a conglomerate with a good deal of silver in it. This is then heated, and the more volatile lead goes off in smoke. The percentage of silver in the residue keeps on rising, until finally there is only a mass of liquid silver mantled in a film of lead, which protects it from contact with the air and thus prevents splattering. When, finally, the lead skin becomes too thin and tears (the silver 'peeks out,' as the smelter says), the lead has done its job and the last of it goes up in smoke.

If we look for the Saturn-lead process in the microcosm, man, we come upon the same comprehensive functions. One of lead's activities is building bone, which involves the death-process of mineralization. The densification brought about by tin in the organism is carried only to the stage of cartilage, which is still plastic. It is lead that carries mineralization to its real conclusion, which one might call a kind of death. But this death enables man to be at home in the realm of gravity, as well as to assert himself against it.

Bone-building is the final stage of lead process in the human organism. Man incorporates death into himself with his bony structure. But at the heart of this mineralized precipitate of our physical selves, at the core of what is most dead in us, we find the scene of life's creation: the red marrow, where new blood, new red blood corpuscles are made.

The lead process is thus linked with the process of death and resurrection in the organism. On the one hand it lends itself to the forces of mineralization active in shaping our bony framework, while on the other it supports independent consciousness, enabling us to co-ordinate our perceptions and relate them to the ego, the centre of each man's personal universe. The lead and silica processes are similar in their influence on this functioning of the sense, which is based on a constant breaking down or dying. Disintegration is continually going on is us, particularly in our nervous systems, but it is just because we are always experiencing partial death that we can become conscious beings. At the moment of complete and final death an unimaginable enhancement of consciousness occurs owing to the sudden setting free of so many formative forces from their bodily tasks. Reports to this effect have been made by individuals who came close to death but were revived. They speak of seeing a tremendous panorama of their whole life, such as cannot be experienced normally.

The lead process is thus related to the most spiritual as well as to the most material aspects of our being: to that maturity of consciousness which manifests itself in the warmth of an all-embracing human understanding. When the lead process within us is thrown out of balance, we lose the firm footing of an ego-directed soul life, as can be witnessed in the poor memory of sclerotics or in the brittleness of bone and the failing senses of old age.

The wide range of properties inherent in lead makes it a valuable medicament in cases where, on the one hand, the process of densification proceeds abnormally, or on the other, consciousness is disturbed in the ways just described. Used in high potencies, it has given good results in the treatment of various sclerotic and related conditions.

In ancient times, this twofold character of the Saturn-influence was well known. Saturn was regarded as the representative of death, of the forces responsible for aging, but equally of the deepest attainable wisdom. The Greeks looked upon Chronos-Saturn as the creator of time. But time harbours new beginnings as well as endings. Time is known as the great healer, the overcomer, who offers resurrection after every death.

It was natural to fear Saturn, for this border-guard who constantly patrols the boundaries of our planetary system is also the guardian of a treasure of ultimate knowledge, to be attained only at a cost of the greatest sacrifice. Suffering and loneliness are awakeners of knowledge.

Lead is in a profound sense the final stage of a great cosmic evolution.

Quicksilver

Quicksilver, the metal of Mercury, is like iron in some respects as it is opposite in others.

It is found in nature in the same state we are familiar with from the use of mercury in thermometers: as a liquid metal. It occurs in smaller and larger globules in the matrix rock, often in the company of mercury sulphide, more familiarly known as cinnabar. The globules tend to unite and form larger ones, which shatter at a tap. The liveliness is a wonderful sight. Quicksilver's ancient name, 'Mercurius vivus,' is truly deserved. And this mobility is demonstrable in many other physical and chemical phenomena.

One of these is the narrow margin between quicksilver's freezing and boiling points. It changes quickly from a solid to the fluid or gaseous state. It drops only 399° C. from the boiling point to freezing, as against gold's 1,537°. Mercury's quick passage through the different states makes it akin to water, which also exhibits a great variety of phenomena in the interplay of the elements, producing steam and clouds, fog, rain, hoarfrost, snow, and ice, and leading each over into the next. 'Hydragyrum,' the Latin name for quicksilver and the origin of the symbol Hg, acknowledges this kinship.

Lively, liquid quicksilver is 'young,' compared with other metals. It has retained the fluid form of earlier conditions of the earth and held out against aging and solidifying. In the table of metals it is abnormal for being a very poor conductor. It is only externally lively, not having yet achieved the inner mobility of conductivity. When the temperature is lowered below the freezing point, however, its conductivity increases markedly. In this solid state it thus comes to possess all the properties which its position in the table of metals warrants.

Quicksilver's reactivity to warmth is expecially notable. It expands and contracts in exact proportion to the rise and fall of surrounding temperatures. It is not a carrier of inner fire processes, as lead and iron are, for it simply reacts to changes in temperature with speed, precision and agility.

Its most significant quality is its capacity to dissolve other metals, making alloys known as amalgams. Only one metal has the power to resist this amalgamation, and that, strangely enough, is iron. For this reason, mercury is kept in iron flasks for storage and transport. We need not be surprised at iron's resistance. Mercury did not participate in the last stages of earth's densifying and remained a fluid, while the force that leads most deeply over into earthiness, transforming the cosmic into the telluric, the spherical into the radial, is that of iron.

Now, if we compare mercury with iron, searching out their likenesses and dissimilarities, we come upon a clue to mercury's globule-forming tendency: it signifies both a retaining of the cosmic sphere-form and a leaning toward individualization. Here we see a perfect illustration of the opposite directions taken by iron and mercury. Mercury's splitting up into numbers of small globules and its tremendous mobility are in the greatest possible contrast to the consolidating power of iron. Iron carries forces of embodiment which, if they go too far, lead to mummification in the sphere of life and to egoism in the soul sphere. On the other hand, quicksilver represents the force that combines small entities into larger wholes, making one large globule of many tiny ones. This is the basis of the capacity to amalgamate, which, overdeveloped, ends in erasing identity.

Chemistry presents phenomena that well illustrate these mercurial characteristics. The reaction of chloride of mercury with potassium iodide precipitates a glorious red mercuric iodide. An excess of potassium iodide, however, has a surprising effect: the red precipitate disappears, leaving a clear, watery solution.

Chemists call this strange association of the elements 'double-salt-forming.' But this explains nothing and does not even describe the nature of the occurrence, especially since the quicksilver here can scarcely be detected by ordinary analytical methods. Moreover, it takes up other substances, such as ammonia (Hg_2ONH_2I). The phenomenon can be explained only by bringing the whole nature of mercury into account. Its most characteristic chemical trait is that of association, a feature already noted in our discussion of its readiness to form alloys, or amalgams.

Quicksilver draws into chemical association substances that otherwise show little affinity for one another. Sometimes there is such tension in these large groupings of elements that the least disturbance sends them flying apart. If mercuric chloride, for example, is mixed with ammonia under certain conditions, a highly explosive compound (Hg_2NOH) is produced by way of the so-called Millon base. Similar compounds result from the chemical reaction of mercury with nitric acid and alcohol. The product is mercuric fulminate ($HgC_2N_2O_2$), an association of dissimilar and conflicting substances which explodes at the slightest tap. This makes it suitable for use in fuse caps for detonating explosives. An interesting point is that nitrogen, though certainly essential to the explosion, lacks the power of combining these heterogenous elements. For that, mercury's associative capacity is needed.

The god Mercury was the divine messenger whose mediation connected earth with heaven. He was also the god of commerce, thereby bringing men into association with one another. This, too, can be harmful in excess. Nowadays there is a tendency to form large cartels and amalgamations on all sides. Companies, so aptly termed 'sociétés anonymes' by the French, tend to lose any personal character when they expand into huge concerns and giant trusts. Excessive amalgamation dissolves the personal element.

When 'iron will' and the 'mercurial temperament' work harmoniously together, they produce capable and well-rounded personalities with social gifts. But imagine an excessively mercurial temperament, with the capacity to organize and manipulate large combines, and dominated as well by an egoistic will. What a perfect constellation for producing a Kreuger or a Stavisky!

The god Mercury represented qualities which, in their finest flowering, make for the building of true human community, but they can also lead to an Armageddon if misused. And these divine mercurial qualities in human nature are perfectly mirrored in the physical and chemical properties of quicksilver.

The mercury process is a very important one in the human organism. Any and every 'amalgamation' process that goes on there can be looked upon as mercurial. The term, of course, is used here to designate a force—a force which, carried to the ultimate point in nature, produces the metal quicksilver.

Two important functions of the human organism are easily recognizable as mercury processes. One is digestion. After nutrients have been broken down to a considerable degree by secretions of the mouth, stomach, and intestines, the homogenized mass is absorbed through the intestinal wall into the lymph and blood stream. In the course of this, an amalgamation of external nature and the human self takes place. Digestion is thus really a fusion of two spheres of energy which merge in the human body-building process.

The second process takes place in the breathing organs, where human nature and external nature also come together. Through the air we breathe we share in the atmospheric life of the whole earth. All humanity breathes the same air, which enwraps all of nature. This fact can be recognized as the true basis of a feeling for an understanding of nature, as well as of the communal sense that breeds truly social conditions.

Even the build of the lungs is mercurial. They are like little trees made of tiny hollow drops. Innumerable spherical spaces thus form a common breathing surface.

We see the imprint of the mercury process on the organism wherever glands built of cells function together as described. Separation into droplets, out of which functional wholes are built is the signature of the mercury forces everywhere. On the human physiological level they control the life of cells. Cellular liquefaction and proliferation are both due to disturbances of the mercury process, which normally maintains a state of balance between the total human organism and its single cells.

Silver

In many of its properties, silver is just the opposite of lead. Lead's resonance is as dull as its lustre. It melts easily, can only be cast, and is a poor conductor. Silver gives out the most ringing of metallic tones and gleams most brilliantly. It is very subtly workable, melts only at high temperatures, and has the highest degree of conductivity. The two metals occupy opposite ends of the table of metals, like Saturn and Moon in the planetary order. The moon's speedy orbit and ever-changing path give silver an inner mobility. But silver manifests this trait quite differently from mercury, as will be seen.

The chemistry of silver paints the first strokes of its portrait in the striking phenomenon of its mirroring capacity. Everyone who has stored silver nitrate has certainly noticed a very fine film of silver appearing on the glass walls of the container. The coating gradually grows thicker, until finally it forms a real mirror. This precipitation process can be hastened by various reducing chemicals. The tendency to form mirroring surfaces is one of silver's chief characteristics.

The chemical reactions of silver show the same tendency. It reacts, for example, with chlorine to form white silver chloride. Under the influence of light it throws off the chlorine with the same energy with which it first attracted it, returning to its former pure metallic condition. Finely distributed, it now appears black. This process is the basis of photography. Photographic plates are coated with an emulsion of white silver chloride, which is sensitive to light. When light streams through the camera lens onto the coated plate, the illuminated parts react, while the rest stays unchanged. The process is completed by developing, which gives us the negative with its black (silver) outlines. The parts that were illuminated are now black, while those untouched by light are still covered with silver chloride in its unchanged white. The fixing bath which the negative is now given removes the silver chloride, so that the dark objects on the plate seem transparent. (A solution of sodium thiosulphate, which dissolves silver chloride, is used for fixing.)

To get a positive print from the negative, the process is run through again. Printing paper is now exposed to light, acting through the negative, and given the same further treatment as the first plate.

This, then, is how photographs are made: they could be called mirrors of the past. A mirror process is certainly also involved in their manufacture.

The Liesegang ring phenomenon helps to round out our picture of silver and of the inner mobility that accounts for its reproductive power. When a drop of silver nitrate falls on a glass plate coated with chrome gelatine that has not quite hardened, the silver reacts with the chrome. A round reddish-brown spot of silver chromate appears. It spreads in all directions, not in the even way an inkspot does, but in wave after wave, each one of which makes a concentric red-brown ring around the original spot. What is characteristic here is the rhythmic repetition that forms concentric spheres, where one might have expected to see just a single sphere as the spot spread out. There is an outflowing motion with a rhythmical wave impulse, like the spread of a musically vibrating sound. This is another example of the kinship between chemical forces and music; the chemistry of a substance is like an inner music that organizes matter into ordered patterns.

The Liesegang rings recall the concentric ripple patterns that spread out in rhythmically expanding waves from the place where a stone is thrown into still water. We might call both reproductive.

When an object is reflected in a mirror, we speak of a pictorial reproduction. When we stand between mirrors we see countless reflections of ourselves, very like the concentric silver chromate rings in the chrome gelatine. Ceaseless repetition and wave-like reproduction of some motion or condition of matter are characteristic of the silver force.

Reproduction means, in a narrower sense, the renewal of species in the world of nature. Just as the silver reaction described above spreads and spreads in concentric circles, nature brings forth cycle after cycle of budding, germinating life, as species reproduce their kind. And even in the single organism the same living rhythm of growth goes on. The annual rings seen on cross-sections of tree trunks are an expression of the same force that makes Liesegang rings. Grains of starch seen under a microscope or the cross-section of an egg reveal the same outflowing rhythm.

The silver process is the force responsible for all these life-rhythms. We are referring here, of course, to the action of a universal force that finds material expression here on earth in the substance silver.

In this connection it is natural to find silver tending more than any other metal to the colloidal state. A silver salt need only be treated with a protein solution to produce pure colloidal silver. We know that a colloidal solution can be described as being neither completely fluid nor yet solid. It has a potentiality for either state. This is an essential characteristic of the living. Our blood, plant sap, and all other fluid carriers of vegetative functions, are colloidal in character.

These silver forces are active in all growth and body-building processes in the human organism, and most strongly, of course, where physical life is reproduced: in the sexual organs. The silver process works on a higher plane in the brain, the organ that enables us to reproduce thoughts and to mirror the world in our conceptual life.

The properties of silver as an early condensation of moon forces indicate its therapeutic uses. It proves valuable as a medicament in the treatment of regenerative and reproductive disturbances, providing valuable support for recreative functions and permeating the fluid organism with its vital rhythms.

Its many-sidedness leads to its use in a great variety of other special therapeutic applications.

Just as lead brings the forces of Saturn to manifestation, so the silver process reflects the action of the moon, whose immediate influence on all the rhythms in man and nature is everywhere evident.

The rhythm of the tides is currently regarded as a product mainly of lunar gravitation. This could be correct, although the assumption leaves some difficult problems unresolved. In any case, there can be no doubt that the primary cause of tidal ebb and flow is the moon's law of rhythm, noted in all manifestations of the silver process. We know that sea water contains silver in a ratio of 10 mg. to a cubic metre. It may be that silver acts as a focus for lunar influences, and as a medium for transmitting moon forces and their rhythms to the tides. And just as sea water rises and falls in accordance with the laws of lunar rhythm, so is there a tide of sap in plants, both during germination and in later growth.

Plant growth is accompanied by a rhythmic increase and decrease of substances, a tidal emergence and disappearance of matter subject to a monthly rhythm. Certain disturbed states of consciousness, such as epilepsy and somnambulism, worsen or improve with changes of the moon.

In some regions there are still farmers who cling to old traditions and regulate the times of planting, harvesting and other such farming activities by the moon phase. This could well be called superstition, if the method were not proved right by the author's own observations and experiments.

Now we might call silver a dense form of moonlight. It is a substance very like the moon in brilliance and reflecting power. The moon reflects the light of the whole universe. Starlight as well as sunlight comes to us in moon reflection. We need hardly be surprised that this dark satellite reflects the sun most obviously. Like a true mirror, it always turns the same side towards us. Its surface is very like that of a frozen flow of silver which has 'spluttered' while getting rid of the quantities of air it absorbed while in a white-hot state, and comes finally to resemble a room landscape sown with craters.

Gold

Gold occupies the middle position in the list of metals. Since it is the sun metal, we may expect to find it possessing all the contrasting properties of other metals in a harmonious and balanced form. As the sovereign and highest expression of the world of metals, it also exhibits unique capacities.

Gold is most often found in a pure state, usually in a quartz matrix. It almost invariably occurs as a 'pollutant' —if one may call it that—of pyrite. Pyrite, with golden-glinting five-sided dodecahedrons, always has some gold in it, and its very form reflects the twelvefold rhythm of the sun's course through the Zodiac. It is an interesting and significant fact that gold always occurs very close to the surface of the ground. Gold miners know that they find less gold, the deeper they tunnel. Atmospheric, hydrospheric and geospheric action sometimes wears away the parent rock, exposing the gold. That is why it occurs in the sand of rivers, seas and deserts. The Egyptians, for example, got their gold from the Sahara and the Nubian Desert.

Gold is recovered by reducing the parent rock to sand and then separating out the grains of gold in the age-old process known as washing. This method, whether applied in its most primitive form by the gold-panner or in great technical perfection, rests on the simple fact that gold is heavier than the ground matrix, so that the latter can easily be carried off by a stream of running water. Chemical recovery by means of chlorination and amalgam processes is a thing of the very recent past.

The amalgam process makes use of the ability quicksilver has to dissolve metals by forming amalgams: gold is simply dissolved out of the rock by quicksilver. In the chlorination process, chlorine performs the extraction. Chlorine is the only chemical agent other than cyanide capable of having an effect on gold.

The power gold has to resist virtually every sort of chemical attack entitles it to be ranked among the precious metals. Only a special mixture of concentrated hydrochloric and nitric acid, such as produces nascent chlorine, has any effect on gold, converting it into water-soluble gold chloride. This hydrochloric and nitric acid misture has long been known by the very suitable name of 'aqua regia' (royal water).

To call gold the 'king of metals' is to use a figure of speech that means little to the modern chemist. But we shall see that a closer study of gold and its less obvious qualities proves its right to this exalted title.

Gold occupies the central place in the table of metals arranged with reference to such dynamic properties as lustre, resonance, conductivity and malleability. Like the sun, which is the harmonizing center of the heavens, governing and ordering the curving paths of the planets, gold is an expression of the harmonizing force in man and nature. Gold's aristocratic nature keeps it free of entanglements and enables it to mediate between extremes. If gold were to form chemical bonds with all sorts of other substances, it could not rule over them as king.

How impressively the changes of colour which gold undergoes in its various metamorphoses reveal its all-embracing, universal nature! The metallic gold we are familiar with in ornaments and tableware has a warm lustre, like a sunny late-afternoon in summer-time. When it is hammered into paper-thin gold-leaf, however, it becomes translucent and turns a glorious emerald green against the light.

Goethe's theory of colour can help us understand what this phenomenon signifies. Goethe pointed out that pure yellow and pure blue are the colours most closely approximating to light and darkness, and are thus polar opposites. Red and violet are intensifications of these poles. Green in their harmonizing. The earth's green vegetation which the sun conjures forth is the harmony of light and darkness, sky and earth, in living matter. This could explain why gold occurs right at the surface of the ground, where earth and cosmos are evenly balanced. Summer's glorious display of green foliage seems conjured forth in light's transformation by the sun-gold process. Everyone knows what a soothing effect green has, both out of doors and in green-painted rooms. Green stands calmly poised between red's aggressiveness and the nostalgic yearning, the solemnity, the exaltation of blue-violet.

But there is another color that creates a harmony between red-yellow and blue-violet: purple. This is not a simple mixture of two polar opposites, but a synthesis on a higher level. Purple may be called a higher metamorphosis of green. Green sustains and carries us. We stand on the earth's green surface and find security and peace of soul in green. It conveys a sense of earthly balance. We can experience the polarity between red-yellow, with its glowing activity, on the one hand, and on the other the quite remoteness and sublimity of blue-violet.

Over this lively interplay of colour, purple reigns supreme. There is scarcely a human being who does not sense the majesty of this indescribable colour. From the earliest times it has been used in the trappings of dignitaries as a mark of distinction and high office. Kings and priests, as leaders through whom the divine will spoke to humanity in times gone by, were robed in purple. Purple seems to open a door through which a higher world can enter human souls. But the purple we see with physical eyes is little more than a dark shadow of the true colour, which Goethe called the heavenly child of Elohim. He says: 'A great secret will begin to reveal itself to us when we rightly conceive the moving apart of blue and yellow, giving special attention and appreciation to the intensification towards red, for opposites here bend back towards each other, uniting in a third hue. The spiritual import of these two separate and opposite beings begins to dawn on us. And as we see them bring forth green below and red above [in our designation, purple] we shall scarcely be able to resist the thought that below we behold an earthly colour; above, the heavenly offspring of the Elohim.'

This pure purple is the colour gold assumes in the colloidal state. The reduction of a watery solution of gold chloride makes it possible to produce every shade of purple. The more it is diluted, the more delicate and glorious the purple grows. A colloidal solution of one part gold in ten million parts of water has a marvellously subtle purple tinge that approaches peach-blossom and is like the indescribable bloom in healthy children's cheeks.

Gold-purple was used in the Middle Ages for staining glass. The glorious purples that shine with all the magic of a long-forgotten art from old church windows, such as those at Chartres, were made of this gold-purple. Present day glass-stains derived from gold are not to be compared with the medieval product.

As the sun affects the development of physical life, so has gold affected the history of man. In ancient times gold was held sacred, for it was looked upon as belonging to the highest gods. In ancient Egypt, the private ownership of gold was forbidden. Gold was kept in the temples, and priests and kings as earthly representatives of gods carried it during ritual celebrations.

Later on, when men began to hanker after the ownership of gold, it was gradually degraded to a symbol of personal wealth; the full extent of the curse that accompanied the plunge into egotism fell upon it. Things have now gone so far that all the gold has disappeared into the vaults of national banks, and pieces of paper are used instead of it. Is there not a striking parallel here with the gradual change from divinely guided consciousness to abstract individual thoughts, which are often as far removed from reality as paper is from gold?

Gold will be freed from these fetters of expediency to the degree that mankind works its way out of abstract thought to a new and active consciousness. We saw the first steps being taken in this direction when the gold standard was abandoned and currency was based instead on real values created by human industry and effort.

The properties of gold described above are also apparent in its use as a medicament when the various physiological functions have got out of balance. It is especially valuable for disorders of the heart and circulation.

Gold reminds us of the aluminum process, which it resembles in its capacity to harmonize polarities. The quintessence of forces of harmony exhibited by aluminum in precious stones appears again in the precious metal gold, but in closer relationship to us.

Special reference was made above to one gemstone, tourmaline, which is seen in cross-section to have both green and purple colours. There are the colours that reveal gold's all-embracing character in the translucent green of gold-leaf and in gold-purple. A tourmaline set in gold thus comes to seem especially symbolic of harmony between earth and universe.

Robert Kelly

AN ALCHEMICAL JOURNAL

The car came for me today.

*

It is only those who are in some way in love with death to whom the Queen's agents come.

*

Silence as instruction. Two kinds of Silence. Negative: silence as abstention from utterance [how to teach poetry]. Positive: silence as a shape to ram down their throats. In their ears. Their bodies. Eyes. Shaped silence, against time.

*

Harpocrates is the Aion too. Silence of Hokhma. Silence of Binah. Michael Angelo's grieving women. Tomb of Giuliano de' Medici, my initiation into the sphere of Binah, into the urgency of poetry. Trey of Spades. Pique-Dame. Prick this woman. Grief. Something held to the lips. Aion. Eis aiona. No time.

*

Silence is the instruction. Al & Carola had a long way to drive. Overweening oracles. Naufrages. Simplicity. I remembered a story. Why I was there. Why the sun shone. They had a long way to go. Presence fills her. Her body turns over, she sees me watching her. How much is part of the automatic instructions. I will never ask or tell her, she will never tell or ask me.

*

Wanting to say brass ash tray she said *brash ass*. Her body turns over. Tambourines, as if those were silence. Whir of the fan. What the adept learns is that waiting for the right time is the same as making things up.

*

Rebels are walking the streets. "Anti-government forces, Boy Scouts & others who make up the rebel core." Militant Buddhist youth organization. Her body in the sun. I dont want to look at gentle ease or suntanned knees. I want a gun, I dont need a gun, I want an enemy, I want a war. Kill the elms soft with green. Italic day, signature of the earth.

*

They are dead. That is they do not answer. What is this busyness of theirs they do not answer to our calls?

*

What a wonder Thomas Vaughan is, priceless consecutor of the real, of the plain & hidden flesh of man. How he hates Aristotle, disdains the feeble *Weisheit* of Tyanaeus. He is here, he is here. The open eye of Matter. O you devil you, you beauty.

*

Today I look in the mirror. I see that my beard has billowed out & swarms around my eyes. Earlier I stood gasping for breath in the icy shower, only the lattice work wood floor of the stall separating me from the rough earth hole beneath. Between air & water I stood on wood. Between earth & air I stood in water. Only my breath was fire. Since then my hair has lain flat & wet, slow-drying in the grey wind. But my beard!
L'homme dans le miroir m'a dit:
Je suis l'homme à barbe rouge.
You can't do anything with me.

*

Outside there is a doghouse from which the dog has been removed, or from which he has wandered. It has plywood walls & a shingle roof. The gap in the front is irregular, the size but not the shape of a dog. It is a perfectly good dog house, small for me but ideal for a dog. Dogs go everywhere & do everything. I have never read a story anywhere about a dog getting into a fight with an eagle.

*

It's on a hillside, & so much has been in or on or under hillsides. I meant *on* hillsides but the others came, *in, under*. I think of the raths & hills my Irishes knew, backparts of my blood, fair dark-haired red-haired men like me who spoke no language I could understand & were my fathers. What if a man desires the acquaintance of his remotest great-grandmother, and she a mere girl, in the mattins of the world, walking on the dewed grass of Ireland. What does it mean if a man wants to go into that time before him (though our language says two different things with that word before: "Before Abraham was, I am" but "Before my eyes"), what does it mean if a man wants to step lightly across the Galway field, earliest morning, up to where the mother of his blood walks just as lightly, & to slip his arm around her slim waist, but with his wrist so flexed that the tips of his long fingers brush, press, & half-support the fullness of her right breast, soft loose in her dress?

*

Whoever that man was I would in that fashion have slightly been, whoever he was he knew the hillsides, had maybe walked inside them beyond the tradition of easy enchantments, had maybe seen those cities, worships, inconceivable entertainments, above all had maybe felt the *speed* of Faery. And if I say all that's in the hill is hill-stuff, molecules & subtle motions, I have denied nothing.

*

The earth, puzzled & dismayed by the ease with which we forget her, rears herself up in hills & mountains to present herself to our eyes, catch our attention. Greeks with the chthonian rites, their blood breakfasts spread for earth, had no mystique of hills, mounts or 'nature.' Logres (old Sumer, our summer-land) which spilt no innocent blood, had need of celestial mountains, hills of the first *sidhe,* bewildering forests piled between man & heaven, a sign, a reminiscence. Mother calling.

*

Somewhere in this country a girl lives behind a door & has her name & mine conjured together in pencil on that door, a psychotic scrawl that hints the sacred mystery of the truth. Its inscriber got the story right. But the names wrong.

*

What he & I had to figure out together before we even talked was this: that the central problem of the alchemic Work is the same as the social, psychological, problem of Jealousy. Who gets into whom. Why? May I plant these seeds in your garden?

*

And now we have been in the rain. She pulled her shirt off & ran before me up the slope, turning back to note how fast I followed, the eagerness of my address to this step of the operation. There was no measure to this time, no bounds to my eagerness, hence no measure of it, hence no *seeming* to run faster though I pursued. It was quiet in the place she ran to, very dark grasses tufted across the ground, given among black rocks. The rain had been sturdier before. But what was mostly was that she didnt know what she wanted. She was so silent her silence startled her, made her uneasy as an animal is startled by its own shadowy reflection in a still puddle. She showed me a bird's nest from which the small blue bird she'd seen in it last week had now flown away. On the way back she showed me a big wet grey toad. We stared at it till I couldnt see it any more. Then it jumped. I thought of the *Hypnerotomachia Poliphili,* how there is One who leads, & one who looks back (wet hair & broad shoulders) to see if another follows. But then I very often think of that. Perhaps this was at last the right time to think of it, though there had been *right times* before, & will be after, God willing. The right time is more frequent than I think. Even the toad had something to speak:

Eines abends spöte
Ging ein Mann einen steilen Weg hinan.
Da sah er eine Kröte—
dies Gedicht ist nicht von Goethe.

Dialect & substandard forms. Popular songs. Old popular ditties. Songs my aunts & uncles knew. Peg o my heart unwobbling pivot? Our *chung?* It was not enough that I followed, however fast. She had to lead. Poliphilo waltzed with the strawberry blonde. Alchemy is the science of finding the right year to be born.

*

Only now is it clear that I was walking on that hillside. Midway up the woods there is a fence, & by it a black wet tree. We stopped & planted seeds there, in the middle of the air. There was such silence in the woods, in the wood, & that's what I'm trying to get away from now. No need for all that silence, no need for all this secrecy, as far as I can see. And there are houses where women sleep. Were we sad because we were silent, & silent because all the secrets had told themselves into the listening rain? Anybody seeing me would have known what was on my mind.

*

One of the girls was of gypsy parentage, & in the set of her body I saw an intimation of the origin of the Cards. These postures are the way we must be, things being as they are. Yoga will teach a man to live without pulmonary breathing beneath the ground, or extend his subtle nervous system to any distance, or live three hundred years. But it cannot teach him to bend his shanks out forward from the knee, or chew one single grain of rice by grinding down with the upper jaw. This intimation in fact I did not see then looking at her, but only now, reviewing the event. What reckoners we are! Runs hits & errors. Secrecy of the pitcher's mound, the Magus of Tiphareth rears back & hurls. Yesod's last chance to knock it over the fence, perimeter, parameter, paramita, into Malkuth, the actual world. In the shell of the catcher's mitt, demonmask of his tantric form, the Qlipoth wait. Or if a man should one day mislay his member, he would find it on the Moon. O what liars we are.

*

Several years ago a team of clinicians discovered that blood of dogs poisoned by carbon monoxide would re-oxygenate faster (in many instances critically so, saving the animal's life) when exposed to the light of a mercury-vapor lamp.

*

A moth the size of the ice-box carries the ice-box away. So what it has to do with is that Greek word *isos*, same as this, same as that. Isomimetic, a man steps through society & enters his house. Shooting methedrine, the bad green heart. Held together by starch. Shooting starch. Filling the lungs with starch.

*

Riding the forest:

1) Who or what does the River serve?
2) Where does it hurt?
3) Will I be ruled?
4) When it rains who is it I hear laughing in the night?

Know the inflammation by these signs:

    Rubor
    Dolor
    Calor
    Tumor

a redness a pain a heat a swelling) --- riding the forest, preserving the memorials of the days.

*

The dream said: *And overnight the instrument is changed.* But night was a year & a day, & what is an instrument was never an instrument before. How we change. How we use ourselves.

*

There is beating on the doors of heaven. I am fooling myself. There is beating on the doors of hell.

*

When I get down to it, there has been little I could really believe in but the heat itself of the process. Baseball game. Today the rodeo: horses quivering in the breathless heat. A shame to use us animals so. The riders. The ridden. The watchers. Gasping the thick valley air, the dust.
                                                      The calcination of horse & its rider. Spectre of Animal beauty raised in the dust-filled vase, spectre of use, spectre of lost blood.

*

As another process, not the casting of bronze, is called *sang perdu*, lost blood, lost bread, the song *perdu*, the elided melody of all-my-life, a purple flower, iris, orchis, testes. A sign & proof of the truth whereof it is the signature. A process of lost blood, choking the vessel, lost.

*

A man of 85 in Northern Dutchess Hospital with aplastic anemia. Given a transfusion, congestive heart failure followed from surfeit of liquid. Given a transfusion of centrifuged blood solids without much plasma, congestive heart failure followed again. Digitalis & mercuric diuretic administered intravenously. "Perhaps the marrow of his bones wore out, as another man might lose his hair."

*

How much can a man lose? If blood is lost in the tree, what of the fruit? I had asked the second question of the afternoon. It was not enough.

*

Wolfram has Parzival finally ask, "Uncle, what's the matter with you?" And that, no more than token, recognition of the reality of the *other* is enough. After all the struggles, romantic & terrible & all, through the deserts of the self, at last, after years, after a Good Friday spell & spell broken,
                                                                                                          after the spellbound repentences,
                              to be able at last to see the tokens perish, & seeing instead an other person, even an *uncle*
                                                       (a right-angled relative, a perpendicular to the self), & make an utterance *to* him which is also *of* him: *Oeheim, waz wirret dir?*

*

What is the matter? we say in English. But Parzival, in Middle High German has to ask, *What troubles you, what's ailing you, why are you perplexed?* We want to know the answer to our own question, what *is* the matter?
                                (Which is not: Why is James James' mother never heard of since she went down to the end of town? Where did his mother go? To The Mothers?)
                                                    But is: what is the *matter?*

*

Everything that we know makes free.
                         Genealogy, accepted or chosen or in-

vented, always limits. Ancestor rites. Joss sticks in brass bowls. Dust on the calendar.

*

But to be in the world means come on harder. Talk with a hard on. Showing them the pictures. Because I want. Words extract themselves from the air as bears eat honey. We'd been at her place for two hours before it struck. What alphabet was it?

*

He reads the blotter's backwards forward in a mirror and becomes a sage.

*

Being in this city under the sea was submitting himself almost to Ordeal, a testing of a Self (which did not perhaps need to be tested) in the midst of the irrelevant, the unnecessary, the irritant, the abominable. It was a sorrow to be here, to turn from what was his, the terrene airy life he lived in the heart of, to put himself in this fix, the half-day journey down, the being-there in the hopeless knowledge of having to ungo the whole way to get back where he had been, no further, except the furtherness of self-betrayal; yes, that was it he thought (his pen blurring in the hydrosphere), *in the destructive element immerse* (he quoted), yes, that was it, his joy had been to taste of self-betrayal, see darkingly how far he could go in without destroying the self, as he had as a child sometimes, breathing fast & prick erect, daringly stayed seated in the car when the el train came to his stop & the doors opened & he sat there & the doors stayed open & he sat there knowing they would close & all his body trembled with the lust of his confusion, delay, desire, self-torture & still he sat & then the doors *would* close & he would be trapped in the kingdom of his own consequence, bedded down with the sheer whore voluptuous *effect* (who was also Love & goddess & wife of his manhood) of his action. Or as he would, long afterwards even, fantasize a girl in a public place taking off her clothes in a daring, trembling, smile-faced deadly flirtation with the irrevocable, how she would strip off shoes & stockings & coat & blouse & skirt & slip (& thus still be clad, though wildly more sexually, as chastely as herself in a bathing suit) & then with the same smile & the saliva drying on her full wet lips & with a shiver of total wild self-abandoning glory loosing the straps of her bra & pulling it off & letting her breasts swing free in the fierce wind of actual crime, then wriggling her panties down, rubbing her hands down into her fur as she writhes her naked ass out at the world, at policemen & god & teachers & nuns & soldiers all running to beat at her with savage reprisals --- she has dared & gone beyond, she has committed irrevocable nakedness.

Yes, that was it he thought, the Daring the Irrevocable; he understood the secret meaning of what Apollo's torso seemed to say in Rilke: *Du musst dein Leben ändern,* you must change your life, strip to the nakedness of a statue, strip yourself of arms & legs & be a torso, gouge out the flesh, murder flesh & blood, burn the earth in the ferocity of changing.

*

The course & sense of narrative; *he* becomes *I*; in a different way ('in a mystery,' as old Arthur would have said), I becomes he. Overwhelmed in the embarrassments of revelation, "I" take "refuge" in "rhetoric."

*

In 1955 I & some school-fellows attempted a revival of *Batman* as an object of inquiry. It does not feel good to have been in the avant-garde of kitsch. Yet my fingers smell of *her* authenticity, She Who Is To Be Obeyed, She who is wet.

*

These are the books: The works of Gerhard Dorn
                                    Michael Maier
                                    Jakob Böhme
                                    Robert Fludd
                                    Thomas Vaughan
Not one of them but wrote with a goose-quill. Over the hen-yard, the scream of the chicken-hawk. Over the stream (Hortonville 1939), the blue scream of a kingfisher. Men who like to read books & watch birds. Presidents of the United States. Men who blow fine glass flasks with wild birds inside. Cégeste (F*lc*n*ll*'s name in the special bars of Toulon) worked it out just fine: L'oiseau chant avec ses doigts. Which means, when it comes to the Vessel of the work: the ouzel chants a wake six dights. Six nays. And on the seventh, breasts. Or casts a storm spell on the Wash. The Wish. They come to life again. L'auzel. L'aura amara. We picked the right road & the wrong goal. For a long time the kingfisher sat on the branch.

*

Peonies in the olive jar, white water. Wise men read the labels. Water salt & acid added. But they are peonies, her holy flower, how the rain stinks of them. I love her. Wise men need no labels.

*

There is something about new morning, dew on the sun & the people out on the loose again, that moves the bowels.

*

After all this crap, time to understand. Yes, that was it; the Daring. The Irrevocable. Death as game. You will notice I do not speak of Death. I do not like that game. If you go on playing it I will take my life & go home. The Gnostic says. When I was a child I heard several sermons each summer (though once in a life would have been enough) about the boy who wilfully missed Mass on Sunday to go to the beach, & came back in a box. That's the way they always said it: in a box --- & there was no doubt what that meant. It is only now, in my thirty-first year, that I begin to doubt the relevance of the priest's report. Yet each sin measures me & limits my work. When I have sinned I write in a box.

*

We made love by the waterfall. Later we saw a snake. It was eating, ugly. I had no compassion for its hunger. Forgive me.

*

As a strong man, I love to receive the commands of beautiful women.

*

The course of love-making follows the phases of the moon. An ignorant girl wrote: 'My dog flowed me to school.' Dont everybody laff at once.

*

What did she mean coming into my office & seeing the big picture of the fish & asking me if I were the Fisher King? Yet she was beautiful. I clapped a hand to my thigh & worshipped --- for the length of that casual, meant-to-be-humorous gesture --- the woman secretly inside it. O unborn twin sister of mine, o death in my body come to life. I was black & blue from the injections, etc.

*

So many birds of morning. Elephant on the desk. To each unit of the biological world belongs its proper gesture. We call it *lucus*, 'grove,' *a non lucendo*, from the fact that it is not bright inside it. Dark birds. The traveller asked for an empty glass. One tusk is longer than the other. In a poem of René Char's we read of *deux pointes semblables*, sun shining on two like tips, of the horn of the bull, of the sword that kills him. I have kept him all these years at the door, waiting for one to become empty.

*

Its earliest glyph was the Ka, the upraised hands

When we leave our house, only the wisest of us throws up his hands.

*

The most remarkable event of the week was a mock crucifixion wherein a young man was lashed to a yellow cross propped up before the people. After saying or pretending to say certain words, he pretended to die. If one pronoun had slipped out of place, I honestly declare I would have lost my mind.

*

But I didnt say what it *was*, of which the *Ka*, the upraised hands, was symbol. Call it in the simple jargon of our time, my time, a process. *Fresh & light-footed* Dante called Guinicelli's love poems.

*

All things are finally brought into the Furnace of Love. We have that assurance. The temperature.

*

Mosquito bite on my thigh, a gentle enough punishment for all the thighs I've bitten. I mean all the times I've bitten thighs.

*

In a play of Joel Oppenheimer's, the classical historical western desperadoes look down from cowboy heaven on the struggles of the characters of the play. At times they speak. When I saw the play performed, the desperadoes were enacted by poets. The fertility of a contrivance is out of all proportion to its meaning. Or a sentence.

*

Hoping to learn by a sign how the Work prospers, I look out the window, first moving the curtain on which the terra cotta ♀ Mirror of Ashtaroth reflects no image

*

I'll try again to say it straight. Hoping to learn by a sign how the Work prospers, I move the curtain & look out, morning

*

The language has roots in me, by it I am grown, leaf & hand & tongue. What is this language? *Who is this King of Glory?* I have sharpened my pen. I have opened the gates of the Temple.

*

The third time, she tells me, is the Charm. I try again: Hoping to learn by a sign how the Work prospers, I look out into the morning & see a black hen, her white chick.

*

What does she do now she is naked? Is this anti-climax? What did I do when the el train rolled on? What was that kingdom of my Consequence? Climax & anti-climax. The ladder & what the ladder leads to, a sloping roof, ridgepole high. You can straddle the crest, or stand for a time on the declivity, then fall.

*

What I have to do now is to lecture on

hsin, the heart. There is an intensity of energy where energy, εv.εργον is the work-within, the force from which all things are outered.
Now since energy (force, virtu, tê) is a *process* (not a *thing*) it cannot to be conceived of as *in* a place, only *as* a place. This is the inside, or *inside* the geometric point; the inscape of the point is the heart of God --- *primum mobile*.
(She held her arms out before her, then snapped them back to her sides, elbows down, clenched fists hitting the shoulder. That was *sin*, she said.)
Woman I love you for the force within you that sometimes joyously outers, is not exhausted, draws me to it as to center. When we were married she said: I will be abundant.
But *hsin*, the heart, is not the romantic heart; it is the well-primed & steady pump that runs the organism of our intellect. Draw me a picture of *intelletto*, draw me a wolf stealing meat from a boiling pot, using a long-handled spoon. Fork. We pace the heart that paces us. The heart pumps blood to the brain from which Hermes the Pacemaker descends to pace the heart. Feed me, feed me, cries the human intellect. Overswarming the deserts of the Pleistocene, man reasons about the weather, becomes man, grasps & eats.
Somewhere we are all naked under our clothes. Nakedness & hunger, the sovereign gestures of the intellect, concealing & revealing, are the heart's work, heart's en-ergy—our strength.
The body. Robe of concealment. Robe of revelation. End of the lecture on *hsin*, the heart. But

the audience does not leave, does not end. They repose in their seats, notebooks on the writing-arms of their chairs: "Before you send us away, you must tell us what place this is in which we are." I answer them: you are in the college of the Jesuits, in the Society of Jesus. The picture on the wall is the emblem of the Order: under the guise of two wolves, the Body & the Intellect steal the energy of the Heart. Yeheshuah hangs before you on a Roman cross. Crucify the heart.

I wake up past noon. I come home in a box.

*

Even then the treatise was not over. Rabbi Dobh Baer (= Bear Bear) had a word or two to say. "Why did they call my *Commentary on Enstasy* a tractate on Ecstasy? Wont they never learn?" Jesus is taken down from the cross by a party of rabbis, who grieve over the dead man. Miles away, Simon of Cyrene stumbles under the burden of no cross.
"Null-Cross,"
Dobh Baer cries,
"they criss-
crossed us;
no enstasy?
crossed out our hearts."

*

To answer my earliest question: it would have been enough to see the sun rise.

*

They misunderstand Chance. Dont you see (dont I see) that once you reckon Chance in the system, *all* other possibilities are annulled? Chance is total if it is at all. By chance, internally coherent systems may arise. Once Chance is reckoned with, the presence of order is no evidence of design. As Chaucer knew; any man who has the Miller follow the Knight is some bloody kind of atheist, a Christian atheist perhaps, or godly bolshevik. Outside his book, Crisseyd gets leprosy from screwing around. Lives in a box. Contaminates the sea. Whose ass do I kiss? Exactly twenty years ago I heard them saying Hubba Hubba. Sator Arepo Tenet Opera Rotas.

*

O my first love forgive me that I can call you first.

*

It was unrealistic. There were the four of us, myself & the three women. I brought them to my secret home & showed them my colleagues & fathers & priests & pupils under the maples, grey-haired old men warming benches, young men studying the veins of trees, astromony of tree bark, the 365 poetic meters & the famous lost fractional meter that completes the year --- was that Silence, or the quarter-rest, the time the sun takes out to turn? Jesus Christ how old I am! I who remembered when this maple had been an Indian *ficus*, & before that a frond-tree of Shamballa, I who had been Naciketas before the world was changed now turned to the blonde young man & said Naciketas, I am bright death inside your skin, hearken to me & learn all. Then I fell silent. He held out the horoscope I had invented for him; I saw Lincoln in the Tenth house & Antinous rising. Dante sang in the hell of the Eighth. On the cusp of the house of marriage was the Thirteenth sign, unknown in Judeo-Christian times. Saturn slept. I reached in & twisted the Neck of the Serpent till his venom dropped down & woke Loki. I burn, I burn, he said. This is unrealistic, the women said. Who is the naked picture of the young man on your wall? He is a great American actress, my ladies, & you have seen, albeit unworthily, one of the few revelations of the Secret College of the Holy Spirit. A bunch of pederasts if you ask me, one of them guessed. I resumed my smoking cap, held my peace & led them away.

*

There! That was Major Hoople talking, Roma 1942, Annandale 1966. I would honor specifically here Gilbert Sorrentino, who got there before me. Furthermore, practically anybody can beat me at pool.

*

When I got back to the motel I tried to explain to her what the Collegium Spiritus Sancti was, how from Pleistocene times at least the angels who watch over men have seen to the continuity of certain spirits who incessantly re-dwell in our midst, & how I had long, long been one of these beings. She doubted my powers; I changed myself into a phallus & futtered her into silence, o holy swastika. She sleeps now while I write. Outside, a busy highway connects New York City with the moon.

*

A flute is played. Shakuhachi. If it is played long enough, there is an end to fictions. After her dance: *kill this woman!*

*

He read, then wrote, about Sandalphon, angel of Earth. Angels in jeans, blue & white & otherwise. Pun.

*

A lifetime supply of goose-quills. Ocean of ink. First lessons in chancery cursive. Have an erection. Keep it up. There's your College of the spirit sank, she said, keep talking big boy.

*

It has been my intention to banish all learning from these pages. Only what I have stood under will serve our purposes, gentlemen. Say the blessing & we will begin. When in the course of human events it becomes necessary for one being to sever the biological bonds that have held it to life & amber waves of grain. The purple mountain's majesty (Yesod) above the fruited plain (Malkuth). Learn the colors. Defer invention. Isnt it just like a burnt-out painter to invent the telegraph. What hath man wrought indeed. I know so little of history I can almost breathe. Remember that old crap about George Washington Carver getting stoned on cotton gin & inventing the peanut whistle? Remember? Remember? God be gracious to my soul, forgive me my inconstant seductions, my imperfect adulteries. The Oracle spake it: *Now beating the drum, now blowing the flute, by fits & starts he weeps & sings in turn.* God, I'm beautiful! Forgive me my constancy.

*

The sun sets irrevocably. That's what it means.

*

The beautiful thing about time there is no mistaking it. No mistake in it.

*

Discipline of the heart. *Hsin* rapturous devours. A sentence without commas, leading to the end of the world.

*

I asked the angel why he had been sent. He took off his robe & said: I will become one just man, there are yellow flowers in a jug, pink peonies in the olive jar, tiny white flowers floating in a blue bowl. There *is* a way. Let it find you. Be glad.

*

It may be that every man is set upon the earth to find one new method of divination. That is, to write one sentence whose syntax is total. Because (this idea is familiar) syntax is the heart of divination, to locate the function of a thing in the structure of process. We must remember that. Who are we?

*

They bleed every month to renew the earth. Every woman is under the obligation, from at least Pleistocene times, to let some of her blood fall on & feed the earth. And if a woman do no more than this, even no more than throw her kotex into a wood or river or ravine, she shall be blessed & fertile & glad in white water. Conscious of my own temerity, I proclaim that the purpose of most human religions is to hide or deny the secret efficacy of menstrual blood. In all parts of the work. Work is the Earth.

*

What does the Martian astrologer make of Earth? Through his zodiac he must delineate the positions & influences of Sun, Phobos, Deimos, Mercury, Venus, Earth, the Asteroids, Jupiter, Saturn, & perhaps the remoter planets. I read in a Martian treatise on genethliacs:

> [Earth] - native name: Tlas, Tellus;
> color: blue; god: Poteidaan
> [Poseidon?]. A lesser malefic,
> of the nature of Venus and Saturn.
> The Earth is above all the planet
> of work, of making things. If Earth
> be at mid-heaven, the native will
> prosper in all arts and crafts.
> Our traditions tell us the inhabi-
> tants of Earth are called *poietai,*
> or makers. Metal: antimony.
> Precious stone: Jade. Earth rules
> the sign Virgo and some attribute
> to it the sign Scorpio as well.
> It is exalted in Capricorn and
> dignified in Leo. Begin no process
> or task when Earth is rising, or it
> will never end. To attract its influ-
> ences, wear a talisman made of antimony,
> copper, & lead in equal measure, and
> on it inscribe, when Earth is at
> mid-heaven or conjunct Saturn or Venus,
> the inverted pentagram ⚳ with a bronze
> stylus, and around it these words:
>
> ARA ORA
> OPERA
> FAC.

*

It may be that too much of the writer's energy is spent on satisfying curiosity. Herman Melville. Peonies in white water. It is four o'clock.

*

From the brow, Athena rises out of each man to refute his lie.

*

It was almost time for me to be reborn. Him to be reborn. The colors.

*

They waited at the tree where they would give us wine. Water if we wanted it. I watched her there & tasted the lines of her body. Limes. Lemons. Tomorrow, she sang. I washed in the stream & rubbed lemons against my chest. I waited for tomorrow. Her body tight as   taut as   tart as a   lemon. Ho ho, a song.

*

Lying down into her arms this said itself in my mind: *Testimonium perhibere de Lumine.* I have come into this world to bear true witness to the Light. Of the light.

*

So having been born in the right year all things continue to happen at the right time. So here I am in my true love's house, & watch this Sunday evening go to grass greyly outside. As I write I am aware that not many miles from here my true love sits in her house & waits for me. And further, while I sit here, we sit here, we sit everywhere, that that other one, my true love, radiant in all other colors, knocks at the door of my house, finds me not at home, leaves a cryptic love note jammed between door & frame, goes away.

*

It is time for me to speak praise of pale women: there are houses where their almost plumed skin gleams beyond any dark that dying day or nature can impose. Through shadows she walks, the house is cold, there is a triumph in her easy quality. But this is the wildness of first fire when the tongues of tenuous flame run up the branch, this is first fire. *Our fire,* the philosophers say of it, *fire of the wise.* From this fire (which is all we know of Light) all things are moved to assume their forms (*rupa*; form's motion) & utter themselves (*nama*; word's emotion). This is a praise of blonde women. First fire pale along the branch. Now this living tree will be consumed, & from its blackened fingers Jean Dominique Ingres will sketch in charcoal the perfected outline of a serene blonde highwaisted enigma, her face turned away, her flesh the first implication of clarity in the physical world. This is the first fire, fire of Aries that begins all years, all possible years, all possible processes. Paleness of blonde women the *ground* of language, *arupa,* the unformed formative syntax of the world.

*

The rhetor crossed his legs, relaxed all zeugmata, untied chiasmus. She waited for him all night while he parsed two highways & conjugated a deponent girl. And at full dawn she told him, when I call you silly I mean you are holy too.

*

There are no years, there are no processes. Eve's apple was the knowledge of subject & predicate as different from each other, different from 'their' verb. Adam shared.

*

She blows smoke towards me, goes away thinking I'm so engrossed I dont notice. Tomatoes in the sun. Getting dark under the trees. The first flicker of boredom quenched in the specific. Sweet coffee. The presence of them, o god the womanly presence!

*

Grind it twice, until it is powder. In our secret instructions, "twice" means to do it right the first time. Grind it twice & cast it on the surface. Long afterwards, when all the process is done, you'll find that the macerated powder has accepted half the volume of the water. But now, when the powder is cast upon the seething, let the heating be stopped, then seal the vessel, & let it remain sealed during the saying of the psalm *Confitemini domino*. Open the vessel, & pour out the infusion. Strain it through sand or sable, muslin or organdy, June or September. Let the grounds or faeces remain in the sieve. Bring to the black water what is white, & to the bitter water what is sweet.

*

The Divine Thighs straddle the Hudson, the Divine Calves along the banks of the river. God kneels. *Allah* means: The One Who Grieves.

*

And I have come to bear what kind of testimony to the Light? What do I know of the Light? She believes at times in an actual hell, where people are fried for being bad; for doing those things we must do? But it all begins with light. Cardinal Mercier, whoever he is, spoke the truth of Christianity for the first time in 2000 years. Sanctity, he said, is taking literally the words of Our Lord. A parable is hard to understand because we are not used to being literal. I am the light of the world.

*

I hold this one's breasts & this one's thighs & press myself on this one's mouth & ask each one in turn: What is it that happened between us at the Pinner in

Wakefield, three hundred years ago, September? We learned the secret, & it cost us our deaths. Back, far down in my blood, an orchestra tunes up. My dearest wife, I will hear you forever & sometimes heed you. I sign this letter in perfect ignorance of the date.

*

All this was the right time. Can I hear what I'm trying to say? At this very minute *She* is waiting for me to come to a door miles away & open to her. Do I hear me, do I hear me?

*

She is at the door, her hair is yellow, her looks are free, her skin is white as. Liberty? As. As.

Just as the rocket burst over the tangled carnival throng I saw the Queen of Cups whirl & send her raving servants in among the crowd. Before the glare had faded she was down the water steps & away in the Chris-Craft. The night came back over the rages & howls & agonies & love-cries of the victims. He turned to me with a strange smile & said, We have put her living in the tomb.

*

She is at the door. How surprised she'll be when I call her Mommy. Long an only child, I first learned of the disease during my mother's second confinement. When she came home I peered into the deep pores of her face, terrified that the skin might show ravages of the imagined ailment. But now there is my true love at the door. Her hair is yellow. She is not free. Her skin is white as

*

All the while it is her wildness I love. It is time I speak in praise of. Wild wet. The sea is all colors. I am afraid of my strength, I mean that strength in me. I fear only certain woods at night. Only certain serpents, brown ones, ones of no color. Only certain dogs, who come along in the darkness & mess around in the lab & tear the throat out of the Work. I do not fear the sea. I do not fear the wind. I do not fear even the sea wind squirming in the cattails, even her sand scouring my stone. Every year must have a beginning. We have the assurance of water, time can do nothing to us.

*

I confess the exaltation of this instant. What matters is that it is. Was. This comes terribly close to a false simplicity, the cost of which would be an easy mistake. Of all things the sun shines on, there is none more worth to be cherished than that the sun shines upon all things with the same light & each thing is different. There is a race of beings who make things new; they are

Children of the Sun. It is they who in the language of Beulah are shown in the Nineteenth Trump, hand in hand in the heat of their primary. In science they are called planets, in religion they are called The Gods, in history they are called Men. I know them by a different name.

*

Let me be clear about this: my Desire is the only vessel strong enough to contain you.

*

I & you, back to that again. of "I" it is able to speak. Who will learn the language of mountains? Studs, seducers, folk on the make, how simple they are: Viva la Libertà, cries Don Giovanni, as if it meant something. She believes at times in an actual Hell, where Giovanni's lust is cauterized, his skin blemished with consequence. They fry you there. Now this is important to me: there are some cookies, a friend once told, such that all of a sudden you eat the fatal one, the one that instantly turns the stomach & makes the joy of all that came before into a queasy, not quite dead weight.

*

In the burgeoning optimism of unlimited desire, I reach out for universal intimacy: I will go to hell, where hell is false repetition, to have lusted for meaning & to have passed, in the ferocity of my desire, right through the thing Meant, right out back into the boondocks, the Qlipoth, the provinces of diminished reality.

*

I'll say this for IBM: from them we may one day relearn that there is no number but One, no repose but Zero.

*

So at the proper time the Vessel is opened & the house is filled with a simply wonderful aroma. We are told that in the Book. Man's fire is poured out on Hamburg, London, Nagasaki, Hanoi. After she had made me into Love there was silence in Heaven the space of half an hour. So also was there one who in a shirt of silver stood before the people & received their worship. Him ate the worms. There is said to be a moral in this story. In this Syntax. Morality of syntax, pause to recover.

*

The anguish of the Work is the discovery of the correspondences. Once they proclaim themselves, they never let the Philosopher rest. The Correspondences.

No man is allowed to die till he has met every god & every goddess & has had his chance with each one of them to revere or to reject. This is the assurance of Love (the Furnace, the Human Body, the World).

*

As on another night we sat up late at the motel trying to find out who Minerva was. My lungs holding the opium down, I went outside & stood by the sea, wanted to cast *her* my seed, got no answers. Waste of the drug, of the potion? Sea a potion?

*

Boil It Down.

*

It took us an hour to get through Hartford, city of lovers. A gold dome on what I was told was the Temple of Venus Percasta. Love assures. As I write down these lies, a little grey moth walks on the page, avoids the wet ink, or is it my words?

*

I love her exactly because she looked everywhere for signs & read them out loud, kept their meanings. Am I godlike because I love exactly? There is no lust like the lust for meaning.

*

Questionnaire

Ouranos
Gaia

Kronos
Rhea

Zeus
Hera

Apollo
Dionysos
Athene
Poseidon

Pluton
Demeter
Aphrodite
Hermes
Hephaistos
Persephone

Fill in the identities. Die.

*

Plainly those 365 bardic metres were no metres. They were each day's measure of itself, each day's song of itself into the specific ear of the poet. Free verse, if you can call it free --- is the child newborn on Christmas free of Capricornus, is the dying old man free of the Moon? But those priest-poets sang each day; their training was directed to making them perfect instrumentalities of music & emergent meaning. Obviously I am making this up. Obviously I am writing in the middle of a wood, at night, when the moon rises she will be seen to be nearing her full, maybe she has risen already, all round me are the scribes & scholars of the College of the Holy Spirit, resting from their carnival appearances or conning the sermons they will whisper, o holy poison, in the ears of sleeping dominies.
These are men who live for nothing but truth & love. Which is true of everyone in the world, but these men know it.

*

They are going off to sail up a river. They have no idea who will be the boat. Or down a river. Or have they? Suppose I said the river you can sail on is not the real river. Would you believe me?

+

I set up this stone to aid the Sun our Lord in his interminable Battle.

*

I knew it was she because of my frequent dreams. From the other side of the paper a wind was blowing. When I was young I was a tamarack was what it said. On the other hand, when I appear in her dreams it is as one who drives a car. What if Heurtebise were Mistress Death herself himself? What if the Chauffeur were the car? The man who makes things hot. They listen to me because I have more fun than anybody. A double-bodied treat. And glory?

*

And Mr Corry, who said his name where he comes from rhymes with *sorry*, told me of Roosevelt's death. FDR sat at a card table signing his outgoing mail. Laura Delano was in the kitchen arranging flowers. Soon they were going to have lunch. Far away from Roosevelt the Russian lady painter worked. Miss Suckley looked up from her own work & saw Roosevelt's head down on the table, his arm towards the floor. She thought he had dropped his cigarettes & hurried over saying Have you dropped your cigarettes? But he touched the back of his head & said *I have a terrific headache.* Later he died. On four sheets of yellow lined legal pad paper, the President had written in pencil, under date 26 December 1937, his instructions for the disposition of his body should he die in office. Among other things he wanted to be buried almost immediately, plainly, without being embalmed. By & large his wishes were not obeyed, since Mrs Roosevelt did not want to open the sealed envelope, containing the memorandum, addressed to James Roosevelt, then in the Philippines.

*

I'm me, that's the point of it. I am at your disposal.

*

She was at the door, I know it, wrote her letter to me, sealed it in the wood of the door with a kiss, has gone away. We are at the disposal of every body.

*

The books give different numbers for the phases of the Work. The books appear to contradict themselves. In such a welter, what can the Operator do but rise in the morning & survey the streets and fields. If his eyes are unusually clear, he may see a different number today. Tomorrow.

*

At times I wonder where our instructions begin. She did not wait long at my door. Time will have its own way with these matters.

*

And there are affectations we are not permitted. What a mouth full. The doghouse deteriorates in the dog's absence. Some mornings I didnt even bother to look. Mortal Sin. She said I was very scary sometimes. Faster, faster this month full of moons.

*

Americans capitulate into matter. There is a different possibility: Al &

Carola, their difficulties with cars & clocks & highways. If they speed, they will have an accident. When the wise men wished to protray longevity, they drew a carp, since that fish goes on living until someone kills it. One swims today in a monastery pond in Germany, I believe, & in its tail a dated metal tag was placed two hundred years ago. An old fish, but the greatness here is a species greatness. So the wisemen didn't speak of Noah or Methusaleh because those were gifted individuals; they drew a carp because carp after carp can do this, go on living. They direct our attention to the *species* possibilities of man. Which are thus specific possibilities.

*

Though each man does his own work, there are no individuals in the work. Or only one individual.

*

What do I know about it? Off in the trees, a horse's full tail is waving & tossing, in & out of the sunlight.

*

So finally they were there all alone together on the boat. I think it was Long Island Sound. People seek identity in the strangest places, but these two were wiser, & sought only the wind on the water, the way the banks came down gently to eat. So much of life is lateral movement, she may have thought.

*

An eagle who has carried off a dog learns to know better. In the bones of his children, revenge replaces marrow. The generations of the work try to subdue us. Yet they are the Work. They must subdue us. Yet we struggle, successfully, not to be subdued. The old man goes on living without marrow or blood. This was called human sacrifice, or the slaughter of the holy know-nothings.

*

Homeopathy begins in lechery; (Il faut chasser une passion par une autre) love-sickness cures itself in love. This morning a great inch-long insect, strong grasshopper legs, strong forearms doing work. From the tip of his face soared back two huge feeler plumes almost the length of his body, delicately curved, antelope horns, masks of Set, the typhonian animal no animal. The god of yoga, torture, lechery & death was the first insect we see in the morning, hard at work. Sublime success. No blame.

*

The whole horse trots out of the woods, sun on his back. No blame.

*

"Diamond Crystal Kosher (Grobe) Zalts. Kosher le Pesach. 3 funt net vag. Sprinkle... covering meat like a light blanket of snow. Inside, too, with poultry." The snow. Inside. The fire next time. No blame.

*

A long time ago I made a list of persons & properties essential to the work. I found upon examination that it contained nothing but the names of women. Yet there is darker still. I write now & ever from angelic informations. Angels who are informers. But the girls' names ride like swans on the paper.

*

No sense of decorum, none at all. Of all things needful to the work, the Dwarf packed his bag of needments. Easements. *K'un*, woman upon woman, abide. I hear the organ, a follower of Sweelinck. When? When? Citius citius currite noctis equi. The true lover says. In all faces I have found dawn nowhere else.

*

From the dark of your distance, dark of your place inside me, I hear you tell there is no need to address you, you will hear the words, you will be curator of specific meaning.

*

From a magical manuscript: "The brethren (nor shall this term exclude women) or lovers of this order will wear gowns of unbleached muslin, fuller's earth will have cleansed them enough, let them be wet, let the sun dry them. Upon the left breast let *O mega* be applied in red silk thread. Seldom will they wear their hoods, the hoods will rest on the nape to conceal the small cross, likewise in red silk, sewn over the nape nerve. In their cuffs let nothing be hidden except the book of the order & one simple cloth to wipe the brow of the dead with & so restore to life. Let no man see the staff."

*

Omega express. Take the A train. Uptown, where the proasteioi do not come, but rule through untrustworthy angels, & benefic confusions arise.

*

Beaver in front of me, in metal replica, & I remember being told beavers need nothing to construct a lodge (we see it as dam) but the materials & a suitable neck of water. The blueprint is the beaver himself, in a mystery we resolve without solving: the beaver does it by instinct. We say. What, if anything, do we make by instinct?

*

Faster faster run ye horses of the night into the availability of dawn, the form of the work perceived again. Seen. A heavy rain brought the temperature from 100° to 86° in a few minutes; it mattered. This is the hottest weather I've known in this place. The words are always the same.

*

First learning that books were, I found a book's name, *A lion is in the streets*. This promising title concealed nonsense about some syphilitic French author. No lion. The child's disillusionment is still with me, & reveals a perilous fact about the nature of literature, of metaphor. Bother with no writer who will not stand by his words, to death if necessary. Trust only the literalist. Take the words of Our Lord literally. Any Lord. This is a narrative in which the man with red beard appears, seems to foil his own work, stands in sight of the end. This is Mt. Nebo, mountain of prophecy. The 'hill of dreams.'

*

Life is preparation for taking leave of the work.

*

Or her body, naked in moonlight, ready to receive.

*

It is at some point, not first or last, the healing of metals, curing the leprosy of matter, restoring the elements to splendor. Syntax lends its magic (=substance). The things that are said that cannot (Aristotle) be thought. It is commonly the 'words' that are blamed, or 'language.' Yet language is the only system in which the truth is stated. Logos, or understanding what's happening, or making things up.

*

Our brains are imperfectly filled, imperfectly ordered. Yet language (not 'words') is the plenum.

*

I fear only certain words. At night.

*

     It was in front of the cathedral that the lepers gathered, the same in every city. They were the imperfections of the system, hopefully consigned outside it, segregated, wished to death. They showed themselves to men while men were on the steps of the place they went to show themselves to God. *Heal me* cries the burnt tree. *Heal me,* the new-born lamb.

*

The phone rings twice eight times. Party line. They're getting the car ready. Four Queens. Four Kings. Four Princesses. Four piebald serving men. Four times four. 4! 2 = 3.

*

Scholars of the Collegium Spiritus Sancti are born under an extreme elongation of Mercury from the Sun, or when Mercury is in the Heart of the Sun. Melville is an example of the first, Egypt of the second. But when Aquarius ascended at nightfall Nile flowed us his waters. Yeats watched his cold moon rising. There are Arabic terms for all of these things. Ibn al-Arabi for instance said the most accurate *vision* of God was in of & as woman. If you add enough prepositions, they approach that totality wherein the relations they designate cease to exist. This is called coming home.

*

Four fields? There was a fifth. Let her right side from upraised shoulder to waist be called Connaught, her right side from buttock to toe Munster, her left leg increasing to hip & flank Leinster, her left breast & chest & heart & head Ulster. Where all four fields come together, womb=well, sheath of all forms, was the fifth of the four, where even becomes odd & the world is saved: Meath, the mid-ground, the High King's own.

*

Summoned from the access of sleep by repeated instruction, I rose & looked out that window indicated by the voice. Across a continuity of dark there grew one lighted space & into it what seemed a young woman came & took all cloth away & joined her hands beneath tender small fresh breasts. Some say I saw the moon, but I say I saw a different thing.

*

It would end if I heard the horn, if I looked out & saw her in the backseat, waiting quietly. They go for me, my emissaries to an unrelenting world immediately above my own. Below. They are the bondsmen, bailiffs, dunners, process-servers, revenuers; they pay all debts; they say they work for the Queen. I say the Queen wears a red Dress & her neck is white above it as ermine & there is a crown of my desires round her head. Some leaf-shaped, some masoned square, some like the tips of lances.

*

"All these old letters of my Book are aright; but Tzaddi is not the Star." Tzaddi is the *woman,* kneeling under the star, reaching 'down' through the worlds for starlight, stirring the waters of our lake (Dante's lago), the pages of our secret books. Tzaddi is fish-hook, *hamus hermeticus,* to angle in the genetic pool, catch the fish of justice, Maat the feathered fish, eat in one great blaze of hunger the consequences of all our acts. The quotation is from the Book of the Law given to Frater Perdurabo in 1904. It took Aleister Crowley a full forty years to articulate his misunderstanding of the instruction. This is a very important contribution to the praxis of the tarot. As a beautiful old musician once said, when told his fly was unzipped: The cage may be open, but the bird is dead.

*

To stick to the work like a fish to water.

*

"I saw myself & some of my company riding by the shores of the sea, & lo! the sea had folk living in it, each mating with other, yet nothing conceived or brought to birth; trees they planted, but none bare fruit; seed they set down that did not grow."

*

There is a city on or under the sea where men sleep with men & children do not come. Its king was a fish, or a fisherman. We were driving one summer & came to it; I sized that town up pretty quick: no women in the streets, women they needed. At considerable personal expense I performed with my company certain acts of sexual polarity on the beach, in the waves, on the rocks, full privily in the heart of their houses in word & thought & deed. They do not love me in that City, because they rightly associate me with the changes that begin, though little do they comprehend them as yet. "Strange things are happening in this City," one of its folk told me. Praegnating winds, the moon declining, new faces in town, an energy. At winter solstice a child will be born. "O our sterility dies away, as a live ocean sucks at the sterile sand," they say.

But I was ignorant too, & knew only the Queen & how much stronger than the king. God is our mother. Alchemy is the science of associating yourself with the 'movements' of time.

*

The arrogant magician imperils his own seed. Some people think that sex lies behind magic, that all magic is sex magic. That would be true if we truly knew sex, the dynamic behind the metaphor of intercourse, impregnation, love. If men love their wives the City is fruitful & masters Ocean. Love your wives.

*

To my delight, the chauffeur was a girl, a tall young lesbian soft-skinned under her green silky mannish uniform. I thought of the softness of her calves inside the boots, & went so far as to insert a finger. She smiled in a business-like way, but made me sit in the back. I could watch her through the glass partition. She would not talk, but did answer specific questions I asked over the intercom. At first I was able to relax, but the drive was a long one & I soon grew nervous. I examined with the minute attention of boredom all the accessories & conveniences installed in the car. This entailed fiddling with the short wave radio, watching the six-inch television screen until the news telecast terrified me, raiding the ice-box for cheese & crackers & a little bottle of champagne, pressing the taps for hot water & washing my hands, for ice water & drinking some, putting a tape on the machine & listening to Charles Ives, then to *A Winter's Tale*. I found the cigars, but I do not like cigars. Fishing in the sapodilla wood cabinets in front of me, I detected on a bookshelf a tantric text I didnt know. When I tried to pull it forward the whole bookcase section swung out, & there before me were the buttocks & hips of the driver. I reached in & felt them repeatedly, they were warm & almost damp from contact with the leather seat. She gave no indication that she felt me. The aperture through which I was feeling her up was so small that I couldnt reach out around to her thighs or lap. I couldnt let go of what I held; hungrily I pressed & squeezed & stroked & pinched, though the flesh was not even soft now, the muscles compressed by her position. For a long time I fidgeted at her, but she gave no sign of notice. Finally I stopped & closed the cabinet, settled back in my seat, lit a cigarette, my fingers trembling with shame & frustration & boredom & worse than these. I smoked constantly, could not look up at her green eyes that occasionally, in reflection, passed through me in her rear view mirror. Couldn't even look long at the nape of her neck, the smooth blonde hair beneath the cap. I dozed, woke to see the cigarette burning my fingers. The car was still moving. I grabbed the intercom & shouted I'm sorry please forgive me I'm only a man I'm too strong, I need, I want, I dont know what I want, I'm sorry, forgive me, please forgive me. What have you done that merits forgiveness? She asked. I thought about that all the rest of the trip.

*

Vear surdan words at nighd. All the drees mound around be. Rangoom Leber Asylum I saw the words. The gade of wroughd irom, spikes on to po vit, runed hands & davaged faces phases reatching through the bars ad me. They all said the word I veared, lep ro sy they said, say it wiv us   lep   ro   see, let rose see the garden, leap roses, thorns tear, thorns dare, lap us we are lep ers, lep ards walk in the gar den, leo is a lion, our faces are lion masks, we have no phases, when you ged like us you're stuck, roses stuck, lep rush roses, say it wiv us lep ro sy. Do you wan to see a lep   er, do you wanna be a lep er, we've stugck wi this lep ro sy, you fin dus every wear, our names are in all your books, you cand flee us in books or in trees or in gardens or in caves of even in the sea the lep ro sea.

*

Childhood dreams, the dead black leopard became a leper, heuristic terror of like sounds. Alchemy is the science of having silent dreams, having no dreams. Only syntax can tell you apart, you menacing words-of-power, only syntax can heal the wound, right the warp you leave in the child's mind.

*

We stopped at the gate so she could tell the sentry, This is Kelly, he's coming to pay his debts. The sentry scowled at me but handed me a flower. A rose, upon examination. We drove up a long curving gravel drive, pines at our left & a vast meadow at the right, a pond in it far off, movement as if of ducks on its surface, geese rising or coming down. She made me get out at a new cinder-block cubical building. **Debriefing** it said over the door. A man came out & led me in, sat me down in a chair, gave me a glass of water, & took my syntax away.

*

Days or hours later I woke up still howling with pain. One came to me & bound my noises, forced a bitter thing between my teeth, & left me to sleep.

*

Most things can be done without machines. Enough suitably intricate vacant circuitry is available inside us to obviate external mechanisms. The adjusters of these circuits are called *angels,* the program tapes fed in are called *reality,* or *time.* Whoever the programmer may be, he or they or she are anxiously awaiting the outcome of each run. Alchemy is the science of becoming aware of the whole project in which we are being engaged. Alchemy is the science of being used. Alchemy is the science of use. Its name probably means *the art of the black,* & alludes in all likelihood not to the black soil of Egypt but to the black blankness of the unknown brain, the 'silent areas' in which the Operator, bent night & day over his fire, eventually kindles a Voice, one that guides him in the science of penetration, science of final separations.

*

Everyone who has gone there knows there is an utter darkness in the back of the brain where the Images go to die. This is called the Elephants' Graveyard. Follow the dying animal, learn the valley where all things perish but ivory, gather the ivory. *Transformation* is peeling away the irrelevant. A matter of time, as they say. (But Elephants, to speak only of elephants, live a long time, have excellent memories, & mate in secrecy. Christ, the power & beauty of elephants!

*

Of women, my angels. At very least I will say this of them: they are distractions from distraction. What this means is: Glory. Glory a woman in her womb. A man's heart is an imperfect womb, but glory a man in his heart).

*

When came to again was no pain. They brought me a rough white robe, led me out into the bright, a cool wind from the shadows, led me up a long rising lawn towards three maples. Under the trees white chairs & wicker tables. Women moved there & soon moved among them. They had left only one word in my head, Glory, it kept saying Glory over & over. The women looked at me, some with desire & some with aversion & some with no trace of movement on their faces. One woman came to me smiling broadly, & speared white & blue feathers into my hair & beard & robe, then took me further up the lawn, up to where a great house stood on the knoll. Kept looking back at the women left behind, kept saying Glory. Her hand was soft & held me tight, she bumped against me as we walked. Glory. Saw our shadows in front of us, & followed them. She led me right up onto the terrace. The door of the house opened & another woman came out, older than the first but not less beautiful. Between them brought me into the cool hallway, led to a small table with a green cup on it. The woman handed me the cup. Drank it all. It was warm & deep & sweet. Recognized the smell & tried to find its name. They led me between them up the stairs. Its name was Glory.

27 June 66 End of the Alchemical Journal.

Diane di Prima

14° SAGITTARIUS
    for Grant

whether it is one storm
or several storms
is a moot point/ it continues
interrupted by
flashes of sun, they last
sometimes for half a day

whether it is winter solstice or
old tears in my bones, I sleep
the wind
rattles the house, the ground heaves, shelves
fly off our walls. Whether
the sun shall ever come out again to stay
over this peninsula is not
the case in point. Matter
the books say, that remains
after calcination can be recovered
by repeated percolation, it is

metallic seed which works
in dark & frigid substance/ salamander
that dances underground in black
& cavernous Fires of beginning (like the wind
calling the earthquake to come out
& play. It will & we shall see
the peacock's tail stream colors in this alembic
of earth & sky

                                                                San Francisco
                                                                 Dec. 1972

MINNESOTA MORNING ODE
    for Giordano Bruno

The City of the Sun is coming! I hear it! I smell it!
here, where they have made even the earth a jailer
where not even the shadows of animals sneak over the land
where children are injured & taught to apologize for their scars

the City of the Sun cannot be far now—

(that's what you said then, brother, waiting in prison
eight years to be burned, to find the sun at last
on the Campo de Fiori—FIELD OF FLOWERS—yes)
how could it be far?
isn't evil at its peak?
(you asked 300 years ago) has not
the descent into matter reached a nadir? & here
5000 miles later, Northern Minnesota
a forest once, now wasteland
where they mow grass, rake leaves:

I vomit lies like the rest, not knowing
whom to trust, here where betrayal is taught as virtue
I weep alone for the words I would like to say
& silently put the faces of the old gods
into the hands of the children; hope they recognize them
here in this Christian place, where Christ the Magus
& Christ the Healer are both forgotten, where the veil
of the temple is rent, but no resurrection follows...

THE CITY OF THE SUN comes soon, cannot be far
yes, you are right—what's a millenium
or two to us, brother? The gods can wait
they are strong, they rise—the golden tower
flashing the light of planets, the speaking statues
that guard its four gates, the holy wind
that carries the spirit of heaven down through the stars

it is here! it is here!
I will build it
on this spot. I will build it at Attica
& Wounded Knee
on the Campo de Fiori, at the Vatican:
the strong, bright light of flesh which is the link
the laughter, which transmutes

Minnesota Home School
Sauk Centre

Harvey Bialy

notes from the praxis—(alchemy

Heka   sunshine / magick

in the *Amduat,* behind the Eldest Magician
Set is hidden

proposition: the earth is alive

                           develops solar (sixth sense)
                           sensitivities, & as such
is endless.
        but the operator envisions
an end

"you never agree with my visions" she said
"what do you want
consensus or a vision?"

& that other "science" which seeks to understand process without
                                           becoming it
is equally problematical.
the source of my own root & rooting in the living black earth.
warned off discrimination and knowing the absolute falsehood of
                                                 the singular

Jung writes of this as part of the mystery of the calendar, 12,
                        (4 and 3) &
what appears to be a main energy path in us to seek this sterile
                               1, as if anything
could be completed. so it would seem that on this score the
                                     technologists *are*
better off
         as the chinese waiter said to the Duchess

the danger is losing touch with the basin

in the carbon after bread is there is power

build a gangplank to the ship of millions

the flux. the catalyst. the protein.
protean shaft of the Sun

the mirror in which "one sees that muck is muck"

what's mind from it is equally alive
all stones & metals precious
an iron knife
you forge yourself from gold

Charles Stein

THREE NOTES ON THE MAGNETIC SENSE

I

For vocabulary suppose the metals and planets: what they are to those who spoke of them and meant them to be measured exactly -
alchemy is at once metaphor and praxis:
trying to tie down the mind, what it is exactly, keep it still, together, whole, of one piece, is like trying to keep mercury together, the silver balls of it fall apart, spread all over the paper I hold it in.

Dee speaks of two mercuries and gives a different hieroglyph for each of them:

that is, the moon over the earth, or over the four elements. The physical constituents of the mind's being. The moon, whose turning in its phases makes it like the mind's changeableness, its periodicity, the phases it goes through.
So this first symbol, mercury as it is natural in us, the mind in its parts, changing.

But then he adds the sun to his symbol:

The sun interposed, put in. The source of the elements, of all turnings, itself enters the operation—our Mercury—the mind made wholly "Ours," at our service. What was volatile is now fixed by the recognition and entrance of its source.

In the Tarot, mercury is the Magician. The distinctly conscious, individual Will as it acts—as it is directed.

I want to make clear what is metaphor, what can be stated as simile now, and also what has a complexity such that it cannot be broken down in this way. The Tarot is not metaphor but archetype—image of a posture in the imitation of which one can come to its meaning.

The Cosmic Images were not really metaphors, though we can see something of what they were by treating them as such. For the entrance of the sun into 'moon-like elements' of the psyche was an event involving the actual sun itself. The sun might be experienced as burning intensely in the head's center or as radiating from the center of the chest, behind the heart, the heart center. In this event, the whole meaning of the sun changes: now looking at the sun in the sky, one immediately becomes conscious of the sun in the body; thinking about the sun in the sky excites its presence in the microcosm. And the two suns are sensed finally as being identical: 'through' the physical body, one comes to the place of the sun.

II

It is not the symbology of the moon that holds my attention so much as certain physiological events—certain changes of consciousness the moon effects.

Looking at the full moon in a cloudless sky, or, now, even imagining it there, a cool flow begins to move from my medulla down my back to the region of the subcardiacal ganglion. It is like cold water, as if my spine were a tube or column of sensitive material the moon itself poured cold water down, cooling the flesh of my body, drawing me into its moving.

In Ouspenskian astrology, as I understnd it, it is only those certain "advanced" or highly "evolved" persons who receive the influence of the moon and the planets, the inverse of conventional astrology, where the adept strives with all his will to overcome the domination of his horoscope, break out of his karmic self,
    —that as our sensitivity increases and our consciousness becomes wider and deeper, our connections with the cosmos become *more* firmly established, more deeply set also.

    And our freedom is
not escape into realms unconnected or estranged from our old existence, but a freedom of locomotion as it were, a freedom to conceive ourselves more widely and deeply involved with a universe from which we cannot be estranged.

III

    Meditation is a process of subtilization and thus of magnetization: making the body *attractive/*

    (in all worlds) notice how the meditator's eyes become clear, his skin smooth, his breath regular and his mind calm during and after his meditation.

    the musculature particularly is sensed by the meditator as becoming lighter, quieter, of a finer stuff than it seemed when, at the outset, he set his attention on it. And at the point in the heart or the head when the process of subtlization is well advanced, a light begins to pull the meditator towards it, a positive brilliance draws him *become light,* up.

Moon work, letting
the body be.
   Subtle. Light
      The sun will
appear, electric source
to fill the body made moon.

Helen Ruggieri

THE ALCHEMISTS WEDDING

When the mother is joined with the son in the covenant of marriage count it not as incest for so doth nature ordain, so doth the holy law of fate require, and the thing is not unpleasing to God. —*Delphinas*

>you are the bridegroom
>the rapist, the son
>coming from the right door
>waiting at the altar.
>on the right side,
>your family, your friends —
>a young bull
>a green lion.
>I stand for the left,
>at the left.
>my friends are on the left side —
>hookers and prophettes
>a dolphin, a unicorn
>my mother, sister, daughter.
>on my left hand you slip a
>gilded snake biting its tail
>the priestess raises her left hand
>in benediction
>the sorcerer pulls a rainbow
>from his right sleeve to surround
>you, me, the guests, all
>in a perfect circle.
>a beautiful ceremony

ISCHUA

"Grind the stone to a very fine powder and put it into the sharpest celestial vinegar, and it will at once be dissolved into the philosophical water."
—*Art Aurif*

>willow trees
>leaning over the water
>trailing in the water
>mud at my bootheels
>with its fierce suck
>to the bank

stumbling over willow roots
at the edge of the brown river
rising by the clear runoff
from the hill across the road
seeking this meandering river
to swell it
over the mud flats
banks, willows, choke cherry trees
to the banked hedge of lilacs
between the garden and the house
old river
under the willows
breaking the water
breaking loose
in the passing swell
sentenced
until I am full
filling my thirst
on the willow bank
suck of the mud holding me
drinking in the river
filling
spreading
dissolving in its spring force

SHADOW

"Keep your hands from that which has a black tail for it belongs to the gods of the earth." — *Ficino*

I walk through
sets, backdrops
scenes
with her in tow
this dark stranger
who walks these
dreams with me
giving me
suggestions
my cue when I
forget my lines
to help or hinder
I don't know
when I turn to ask her
she's behind me again

STONE BIRTH

"(the stone) can neither be melted nor penetrated nor mixed, but is made as hard as glass." —*Ademanus*

stone nova
between my legs
blue obsidian
head heavy splatters
redding out a
jagged halo
blue cast stone
saphire
opal
lapis lazuli
blue glass
blue born stone
I have been a
long time full
with your weight
birthing mineral
to hollow out a
victory of sorts
blue born stone
what shining element
I don't know

Robert Kelly
THE ALCHEMIST   *for Robert Duncan*

The origin, far side of a lake
is always shadow

                        the voice goes around
                        it easily in one hour

given: man, the
origin, dark side of a lake, the sun
breaks on it, walks in it, drives
out the human face

the sun walks in the deep water
where the shadow of origin touches bottom

the lake silent in a cold without snow
where the further shore is invisible & there are
no hills   but cranes
spread out on it if there are cranes
if there is anything for them to eat
                        IF ANYTHING GROWS THERE

(making me whatever I do,
where he is or is about to be
not even letting the long afternoon grow under him)

           SINCE OUR OWN EYES ARE NOT STILL
           a song that some of us are singing in the ditch...
           totum incognitum
           sum of what we don't know for ourselves)
           of ourselves

                        the inquisitors' faces
                        sheathed in rare earths,
                        the old religion, our
                        god in his own horns, a
                        spring freshet in Spain
                        uncovering Altamira,
                        baring elements in

The alchemist
(twenty years over the alembic)
his left hand fisted, snotrag on cheekbone,
who shall weep

                        and wake up in the morning

selling flowers in the veins of his arm
crying down the street jonquils jonquils
the needle stuck in his brain
inventing true north

       as the Chinese the southpointing carriage,
       the wheeled cart with a figure that
       would go on forever pointing south,
       however the cart was turned

or Sung and Wei divided, north by south, Sung & northern Wei.

Sung: Mu Ch'i and his persimmons, a measurement of light

    remote into a thing

  made into a thing

(six things, and a painting is not about them)

     but the task of a carriage to go on riding north

     wherever the figure is pointing IS south

& ride northward through the hemispheres of his brain
apple in the cracked skin   o madness

     will we reproach burnt flesh with a mirror,
     turn away Antichrist, reject the imposed form,
     with a clear clean painting however composed
     or organized, if the light be anything else but
     fragment?

& if we do not get up and destroy all the congressmen
turn them into naked men and let the sun shine on them
set them down in a desert & let them find their way out,
north, by whatever sexual power is left in them, if we do not
seize the president and take him out in daytime and show him
the fire & energy of one at least immediate star, white star,
hammer that down in his skull till he can hear only that
rhythm & goes and enters the dance or makes his own,

we will walk forever down the hallways into mirrors and
stagger and look to our left hand for support & the sun
will have set inside us & the world will be filled with Law,
and it is that exchange we must sweep out of the temple,
the changing of gold and power & the figure of Christ into Law,
till the leaf is subject only to the pattern of its own green veins

which out of all patterns only will feed it when I am dark

light contained in the persimmons, six powers of light

        folly of alchemists
        stretched out on the snow
        unlivable abstraction of his skin

in the robe covered with suns, moons,
motions we call 'planets' and do not know
the green life in their valleys, geysirs
of wet light at the exact temperature of orgasm,
brown breath, brown blood wreathing the heart muscles

        he holds to his eye

                The alchemist

            at the top of her A her
            voice, breaking,

            Calaf's name is 'Love'

            Stir well little
            chew thoroughly
            boy in the fire /
            to sing in the
            fire

where the streets run north
roughly but Broadway to the true north?
and asked

        what corner is he on today with his music?
He was here yesterday and
sold daffodils

            NAME IS LOVE

movements somewhere in time
since our own eyes are not still

in the sleepless dark
to travel with made light

holds his hand to his face & weeps for the lost struggle
wasted in the snowfall in the crucible, only the fire of Law
burning off sulfur & mercury and this fire is earth's face

                recognizable in the plain light
                the failure of self to go into gold,
                unaccountable. The alchemist

weeping in the Spanish field
in a cloak chewed into rags by its symbols

                        a body,
                        under it,
whose name is love & which only of all light love can eat

[1961]

Gerrit Lansing

THE HEAVENLY TREE GROWS DOWNWARD

Who bury the dead
must from the grave
establish a habit

Who bury the dead
lead forth the bride
stainless in dress

the morning-
glory creeps
stone
lizard

Who bury the dead
in fetal position
knees pulled up to chin

Who bury the dead
to rise again

IN NORTHERN EARTH

The graveyard overgrown and memory efffaced,
cats of many colors run among the sumach
that roots in human stomachs long gone back
to long enduring earth, and what is length
of days or seasons in astronomy of death?
Endurance is calamity if earth speaks true
and the measurement of time is not posterity.
How the line must lengthen while the sun endures
and the poem report advanced celebrity!
Dissolve, coagulate, the chemists say:
but the first darkness blinds the human eyes
that climb the ladder of the visionary spinal chord to issue in
                                        the thousand-petalled sun.

Jed Rasula

THE BATH

Rubeous transactions of sun & moon
   convince the waters of earth to boil
   & heart to bubble with slime from the bath

the vessel that drops a bird from a cloud
   sealed its heartbeat web in my brain
   steering the scandal from cell to cell
     abruptly harmonize sprigs of light

     & equally suddenly recede

     to bring the metals to life
   with ash extracted from ash
     to fleece the furnace
& draw the lion up out of the bed of coals

the branches & leaves   shake & filter the light

my green lion wavers & pales or brightens full risen
     designs of the sun descending

   boca this book, beckoned from branches

the stars are fumes & spices of animal sky
the light a continual appointment
the life that is mostly mine as it seeps away
back in the porous mass, locked in turbulent water
   splashes out nectar on a stick
 a film of pollen on a wrist of plum
 scatters & the dust is a blaze of petals in spring

by the speed of Hermes the stars have come down
    to shine in these opening eyes
whose smile's a fruit fresh cut
     solved in a splash of the lion's bath
   as beating drops extracted

Diane Furtney

PAIRS

Near you again; and I think of red
and gold, the crazy matches they make—

down the street there was a late
patchwork lantana spread at the elbow

of a redheaded gardener, a gold pin
that dangled from his sunburned ear;

long bright clouds were bending
north of the low red sun,

my Irish setter kept shuffling
yellow leaves in the gutter—

I could go on: up to the dim brass newel
and red stair-rug to your door,

even this heated, rusty tea
held close in your gold hands.

I've left out your Flemish paintings
and the two colors of distress,

your Arab rug, our long months of yes
and no; but now I wander too far off.—

As it happens, today I'm crazy about you
rather than the other (red? gold?) way

around. And I think a list in medieval magic
said the nature of gold stays still, red's

quick: that gold leaf can calm a painted
manuscript scene, but red pushes into depths,

that for balance the alchemist's dark
red robe had to glitter at the wrists

and certain elixirs could only drip
in the red hours of the day—

(You talking by the window now, your hair
glazed, while I stand, tense, on your rug

or pace). I think some illumined formulae,
contraries, dissolved long ago into blood, in bits,

or say they did: leaving that yellow pencil, for
instance, sprawled on your brick coat on the floor,

both objects exact and sure of their possessions,
but us here, conflicted, mixed—

if for us it's a dark-and-light stirred age?
OK: If I'd turn to you again, describe out loud,

claim that red is yes, would some
bright business in us not stay away?

Human life is in danger right from the beginning: It is promised neither on an archetypal nor a biological plane. It must come into being of its own material and make its psyche and spirit out of itself, its body. No matter how many transcendental planes there may (or may not) be, we cannot overlook or escape the sheer immensity of creation on a purely physical plane. The alchemists who sought to raise spirit and soul ever out of matter, uncommon substance out of common, and gods themselves out of ashes, understood implicitly that we are bound by our mortality. The decay and pain around us is not the wasting and grief of a mere residual world in which we chanced to occur; it is the decay and pain of us, the fact of our substance. We put on the mortal coil with great difficulty and minute precision; we cannot be abstracted from it, and we cannot idealize our wholeness and mentation as if it were solely angelic or metaphysical. The crisis of our becoming is real, not the image of a higher dimensional realm and not the symbol for another immortal mortality.

—Richard Grossinger

Et sic in infinitum.

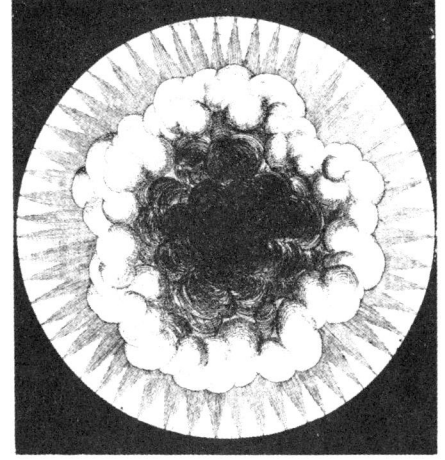

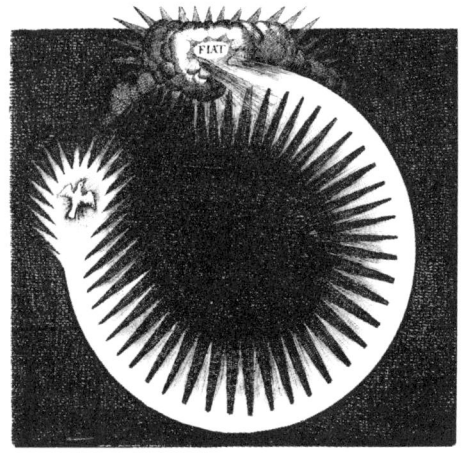

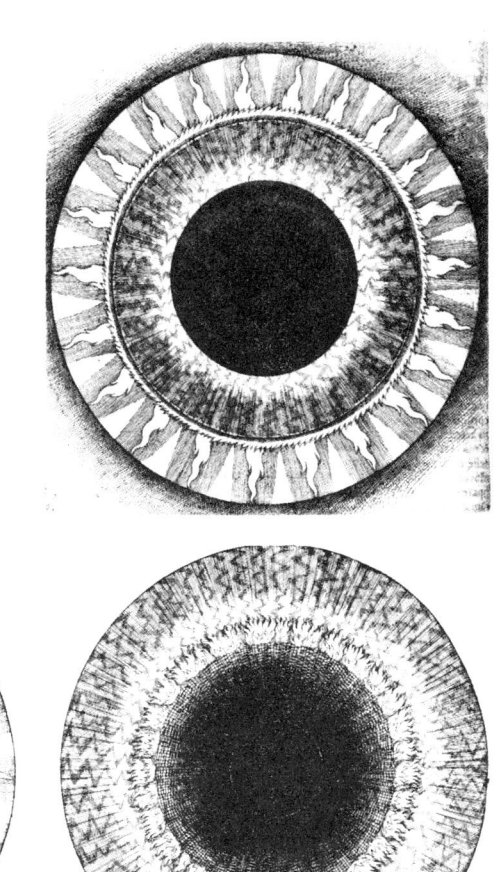

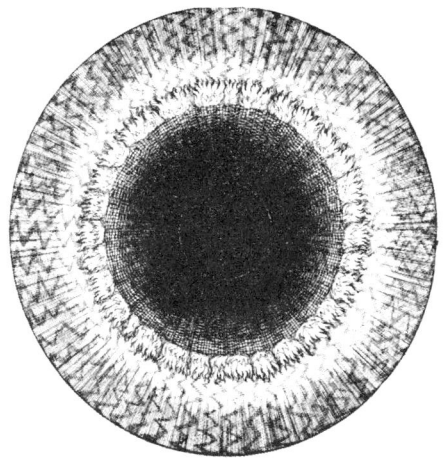

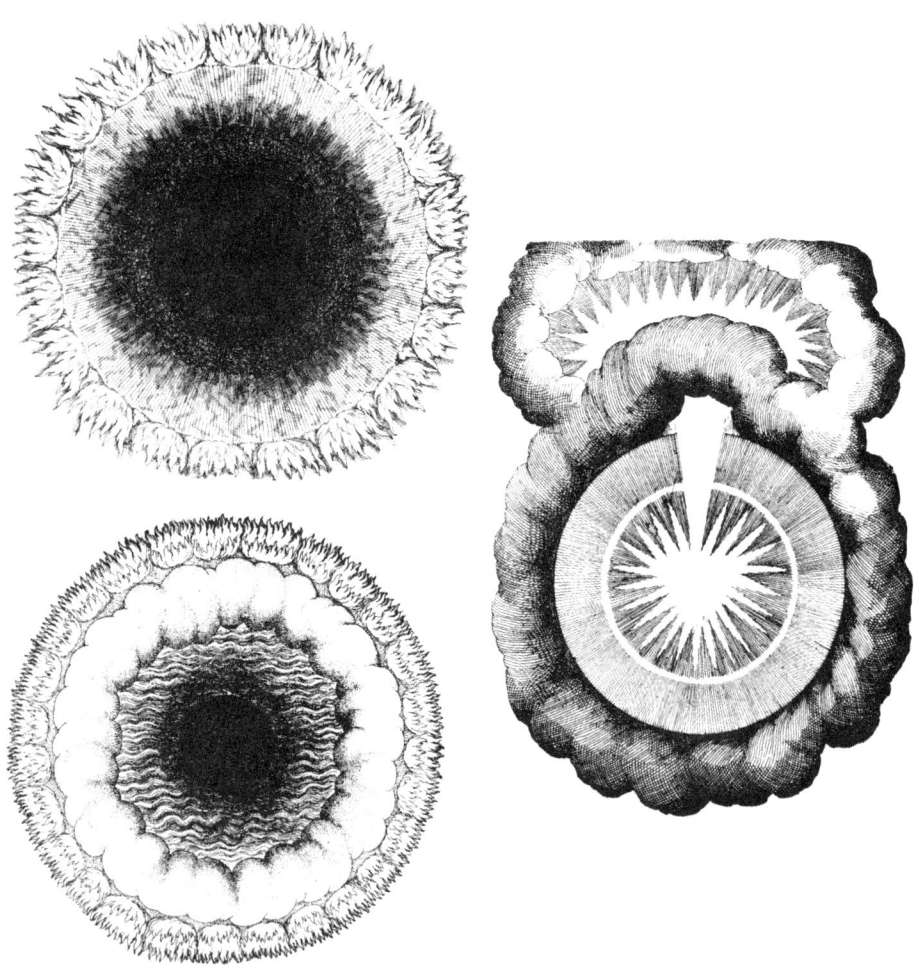

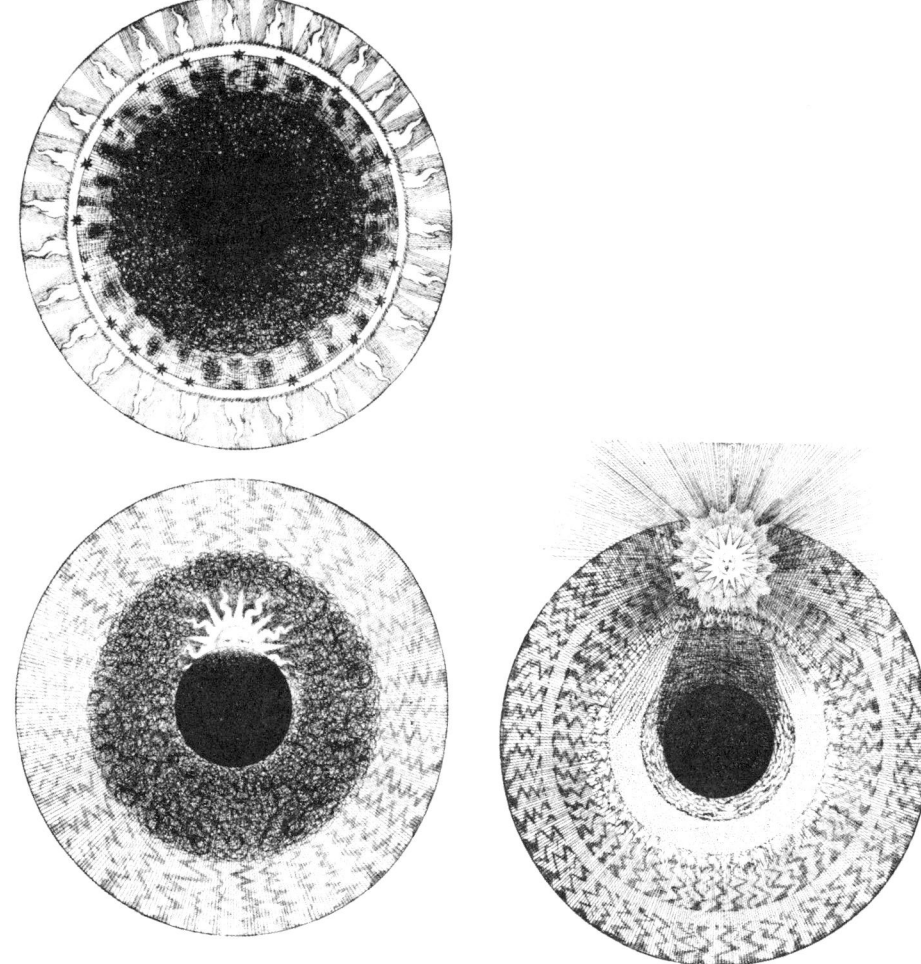

Figura I.

CHAOS VETERUM

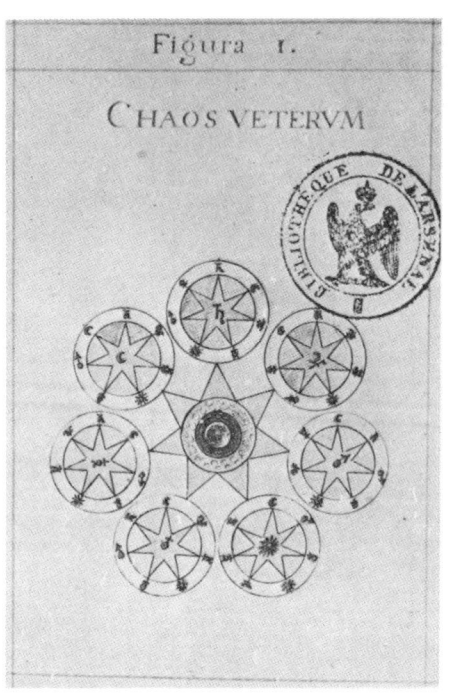

Figura II.

SUBIECTUM CHIMICUM

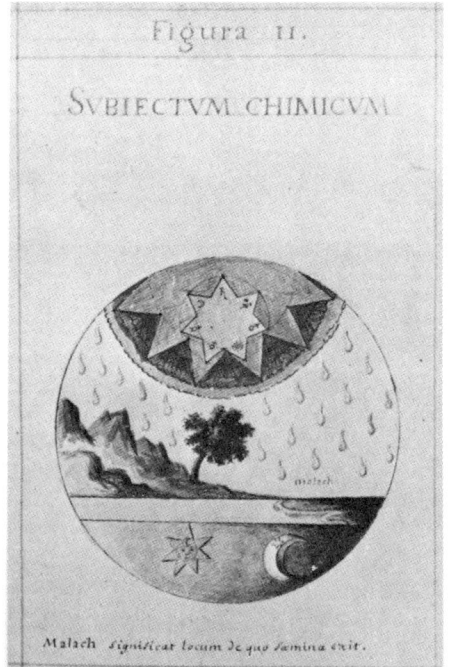

Malach significat locum de quo fæmina exit.

Figura III.

DISTILLATIO PHYSICA

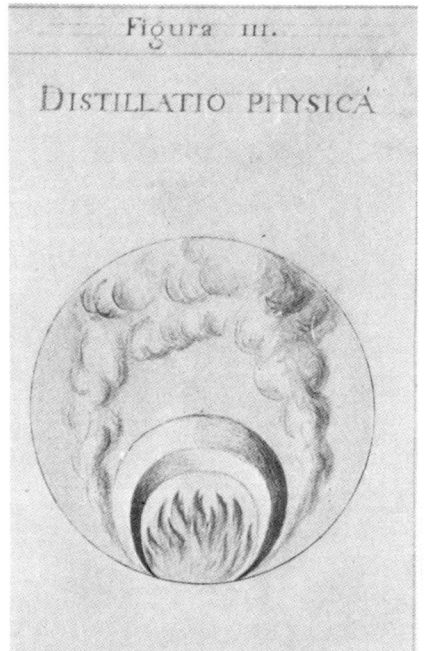

Figura IV.

PRÆPARATIO PHYSICA

Figura V.

DE DIVISIONE

Figura VI.

ACVATIO

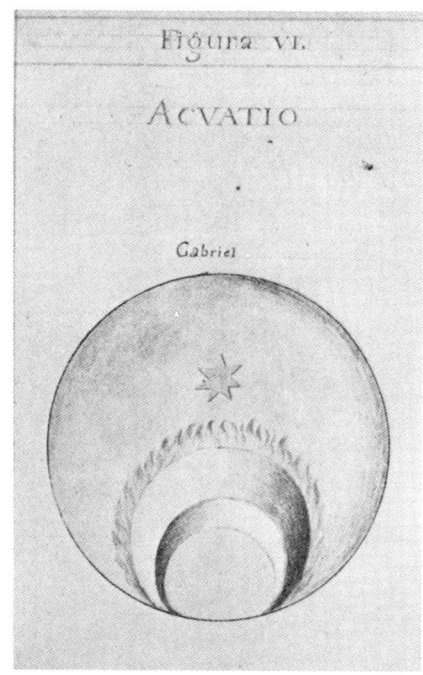

Figura VII.

LEO VIRIDIS

Figura VIII.

COITVS

Figura IX.

LAPIS TRI-VNVS

Figura X.

CALCINATIO

Figura XI. SVBLIMATIO

Figura XII. SOLVTIO

Figura XIII. GENERATIO

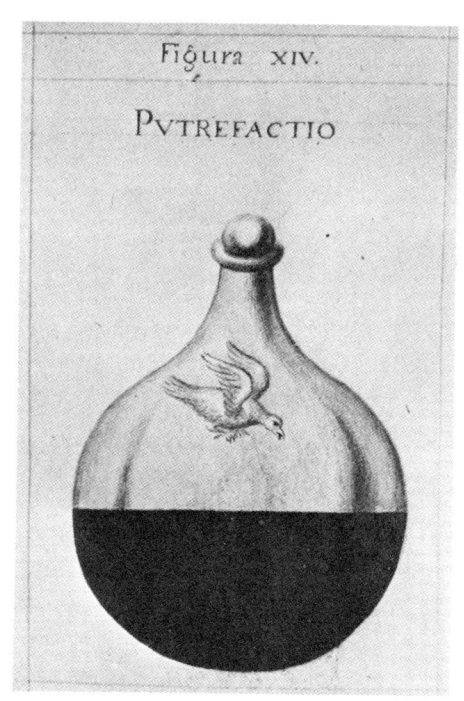

Figura XIV. PVTREFACTIO

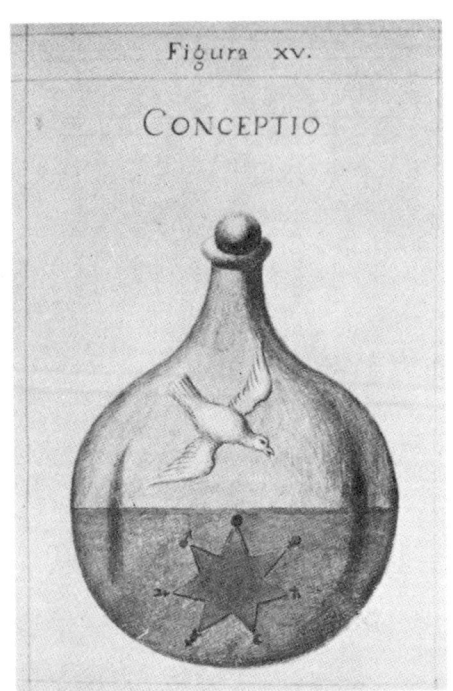

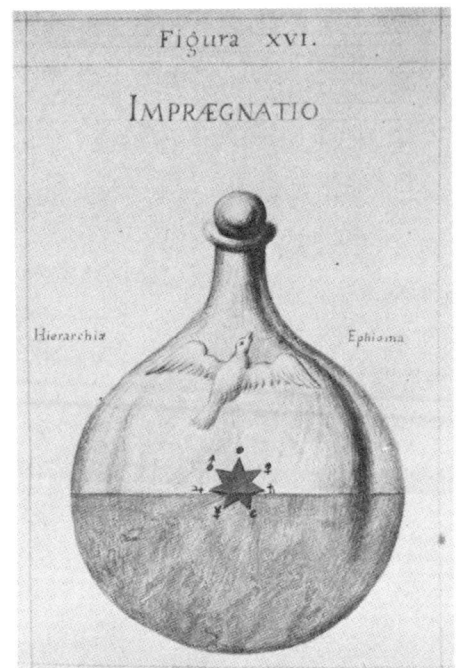

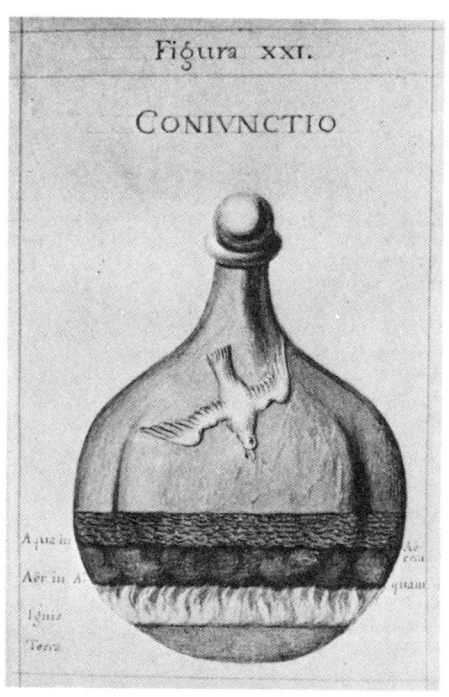

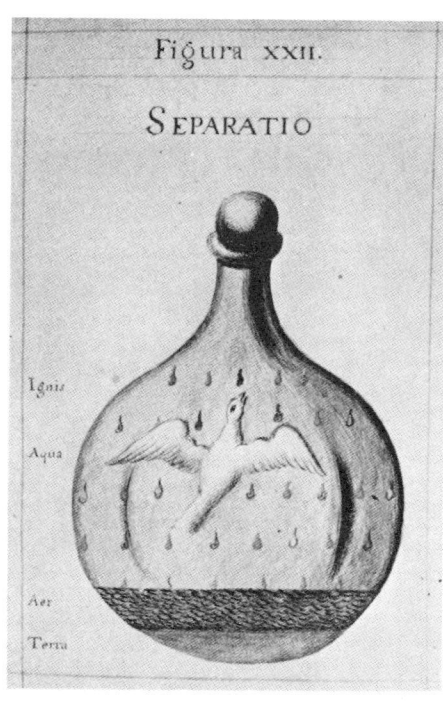

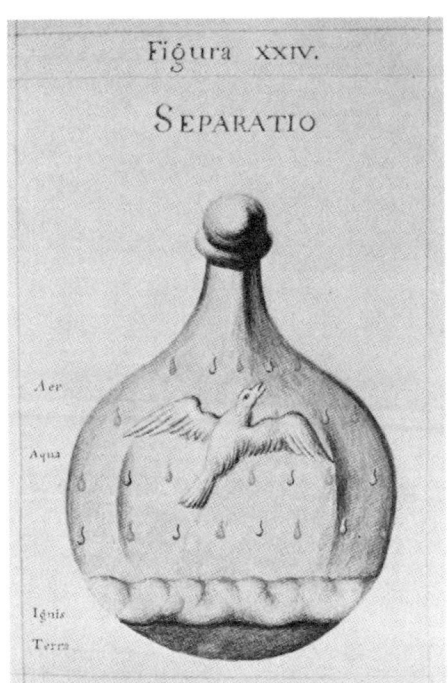

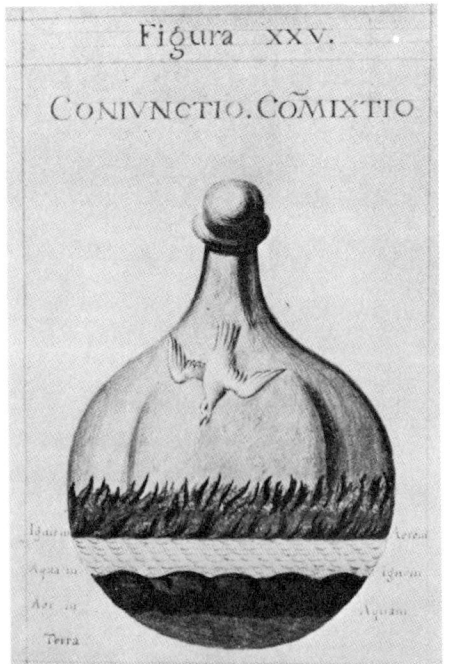

Figura XXVII.

IGNIS INNATVRALIS

Figura XXVIII.

ORTVS

Figura XXIX.

FERMENTATIO

Figura XXX.

PVRGATIO

Figura XXXI.
SEPARATIO

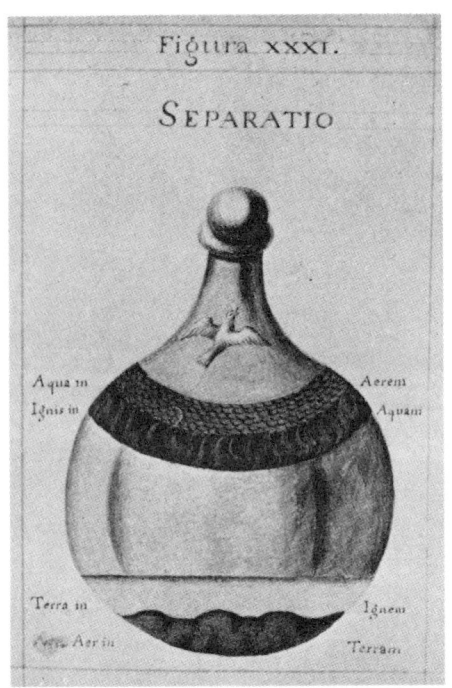

Figura XXXII.
CONIVNCTIO

Figura XXXIII.
SEPARATIO

Figura XXXIV.
CONIVNCTIO

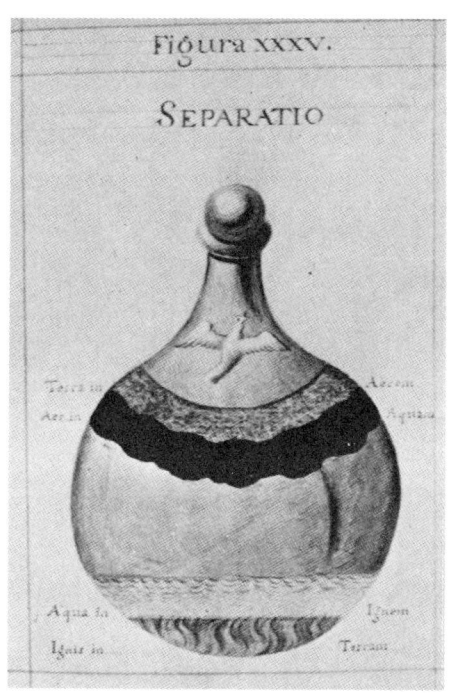

Figura XXXV.

SEPARATIO

Figura XXXVI.

CONIVNCTIO

Figura XXXIX.

FIXATIO

Figura XL.

PROIECTIO. CERATIO

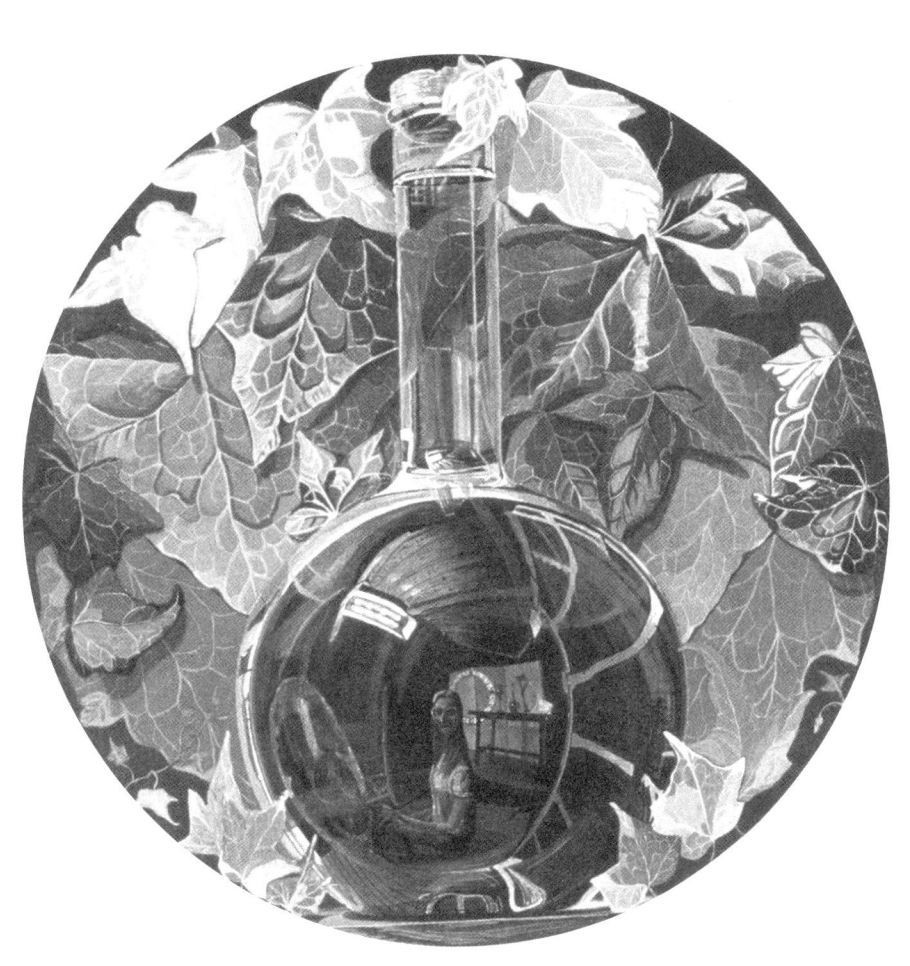

dens, inseritur.

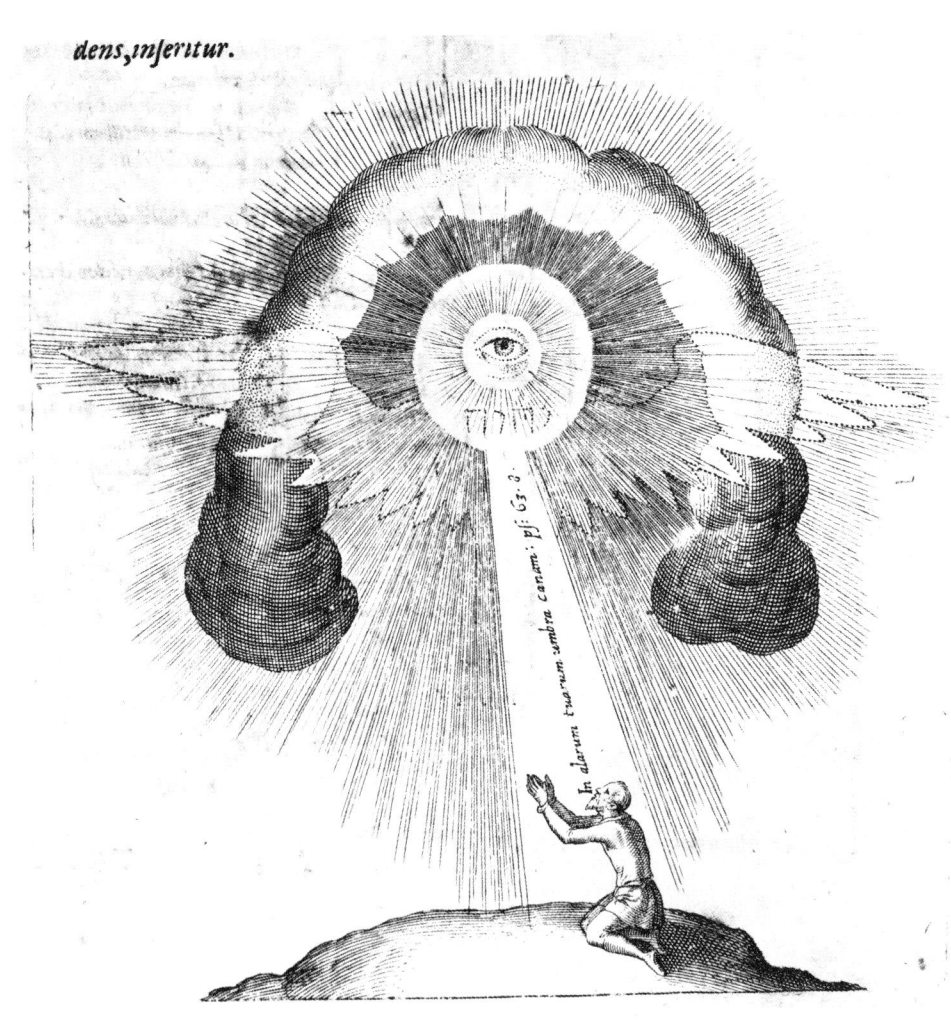

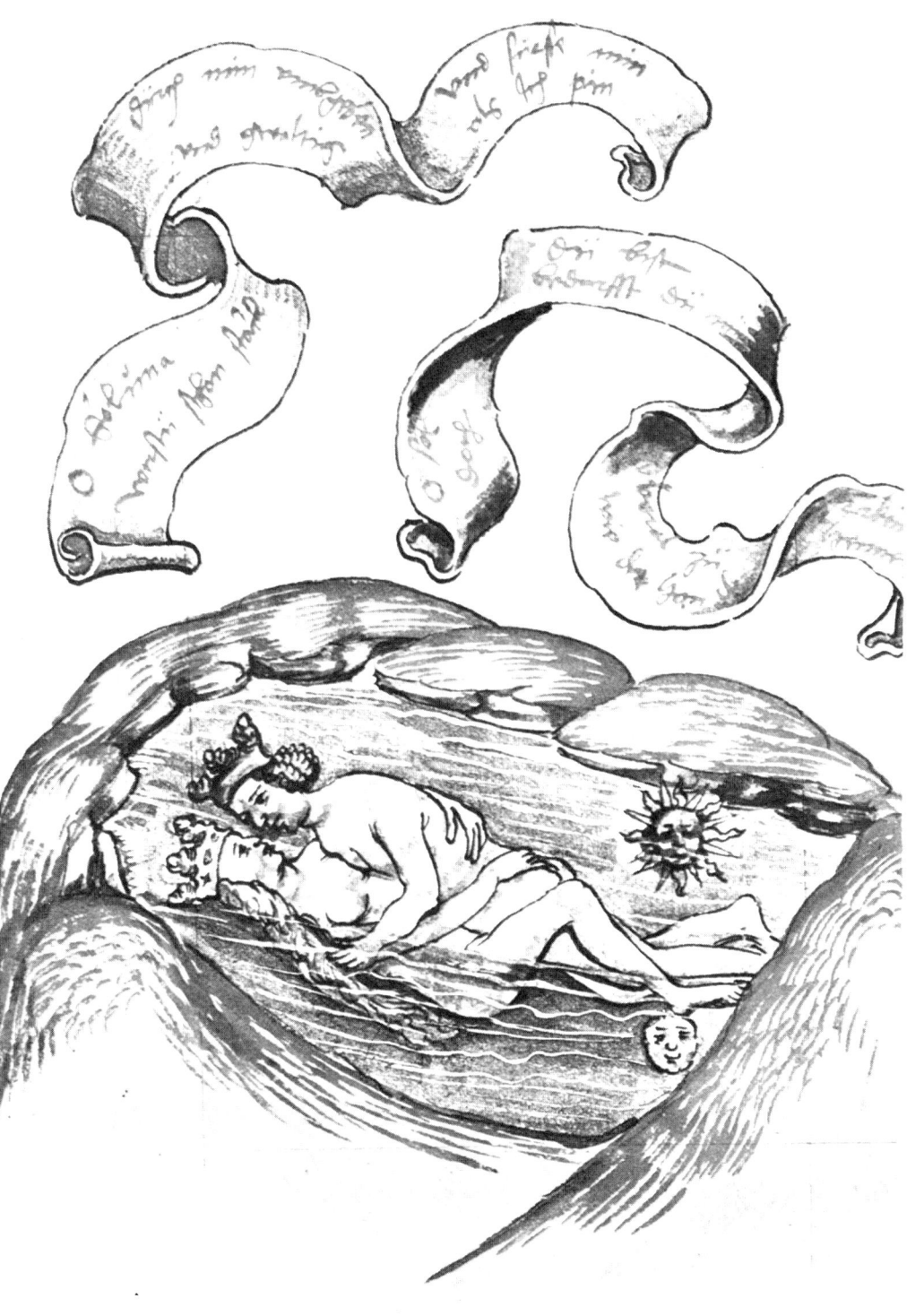

Τοῦτ᾽ ἐστὶν τὸ μυστήριον ὁ οὐροβόρος δράκων
ἤτοι τοῦτ᾽ ἐστὶν ἢ λάβωσις τῶν σω-
πάντων τῆς ἐργασίας
αὐτοῦ

Τὰ δὲ
αὖ

Τὸ δὲ

Τὸ
οἶδέ
που
σύμβε-

φῶτα τῶν μυστηρίων τῆς
ἐστὶ ταῦτα ἢ ἐὰν θώσϊν·-
τρασίγον αὐτοῦ ἐστὶν ἰώσις·
τὴν ἤοσίγας αὐτοῦ:-
πόδες αὐτοῦ οἵ τέσσαρες θῖν
σώματα τῆς τέχνης

τέχνης
του
ἤτε
του
μας

Τὰ δὲ
τὴν αὐ...

Σὺ δὲ ἐν τούτοις πίστου τὸν νοῦν ἔχων ὦ φίλτατε

ὡς ἴσα αὐτοῦ
θέλξαι κοῖα

αὐτοῦ τοῦτ᾽ ἐστὶν τὸ ὁ·

Δράκων τίς παρακάθηται φυλάττων τὸν ναὸν τοῦτον
τὸν χρυσοδμήνον· πρῶτον θῦσον κι ἀπόδερμά-
τοσον, κι λαβὼν τὰς σάρκας αὐτοῦ ἕως τῶν ὀστέων,
πρὸς τὸ στόμιον τοῦ ναοῦ ποίησον αὐτὸ βάσις
κι ἀνάβηθι κι εὑρήσῃς ἑκεῖ τὸ ζητούμενον χρῆ-
μα· Τοῦ γὰρ ἱερέως τοῦ χαλκάνου μετέσβη τοῦ
χρώματος τῆς φύσεως κι γέγονεν ἀργυρανθῦ-
ον μετ᾽ ὀλίγας ὡν ἢ ἡμέραν ἐὰν θελήσῃς εὑρή-
σεις αὐτὸν κι χρυσανθοῦν· τὸ εἰ τοῦ θείου ἀκώως
λαβὼν θεῖον ἄπυρον λεώσον οὔρῳ ἀφθόρου· εἶτα
λαβὼν ἄχμην δυνάμει ἔψε ἕως ἱδὶ πλεύσῃ κι γί-
νεται ἄκαυτον· δοκίμαζον κι ἕτερον κι βλέπων

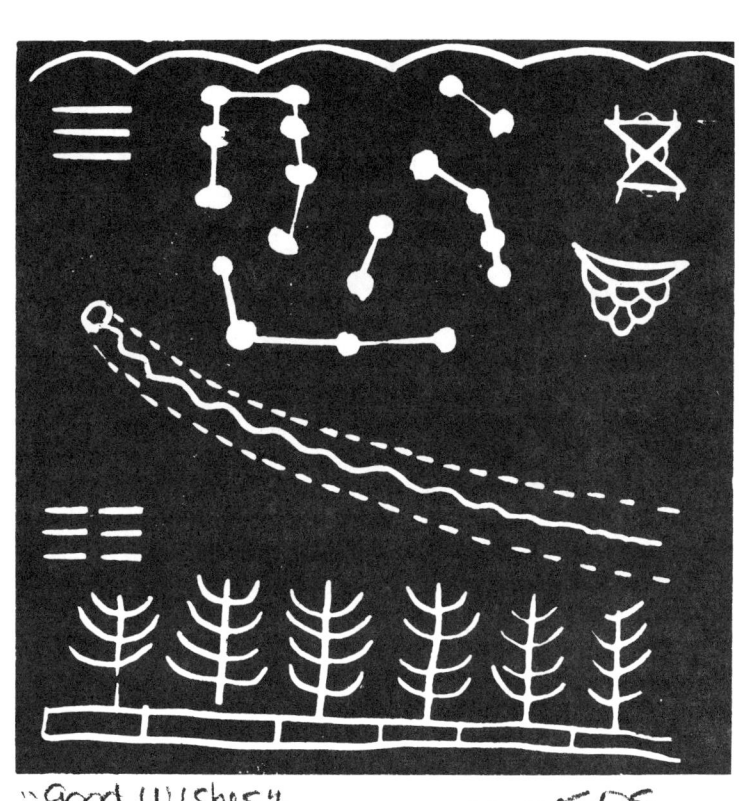

"Good Wishes"
"An Auspicious Omen"

"Cosmic Seal" EDS LEIDEN 7/69

HEAVEN and EARTH   CDS

The Vault of Heaven, and the Silver River float over thirty three Islands.

COS LEIDEN 7/89

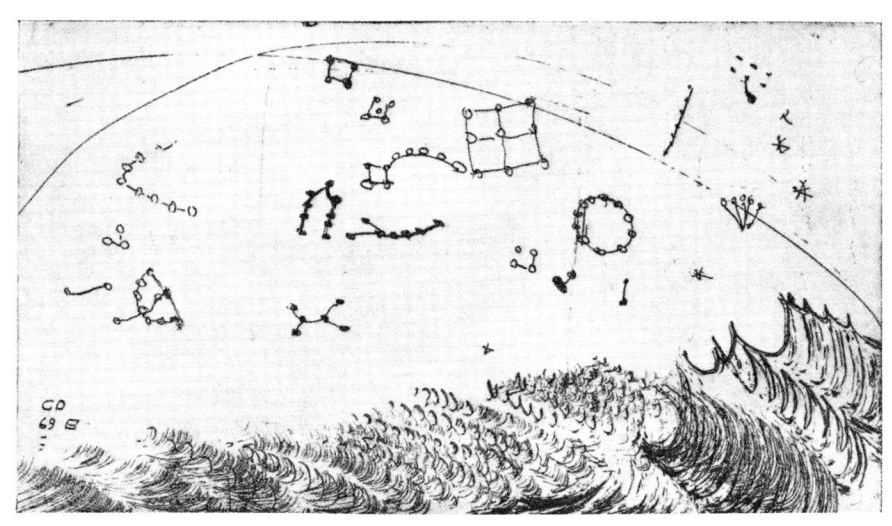

"The Sea Rises under the Constellations"

F. SOLVTIO PERFECTA III.

F. PVTREFACTIO IV.

Charles Poncé

THE ALCHEMICAL LIGHT

The alchemists believed that nature contained an illuminating principle reminiscent of the soul's power concealed within the elementary world stuff. Because individuals were also thought of as composed of this stuff, it was expected that this luminary could be found within them as well. The light, according to their belief, was the archetypal principle that preceded all things and could be experienced by a turning about within.[1] Thomas Vaughan, admittedly elusive about the matter, wrote:

> "The almighty God placed in the heart of the world, namely, in the earth—as He did in the heart of every other creature—a firelife, which Paracelsus calls the Archaeus and Sendivogius the Central Sun... Over this Archaeus or central fire God hath placed His heaven, the sun and stars, He hath placed the head and the eyes over the heart. For between man and the world there is no small accord, and he that knows not the one cannot know the other."[2]

The Paracelsian term Archaeus is defined by Ruland as, "a most high, exalted, and invisible spirit, which is separated from bodies, is exalted and ascends; it is the occult virtue of Nature, universal in all things, the artificer, the healer."[3] According to Vaughan, Archaeus is the central sun contained within the heart of every creature and takes the shape of an invisible spirit that is the active principle in Nature. Ruland further identifies this spirit with another Paracelsian term, Adech:

> "Adech is our interior and invisible man, who raises up in our minds the images or archetypes of all other things which our visible and exterior man copies and forms with his hands. Each works after his own nature, the invisible things unseen, the sensible, under form sensible, those things which are within the domain of the senses."[4]

The Archaeus and Adech have up to this point been described as a central and invisible sun that creates images which are then transformed into concrete realities. It is in this sense an independent creative principle that gives shape and form to the phenomenal world through the agency of the human mind. We come closer to understanding exactly what this principle is when we read Paracelsus' comments on Hermetic Astronomy and discover that the stars of heaven would not be able to affect us if not for the existence of a star within us that acts as a medium between the heavenly powers and our bodies. "There is one star that governs all things... its office is to operate in man... to turn and to change their senses and their minds... This same medium is and must be a star situated in those things where the supreme operates. By this medium is produced an effect on the substance and on the body."[5] This star in persons is imagination,[6] and in that it is described as a complete sun, the illuminating principle in nature.

The star composed of imagination is called a spirit, and, to the alchemical mind, the spirit is that thing which unites the soul with the body:

> "The Spirit produces the Soul from the Body, and returns it when it is white. Therefore it is called the Life of the Soul—*Vita Animae*. Should the Spirit depart from the Soul it could not give the life. The Soul unites and conjoins the married, Body and Spirit; so the Spirit unites the Soul with the Body, so that it is all one thing."

Therefore, the medium connecting body to psyche is imagination. Paracelsus says as much:

> "The Archaeus is of a magnetic nature, and attracts or repulses other sympathetic or anti-pathetic forces belonging to the same plane... The vital force is not enclosed in man, but radiates around him like a luminous sphere, and it may be made to act at a distance. In those semi-material rays the imagination of man may produce healthy or morbid effects. It may poison the essence of life and cause diseases, or it may purify it after it has been made impure, and restore the health."[8]

Thus, the image is a power capable of affecting the human body. We are familiar with the idea of an image affecting the psychological well-being of an individual—such as the poor self-image handed down from a parent to a child that causes a stunting of his or her psychological growth. But Paracelsus implies more than this when he states that the image can directly affect the body. The depth psychologist, R. A. Lockhart expresses this involvement as follows:

> "...bodily organs and processes have the capacity to stimulate the production of psychic images, meaningfully related to the type of physical disturbances and its location."[9]

Paracelsus believed that the image is capable of healing what it has poisoned, and Lockhart reports a case in which a man dying from widespread cancer had a series of dreams so profound that they caused a deep transformation of his personality to occur, after which time his cancer regressed. All of this gives some validity to the alchemists' claim that alchemy is capable of freeing the body from every form of suffering through work on the soul.[10] I do not mean to imply here that the alchemists created a material or chemical substance capable of freeing the body from its infirmities, but rather that the object of alchemy was to bring an individual into a proper and harmonious relationship between psyche and soma. Religious, mystical, and metaphysical considerations aside, if the techniques the alchemists employed did this and nothing more our high valuation of alchemy would be more than warranted. We must allow the possibility that "the medicine of the body is the image of the medicine of the soul, just as the infirmities of the soul are the image of the infirmities of the body,"[11] for such equations lead us toward where body and psyche unite and affect one another.

Commenting upon the importance of uniting feeling and intellect, Jung wrote: "The one must lend itself as auxiliary to the other yet the contrast between them is so great that we need a bridge. This bridge is already given us in creative phantasy. It is not born of either, for it is the mother of both."[12] For the alchemists, he tells us this bridge led to "an intermediate realm between mind and matter, i.e. a psychic realm of subtle bodies whose characteristic it is to manifest themselves in a mental as well as a material form."[13] Plato was aware of the reality and efficacy of this imaginal bridge when he wrote that there is an art capable of turning the soul away from the outer forms of the world toward the inner, and that this conversion of the soul is not one producing vision, but rather one bringing about its proper use of vision. In short, he anticipates Henry Corbin's suggestion that imagination is a trans-sensory organ of perception: "...this organ of knowledge must be turned around from the world of becoming together with the entire soul...until the soul is able to endure the contemplation of essence and the brightest region of being."[14] Apparently the uniting factor between body and psyche, between the outer heaven and the inner heaven, is the medium of imagination. This medium of imagination, the imaginal, is another space, a nowhere that in some way nonetheless meshes with our everyday reality. This may suggest to some that imagination is little more than fancy or phantasy. But what has been evoked is the matter of *work*, of the need to exert an effort of will that essentially calls for an inversion of selfhood, a giving up of self. This demand alerts us to the fact that the initial movement in the direction of imagination was a strict regime of prayer and monastic discipline.

Prayer in this stage was more likely a petition for aid[15] which in time gave way to a mode of contemplation whose emphasis was that of establishing an inner dialogue. As William James put it, prayer "or inner communion with the spirit thereof—be that spirit 'God' or 'law'—is a process wherein work is really done, and spiritual energy flows in and produces effects, psychological or material within the phenomenal world."[16] It is at exactly this point that imagination enters the picture.

Imagination does not merely refer us to a pleasant passage of images across the screen of our consciousness, but a visual dialogue that engages the energies of our psyche to the same degree that it becomes engaged with the phenomenal world. This dialogue serves not only to act as a bridge to the imaginal, but to give it its place as the other half of what we would call our wholeness. This was the great discovery of alchemy: that we can take an active part in the on-going creation of Genesis through the medium of imagination. If the image gives birth to psychic life, and psychic life in turn manufactures the material person-made world from the ideas clustered around the image, then the fullness of life is to be found in an active participation with the image at its own level as well. Whether one wishes to call such an involvement meditation, contemplation, imaging, or prayer—it is a participation in otherness, in the undefinable ground of life.

This is what is referred to in the *Hermetica* when we are told that, prior to being in the world, soul and mind had been Life and Light, and that only those who are capable of recollecting this will "learn to know that you are made of them,... [and] go back into Life and Light."[17] All of this is another way of saying that the image, and imagination, is life. If one can imagine living a day without the experience of those images that normally pass through one's mind, this seemingly metaphysical statement will take on a different and quite concrete meaning. Without even the basic experience of mental images needed to recall where we parked our cars, left our hats, first met a person we have met again, there would be little to us. The philosophic and Hermetic traditions take this one step further: we are essentially dead, prisoners in Plato's cave, as long as we do not engage in the imaginal life that has given birth to our psyches in the first place. "Image and meaning are identical,"[18] so the degree to which we give emotional validity to the image is equal to the meaning we are capable of discovering in the life that the image creates.

But the process is not without its dangers, for what we are speaking of here is the petitioning of a dimension capable of shattering all that we identify with consciousness. The alchemical demand of sealing the vessel refers us to the importance of keeping this experience in some way separate and distinct from our everyday existence. One might say that it is overlapping of these two dimensions that turns the mystical or transformative into the pathological. The alchemical vessel, or rather its employment in a symbolic sense, was a way by which the impersonal reality of the soul—which could lead to a depersonalization experience of pathological proportions—could be kept from contaminating one's relationship to the world outside. Thus, we find a petitioner asking how one might arrive at the 'Supersensual Ground' without the destruction of his personality:

> "How am I to wait for the rising of this glorious Sun, and how am I to seek in the Centre, this Fountain of Light, which may enlighten me throughout, and bring all my properties into perfect Harmony? I am in Nature, as I said before; and which Way shall I pass through Nature, and the Light thereof, so that I may come into the Supernatural and Supersensual Ground, whence this true Light, which is the Light of Minds, doth arise; and this *without the Destruction of my Nature, or quenching the Light of it, which is my Reason?*"[19]

So we see that the alchemist and the mystic were well aware of the necessity of keeping these two worlds separate and distinct. It is apparent such observations were not spontaneous revelations but the result of painstaking observation and experience. The stuff of present-day psychology obviously had its beginnings with such experiments centuries ago. The problem is that psychology does not set out to define the imaginal, but rather the degree of our pathological relationship to it. There is no geography of the soul or spirit available for those who would wish to journey there. The creation of such a geography obviously demands travellers who have made the journey. The most we can do until their arrival is piece out the descriptions left to us by those who have been there centuries before.

The opening stages of the journey demand purification, meditation, and the withdrawal of attention from material sensations up to the point when

> "the imaginative faculty will turn your thoughts to imagine and picture

[mental contents] *as if* it ascended in the higher worlds up the roots of his soul... until the imagined image reaches his highest source and there the images of the [supernal] lights are imprinted on his mind *as if* he imagined and saw them in the same way in which his imaginative faculty normally pictures in his mind mental contents deriving from the world..."[20]

Here we arrive at the complicated issue of imaginal geography, for whereas in the stage where the soul was to be pulled back from 'out there,' from the world of phenomena, it was assumed that its withdrawal landed it 'in here,' in psyche. But no sooner is that achieved when we are invariably presented with images of ascension. The difficulty has to do with the fact that, to our way of thinking today, 'up there' is associated with 'out there.' What we have to be reminded of here is that the imaginal also describes itself in terms of spatial co-ordinates; the famous alchemical dictum, 'that which is below is as that which is above, and that which is above is as that which is below,'' directs us to the placement of the imaginal world relative to ours. There is no reason we should not expect to find an above and below in the imaginal without reference to our spatial position in the phenomenal world.

And yet the experience of ascension and descension (as it transpires in the imaginal) expresses itself through our bodies—that is, through our sensory system, to give us the impression that it is happening 'out here.' That these imaginal happenings do cause the individual sometimes to believe that their expression is happening 'out there' is clearly shown in those Ecclesiastical depictions of saints and other mortals receiving an influx of spirit pouring down from the sky.

Such distinctions are important, for they help us separate the experience of the imaginal from the phenomenal without losing the quality of the experience, while at the same time safeguarding against a destructive inundation of the imaginal. As we should recall from our earlier pages, this was of major concern to those who wished to experience the 'Supersensual Ground' without the loss of their reason. It at the same time serves to 'locate' imaginal activity in much the manner that mythology locates gods and goddesses at a variety of geographical points on the earth. In the same way that a favorite spot in your garden might elicit memories of activities you had undertaken there, so too does locating co-ordinates within the imaginal allow recollective memory to become activated. For this reason alchemical treatises always abound in descriptions of Biblical or mythological places. Such landscapes serve as catalysts for the interior process.

Returning to the Safed Kabbalist Hayyad Vital's account of the soul's ascension, we are drawn even further into the geography of the imaginal. We should note in particular his statement that the meditator ascends towards the *roots* of his soul. The source of the image is Plato:

"As concerning the most sovereign form of soul in us we must conceive that heaven has given it to each man as a guiding genius—that part which we say dwells in the summit of our body and lifts us from earth towards our celestial affinity, like a plant whose roots are not in earth, but in the heavens. And this is most true, for it is to the heavens, whence the soul first came to birth, that the divine part attaches the head or root of us and keeps the whole body upright."[21]

As our account from the *Gloria Mundi* clearly shows, this same image was taken over by the alchemists: "Man may be compared to an inverted tree: for he has his roots or his hair in the air, while other trees have their hairs, or their roots, in the earth, and as the Sages say,...the root of their minerals is in the air, and their head in the earth."[22]

Whereas in Kabbalistic accounts the roots of the soul contain the supernal lights, or the sefiroth, in the *Hermetica*[23] we are told that the ascending soul must pass through the planetary zones in order to be stripped of the dark qualities originally assigned to it by each planet. This idea is implied in our passage from the *Gloria Mundi*, for the minerals contained in the roots of the inverted tree-soul refer us to the planets whose attributes they symbolize. In each instance, therefore, a journey must be undertaken through the planetary zones, or what Plato refers to as "those circuits in the head that were deranged at birth."[24] These references are particularly important when we recall that the alchemists thought of the planets as contained within us: "For it is true that the external stars affect the man, and the internal stars in man effect outward things, in fact and in operation, the one on the other."[25]

We inherit a two-fold image: the alchemist and the philosopher draw the nourishment for their souls from the imaginal, where the roots of their souls are planted. This is accomplished through imagination which allows the alchemist to journey to each mineral contained in the tree's branches in an attempt to turn each to gold.

With these few references to philosophy an alchemy we can now easily discern the meaning of the imagery offered us in the following excerpt:

> "If any one were to take common metallic gold and silver, and tried to resolve those metals into mercury, he would be doing a very foolish thing. It is a result that cannot be brought about by any chemical process... But these sages did not speak of common gold and silver, which must always remain what they are, and can never become anything else, and certainly cannot aid the development of other metals... No, the *living* fruit (the real living gold and silver) we must seek *on the tree*, for only there can it grow, and increase in size, according to the the possibilities of its nature. This tree we must transplant...into a better and richer soil, and to a sunnier spot... I wish you to understand that Mercury, which is a most excellent tree...must be taken and transplanted into a soil that is near to the Sun...—in the garden of the Sages, the *Sun* sheds its genial influence day and night... There our *tree* is watered with the rarest dew, and the fruit which hangs upon the trees

swells and ripens and expands."²⁶

Our writer begins by stating flatly that the gold and silver to be created are not the common gold and silver but a living fruit to be found upon a tree identified as Mercury, the spirit *par excellence* of alchemy whose identification with flowing and reflective quicksilver easily brings to mind the idea of imagination—that which flows and reflects images. This tree must be uprooted from the barren soil of the commonplace activity of imagination and replanted in the garden of philosophy. There in the garden, true gold and silver may be cultivated.

Imagination is spirit; in some of our selections it is referred to directly as such. The reflective and fluviant quality of the Spirit Mercurius in its alchemical depiction as quicksilver aptly symbolizes the activity of imagination: it flows, it fragments, it reflects. But we could just as easily bring alchemical material to bear on the idea that the soul is imagination, thus reminding us of the alchemists' statement that "Also the Soul is called Spirit, and the Spirit is called Soul."

Jung tells us that there are five instincts: hunger, sexuality, drive to activity, reflection, and creativity. The first three are easily understandable and need no explanation. Reflection "is the cultural instinct *par excellence*, and its strength is shown in the power of culture to maintain itself in the face of untamed nature,"²⁷ in its ability to interfere with stimuli whose tendency is to trigger instinctive discharges. Whereas in other creatures a stimulus is followed by an impulse to act that immediately discharges itself into the world, this 'specifically human'²⁸ instinct carries the impulse over to a psychic realm where it is either held in check or dissipated. The charge that would normally move outward into this world becomes turned inward, toward the psyche where it becomes the object of reflection in the form of images.²⁹

From what Jung has said, we might surmise that there occurs a radical alteration of impulse from what might be thought of as instinctual concreteness (making real the impulse) to a state of pyschic immateriality, or a transformation of the concrete into image. Jung describes this latter process as psychization, but the mystics would have and did call it death. In Jung we find, "In spite or perhaps because of its affinity with instinct, the archetype represents the authentic element of spirit, but a spirit which is not to be identified with the human intellect, since it is the latter's *spiritus rector*."³⁰ So psychization might be thought of as spiritualization:

> "Psychic processes therefore behave like a scale along which consciousness "slides." At one moment it finds itself in the vicinity of instinct, and falls under its influence; at another, it slides along to the other end where spirit predominates and even assimilates the instinctual processes most opposed to it."³¹

The alchemical and mystical demand that the gates of the senses be closed (and the soul recalled from its materialistic involvement with the world) directs us to this psychological process of reflection. The 'death' of an instinctual response and its psychization, a process in which the response becomes image, is in direct correlation to the retrieval of the soul for the purpose of its ascension up the contemplative ladder of imagination as described by the Kabbalist Vital several pages back. It also fully answers the description of the alchemical nigredo in which the body dies and the soul ascends.

Another way of putting it is that the plane of imagination is created by death—it is the death of the soul's bodily impulse that turns it into image and thus subject to spirit. Remembering that imagination has been spoken of as illumination and as a brightness by the alchemists, it is not without interest that in Plato the pure soul is compared to light[32], and that the place where all souls go to in death, Hades, is described like the soul: "glorious, pure, and invisible."[33] Thus, Soul and Spirit are not only connected by death, but by imagination. In fact, the implication is that without the interplay of soul and spirit there would be no imagination. Imagination might be compared to the *idea* of a mirror whose existence could not come to pass without the silvering substance of mercury on the one hand, and glass on the other. The combination of the two creates a place of reflection. Thus, the combination, the reflection and clarity, of soul and spirit create imagination.

We have given indications that the alchemical process heavily relied upon methods that called for an immersion in imaginal processes. We have also indicated that these processes lie far beneath the threshold of what we normally identify as consciousness, and that because of their foreign nature to the twentieth century mind they often burst upon us in a manner not to excite as much as to terrorize and break down the boundaries of personality. It has also been implied that such breakdowns of our ego defenses have often been referred to as a prerequisite for any type of transformation along the lines that mysticism and alchemy have laid down. Our difficulty today, therefore, is to be found in our attitude towards such intrusions of the imaginal. Textbooks warn us of pathology—and in many instances such intrusions properly answer that description. But the reason why this is the case has not so much to do with the events themselves as with the reception of the event. A psychology or religion that holds the imaginal at bay is bound to suffer at its hand. One cannot adapt a religious mode of being without at some point being forced to experience what one is talking about, nor can one admit that one is a psychological being without experiencing the fullness of one's psychology.

Religions and psychology, alchemy and mysticism, all deal with similar issues. The difference lies in the terminology and the ritual engagement. Whether one goes for guidance to a priest, a doctor, or one's dreams, they are in all instances deeply engaged with the nature of being. To deal with only those aspects that link us to the phenomenal world is to deny and ignore the deeper and far more personal issues of life and death. Alchemy is a tradition that found itself almost unwittingly attempting to incorporate these issues through the phenomenon of imagination. Admittedly, the method was not created out of a body of doctrinal beliefs. Each alchemist appears to have discovered the method for himself—and what he discovered was the operation of what he called Nature: a natural process in psyche. Whereas in the East this process was worked into a method such as yoga, here in the West it was allowed to develop with very little modification or restraint. In the East, when an incorrect employment of such methods would yield what we would call pathological phenomena, such phenomena were regarded as the outcome of wrong techniques—not as illness. Perhaps it is because we have no technique, no guiding rules for the experience of the imaginal, that these phenomena that historically produced mystical or religious doctrines, instead became the science of psychology. That is, because the experience of the imaginal had no containing ritual, no alchemical vessel, it came to be seen as a disturbance of persons rather than a disturbance of methodology. Therapy as we know it today may be nothing more than an attempt to compensate for the absence of a containing ritual or religion that would receive and portray these experiences as transformative rather than degenerative. This might explain the striking similarities to be found between certain aspects of mystical and pathological experiences, similarities suggesting that they are, in fact, the same experience.

As can be seen by what has gone before us, the tangle of images that form the body of alchemy have their source in a number of traditions that, at first sight, seem to have little to do with alchemy. That alchemy, however, has served as the receptacle for practically every type of speculation about the nature of the soul, spirit, and body indicates that in it we have a drawerful of imaginings about what is basic in being, whether or not we accept the poetry of the terms employed to define it. At the very least we have discovered that alchemy is a legitimate expression of a Western mystical tradition that appeared just before the emergence of the Scientific Revolution. At the most, we might discover that the alchemists were involved with a never-ending Genesis, an imaginal world without end.

FOOTNOTES

1. "O Man, thou art with thy soul in the inward; but thy soul's will hath turned itself about with Adam into the outward; therefore, if thou wilt behold God and the Eternity, *turn* thyself about with thy will into the inward, and then thou art as God himself." *The Works of Jacob Behme*, William Law, tran., London, 1781.
2. *The Works of Thomas Vaughan*, Arthur Edward Waite, editor, Theosophical Publishing House, London, 1919, p. 403.
3. *A Lexicon of Alchemy*, Martin Ruland the Elder, Arthur Edward Waite, trans. and editor, John M. Watkins, London, 1964, p. 36.
4. *ibid.*, p. 6.
5. *The Hermetic and Alchemical Writings of Paracelsus*, Arthur Edward Waite, trans. and editor, two volumes, James Elliott & Co., London, 1967, vol. II, p. 285.
6. "The imagination is the mouth of the body which is not visible. It is also the sun of man which acts within its own sphere after the manner of the celestial luminary. It irradiates the earth, which is man, just as the material sun shines upon the material world...And as the sun sends its force on a spot which it shines upon, so also the imagination, like a star, bursts upon the thing which it affects." *ibid.*, vol. II, p. 7.
7. Ruland, *op. cit.*, p. 31.
8. *Paracelsus: Life and Prophecies*, by Franz Hartmann, Rudolf Steiner Publications, Blauvelt, New York, 1973, p. 133.
9. "Cancer in Myth and Dream," by R. A. Lockhart, *Spring* 1977, p. 10.
10. "Our Art frees not only the body, but also the soul from the snares of servitude and bondage; it enables the rich, and comforts and relieves the poor. Indeed, it may be said to supply every human want, and to provide a remedy for every form of suffering." *The New Pearl of Great Price*, Arthur Edward Waite, trans. and editor, Vincent Stuart, Ltd., London 1963, reprint of 1984 edition, p. 119.
11. *The Epistles of Ali Pul*, J. W. Hamilton-Jones, trans., John M. Watkins, London, 1951, p. 5.
12. *Psychological Types*, by C. G. Jung, Harcourt, Brace & Company, Inc. New York/London, 1923, p. 77.
13. *Collected Works of C. G. Jung*, Routledge & Kegan Paul, London, 1953, vol. 12, par. 395.
14. "The Republic," in *The Collected Dialogues of Plato*, Edith Hamilton and Huntington Cairns, editors, Princeton University Press, 1973, Book vii, par. 518d.
15. "Then fall upon thy knees, and with a humble and contrite heart render to Him the praise, honour, and glory due for the hearing of thy prayer, and ask Him again and again to continue to thee His grace, and to grant that, after attaining the full and perfect knowledge of this profound Mystery,

thou mayest be enabled to use it to the glory and honour of His most Holy Name, and for the good of thy suffering fellow men." from "The Sophic Hydrolith," in *The Hermetic Museum,* Arthur Edward Waite, editor and trans. John Watkins, London, 1953, 2 vols., reprint of 1893 edition, vol. I, pp. 74-5.

16 *The Varieties of Religious Experience,* by William James, Longmans, Green, & Co., New York, 1910, page 389.
17 *Hermetica,* Walter Scott, trans. in 4 volumes, Oxford, 1924, vol. I, p. 17 & 21.
18 Jung, CW 8 par. 402.
19 Behme, *op. cit.,* vol. IV, P. 89, my italics.
20 Hayyim Vital, quoted in *Joseph Karo: Lawyer & Mystic,* by R. J. Zwi Werblowsky, The Jewish Publication Society of America, Philadelphia, 1977, p. 69.
21 "Timaeus," *Plato's Cosmology,* trans. by Francis Macdonald Cornford, Routledge & Kegan Paul, London/New York, 1971, 90a, p. 353.
22 *Hermetic Museum, op. cit.,* vol. I, p. 218.
23 "Timaeus," *op. cit.,* 90d, p. 354.
25 *Hermetic & Alchemical Writings of paracelsus, op. cit.,* II, p. 285.
26 *Hermetic Museum, op. cit.,* vol. I, pp. 144-5
27 Jung, CW 8, par. 243.
28 *ibid.,* par. 241.
29 *ibid.,* par. 242.
30 *ibid.,* par. 406.
31 *ibid.,* par. 408.
32 "Republic," *op. cit.,* Book vii, 518.
33 "Phaedo," *Collected Dialogues of Plato, op. cit.,* 80d.

Edward Whitmont
NON-CAUSALITY AS A UNIFYING PRINCIPLE OF PSYCHOSOMATICS—SULPHUR

"There is no such thing as an inert substance. Everything in this whole cosmos has power and corresponds to a human condition. All over the cosmos are formed patterns that are hidden in various substances and correspond to the states of human beings. Our being itself is spread out over the cosmos, and our disease fields, our disorders, correspond to field patterns around us."—*from a talk in 1983.*

The concept of causality, namely the linear association of phenomena by cause and effect, has always been an unquestioned logical category; in scientific work, especially, it seems to us the only possible and thinkable one. To satisfy our scientific logic—the causal relationship of events has to be established before we can reasonably assume an understanding of the phenomena in question.

Thus we ask whether physical disorders are caused by mental ones or vice versa. We ask why a potency acts, why a similar drug removes a condition which it can cause; whether prescribing on the basis of symptom similarity removes also the 'cause' of these symptoms, namely the 'illness.' In attempting to find a logical order in the maze of symptoms of our Materia Medica we have to ask such questions as what causes the 'ragged philosopher,' *Mr. Sulphur*, to have eczemas, and why that same *Sulphur* constitution should also be characterized by varicose veins and an aggravation from heat? What causes what, and how so?

At best, these questions prove unanswerable. But, actually, they involve us in more and more illogical paradoxes. The very law of similars itself is such a logical paradox when looked at in terms of causality. That, seemingly, cause and effect could be reversible—such as emotional states causing organic conditions or organic derangements causing mental disorders—seems equally bewildering. More or less despairing of ever finding satisfactory answers, we have embarrassedly stopped asking such questions.

It has never occured to us that the very mode of reasoning which we have come to take for granted may itself be a barrier toward a real understanding of the phenomena of life. Astounding as this may sound, it is precisely the conclusion with which we are confronted by modern scientific insights. Non-causality, as a scientific principle suitable for a better understanding of nature, has been advanced by the exactest of all sciences, physics, and more recently also by analytical psychology.

W. Heisenberg[1] who introduced the so-called 'uncertainty principle' into physics expresses himself as follows:

> In the statement that whenever we know the present exactly in every respect, we can predetermine the future, it is not the conclusion that is wrong but the premise. As a matter of principle, we cannot ever exactly recognize the present.

The basis for this statement lies in the fact that, in atom physics, the very process of observation itself has been found to disturb and thereby change the course of the events which are to be observed. One may determine with approximate exactness either the course or the impulse of an electron but not both; the accuracy of determination of the one diminishes in relation to the gain of exactness of the other. Never having had a firmly exact premise from which to deduce an effect, the laws of energy had to be formulated in a different way by quantum physics.

Thus we may understand Planck's statement that the law of causality has finally failed us in its application to the world of atoms. The arrangements of energy quanta and the phenomena of radio-activity are defined by modern physics as causeless phenomena, namely, *a priori* basic arrangements. Statements about the electrons cannot be made on a linear cause and effect basis, for instance, by deducing a certain action as effect from a given course and energy charge. Rather, the laws of atom physics are expressed in terms of a generally descriptive statistical probability which lists courses, energy charges and actions as *coordinates* on equal levels instead of subordinating action as an effect to courses and charges as cause. Thus, a totality of a phenomenon, namely, an indeterminable number of electrons, shares on a statistical basis in the known qualities, some having the expected courses, others the energy, others the action, etc. It is undeterminable, however, in what way a given individual electron may express the general statisical law in which it shares.

Each individual case is an unpredictable instance of a totality of a general law of arrangement under which phenomena are related to each other, not as cause and effect, but individually and unpredictably expressing different aspects of that general law.

In a recent essay[2] C.G. Jung, referring to the above facts of physics, states that

> ...since the connection of cause and effect turns out to be only statistically valid, namely only relatively true, the principle of causality is only relatively usable for the explanation of natural phenomena and thereby implicitly presupposes the existence of one or several other factors necessary for explanation. That means that under certain circumstances the connection of events is of a different nature than causal and thereby demands a different principle of explanation.

This different non-causal principle Jung terms 'synchronicity.' He defines it as "the timely coincidence of two or several events which cannot be causally related to each other, but *express an identical or similar meaning*."[3] He remarks that in the macro-physical world we would but look in vain for non-causal events simply because one cannot even imagine occurences not causally related. On the other hand, in depth psychology experiences with the phenomenon of synchronicity kept accumulating from year to year in the form of the observation of coincidences of inner subjective psychological states with objective outside events, meaningfully related to each other in such a way that their merely 'accidental' association became a statistically determinable improbability. These coincidences can generally take the form of the coincidence of an endopsychic condition of the observer with a simultaneous objective outer event that directly corresponds to his psychic content (an example of this is the story quoted later on) or with an event that takes place outside of the observer's field of perception (for instance, the burning of Stockholm coinciding with Swedenborg's vision of it) or as the coincidence of a psychic state with a corresponding not-yet-existing future event which can be verified only subsequently. For brevity's sake we have to omit the numerous observed instances which Jung quotes as examples.

Jung comments that these experiments prove that to a certain degree the psyche can cancel out the factors of time and space and that the motions of inanimate bodies can be influenced psychically. Since distance in no way affected these experiments, the idea of a transmission of energy had to be discarded. Moreover, as Jung points out, the concept of causality does not hold, since we cannot imagine how a future event could 'cause' an effect in the present. Thus, one has to assume, at least provisionally, that improbable accidents of a non-causal nature, namely, meaningful coincidences, have entered into the picture.

Jung goes on to state that in the course of his investigations of the collective unconscious he ever and again came up against connections which he could not explain as merely incidental groupings or accumulations, since the connections of these 'spontaneous coincidences' expressed a common meaning in such a way that their accidental concurrence would represent statistical improbability. (For Rhine experiments the statistical improbability has been figured out from between 1:250,000 upto 1:289,023,876).

In giving characteristic examples from his own vast experience, he warns that nothing would be accomplished by an *ad hoc* explanation, since he could mention a great many such stories which in principle are no more surprising and incredible than the irrefutable Rhine experiments and which would show that every case calls for its own different explanation, a causal explanation, however, being inadequate in each instance.

One example out of the many he gives we shall render in his own words:

> My example has to do with a young patient who, in spite of the efforts we both made to overcome the resistance, continued to remain psychologically inaccessible. Her difficulty lay in the fact that she always knew best about everything. Her excellent upbringing had provided her with a weapon ideally suited for this purpose, namely, a sharply polished, Cartesian rationality with a concept of reality that was 'geometrically' beyond question. After several fruitless attempts to temper her rationalism with a somewhat more human common sense, I had to confine myself to the hope that something of an unexpected and irrational nature would happen to her, something that would succeed in breaking the intellectual retort into which she had sealed herself. I was sitting opposite her one day, in order to listen to her flow of rhetoric, with my back

to the window. She had had an impressive dream the night before in which someone had given her a golden scarab (a costly piece of jewelry). While she was still engaged in telling me this dream, I heard something behind me gently tapping on the window. I turned around and saw that it was quite a large flying insect which was beating against the window pane from the outside in the obvious effort to get into the dark room. This seemed to me very strange. I opened the window immediately and caught the insect in the air as it flew in. It was a scarabaeid, cetonia aurata, the common rose bug whose green-gold coloring most nearly resembles that of a golden scarab. I handed the insect to my paitent with the words: "Here is your scarab." This experience punctured the hole we had been looking for in the thick armor of her rationalism and broke the ice of her intellectual resistance. The treatment could now be continued with satisfactory results.

In summarizing his concept Jung admits that synchronicity represents a highly abstract, not readily visualizable (*unanschauliche*) entity. He points out that, since the meaningful or intelligent behavior of low forms of life which have no brain and even of lifeless bodies falls within its scope, it forces us to abandon the concept of psyche as associated with the brain. Rather, we seem to deal with a formal or formative factor of meaning, independent of any brain activity, which expresses itself equally through lifeless things, body and psyche. This again is in complete agreement with the conclusion of nuclear physics, as expressed by Schroedinger[3], that form not substance is to be the fundamental concept underlying the dynamism of matter. We are encountering here the dynamic of what medieval philosophers called causa formalis, ordering power of an inherent form intent or "entelechy." Thus we may come to understand the psychosomatic interplay as but one instance of synchronicity, namely, of the expression of a formative or meaningful element, rather than as a linear mechanical cause and effect interrelation.

Jung goes further to add that the fact of the 'absolute knowledge' that characterizes the synchronicity phenonmenon—a knowledge which includes future and space-distant events and which is not transmitted by any sense organ—suggests to us the existence of a *per se* meaning of a transcendental nature that "exists in a psychically but relative space and corresponding time, namely, in a non-visualizable space-time continuum."

His conclusion is that, in view of the mutually closely supporting findings of atom physics and psychology, it becomes necessary to add to our basic categories of scientific thinking causelessness or synchronicity in addition to the categories of space, time and causality. Just as absolute unformed and indestructible energy relates to its perceptible manifestation in space and time, so relates the principle of non-causality, namely, the inconstant indeterminate contingency, expressible only symbolically through analogy, similarity and meaningfulness to the constant determinate relation of cause and effect.

The two approaches along linear causality and synchronicity are not mutually exclusive but rather complementary. The nature of the phenomenon, not arbitrary choice, determines which of the two applies. In the realm of macrophysics and our consciousness of the daily observable happenings, the concept of ordinary causality holds. On the other hand, in the subatomic sphere, in the realm of the unconscious and in the very activities of the life processes, causality ceases to be applicable and may be replaced by the principle of inconstant, non-causal connection through synchronicity or meaningfulness.

How does this principle of 'meaning' actually and practically enter into the observable life and psychic processes? The spontaneous, discontinuous occurrence of 'bundles' of events analogous to the quanta of microphysics represents a phenomenon, the biological and psychological expressions of which G.R. Heyer compared to the effects of the 'field' of physics.[4]

A field is described as a kind of tension or stress which can exist in empty space in the absence of matter. It reveals itself through the fact that material objects that happen to lie in the space which the field occupies respond to its forces in a characteristic way. This response is determined on the one hand by the type of the field (for instance, the different patterns of iron filings in a unipolar and a bipolar magnetic field), on the other hand by the characteristic responsiveness peculiar to the object (for instance, a magnet needle responds mechanically with deflection, a neon tube with a light phenomenon to the same electric field. A piece of wood will not respond at all). Thus, the field is a kind of a transcendental entity never directly observable which we know only through the peculiar behavior of the objects which it affects and through which it manifests itself.

Similarly, the transcendental 'meaning' underlying the synchronistic occurrences manifests itself to us only through the objects which it affects and which, each in their own and characteristic way, give it expression. Thus, whenever a 'field of meaning' arises in the course of living existence, or perhaps we might say, when one's course of life passes through a 'field of meaning' this field manifests itself through events on various levels (for instance, psyche, soma), all of them in their own different fashion giving expression to that same formative factor. Borrowing a mathematical terminology, we may say that the synchronistic occurrence of $X1$ $X2$ $X3$, etc., namely, meaningfully associated analogous phenomena in psyche, soma, outside nature, etc., not only postulates the directly unknowable transcendental factor X but also offers us a way to at least approach it indirectly by establishing through a process of imagination the common denominators of $X1$ $X2$ $X3$, etc. Obviously, also, the concept of the 'field of meaning' is itself but an attempt at symbolic representation of something non-visualizable that can never be directly observed. What Schroedinger says of the atom model equally applies to our concepts here:

> The pictures are only a mental help, a tool of thought, an intermediary means...from which to deduce a reasonable expectation about the results of new experiments...We plan them for the purpose of seeing whether they confirm the expectation—thus whether the expectations were reasonable and thus whether the pictures or models we use were

adequate. Notice that we prefer to say *adequate*, not *true*. For in order that a description be *capable* of being true, it must be capable of being compared *directly* with actual facts. That is usually not the case with our models.[5]

In the following, a comparatively brief example is given of how the above concepts, hypothetically applied, might enlighten us about the scope of the 'field of meaning,' a partial manifestation of which we are familiar with in the symptomatology of our drug *Sulphur*. In attempting to abstract a 'common denominator' from what we consider but partial manifestations of the 'field of meaning,' that is from the mental, constitutional, physiological, chemical, etc., known qualities of the drug, in addition to whatever other material we may glean for amplification from other sources, we follow the purely descriptive enumerative method which Hahnemann's genius anticipated and which now has been adopted also by modern physics. The understanding of the broader formative law of the field may enable us to anticipate the nature of events to be expected—on the basis of statistical probability, however, but not specifically for the given case. Similarly, we may, after recognizing a certain drug picture in a patient, anticipate a possible scope of further symptoms that may arise, without being able to predict specifically for the given case which of these possible symptoms he is actually going to have, if any at all.

Moreover, mental and physical symptoms being synchronistically, not causally, related, may substitute for one another and thus one may appear to be able to cancel the other. Thus we get a first glimpse of an understanding how also illness and 'similar' drug energy, as synchronistic entities of the same 'field' sharing a functional likeness, may perhaps substitute for one another and thus functionally cancel each other.

It is not intended, before an audience such as this, to waste many words about the well-known details of the symptomatology of *Sulphur*. In synthesizing these details into a meaningful relation we may describe a constitution which is prone to stagnation: slowed circulation, insufficient oxidation within the cell and delayed elimination; on the other hand, we have also to describe its extreme opposite, turbulent impetuosity: increased circulation, ebullitions, active congestions, inflammations, states of increased, exaggerated oxidations and combustion, tissue breakdown and neurovegetative overstimulation.

Into the first category we may place all the symptoms of toxemia, offensiveness of skin and discharges, lack of vital reaction, suppressed and relapsed states, air hunger, poor appetite with increased thirst, the venous, abdominal and general plethora, obesity, ptosis, and degenerative states, as well as the improvement from motion.

In its opposite belong the classical ebullitions of heat, burning, itching, tissue breakdown, poor nutrition and assimilation, the weak, empty, all-gone feeling, the hyperthyroid, tuberculous, catarrhal, hyperpyretic and inflammatory states, as well as the general and nervous hypersensitivity, the aggravation from heat, the desire for high caloric and spiced foods—to name but a few typical symptoms.

We find that an analogous pattern of polar opposites characterizes also the mentals and the personality type. One group of *Sulphur* patients are rather non-intellectual people, often of the labourer type, heavy, earthy and prosaic; swarthy, rough or obese. They may even be mentally quite dull, slow and disinterested without any introspective tendencies, concerned only with the material and physical facts of everyday life. Psychologically, they could be classified as belonging to the extroverted, sensory type, a type whose main adaptation is by means of perception and orientation through the physical senses of immediate material facts.

Their material opposite is the extreme mental type, the philosopher, scientist or impulsive artist, concerned only with problems of mind and spirit, of art and philosophy, worrying about who made God, bubbling over with new ideas, impatient, nervy and restless, even psychologically itching and burning, driven and driving everyone else, inspiring, enthusiastic, an inventive genius full of initiative, poor in execution, unreliable and unstable. Disorganized and confused, they are utterly oblivious of things physical and material which they also are not too capable of handling properly. They are careless, unkempt and dirty. In short, this is the type of Hering's 'ragged philosopher.' Living in a realm of imagination and always having to reform the world, they also lack real introspective ability and critical evaluation of themselves. Psychologically, they represent an extroverted intuitive type, whose main adaptation is through the ability to 'smell out,' as it were, the invisible possibilities inherent in a situation; they are the polar opposite of the sensation type, blind to all the material things of today, always perceiving hunches and ideas of what might be tomorrow.

Thus far goes our own imaginative knowledge of the person who manifests the *Sulphur* 'field.' If we are to fathom its 'meaning,' we need other manifestations on different levels in order to abstract a common denominator. One source of such information offers itself to us in the experience of this same entity as a purely psychological phenomenon as we find it reflected in the alchemistic concepts of *Sulphur*.

Contrary to general popular opinion which considers the alchemists simply as charlatans or, at best, but primitive pioneers of modern chemistry, C.G. Jung has conclusively demonstrated that the alchemists were the psychologists of their day, searching for a synthesis of human knowledge. Their truest practitioners were seeking the 'philosopher's stone,' the mysterious 'lapis' that symbolised the total man. Analytical psychology describes this total man as the 'self' whose phenomenology coincides exactly with the rich and varied symbolism to be found in alchemical literature and in the affiliated pagan, gnostic, and Christian writings. In working with their materials, the alchemists' unconscious psyche reacted in calling forth concepts, images and visions which the alchemist projected upon his substance—namely, ascribed it to the substance as its quality. Whereas, to the modern chemist these phantasies are absurd and meaningless, for the analytic psychologist they refer to definite formative elements of the unconscious psyche; since these are to be found not only in the alchemist's phantasies, but also in the average dream material of people of our own time, they are meaningful and practically applicable for the diagnosis, interpretation and treatment of contemporary psychological problems. Thereby, they give evidence of their psychological truth as timeless, transcendental, meaningful entities of the psychic realm.

In passing, it may be mentioned that the analytical psychologist views the alchemistic conceptions only as psychological projections, namely, endopsychic stirrings naively ascribed to a substance; in psychology the question has not been raised at all whether the substance may not have something to do with the images it seems to call forth. For the modern psychologist, limited in his understanding to the usual concepts of chemistry and medicine, knows as yet little about the dynamic tendencies of substances in terms of constitution, personality and psyche just as the average homeopath knows little about depth psychology. However, by bringing together these two fields of experience, a fuller comprehension of the 'field of meaning,' the psychosomatic synchronicity, may be gained.

To the alchemists, *Sulphur* had a durable nature[7](*Sulphur duplex*): one, the white one, *Sulphur crudum* and *vulgare*, corporeal, heavy, earthy and inimical to the sublime 'lapis,' the philosopher's stone; the other red form and spirit, the fiery sublime material of the 'lapis' itself.

The crude or vulgar *Sulphur* was called earthly filth, corporeal, dense, tough, derived from the 'fat of the earth,' ashes of ashes, dregs, scum and refuse of evil smell and weak power, the essence of decay, corruption and putrefaction and the source of imperfection, causing the blackness of every work. The other nature of *Sulphur*, however, was described as a spiritual principle, the carrier of light and fire, the soul of all natural beings, the 'fermentum' which gives life to the imperfect bodies, the principle of the generative power of the sun, spirit of life, light of nature, creator of a thousand things, heart of all things, creating the mind and the colour of all living things, the principle of desirousness (*concupiscentia*) and aggressiveness.

Moreover, *Sulphur* was allegorized as the 'medicina' as well as the 'medicus,' the physician who receives an incurable wound. This alludes to the ubiquitous myths of the Divine Healer (for instance, Asclepius but also Christ) who always himself suffers the sickness he cures. In the mythogem the god sends the illness, is the illness, is ill (wounded or persecuted), is the medicine, and heals the illness.[8]

In other words, *Sulphur* embodied the principle of universal illness and the potential of its cure... this is not too far from Hahnemann's phrase of 'king of antisorics.'

We may attempt now to interpret this symbolism in modern psychological terms. Nothing less than the basic polarity and conflict of the soul seems expressed here as it embraces and is torn between spirit and matter. One aspect expresses the force of physical instincts that involves us in the material and sensory sides of existence, the level of our animal nature which, yet, is the matrix, source and maintaining strength of our physical existence and the stage upon which our lesson of life has to be learned. However, when the instinct side becomes one-sidedly preponderant, a stagnation results of one's inner progress, a corruption of one's humanness through purely materialistic, egotistical instinct-gratification. The opposite aspect represents the stimulus of the intuitive breath of the spirit which enlivens and quickens existence in a constant process of seething and generating. This process never allows life to come to a rest, it endlessly promotes evolution and development and is always in opposition to standstill and the established order of things. Yet, through its one-sided preponderance, one would lose the ground of reality under one's feet and become oblivious to one's earthly limitations. The person who loses contact with his instinct nature is subject to a psychological inflation as we meet it in the conceit of the 'spiritual' person, preaching, teaching and reforming the whole world, completely involved in mental speculations.

In the elements of these psychological pictures we readily can recognize the elements of the two contrasting types of our *Sulphur* personality and constitution: the stagnating, congested, earthy side and the restless, driving, burning, itching, ragged philosopher with all possible blendings and combinations of the individual elements in one particular person.

Beyond the superficial aspects, however, the polarity seems to allude to the mysterious and intricate intertwining of spirit and matter and the paradoxes of existence which we often experience as moral problems. This is touched upon in the symbolism of the identity of illness: medicine and healer, which looms in the background as a transcendent archetypal principle encompassing and transcending good and evil, life and death, earth and spirit, and forces upon us the almost impossible task of being dweller in two worlds, rendering unto Caesar what is Caesar's and unto God what is God's.

Unconsciously, this may loom as a background problem wherever the conflict situation is brought forth that manifests the 'force field' that homoeopaths or alchemists call *Sulphur*.

What is to be gained by considering the above psychological symbolism? It is hoped that this approach which brings together Homeopathy and depth psychology may help us make a few first stumbling steps toward clarifying some of our bewildering problems, such as the relationship of life and personality problems to illness, of illness and symptoms to the similar remedy, etc.

In the synchronistic, causeless, *a priori* arrangement, the 'bundle' of phenomena that we associate with *Sulphur*—outside events, psychic, somatic, biologic and chemical dynamisms—all seem to express each in its own fashion, a transcendental meaning that, with our human limitation of comprehension, we can but describe as a conflict tension between the above and the below, spirit and instinct, intuition and physical reality, the flame of creative impulsiveness and the inertia of dense matter, the katabolic processes of oxidation, combustion and decomposition and the anabolic life process of quiet synthesis and reconstruction. When, in a predominately extroverted, object-oriented individual, the tension of the conflict exceeds his ability to integrate it by finding a point of balance within that would satisfy the demands of both sides—whenever this integrative ability fails—then either the forces of egotistic instinct gratification, inertia, stand-still, corruption, putrefaction and stagnation prevail or the opposite ones of flighty intuition, conceit, exaggerated spirituality losing the ground from under its feet with restless, burning overactivity mental and physical. Whether this disturbance expresses itself as physical illness or as a personality trait, an analogous pattern underlies the somatic illness or the psychopathology; the same 'field' brings itself to expression on different levels.

Obviously, the conflict thus described is a general human one and does not apply to some individuals only. Yet this would be no more in contradiction to our assumption than the fact that *Sulphur* is a chemical constituent of *all* living tissue maintaining cellular respiration (cystin-cystein transfer) and yet the clinical *Sulphur* disorder which calls for it as a remedy affects only certain people. Similarly, the 'meaning' that expresses itself through the 'force field' is, in its widest sense, valid for everyone. But only for certain individuals does that 'field' become activated in such a way that phenomena of a manifest disturbance are called forth in soul or body: To the psychologist this peculiar dynamism is well-known. To give an example merely by analogy: we all have fathers and mothers and may or may not have encountered difficulties in our relation to them; yet only for some individuals does the parent-child relationship actually engender manifest pathology by activating a conflict. The 'field' may be ever present. In order to be manifest, it has to become 'constellated,' as the analytical psychologist calls its activation, comparable to the 'causeless' discharge of an energy quantum.

Psychologically interesting is the fact that Hahnemann supposedly called *Sulphur* the 'king of antipsorics,' psora being considered by him the universal illness of mankind.[9] Evidently, we meet here an example of how the preoccupation with the same object-matter called forth the same symbolic representations as a spontaneous creation of the collective unconscious. The alchemists spoke of *Sulphur* as the *prima materia* of the 'king' sol and as the *medicina* and the *medicus* who receives as well as heals the sickness, meaning the divine medicine, the panacea for the universal illness of mankind. In spite of Hahnemann's, as well as Kent's, *conscious* committment to the principle of individualization which is the backbone of homeotherapeutics we find that out of the *unconscious* arises spontaneously the archetypal symbol of the panacea, the divine medicine which is to heal the universal illness of mankind, namely, the split between the above and below. Yet, the divine medicine is an attribute of the 'Self,' which is the synthesis and totality of existence. This the alchemists already saw in *Sulphur*.

1   W. Heisenberg, quoted in J. Gebser: *Abendlandische Wandlung,* Verlag Oprecht, Zurich, New York, p. 60.
2   Jung, C. G. *Collected Works 8 (The Structure and Dynamics of the Psyche,* NY 1960), Part VII, "Synchronicity: An Acausal Connecting Principle."
3   E. Schrodinger: *Science and Humanism.* Cambridge University Press, p. 18.

4   G. R. Heyer: *Vom Kraftfeld der Seele*. Origo Verlag, Zurich.
5   Schrodinger: *op cit,* p. 22.
6   John Read: *Prelude to Chemistry*. MacMillan Corp., New York. p. 2.
7   C. G. Jung: *"De Sulfure."* Lecture before the Swiss Paracelsus Society held on Dec. 21, 1947. Private printing.
8   C. A. Meier: *Antike Inkubation und Moderne Psychotherapie.*
9   J. T. Kent: *Lectures on Homeopathic Philosophy,* Erhart & Karl, Chicago, p. 146.
10 C. G. Jung: *Modern Man in Search of a Soul*. Harcourt, Brace & Co., New York. p. 264.
11 C. G. Jung: Foreward to Victor White: *God and the Unconscious*. Henry Regnery Co., Chicago.

Mutus Liber, a wordless book from the year 1677, shows some of the methods of the Art of Alchemy. Anyone familiar with olden small-scale saltmaking or mother-liquor sublimation (see text) can easily detect surprising similarities between the steps illustrated in these ancient engravings and cottage-style salt refining. When salt was traded for gold—ounce for ounce—alchemy was deep into the study of one of the earth's most complex substances: Seasalt. With 84 out of 103 known chemical elements of our planet, to this day seasalt defies synthesis and reconstitution. Contemporary alchemists have shown it to be a restorer of human wisdom and a healing and peacemaking substance.

Jacques de Langre

SEASALT AND ALCHEMY

Salt, the sublimation of the oceans of the planet, has held the highest interest for the alchemists of all past periods. Still, it continues to reveal fragments of its secrets to serious contemporary alchemists.

The much older ideology, astrology, which preceded and ushered alchemy into human consciousness, sought not only to discover the relationship of man to the cosmos and to explore how this kinship could benefit mankind but pointed to the ocean as the strongest manifestation of astral influence on earth. Since alchemy was concerned with man's relationship to terrestrial nature and the phenomena of this planet's elements, salt—through its sublimation by the sun, or by fire in the alchemist's workshop—was the pivotal substance that merited deep study and reverence as the primary transmutation element. One of the most authoritative alchemists of today, Professor Louis C. Kervran, understands transmutation at low energy and has succeeded in discrete experiments in transforming chemical elements. His scientific explanations and formulae are accepted by the scientific establishment and he was awarded the Nobel Prize. Having thus discovered and codified a new property of matter, Professor Kervran has clearly demonstrated alchemy's most noble achievement in the realm of modern medical physiology. For it is in the search for the Elixir of Immortality that the Art finds not only the purest aspirations but also the most measurable success.

Whereas in the West the objective seems to have evolved from gold-making to elixirs of immortality to simply superior medicines, neither the first nor the last of these objectives seems ever to have been important in China. Chinese alchemy was consistent from first to last, and there was relatively little controversy among its practitioners, who seem to have varied only in their prescriptions for the elixir or perhaps only over their name for it. In the West there were conflicts between advocates of herbal and chemical (i.e. mineral) pharmacy, but in China mineral remedies were accepted along with salt pickles, sour plums, etc... In Europe there were conflicts between alchemists who favored gold-making and those who thought medicine the proper goal. The Chinese always favored the latter.

If alchemy, whether Oriental or Old World, has spent countless years studying the use of morning dew to create "the gold of the thousandth dawn," the study of seawater and of its mother liquor proceeds from the same quest and truly accomplishes miracles.

Modern salt-refining technology owes a great debt to the alchemists, obscure or famous, who found the secret of extracting the mother liquor (bitterns) from the dried crystalline salt of the oceans. Called variously *nami no hana* ('the flowers of the waves' in Japanese) or *Eaux-meres* in French (literally 'mother waters'), the riches of the sea contain the essence of all minerals of this planet. Extremely bitter in taste*, this mother liquor not only serves to cure many grave illnesses, coagulate vegetable protein as in tofu making, but also duplicates the human body's most complex chemical assemblage of essential minerals. If it is taken in diluted liquor form, or in the naturally solar-evaporated, clay-bed purified form, "Mother Liquor" effectively serves as immunization against all diseases but it also cures countless illnesses.

The secret of the immortality or the Endless Prolongation of Life has been the subject of deep study, and some of the successful experiments of modern-day alchemists prove that it is not an unrealistic goal: to wit, Alexis Carrell (1873-1912) kept a chicken heart alive for over 37 years by immersing the pulsating heart in a solution of seasalt. Dr. Carrell willfully ended the experiment after a third of a century, having more than proven that living cells could be immortal.

The panacea or substance for maintaining life forever will doubtless remain a secret teaching, but seawater, or its sublimation in the form of light grey hand-harvested seasalt, is a symbiotic culture medium for human living cells; its saltiness is the basis of all body fluids, amniotic water, and plasma. We can find many justifications to consider seasalt the fluid substance that alchemists sought as the regenerator of life or Philosopher's stone.

Jabir ibn Hayyan, a Musulman Sufi alchemist (years 720-800) in his *Summa Perfectionis Magisterii* not only mentions Regal water but makes allusions to Lustral water as well, that form of oceanic fluid that shimmers and fluoresces from the charged energy and all of the 84-odd dissolved chemical elements of life it contains.

The Belgian historian Henri Pirenne observed that during the High Middle Ages, because of the virtual disappearance of salt, the Atlantic Coast was deserted and the entire continent was thrown into a Dark Age of human under-development. While Vespasien and Titus conquered the desert of the Dead Sea for local salt to save their empire, the north of Europe suffered from a salt famine for almost 500 years. The average daily ration of the precious element fell to less than two grams per person and many died from folly induced by salt-deprivation or dehydration.

The chemical demands of the human body require that the salt concentration in the blood and the body fluids be maintained at a constant. If the body does not get

---

*Its name in English is 'bitterns,' but all developed countries' bitterns are a by-product of the salt refining industry. These high technologies start their salt-making process from 'crude' salt which is bulldozer-harvested from concrete cement salt flats i.e. polluted, non-selective, dirty and poison-laden sources. What is even worse, mine, lake, or rock salt are gathered from dead, grossly unbalanced deposits. The only true healing and safe bitterns are those made by adepts from sun- and wind-dried seasalt, sublimated on clay bed flats from the essence of the sea. Their mystery is that, unlike industrial bitterns that are totally anhydrous—containing no molecule of water—the natural bitterns stubbornly retain enough moisture to be deliquescent, thus their name: "Liquor of mother." The method for duplicating hand-harvesting and the making of restored mother liquor is fully described in: *Seasalt and Your Life* published by Happiness Press, Magalia, California.

enough salt, or too much of the wrong, refined variety, a hormonal mechanism compensates by reducing the excretion of salt in the urine and sweat. But it cannot reduce this output to zero. On a completely saltless diet the body steadily loses small amounts of salt via the kidneys and sweat glands. It attempts to adjust to this loss by accelerating its secretion of water so that the blood's salt concentration can be maintained at the level vital for survival. The result is a gradual desiccation, dehydration of the body, and finally death, often preceeded by a loss of rational thinking, dementia, or running amok. The organism literally dies of thirst.

In lack of drinking water the crucial factor—salt concentration in the blood—is the same but the hormonal homeostasis works in reverse: to reduce the secretion of water and increase the salt secretion in order to maintain the correct salt level. Nonetheless, the inevitable, irreducible water loss leads to death. In short, the body's normal craving for salt and for water are both aspects of the same vital needs: a saline internal fluid.

The extent of the salt famine reported by Henry Pirenne caused human flesh to be sold on the open air markets and created an epidemic of crazed people who, to replenish their salt, drank blood from humans they had slain. Quick to exploit this desperate situation, the rulers of Europe grabbed the remnants of stock and exacted exorbitant salt taxes. Heavily burdened by tarifs and gabelles, common salt became a luxury which lured invaders and invited wars. Salt mined from deep pits was substituted for rich seasalt but the lack of balanced trace elements in the rock salt unbalanced the mental equilibrium. When salt complete in trace elements is withheld, the bodily functions that depend on these noble chemical elements either slow down or stop altogether. The magnesium, bromide and iodine salts are found in adequate concentration in the Celtic salt of Brittany, France. Less of the precious minerals are found in white refined salt, mined salt, and that of the Great Salt Lake, and the Dead and Red Seas. As trace elements begin to vitiate, mental and muscular fatigue are soon followed by depression, epilepsy, stress, folly, impotence, and frigidity.

The damages wreaked on humanity by the lack of salt for almost 500 years were considerable but today, in spite of an apparent abundance, this marasmus continues under another form. Since only 3% of the total world production of salt is for food use, to satisfy the demands of an ever growing chemical industry, salt refiners are forced to switch to mine salt, which is cheaper to harvest. Gradually during the past five centuries, salt merchants have exploited the precious liquor without conscience and even refined edible salt in order to extract rare trace minerals for the chemical industry: magnesium for light alloys and explosives, and bromine for anti-knock compounds and chemical fertilizers.

During the long salt famine from the year 500 to the tenth century, alchemists have sought to make salt by any means; it has become a necessity for survival. However, compounding seasalt and duplicating the work of the great oceans of the world, which has taken billions of years, is an unsurmountable task. The present rarity of the substance creates an even deeper respect for the mysterious seasalt crystals in the shops of the Dark Ages alchemists.

The Emerald Tablet is not so cryptic anymore if the crystallization and subsequent sublimation of mother liquor from the seasalt crystals are understood: "Separate the Earth from Fire, the subtle from the crude with much travail... It rises from the Earth toward the sky, and immediately comes back on Earth where it gathers the force of superior and inferior creations. You will then have all the glory of the world and that is why all darkness will leave you."

The "plasma of Quinton," a name registered in 1907 by one of France's most renowned modern day alchemists, is a life-giving fluid. Still made by a secret natural process, it is a far cry from what is being used today in hospitals, the crude Ringer solution that will never reconstitute the true composition of human fluids. Quinton's plasma continues to save lives as it has for the past eighty years. The biologist who began using it for athrepsia created hundred of clinics throughout Europe and dispensed the precious plasma in a victory of life over death for thousands of moribund patients. Detractors from the ranks of modern scientific medicine forced the clinics out of existence but the serum continues quietly to honor its alchemical legacy.

The crisis of Western Europe began with the flooding of the ancient salt flats, a phenomenon called eustatic ebb and flow; it was esoterically countered by the entry of Arabic alchemy first into Spain, then the Mediterranean world. Under Pope Sylvester II (who had read Arabic alchemical works) the newly imported science established its true realm: the technique of salvation, physical as well as moral, beginning with the renewal of salt. C. G. Jung, in his *Psychology and Alchemy*, sees alchemy as seeking to impart the spark of eternal light out of the abyss of the darkness of matter. Mikhaël Ivanov, who rekindled the flickering flame of gnostic thought in our time, symbolizes it this way: "The blood of the Earth is Water. The Oceans are its Heart, the vast planetary heart where plasmic blood is in abundance. The rivers, lakes and streams are the arteries and the veins. The lungs (much more extended than the heart) are the earth's atmosphere where blood is purified."

A German alchemist who died in the 1930's, Max Retschlag sums it up this way: "Our knowledge on the constitution of the human body, the structure of the cells and that of the smallest living entities leads us rightfully to believe that a certain remedy can be found, made up of a latent and concentrated energy, that will act as a universal remedy for all illnesses. Since the vital energy is an electromotive force, this specific remedy must be composed of matter capable of liberating a concentrated electric charge; after that matter has dissolved in the body fluids, just as it occurs in galvanic batteries where certain salts whose dissolution produce a more or less constant current between the poles." From the large number of allusions made by the ancient hermetic masters it would appear that it is those same salts that enter as base material in the preparation of the elixir of life.

Salt, in its broadest meaning, describes anything that crystallizes; according to the ancient masters, it is the very first being, since all matter can be reduced to the saline form. It is the Word of God turned into matter. One particular salt, a celestial instrument and son of the divine solar fire, ultimately unites to passive earth in order to yield a saline incarnation.

This salt is made up of a mercurial humidity and of a sulphureous fat, and these two essences, antagonistic to one another, form the original trinity of life as alkali, acid, and salt.

Salt remains forever true to its form. Retchlag says: "Its crystalline living soul constantly gives birth to the same configurations; only the location and the circumstances of its origin change."

Alchemical medicine thus shuns the material and physical action of remedies upon the mere physical sphere of the organism. It much prefers to effect the cure "from above" as direct action of the constituting forces of the remedy. Whatever the various realms that are covered by alchemical medicine, the preferred manner of the magisters is by the utilization of energy, of light and of vibration.

Alexander von Bernus (1880-1972) quotes an anonymous author from the end of the eighteenth century in a work titled: *The Secret of Salt, the most noble Creation produced by the great Goodness of God in the entire Realm of Nature.* "The salt is derived from the ashes of a great power... and there are virtues hidden therein."

To say that salt is "the word of God" is not simply an allegorical allusion. It is no coincidence that the amniotic fluid that bathes the human embryo is salty like the ocean from which all life on this planet has issued. Nor is it a coincidence that the most healing salt today is a 'total' salt, with over 84 trace minerals, obtainable only by sundrying—and not by kiln or flash pan drying as modern refined salt is. Drying by the sun alone sublimates all of the noble minerals of the cosmos into seasalt, not only macro-nutrients such as calcium, sulfur, phosphorus, potassium, and magnesium but the trace elements as well: copper, brome, tin, rubidium, manganese, iodine, boron, cobalt, lithium, valine, nickel, fluor, chromium, silver, zinc and gold. Both macro-nutrients and trace elements have been removed in total from modern refined table salt. Somehow the alchemist magisters of ancient times knew the fallacy of refinement; they insisted on "total" salt of ocean origin, shunning earth deposits as lifeless and fossilized.

In the Art, sulfur and mercury stand for the two antagonistic properties of matter everywhere in the cosmos. Salt, in this trilogy, represents the means of uniting these two first principles. However, we must bear in mind that sulfur, mercury, and salt are not the chemical elements of those same names but define fundamental *qualities* and *properties*.

The salt that allows the fusion of mercury to sulfur can be compared to that vital spiritual force that permits the union of body and soul, the true *anima* that makes all creatures come or stay alive, like Dr. Carrell's chicken heart.

Hermetic chemistry has been passed to us as a series of symbolic images: sulfur represented by a king robed in red; mercury by a queen gowned in white; and the salt, which united them both, as a priest celebrating their marriage.

The Philosopher's stone, as described by Paracelsus (1493-1541), would "present a dazzling red color, that of rubies, and be sparkling and heavy. It heals the human body of all weaknesses and restores its health."

I have seen such a substance in the form of the traditional salt on a Pacific island—red as rubies and sparkling. It is one of the last hand-harvested seasalts on this planet; yet it can not be sold as salt and the white folks that live there prefer the supermarket's! Its brilliant color is derived from a special clay that the natives mix into the beds as they crystallize under the blazing tropical sun. Through their island-hopping migration from the Orient, these people carried the belief that such salt is the human body's panacea.

A recipe given by the Belgian alchemist Van Helmont, who worked in Vilvorde, and by Arnauld de Villeneuve describes the power of this salty philosopher's stone as; "Having the property to create the form and perfect in infinitely, since the improved form will improve the next and so forth till infinity."

Such is the similarity between the division of living cells to form an embryo and the work of transmutation performed by the Philosphers' stone. The analogy to atomic fission and chain reaction equally comes to mind; here we see the wisdom behind the alchemist's reluctance to divulge the Secret to the uninitiated, the same caution that prompted Dr. E. Orowan to state in *Science Journal:*

"The large majority of earth's population considers that science and technology pose a growing deadly danger to their life. They feel powerless, at the mercy of a minority, as if they laid on an operating table at the hands of, not healers, but of irresponsible boys urged by curiosity or—what is worse—by a desire for notoriety or promotion."

When the first atomic bomb was dropped on Hiroshima, the only true protection —and the substance that saved many who were closer to the epicenter than others who had died—was none other than salty miso, a fermentation of soy beans and seasalt. This could replenish human bodily fluids from the totality of the protective minerals of the ocean.

While such medicinal use might not have been what the magisters of the Dark Ages had in mind, their refusal to allow their science to be disclosed to anyone outside was prophetic in light of the breed of today's mad scientists. The revelation of certain atomic secrets to arrogant dilettantes is definitely putting our entire humanity in grave peril of extinction.

Isaac Newton (1642-1727) was both an alchemist and a "magician." I use the latter term because he saw the universe as an enigma, a secret that could be understood only by the application of pure thought to interpreting phenomena. Sir Newton stated that the indications leading to the solution of these enigmas could be found in the sky and in the transmutation of the chemical elements of the earth and ocean. Newton also valued highly the traditions and secret documents that have been transmitted like a chain, without interruption, since the first cryptic revelation of the Babylonians about 10,000 years ago.

After Newton, the idea that knowledge of the Art implied danger was overlooked and the ten-millennium secrecy of alchemy was broken. When the Emerald Table concludes: "The operation of the sun is complete," its author seemed to know that the planets and the stars draw their energy from the transmutation of the elements. "The operation of the sun" is the very basis of the atomic bomb: Fission - Fusion - Fission. Wouldn't it have been better if the secret of the operation of the sun had remained hermetic knowledge?

The legend that has often identified alchemy with only the pursuit of making gold is false. The true dedicated initiates had little or no interest in gold but found that iron was much more important because iron is the origin, the lever of the universe. A German alchemist wrote: "Eisen trägt das Geheimnis des Magnetismus und das Geheimnis des Blutes," which means: "Iron carries the mystery of magnetism and the mystery of the blood." In 1616, in the *Noces Chymiques*, the formula with the atomic weight of iron isotope was revealed: $A=1, L=12, C=3, H=8, I=9, M=13, I=9, A=1$, total$=56$.

Iron and its dissolving agent, salt, are the essential constituents of hemoglobin. Both of these elements are found, as a single pair or in combination, in the human blood. Iron is totally lacking in sea waters (less than 3 parts per trillion, by weight). The magnetic cosmos is made up of iron with all of the metallic macronutrients and 84 trace elements in the oceans.

In every corner of the globe there have lived men who retained fragments of the secret teachings and divulged them to non-initiates. Here and there, parcels of the Art were revealed: porcelain, gunpowder, acids, and gases. Electricity was jealously guarded by the Baghdad alchemists of the second century, Chinese alchemists produced alumninum at the same time by a process that leaked out only recently. And Sir Newton wrote in 1676: "There are further secrets besides the transmutation of metals and the only great magisters are to understand these."

No matter how improper or dangerous these leaks of part of the great Art were, we must now entertain the possiblity that the new alchemy offers to a cruel world where death roams for all and nuclear accidents lurk at every turn—the chance of recapturing the true source and harmony of life. Alchemy's altruistic attitude is still an exemplary force: It can become a guide and lead all of humanity to hope again.

The day will come when all men will arrive at the full knowledge of alchemy in its pure thought form. It will then no longer be a physical science but an ethic of living.

Most likely before the end of this century humanity will have to take the giant transmutational step predicted by Teilhard de Chardin when he speaks of the "Grand mutation of humanity toward salvation." The secret of "the Flowers of the waves" has not yet been revealed. Modern populations of all the great powers do not have one single crystal of salt that is pure and sweet* ocean sublimation,

---

*The term "sweet" is used knowingly; in the plasma of Quinton, the bitterness of seawater has been naturally transmuted to the sweetness of saliva and other healing fluids of the body. Also natural seasalt dissolved in spring water has none of the bitterness of raw seawater or crude salt.

crystallized by the sun and sifted by the earth. With its very real impact on human sanity and peace, refined salt must not continue to proliferate, bringing with it aggression, madness, loss of equilibrium and harmony. If alchemy is to come out in the open, revealing the secret of the totality of seasalt**, it will have won its ultimate victory.

**The concentrated efforts of a group of researchers today are working to bring back natural seasalt in worldwide usage. Their society welcomes input and donations to strenghten their efforts. For a free packet of information, write: The Grain and Salt Society, P.O. Box DD, Magalia, CA 95954.

Robert Duncan
Chapter 5 of Part I: *The H.D. Book*

This is not the beginning of the book. That was later, or, coming later, it was written earlier. What was to become our study began long ago. In one sense it began before writing or reading began, when as a child I lay drifting in the environment of voices talking in the next room. I would be put to bed among the potted plants by the wall that was all windows of a sunroom or herbarium at my grandmother's, and as my elders talked in the inner chamber, I, outside, could gaze at the night sky where some star was "mine" and watched over me; stars were eyes, or the first star seen was a wish or would grant a wish. My soul, they told me, went out to the stars or to other worlds. I laid my body down in the bed as if it were a little boat and sailed on a voyage I pretended. *"Wynken, Blynken, and Nod,"* the rime went, *"one night*

> *Sailed off in a wooden shoe—*
> *Sailed on a river of crystal light,*
> *Into a sea of dew."*

"Where are you going, and what do you wish?" —so the old moon questions the voyagers. "I know where I'm going and who's going with me" another old song went. The rime was a child's fancy by Eugene Field, a crude versifier, a despised source. In Maxfield Parish's picture—"Show us the picture," we used to ask as Mother read—still glowing in memory, they go out into a sea of stars, into the blue of the night-sky. "I pray the Lord my soul to keep."

The soul, my mother's sister—Aunt Fay—told me years later, was like a swarm of bees, and, at night, certain entities of that swarm left the body-hive and went to feed in fields of helium—was it in the upper atmosphere of the earth or in the fire-clouds of the Sun? The "higher" ascended nightly, and in its absence, the "lower" dreamed, flooded the mind with versions of the Underworld. "While the cat's away, the mice will play." There were not only pretend dreams or plagiarized dreams like making up the Wynken-Blynken-and-Nod Boat of Eugene Field to be one's own, but there were rare dreams of the higher realms, instructions from angels of the Sun, and there were dreams of one's own "lower" nature, messages from the Underworld, rebellious images that flooded the mind in the absence of its King, when genitals or liver, heart or bowels, took over the imagining screens of the brain for their own uses.

My aunt's name, *Fay* or *fairy*, had to do with illusions or enchantments, bewilderments of the mind in which we saw an other world behind or under things, and at the same time with the enchanters themselves, the folk who lived under the Hill. *Fate, faith, feign,* and *fair*, we find, following the winding associations of *fay, fey,* and *fairy* in the O.E.D., are related. From many roots, words gathered into one stem of meaning, confused into a collective suggestion. There is *fay*, too, from *fean*, meaning to join, to fix. In the United States of the nineteenth century it could mean the fit of a garment: "Your coat fays well," the

O.E.D. gives us. The casting of the image is high fairy, *phanopoeia*; but the image itself, as Pound conceived it to be—a nexus, "an intellectual and emotional complex in an instant of time," he wrote in *A Stray Document*, "which gives that sense of sudden liberation; that sense of freedom from time limits and space limits; that sense of sudden growth..." — the image itself is *fay*: an apparition and a joining in one.

The little poem by Field was fay, for it cast its spell. And in the inner chamber, the adults, talking on, wove for me in my childish overhearing, Egypt, a land of spells and secret knowledge, a background drift of things close to dreaming—spirit communications, reincarnation memories, clairvoyant journeys into a realm of astral phantasy where all times and places were seen in a new light, of Plato's illustrations of the nature of the soul's life, of most real Osiris and Isis, of the lost Atlantis and Lemuria, and of the god or teacher my parents had taken as theirs, the Hermetic Christos. This word *teacher*, as I first heard it, before I went to school, meant the same thing as a god. God was not a god, but from His Being He sent out teachers or gods. True teachers, like Christ, Buddha, Hermes or Lao-tse, were Light Beings, Messengers of the Sun Itself. Hermes, Mercury, was the one with winged helmet and winged sandals I had seen in the bronze figure that stood on the piano at Aunt Fay's. He was the god of the high air, of those helium fields, carrying a rod around which two snakes twisted. This wand or *caduceus* meant, Aunt Fay explained, that he was god of Life, systole and diastole of the heart beat. But the real image of the god was the picture Grandmother showed me in *The Book of the Dead*. Egypt was the hidden meaning of things, not only of Greek things but of Hebrew things. The wand of Hermes was the rod of Moses, and my grandmother studied hieroglyphics as she studied Hebrew letters and searched in dictionaries for Greek roots, to come into the primal knowledge of the universe. This god, the Egyptian Thoth, was Truth, the truth of what life is that we know in death. He appeared not in the high air but was a Being of the Sun Below the Earth, a Lord of the Dead. He held the scales and weighed the soul; he judged between the fair and unfair. He had another title in *The Book of the Dead*: He-Who-Decides-In-The-Favor-Of-Osiris.

Fay from *fata* had to do with the dead. The fairies as fates or norns were spinners of the threads from which life was woven, who measured man's span and cut the cord to deliver him into death as once they had cut the first cord or chord when the music began. But the word *fey* too came from another root that meant *fated to die, cowardly,* or *weak*, as the O.E.D. tells us—unnamed. In our common speech it meant "crazed", "touched", and then, "clairvoyant", "in tune with the dead". The lords of the dead were in the Egyptian writing: the Ibis-headed Thoth, Isis with the disc-crown, the lion-headed Sekmet, the winged serpented Sun, showing the animal nature in which our souls had evolved.

Just as, when the rime of Eugene Field's was all but forgotten, in the study of Pound's *Cantos* I was to come again to a "river of crystal light" and in the study of Yeats's or Breton's poetry I was to come to hear of a "dew" or a "sea of dew", so in Whitman's "eidolon yacht of me", in Lawrence's *Ship of Death*, in the "caravel" that in *Helen in Egypt* carries Achilles to the shore where his Helen waits, I was to come again to that "wooden shoe", the Wynken-Blynken-and-Nod Boat. When I was no longer a child but a boy in my early teens, I had found it too in the fairy ship of Avalon. The Boat of Dreams, the Boat of the Dead, was one of the great images of Poetry. In the late Cantos of Pound it appeared as I saw it, almost as early as that other picture by Maxfield Parrish, in the Egyptian picture-writing my grandmother studied: it was the Ra-Set Boat. "And then went down to the ship," Pound had begun the established text of those *Cantos*, moving with the phantoms of Odysseus and his descent to the dead upon a sea of the imagination.

In the fairy-world, the otherness or alien nearness of the dead and of hidden elements, of illusion and delusion in our daily life, the witchcraft of phantasy and the bewitched obsessions of madness, all the psychological dangers, combined as if they were the heart's wish. The specter that haunts Europe, Marx had called the hidden wish of the human spirit in history; the traumatic image, Freud had called the repressed wish of the psyche—the primal scene. The underground uprises into the place of what is above-board. Justice demands it. The verso appears, so vivid that we see the surface of things had faded in the sunlight, and what we most feared we might be we become. The living seem dead and the dead most alive. Men could no longer trust what was fair or appeared fair. The words *fey, fay* and *fairy,* had a meaning I was to learn among schoolmates that in the common usage superseded all other meanings: queer, perverted, effeminate. Old concepts of sodomy and shamanism—the cult that Orpheus brought of mediumship, poetry and homosexuality, from the forest world of the North into Greece—carry over into our vulgar sense of the word *fairy*, where men's fear and mistrust of a sexual duplicity is most active.

The Above and the Below, the Left and the Right—Hermetic doctrine and Cabalistic lore suggested a reality that was duplicit. Love, I was taught, had once been, in an other life, hatred; and hatred, love. There were times when in flashes of anger against my mother's will, I would glower and strike out. That was the law of karma, my mother would explain, that hatred and love were so intertwined. Like those snakes on the magic wand, above which the wings of the mind hovered. Male and female were mixed too, I learned, for we who were men had been women in other lives and understood what to be a woman meant out of the depths of our human experience, the source of sexual sympathies and powers. So, Shakespeare, because he had the memories of lives, had inner knowledge of Lady Macbeth and Macbeth, Anthony and Cleopatra, Hamlet and his mother, the Queen. Being was the ground of an ambivalence that was the counterpart in turn of the ambivalence of the universe at large hidden and disclosed in things.

In the beginning I heard of guardian angels and of genii, of vision in dreams and truth in fairy tales, long before Jung expounded the gnosis or Henri Corbin revived Avicenna. For these ideas were properties not only of the mind above, the high thought of Neo-Platonists or Romantic poets, but they were lasting lore of the folk mind below too, wherever old wives told their tales. Gossip had brought rumors of the divine wisdom into American folk ways. From the popular movement of nineteenth century American spiritualism, where witch tradition out of Salem, shaman rite out of the world of the American Indian, and talking with tongues or from the spirit out of congregations of the Holy Ghost in the Protestant movement, mingled to become an obsession at large, so that in the last decades of the century in town and countryside groups met to raise the dead at rapping and levitating tables, new affinities with more ancient mystery cults of spirit and of a life beyond life were awakened. The theosophy of Plutarch, Plotinus, Pseudo-Dionysius the Areopagite, the hermeticism of Pico della Mirandola, or *The Light of Asia* and the *Bhagavad-Gita,* joined in the confusion of texts and testimonies of libraries that could include accounts written by trance-mediums of travel to past time or far planets, manuals of practical astrology and numerology, or Max Heindel's *The Rosicrucian Cosmo-Conception*—"Its Message and Mission: A Sane Mind. A Soft Heart. A Sound Body."

My grandmother, as a young wife of eighteen, had lost two babies in a polio epidemic, and she came down to San Francisco from what is still backwoods Sierra country, to go from one spiritualistic circle to another, seeking consolation or communication, some continuity of feeling. The Indian guides must have seemed not out of place, for she had been born in Indian country in the wilderness of the Modoc territory in Eastern Oregon, just after the Civil War. My father's family had moved West too, first into Ohio at the beginning of the nineteenth century, and then on, at the frontier or beyond the frontier of America, into California. Tales of pioneer days, of Indian wars and Indian sympathies, lingered on along with the new lore of strange ways. From Modoc County in northeastern California, where she had gone as a young bride, my grandmother brought Indian baskets and beaded belts, feathered charms and *wampum* or strings of shell money, her curios. In my childhood, there were still mediums at times, among those meeting in the other room, talking in Indian voices; but my grandmother had gone on from the spiritualist circles within a year or so, and sometime in the eighties, had joined a group to form a Hermetic Brotherhood.

Their thought rose from a swarming ground prepared by Helena Petrovna Blavatsky. *Isis Unveiled* had appeared in 1877; *The Secret Doctrine* in 1888; Sinnett's *Esoteric Buddhism* had appeared in 1883. Into her alembic or witch's pot, Blavatsky had stirred whatever hints, scrap legends, lore, visions, phantasies, things she made up herself, into a muddle or stew, "Pot and Pan-theism" a contemporary wit dubbed it. Though she ransacked demonologies, histories of magic, studies of religion, encyclopedias of gnosticism and neo-platonism—"about 2100 quotations from and references to books that were copies at second hand...without proper credit," an angry critic writes: "Nearly the whole of four pages was copied from Oliver's *Pythagorean Triangle,* while only a few lines were credited to that work"—the material of *Isis Unveiled*, H.P.B. insisted, was not out of reference books she had read, a matter of her imagination and research, but was revealed to her in the Astral Light. So her disciple Olcott describes how, in the evening when he would return from his office and sit opposite her as she wrote, "with the vacant eye of the clairvoyant seer"—but we see it also as with the vacant eye of one remembering what she had read that day—she would "shorten her vision as though to look at something held invisibly in the air before her, and begin copying on her paper what she saw." Did she pretend, as I used to pretend as a child to sail out in the boat previous to dreaming? Why? Her references were actually all there in books that Olcott and she had gathered in their library in that very room or in libraries of occultist friends. She had an insatiable curiosity and energy in gathering information. She talked with everyone and read everything. In those very years (1875-1877) when *Isis Unveiled* was conceived and written, she drew upon the learning of Alexander Wilder, an American occultist, who had written *Eleusinian and Bacchic Mysteries* and *Serpent and Siva Worship, or A Translation of the Theurgia of Iamblichos*. Blavatsky insisted her guides were spirits. "One such collaborator," Gertrude Williams tells us in her book on Blavatsky, *Priestess of the Occult*, "was the Old Platonist who, remaining invisible, talked by the hour, dictating copy, checking references, answering questions." "The spirit Old Platonist would be more convincing," Mrs. Williams observes, "if there had not been an Old Platonist in the flesh—Dr. Wilder, who also talked by the hour, checking references and answering questions." But the work was not meant to be convincing. It was meant to be upsetting to the mind that would have tolerated Dr. Wilder as an authority in a curious field of thought but would balk at the pretension of a spirit as an authority in a revelation. Her purpose was not to convert but to overthrow the established orders of thought, to set up whatever was doubted, feared or despised in the place of the ruling conventions. Yes, but mixed up with the hysterical impulse to insult and subvert the respectable and reasonable was—also a component of hysteria—the intense sense of how much the society itself was in need of some release of vital powers.

"I am solely occupied," Blavatsky wrote to her sister, "not with writing *Isis*, with Isis herself. I live in a kind of permanent enchantment, a life of visions and sights, with open eyes, and no chance whatever to deceive my senses! I sit and watch the fair good goddess constantly. And she displays before me the secret meaning of her long-lost *secrets*, and the veil, becoming with every hour thinner and more transparent, gradually falls off before my eyes, I hold my breath and can hardly trust to my senses! ...Night and day the images of the past are ever marshalled before my inner eyes. Slowly, and gliding silently like images in an enchanted panorama, centuries after centuries appear before me... I certainly refuse point-blank to attribute it to my own knowledge or memory. I tell you seriously I am helped. And he who helps me is my Guru."

My "Daemon," Socrates had called him; or Genius. The Muse, a poet might have called Isis. But Blavatsky was not, she insisted, musing. Whatever else *Isis Unveiled* might be, it was not to be taken as a scholarly study, a philosophy, or a work of the imagination; it was to be taken as revelation, a dictate of the unconscious. A new specter was raised to haunt the course of Western Civilization.

"The mind is the great Slayer of the Real" is one of the fragments in *Voices of Silence*, "translated" by Blavatsky out of Senzar, the language hidden from the mind. The scholar, the philosopher, the poet, were all men of the mind, and, in the critical distance of their discipline or art, slayers of the real. This "Real" was Isis naked, the Revealed Doctrine. We can read another message in the oracle, for the Mind, the idiotic or autistic dream and will, is also a great slayer of another "real," the common sense. Blavatsky had set out to destroy what Freud calls the reality principle. John Symonds in his book on Blavatsky, *The Lady With The Magic Eyes*, from which I quoted the fragment from *Voices of Silence*, comments: "The *Mind* is here used in the sense of consciousness, upon which all our Western scientific knowledge is based, but which the East regards as only part of the world of illusion." Blavatasky's Mind, as Slayer of the Real, may have stood for the conscious, as Freud was to find it in his study of hysteria at the end of the century, at war with the unconscious. Plagiarism, fraud, perversion by pun, by reversal of values and displacement of content, of above into below, male into female, left into right, before into after—all these Freud saw as operations of the unconscious.

She impersonated the Unconscious, but she also gave her ego over to unconscious—"invisible" or "occult," she called them—guides. She was unconscious of what she read or learned in talking with Dr. Wilder, and accepted the information only in a trance-like state from the unconscious where it had been suppressed.

She was a wishful thinker, and she flew into rages when her wishes were questioned. She did not rage at Nature—Nature seemed to cooperate with her powers—but she was savage when confronted by ways of the mind that others took for granted, by what was proper to think, reasonable to hope for. More, she was outraged by her own disciples, the credulous and ever-admiring Olcott, the reason-seeking Sinnett, for she wanted the mind in following her Doctrine to be convinced by what it did not believe, to submit to the unreasonable. She did not want her theosophic manifesto to be accepted; she wanted men to come by way of what they could not accept into the rebellious impulses that lay back of *Isis Unveiled*. "If you only knew what lions and eagles in every part of the world have turned into asses at my whistle, and have obediently wagged their long ears in time as I piped," she wrote to a confidante.

There is pathos in her scorn. She had wanted to awaken a disobedience in man that would restore the lion or eagle he must be. The hidden Adam restored, man transformed under the dictatorship of the unconscious. You have nothing to lose but your chains of belief and disbelief, she had wanted to say.

For she was bound in chains of belief and disbelief. The imagination was intolerable to her conscious mind. She denied that there was any truth or trust in what a man might create or initiate. Even her book, in order to be doctrine, could not be created by her or have any virtue in her own thought but must be dictated by Masters outside the work, just as the truth of Man could not be immanent in his evolution but must be established in a paradigm, an actual plan given in the beginning and recorded in the eternal—the "Akashic" or Astral Light. "I certainly refuse point-blank to attribute it to my own knowledge or memory," she had said then as if such an attribution would have brought the authenticity of *Isis Unveiled* into question. She would have excluded the more vehemently any suggestion of her own phantasy or imagination entering in.

Whatever came from the individual inner volition was suspect. Over and over again she warns against the elemental and animal entities, the false impulses, that threaten any free life of the psyche as a medium. It is experience itself that she warns against. What does not come from a superior external authority, from Adepts "closely connected with a certain island of an inland sea," what does not come from the teachings of a primal and esoteric wisdom comes from below, from the Left, from the swarming mass of a false science based upon the senses. All the imaging, voicing, personating, creating activity that characterizes the imagination in the ego was denied and mistrused by her conscious mind. Only what was actual and imperative was permitted reality. Her ideas, her intuitions, her voices —the imagined teachers Morya and Koot Houmi—were illusions if they belonged to her own creative life. The Universe itself was Maya if it was created. The real could not be made-up.

Given the chains of belief and disbelief, the alternative of illusion is delusion. The creative was the veil of Isis. To find the hidden thing one had to strip the creative veil away. The magic of Blavatsky, the fascination of her writing, was never then to be the magic of enchanting prose, evoking its life in us to become most real in the weaving of a spell that is also a music with many images and levels of meaning—the illusion of an experience. Her magic was to be, on the contrary, the fascination of an argumentative delusion, the pursuit of proofs and laws behind appearances.

She sought in India and Egypt, she drew portraits, and, finally, she faked evidence to prove that her Masters were not figures of a dream or fiction, creatures of the veil, but actual persons. Anti-materialistic though she declared herself, she could not believe they might be spiritual beings "not of this world." She rejected all sublimations. Proofs lay in materialization—cups and saucers, gloved hands, bells rung, wafts of scents, actual letters received in a spirit post-office. Ideas, imaginings, visions were immaterial; she sought only the manifest. Yet she could live too in "a kind of permanent enchantment," as she writes to her sister, smoking hashish and having, not her own phantasies but hashish phantasies. Given the manifest agency of the drug, so that any suspicion of her own psychic agency might be denied, she could dwell "with Isis herself."

In 1891, a month before her death, she closed her last essay with a quotation from Montaigne: "I have here made only a nosegay of culled flowers, and have brought nothing of my own but the string that ties them." But that string was the thread of her argument, a wish that she and mankind with her might be released from the contradictions of dream and fact, creative idea and actuality, volition and authority, that tortured her spirit. But the string was also the quest for an end of dream, creative idea, volition—if only they could be proved to be their opposites so that what we had thought was moving would prove to be schematic and settled. The string was the obsessional winding of the thread: the double-faced words "Mind" and "Real," the inversion of evolutionary theory, the perversion of geological theory, the transference of fact into fiction and fiction into mode of fact, the subversion of accepted scientific thought, the plagiarisms, the fraud—worst of all, the reasoning of a woman who knows she must be right or all is lost.

With pathos, she added: "Is anyone of my helpers prepared to say that I have not paid the full price of my string?" She had been attacked and exposed, vilified and ridiculed. Her own followers had come to doubt that her Masters "really" existed. But the pathos was Mercurial, for she had meant for her followers in all the stupidity of their conscious minds, bound by chains of Theosophic belief, like her defamers bound by the chains of scientific or respectable disbelief, to pay the full price of her string.

For the price of the string, the price of the wish, the quest, the obsession, lay in an oppressive state. She had gathered a pitchblend of suggestion once her "doctrine" was mixed, in which some radium lay hid. In the mess of astrology, alchemy, numerology, magic orders, cabalistic and Vedic systems combined, confused, and explained, queered evolution and wishful geology, transposed heads—the fact of her charged fascination, her need, remains. Her sense binds: that until man lives once more in these awes and consecrations, these obediences to what he does not know but feels, until he takes new thought in what he has discarded, he will not understand what he is.

Isis Unveiled and *The Secret Doctrine*, midden heaps that they are of unreasonable sources, are midden heaps where beyond the dictates of reason, as in the collagist's art from what has been disregarded or fallen into disregard, genres are mixed, exchanges are made, mutations begun from scraps ("2100 quotations... without proper credit"), towards figures of a new world. In the conglomerate she gathered, things of disparate traditions whirl and take on new shapes for the conscious imagination, separated from their contexts and credits, tainted with foreign meanings. Her conscious insistence that her work was dedicated to the immutable archetypical Reality of the esoteric wisdom hid or veiled her unconscious wish—it was a vital intuition also of the meaning of science, religion and art—as a magic to take over Nature—our own inner nature then—from the Father, and to give birth to a new Nature, to prove What is to be an illusion in the light of What Must Be. The Isis, the Esoteric Wisdom of What Is, appears in the imagination to keep alive the rebellious writer's sympathies with her own nature, Nature then, in the presence of the would-be usurping wish.

So, Blavatsky saw vividly how Science, under dictatorship of Reason, had isolated itself from concern with any world of Spirit, psychic world, and finally from human and animal sympathies, declaring only that world to exist which could be positively known. "We must bravely face Science and declare," she wrote in 1888, "that the true Occultist believes in *Lords of Light*; that he believes in a Sun, which—far from being simply a 'lamp of day' moving in accordance with physical laws; and far from being merely one of those Suns, which, according to Richter, 'are sun-flowers of a higher light'—is, like milliards of other Suns, the dwelling or the vehicle of a God, and host of Gods." Her chapter heading *Modern Physicists Are Playing At Blind Man's Buff* has not lost meaning but has gained in terror in our day, seventy-five years later.

There had once been, she tells us in *The Secret Doctrine*, "on the plan of the Zodiac in the *upper* Ocean or the Heavens, a certain realm on Earth, an inland sea, consecrated and called the 'Abyss of Learning'; twelve centers on it, in the shape of twelve small islands, representing Zodiacal Signs—two of which remained for ages the 'mystery Signs'—were the abodes of twelve Hierophants and Masters of Wisdom. This 'Sea of Knowledge' or learning remained for ages there, where now stretches the Shamo or Gobi Desert. It existed until the last great glacial period, when a local cataclysm, which swept the waters South and West and so formed the present great desolate desert, left only a certain oasis, with a lake and one island in the midst of it, as a relic of the Zodiacal Ring on Earth. For ages the Watery Abyss—which, with the nations that preceded the later Babylonians, was the abode of the 'Great Mother,' the terrestrial post-type of the 'Great Mother Chaos' in Heaven, the parent of Ea (Wisdom), himself the early prototype of Oannes, the Man-Fish of the Babylonians—for ages, then, the 'Abyss' or Chaos was the abode of Wisdom and not of Evil. The struggle of Bel and then Merodach, the Sun-God, with Tiamat, the Sea and its Dragon—a 'War' which ended in the defeat of the latter—has a purely cosmic and geological meaning, as well as an historical one. It is a page torn out of the history of the Secret and Sacred Sciences, their evolution, growth and *death—for the profane masses*. It relates *(a)* to the systematic and gradual drying up of immense territories by the fierce Sun at a certain pre-historic period, one of the terrible droughts which ended by a gradual transformation of once fertile lands abundantly watered into the sandy deserts which they are now; and *(b)* to the as systematic persecution of the Prophets of the Right Path by those of the Left."

The psychic history of the Universe, Earth and Man, was the drama of each in the other, written in traumatic scenes—the freezing of the Hyperborean continent, the submerging of Lemuria and Atlantis, the drying up of the Gobi centers. Just as in the bardic tradition the poet has lived in all things—so that Gwion (Finn) in the thirteenth century *Romance of Taliesin* is not only the hero or god-child Fionn of the land of fairy, but names himself also Taliesin, the ninth century poet, and, again, may be a power of the cosmos, for he claims: *"Chief bard am I to Elphin, my original country is the region of the summer stars;"*

I was with my lord in the highest sphere,
On the fall of Lucifer into the depth of hell.
I have borne a banner before Alexander...

This "I," the poet's persona in his song, lives in whatever It sings of:

I am a wonder whose origin is not known.
I have been in Asia with Noah in the Ark...

—just as in the psyche-mysteries of Freudian psychoanalysis, the individual psyche is seen to recapitulate the psychic life of the species.

"Since the time we recognized the error of supposing that ordinary forgetting signified destruction or annihilation of the memory-trace," Freud tells us in *Civilization and Its Discontents*: "we have been inclined to the opposite view that nothing once formed in the mind could ever perish, that everything survives in some way or other, and is capable under certain conditions of being brought to light again, as, for instance, when regression extends back far enough." Tracing the history of "the Eternal City," Freud then turns to picture the psyche itself as such an Eternal City: "Now let us make the fantastic supposition," he continues—it is one of the creative phantasies of Freudian thought: "that Rome were not a human dwelling-place, but a mental entity with just as long and varied a past history: that is, in which nothing once constructed had perished, and all the earlier stages of development had survived alongside the latest. This would mean that in Rome the palaces of the Caesars were still standing on the Palatine and the Septizonium of Septimus Serverus was still towering to its old height; that the beautiful statues were still standing in the colonnade of the Castle of St. Angelo, as they were up to its siege by the Goths, and so on. But more still: where the Palazzo Caffarelli stands there would also be, without this being removed, the Temple of Jupiter Capitolinus, not merely in its latest form, moreover, as the Romans of the Caesars saw it, but also in its earliest shape, when it still wore an Etruscan design and was adorned with terra-cotta antefixae. Where the coliseum stands now we could at the same time admire Nero's Golden House; on the Piazza of the Pantheon we should find not only the Pantheon of to-day as bequeathed to us by Hadrian, but on the same site also Agrippa's original edifice; indeed, the same ground would support the church of Santa Maria sopra Minerva and the old temple over which it was built..."

To penetrate the depths of the psychic life, Freud resolves: "We shall have no hesitation in allowing ourselves to be guided by the common usages of language, or as one might say, the *feeling* of language, confident that we shall thus take into account inner attitudes which still resist expression in abstract terms," and following clues, like the hero of the detective fiction which is the contemporary of psychoanalysis, he reads in the psyches of his patients the drama of a prehistory or metahistory, like the popular "Mystery." So, in the theosophic mystery, the traumas of Hyperborea or Atlantis may be our own—"those very Monads, which entered the empty, senseless Shells, or Astral Figures of the First Race emanated by the Pitris," Blavatsky writes, "are the same who are now amongst us—nay, ourselves, perchance." *Canto VII*, Pound *"And all that day, another day,"* hearing *"Thin husks I had known as men,/Dry casques of departed locusts/ speaking a shell of speech,"* writing in a period when he was most conversant with Yeats's cabalistic lore, may have had the presence of the *kelipah* in mind, evil that is quickened only by the sin of man but in itself is but the dead residue of creation: *"Life to make mock of motion:*

>For the husks, before me, move,
>   The words rattle: shells given out by shells
>
>...
>
>And the tall indifference moves,
>   a more living shell,

Drift in the air of fate, dry phantom, but intact."

The bardic tradition may be recalled by Graves in his "historical grammar of poetic myth," *The White Goddess*, or the primal scene of Titanic infants playing with fire haunts Freud's *Civilization and Its Discontents*, as the Atlantean transgression of Nature's laws returns to Blavatsky's mind, because we live in a time into which all times are gathering. "The communion of saints is a great and inspiring assemblage," Whitehead writes in his *Aims of Education* in 1929: "but it has only one possible hall of meeting, and that is, the present." We find ourselves gathering what they were or drawn to the idea of them, for we have that wish for a great time or a great space—overpopulated as we are—to love in; and we call up the whole population of mankind to live in us.

"Before the mind's eye, whether in sleep or waking, came images that one was to discover presently in some book one had never read," Yeats tells us in *Per Amica Silentia Lunae*: "And after looking in vain for explanation to the current theory of forgotten personal memory, I came to believe in a Great Memory passing on from generation to generation. But that was not enough, for these images showed intention and choice. They had a relation to what one knew and yet were an extension of one's knowledge. If no mind was there, why should I suddenly come upon salt and antimony, upon the liquefaction of the gold, as they were understood by the alchemists, or upon some detail of cabbalistic symbolism verified at least by a learned scholar from his never-published manuscripts, and who can have put together so ingeniously, working by some law of association and yet with clear intention and personal application, certain mythological images? They have shown themselves to several minds, a fragment at a time, and had only shown their meaning when the puzzle picture had been put together. The thought was again and again before me that this study had created a contact or mingling with minds who had followed a like study in some of her age, and these minds still saw and thought and chose."

Yeats had sought out Helena Blavatsky in 1887 when he was in his early twenties, and he had gone on in other circles to devote his life to the esoteric wisdom cults. But it was the affinity that Poetry in the daemonic tradition has for the occult that moved him, for from the first Yeats had believed that Poetry was itself a secret doctrine. It was the study of Blake that had brought him to the threshold, leading beyond to Boehme and to the Zohar of Moses of Leon. It was Shelley who had set him on his way, for he had read in that poet's *Hellas* of a Jew, *Ahasuerus*, of whom it was said:

> *Some feign that he is Enoch: others dream*
> *He was pre-Adamite, and has survived*
> *Cycles of generation and of ruin.*

"Already in Dublin, I had been attracted to the Theosophists because they had affirmed the real existence of the Jew, or of his like," Yeats tells us in *The Trembling of the Veil*. He demanded, like Blavatsky, that his images be verified. He had come in search of a Master in life who had appeared to him in Shelley's play—the Wandering Jew, Ahasuerus. "Mistake me not!" Ahasuerus had said in *Hellas*: "All is contained in each."

> *Thought*
> *Alone, and its quick elements, Will, Passion,*
> *Reason, Imagination, cannot die;*
> *They are, what that which they regard appears,*
> *The stuff whence mutability can weave*
> *All that it hath dominion o'er, worlds, worms,*
> *Empire, and superstitions.*

It was to increase the dominion of the poetic mind that Yeats pursued his studies in the occult. The doctrine of correspondences that he found there enlarged the mission of metaphor and simile. The concept of the *eidolon* inherited from Iamblichus in which primal and eternal images are the movers or powers of the universe, agents of reality, charged the poet's reveries and visions with a radical purpose, a directive towards the heart of the matter, taken in what the majority of men took to be a literary pastime—at best a function of a cultured sensibility, at worst an idle and childish indulgence in phantasy.

Yeats is often called a symbolist, but the symbol for him was a magic intermediate, having its efficiency in the route it made between the soul and the image, the objective. But it was also—it had—it moved into his mind with—intention and choice. It was also the subject; it presented itself to him. For Yeats, as for Blavatsky, the great images were not imagined in the sense of being thought-up, but came to the imagination. There was a way, he tells us, in which men kept their bodies still and their minds awake and clear so that they became mirrors of the real.

"I had no natural gift for this clear quiet," he continues: "and I was seldom delighted by that sudden luminous definition of form which makes one understand almost in spite of oneself that one is not merely imagining." It was to live in this world as if it were more than imagined, as if it were a poetry that had its authors in eternity, as Blake called them, and the poet in his art projected a like-poetry, a microcosmos of the Real in the medium of words, guided, like Freud, "by the *feeling* of language." The Universe was a great Work or Language, life itself its voice, and all that the poet felt, heard, saw and sensed in the world about him or in himself was a language he must come to read, just as each art had its little language of images, sounds or movements in which meanings were evoked.

In an age when what we commonly call Science, the evocation of a world purely in terms of facts and uses, the dual presumption of mathematical and mechanical imaginations in place of all other imaginations, defined its own realms as the sole Real and all other worlds as unreal, there were men in the arts too who attempted to define realistic claims, working purely in terms of semantic or literary values, at war with unrealistic or animistic tendencies. Turning to the heretical or pseudo-Sciences of the occult, the evocation of a world in terms of a living language, Yeats was turning too from any purely literary or aesthetic interpretation of poetry, to affirm the truth he had found in Shelley or Blake as the most real. He sought not only theosophy, god-knowledge, but theurgy, god-work; and there was magic too, daemonic experiment. Words are at once agents of personal feeling and composition in a poem and also bearers of knowledge felt, evokers of the real and casters of spells.

*

The Hermetic Order of the Golden Dawn, the ritual cult to which Yeats belonged, begun by Dr. Woodman, Dr. Wynn-Wescott and MacGregor Mathers after the publication of Mathers' *The Qabalah Unveiled* in 1888, ten years after Blavatsky's *Isis Unveiled* and the year of *The Secret Doctrine*, gave rise not only to new formations in occultist circles but also to new formations in the literary worlds. There is a first splinter-group, as such mutinies are called in Marxist movements, when between 1900 and 1901, MacGregor Mathers and Aleister Crowley leave the party or are ousted from the party in a furor of legal battles, theoretical arguments and magic wars. Crowley, obsessed since the trauma of the Chogo Ri expedition of 1902 with the terror of the void ("The Abramelin demons, that Crowley had invoked at Boleskine, would seem to have formed a secret alliance with their cousins of the Himalayan Heights," C.R. Cammell observed in his study of Crowley), devotes his life to finding a sufficient nightmare to fill the emptiness. Since the Second World War (where certainly the void and terror opened in the death chambers of the Nazis or the radioactive holocaust of the Americans over Japan would seem a sufficient blackness), in the rise of a Poetry of emptiness and black humor, in the works of Philip Lamantia or in the film-poetry of Kenneth Anger the influence of Crowley begins to appear.

But we have here to do with a later division of the Order of the Golden Dawn into two distinct and even opposing groups among its members. Virginia Moore in her study of Yeats, *The Unicorn*, traces this history. The one, followed by Yeats and Algernon Blackwood, continued along the line of a pantheism in which all gods had reality in terms of the Anima Mundi below and the Great Mind or God above. The other, led by A. E. Waite and including Arthur Machen, Charles Williams and Evelyn Underhill, in 1903 broke with the parent body and formed a group which kept the Golden Dawn name and studied mysticism. For this group, the validity and verification of the esoteric tradition lay in the concern with the power of the Christos—and outside the Christian reality, the esoteric was evil.

For Algernon Blackwood, who with Yeats and the elder Watkins formed, Virginia Moore tells us, a Society of the Three Kings, if we read his popular romances aright, there was a theurgy in the worship of the elements that united him with the region of the stars and opened a way into the elemental realm of Nature, the restored childhood world of *The Education of Uncle Paul*, *The Centaur*, *A Prisoner in Fairyland*. For Yeats, as *The Trembling of the Veil* and *Per Amica Silentia Lunae* testify, there was a magic that opened his mind to invasions of sensation and image, uniting his imagination with the passionate and daemonic life of the Anima Mundi. They may have been—those three Kings devoted, we are told, to "the study of Mysticism not Occultism"—three Magi or Magicians too, studying the magic of the Child. Yeats in his *Autobiography*, like Blackwood in his novels, makes it clear that he seeks what he once knew in his childhood when he dwelt upon the thresholds of an enchantment of *faierie* in Nature, a closeness to the earth and to folk ways.

The Hermetic Order of the Golden Dawn is one stem then of divergent ways in the tradition: the first, is followed by Mathers and Crowley, from *The Magic Operation of Abra-Melin the Mage*, which Mathers had found in the Library of the Arsenal in Paris and translated, led—they no sooner split from the Order than they were at war with each other—to the struggle to become the Master, over Nature, the climbing to the heights of Chogo Ri, or over Poetry, the climbing to the heights, as he saw them, of *Ambergris,* A Selection from the Poems of Aleister Crowley. In the Black Fantasy of Crowley's *Moonchild*, Mathers and his wife, the sister of Henri Bergson, are seen twisted by hatred: "Douglas found his prestige gone, and his income with it. Addiction to drink, which had accompanied his magical fall, now became an all-absorbing vice..." then: "It was the vilest thing charged against that vile parody of a man, his treatment of his wife, a young, beautiful, talented, and charming girl, the sister of a famous Professor at the Sorbonne. He had delighted to reduce her to the bedraggled street-walker that she now was." Among Crowley's saddest delusions is his perception of his own quality in writing. Yeats appears in the poetic insight of *Moonchild* as "a lean, cadaverous Protestant-Irishman named Gates," driven by his vanity to make war on Crowley. "He possessed real original talent, with now and then a flash of insight which came close to genius. But though his intellect was keen and fine, it was in some way confused; and there was a lack of virility in his make-up. His hair was long, lank and unkempt; his teeth were neglected; and he had a habit of physical dirt which was so obvious as to be repulsive even to a stranger." It may be, indeed, that Satan himself gave Crowley this gift of malice for it has turned out over years to be a prose of dirt and leaves, a mirror reflecting only its author's intent.

The second way from *The Golden Dawn* led towards the fictional reality of Yeats and Blackwood, the creative imagination and the search for a magic participation in Nature and the Divine World, an indwelling not a mastery. The third, in reaction to the first two, returned to the orthodoxy of the Anglo-Catholic or the Catholic church, portraying the evil of magic and even the evil of Nature, and interpreting the esoteric wisdom as the higher truth of Christian dogma.

There was another movement after the death of Madame Blavatsky. This time not in the temple of a ritual cult but in the lecture hall of a theosophic school. G. R. S. Mead, who had been Blavatsky's secretary, followed the way, not of magic rite nor of mystic ritual but of gnosis, the teaching in the divine mysteries. In 1896 he published his translation fom a Latin version of the Coptic text the *Pistis Sophia*; in 1900 his study of surviving Gnostic texts and traditions, *Frag-*

ments of a Faith Forgotten; in 1906 *Thrice-Greatest Hermes*, studies in Hellenistic theosophy and gnosis, with a translation of the Trismegistic literature; and then, the series of eleven texts: *Echoes from the Gnosis*. In the magazine *The Quest* edited by Mead, his purpose is clearly to establish all religions as one ground of man's search for a life in the Divine World, to free the mind of man in his quest for the Divine from the inhibiting forces of dogma and church views, and at the same time, to revive the senses of the Divine World as the Real, the source of man's vital life.

Along another path, at Oxford and especially Cambridge, following *The Golden Bough* of Frazer in 1890, both classicists and folklorists found themselves students of the mystery cults. The way led from Bergson's *L'Evolution créatrice*, Jane Harrison tells us in her Preface to *Themis* in 1912: "I saw that Dionysos was an instinctive attempt to express what Professor Bergson calls *durée*, that life which is one, indivisible and yet ceaselessly changing. "The mystery cult was then not only an agricultural rite but a psychological rite. From a second source, Durkheim's *Représentations Individuelles et Représentations Collectives*, she had gathered that not only was the mystery-god an agency of "those instincts, emotions, desires which attend and express life" but that "these emotions, desires, instincts, in so far as they are religious, are at the outset rather of a group than of an individual consciousness."

The texts of the classicist or the folklorist took on new dimensions in the light of ideas of life forces and collective mind. "I was no longer engaged merely in enquiring into the sources of a fascinating legend," Jessie Weston writes in telling of her conversion from the folklorist view in the Preface to *From Ritual to Romance*: "but on the identification of another field of activity for forces whose potency as agents of evolution we were only now beginning rightly to appreciate." Tracing the roots of Grail legend to "the mysterious border-land between Christianity and Paganism," she tells us, the path led from Cumont to Mead where she found "not only the final link that completed the chain of evolution from Pagan Mystery to Christian Ceremonial, but also proof of that wider significance I was beginning to apprehend."

In the Quest Society, as in the person of its leader, G. R. S. Mead, the higher learning and the lower world of the occult meet. Here again, in the pages of *The Quest*, we find the new philosophy of Bergson along with Jessie Weston's Grail essays, Eisler's studies in Orphic cult and the Fisher King, Pound's *Psychology and Troubadours*. And there is not only the study of the *mythos*, the lore, but there is—so the testimony goes—back of the texts some knowledge of the *dromena*, what was done in the rites. "I know, I mean, one man who understands Persephone and Demeter," Pound says, "and another who has, I should say, met Artemis. These things are for them *real*." The mysterious border-land between Christianity and Paganism that Jessie Weston sought knowledge of lay not only in the past but in the present London of 1909: "No inconsiderable part of the information at my disposal," she writes: "depended upon the personal testimony, the testimony of those who knew of the continued existence of such a ritual, and had actually been initiated into its mysteries."

My grandmother was an elder in a provincial cult of this Hermetic movement, far from its center in London. Close to the wood-lore of her origins in frontier life, she had some natural witch-craft perhaps. But then it may be too that all Grandmothers, as in fairytales, are Wise Women or Priestesses of Mother Nature. I was but a boy when she died, and with her death, my father's tie with the old wisdom-way was broken. There was no cult after her death.

There is only what I remember out of childhood: the colored lithographs of Egyptian temples and the images upon the table, the voices talking of "Logos" and "Nous," the old women looking wisely into the Astral Light and telling what they saw there.

My father and mother were initiates, but in their own lives the tenor of the initiation was lost. From the region of San Francisco, they moved to Bakersfield, obedient to the directions of the stars in the Zodiac, as now Zen converts are obedient to the *I Ching*—Fate and Chance. They were isolated from their Brotherhood, their studies changed to studies that were respected by the community into which they moved. By the time I was adolescent, my father was involved in the study of botany and local historical sites. After his death, Mother was relieved, I think, that this way of studying things might be dismissed. New friends did not share her belief—that was part of it—but then, though their belief lasted, her interest did not last.

In my mind it has lasted. The lure is the lure of those voices weaving, as I began to understand words, a net of themes in which knots of meaning that refused any easy use appeared, glimpses from the adult world of words beyond them, as words were just beyond me, such a tapestry as Penelope is said to have woven that was never done but begun again each day, or as Helen wove, in which were all the scenes of the Trojan War. What was the hidden meaning of such a "Troy," of "War?" they would ask. It was not a dogma nor was it a magic that I understood for myself in the theosophic world about me but I understood that the meanings of life would always be, as they were in childhood, hidden away, in a mystery, exciting question after question.

The quest for meanings was a vital need in life that one recognized in romance where the hero must learn the language of birds, overhear the conversation of trees, call up even shadows to populate his consciousness. By associations, by metaphor, by likeness of the part, by fitting as part of a larger figure, by interlinking of members, by share, by equation, by correspondence, by reason, by contrast, by opposition, by pun or rime, by melodic coherence—what might otherwise have seemed disparate things of the word as Chaos were brought into a moving, changing, eternal, interweaving design of the world as Creation. It was the multiplicity of meanings at play that I loved in the talk of my parents in the nineteen-twenties. Two phases of the psyche's development in childhood—the endless questioning and the timeless play—found their reflection or continuation in the adult world of above and beyond.

We shall lose it all if it be not those voices talking over the evening fire. But the voices are gone. The waves throwing themselves down in ranks upon the shore are what I hear.

*

There had been catastrophe. There would be catastrophe. The time in which a man lived was a whirl or drift in a great sea that might rise out of itself into a roaring end of things. In the early years of the Depression, '29 or '30, when I was ten or eleven, I would lie awake before going off to sleep at the summer cottage at Morro Beach, letting the crash of the surf take over and grow enormous in my mind which dwelt at times like this upon the last days of Atlantis, imagining again the falling of towers, the ruin of cities, the outcry of a populace swept under by the raging element. When would it come? When would the long-awaited tidal wave, the advancing wall of water, sweep all before it? Even so the grown-ups talked of Atlantis and of America, as if it were a New Atlantis. The Atlanteans, even as we might, in their science had come to to know too much, the grown-ups said; they had found some key of the universe and had unlocked forbidden, destroying, powers.

Taller than Morro Rock I would think the breakers must be. I would try to picture the flood enormous enough to crash upon the mountains of the Coast Range as if they had been but banks of sand and to drown the San Joaquin. Or I would listen, curled on the ledge back of the seat in the coupe, as Mother drove us home from the movies in San Luis Obispo to the beach, for the fascinating sound above the fascination of the motor-sound, for the sea-roar. Now it will come, now it is coming, pouring in from the coast to meet us.

Born in 1919 at the close of the War, I belonged, I had been told, to an Atlantean generation that would see once more last things and the destruction of a world. There was a repeated dream I had as a child that came to be my "Atlantean" dream, for my mother told me it was a memory-dream. I belonged, too, to the generation that had been destroyed in a cataclysm before the world we lived in began. I had a part in the fabulous.

Sometimes in phantasizing, calling up pictures like this to illustrate an other life, I would rescue myself and set out upon the sea again in a boat. But the boat was now no longer charmed or charming, like the Wynken-Blynken-and-Nod Boat had been. Huddled in the wrappings of my bedclothes, I was never sure how the dark exposed rowboat or life-boat had escaped the holocaust in which it had been said all was lost, but it had been said too that certain adepts had escaped and I would be an adept. I was never sure how the boat was making its way now north and east over a grey and forbidding sea towards new land. The way was alien. I was never sure that this part, going on to rescue myself like this, would work out at all. On and on the boat sped towards some colony or destiny that had no such reality as the deluge, the sea itself, had, but lay ahead unseen and unreal.

We had moved from the Bay Region to the Valley in '28, away from the house my father had designed in Alameda as a young architect before I was born or adopted by my parents, away from the towers of San Francisco where he had worked in a firm as a junior architect; and away too from the circle of Hermetic students. Back of what we knew as children, scenes were being shifted: from the big house with its parties, the garden and the studio, to the crowded little house in Bakersfield where my sister and I slept in the same room; from the conversation at table that was all fabulous history and fantastic science to the admonitions and explanations of the Depression years, the economic worrying and the things-to-be-discussed later. What was left me from the talk of my elders in that antechamber of my childhood was now all my own. My parents, living far from the center of things, were concerned now with security and status, the politics and business opportunities of Bakersfield. Our religion became something we did not talk about to everybody. I talked to myself about it.

I would shake the Mah Jong table and the palace of many gardens and courts, the majestic halls and ramparts, constructed by giant hands from another world, the corridor where the Queen walked in the evening to meet the King, would fall. It seemed as if distant almost real shouts of anguish rose among the tottering ivory walls, and, making my play of earthquake, for I was the genius of the scene, I almost heard the confusion of delicious dismay, grief and fear, echoed in my heart as if bonds of human sympathy united me with the inhabitants of this world I created to destroy again and again. What I would see then was... Yes, I would see the actual mahjong tiles. I had had to build with utmost care and grandeur my little piled-up city or kingdom with many levels, for in the care piece by piece a place for something to happen was prepared, an other realm was built up, each tile the immediate occasion of a life fated to come to its last day. What I would see then was the monolithic real building I was engaged in, coming into existence block by block and yet the blocks themselves coming into existence in the building, out of what they were—the imposing gleam of the red dragon and green dragon walls, the mysterious symbols of the Chinese game with its winds and flowers converted into ancient glyphs and signs of a fated citadel. The Queen again would walk in the shadowed colonnade, the priests would sound their alarms from the tower, the scenes of human panic would flare up in the mind's eye, the pitiful consolation of the Queen in the King's embrace as the walls fell, the... No, he would not get to her! —the crashing house between, the grief and loss. Each time I would experience what the victims of the holocaust experienced.

In the Atlantis phantasy and the Atlantis game or play, the most real emerged only in terms of what was most unreal. It was an experience true and untrue to itself. I could call up these returns of a scene, but I had no will in calling them that could go against the emerging pattern, given in the play. The intense reality, wherever I became arbitrary, dissolved into unreal and unsure elements. I could not name for sure any place as my destination. I could not name for sure any time as my appointed time. So, though I read eagerly anything and everything about my Atlantis, it grew only more suspect in the obsessional proofs of Ignatius Donnelly—I didn't believe in an historical Atlantis—and yet, when geologists and reasonable historians scorned the would-be fact of Atlantis, the sinking land seemed real. Outside of history, there was an Atlantis—the shuddering earth, the engulfing waters, came into their own again.

"In other words, they were not poeticised versions of unique historical events in the life of any individual *hero*," Jane Harrison writes of myths in *Themis*: "but reflect recurrent ritual practices, or *dromena*." The things said over the fire long ago in my grandmother's rooms, or the talk at table in my childhood of planetary influences, elemental powers, lives before this life—the whole pictured island of lost consciousness under the sea waves that might rise once—Atlantis—was not false history but spoke of a feeling about the course of life itself. My grandmother died in her drama, her *mis en scène* of the Hermetic cult, and those who had lived in the enchantment of her stage survived to defend, to prove, to suspect or to put away what, when she had been alive, had been the language in which her living was written.

It is in the dream itself that we seem entirely creatures, without imagination, as if moved by a plot or myth told by a story-teller who is not ourselves. Wandering and wondering in a foreign land or struggling in the meshes of a nightmare, we cannot escape the compelling terms of the dream unless we wake, anymore than we can escape the terms of our living reality unless we die. There is a sense in which the "poet" of a poem forces us as writer or reader to obey a compelling form, the necessities of the poem, so that the poet has a likeness to the dreamer of the dream and to the creator of our living reality; dream, reality and the poem seem to be one.

The dream that was called my Atlantis dream was not something I thought up or that derived from the talk of my elders. The sequence remains emblematic and puzzling. Had my parents been Freudians instead of Hermeticists, they might have called it my birth-trauma dream. My mother had died in childbirth, and in some violent memory of that initiation into life, she may be a counterpart of the mother-country that had been lost in legend. But for me, the figures of the dream remain as if they were not symbols but primal figures themselves of what was being expressed or shown. Memory of Atlantis or memory of birth-trauma, phantasy of Isis or play with words—these are not what the heart fears and needs, the showing forth of some power over the heart.

First there was the upward rise of a hill that filled the whole horizon of what was seen. A field of grass rippled as if by the life of the grass itself, yet I was told there was no wind. When I saw that there was no wind it was a fearful thing, where blade by blade the grass so bowed of its own accord to the West. The grass moved towards the left. The seer or dreamer then was facing north. There may have been flowers—day's eyes—the grass was certainly in flower. The field was alive and, pointing that way, across the rise of the hill to the West, gave a sign.

Was I four or five when I first dreamt this dream? It came again and again as if to cut its shape for sure in what I would be. "For these images showed intention and choice," Yeats says of such showings-forth. When I heard the story of that nymph who fell hopelessly in love with the Lord of the Sun, Helios, I was drawn to identify with the Sunflower that rooted in her passion turns her head to follow the

Sun's way, for there was some faint reminder there of the grass I had seen in my dream bowing to the West. But in my dream there was no sun. The light was everywhere, and I can not be certain it was morning, evening or high noon.

Then in a sudden almost blurred act of the play, there was a circle of children—sometimes they are all girls or all boys, sometimes they are boys and girls—dancing in the field. They choose or have chosen someone who is "IT" in the center of the ring, but I see no one there. The Dreamer is in the Center, the "I" or Eye of the Dream. And just here, I realize that this "I" is my self and second that I have been "chosen," but also that in dreaming I am the Chosen One, I have been caught in the wrong—a "King" or victim of the children's round dance. Ring a round of roses. Pocket full of posies. Or is it poses? for I had been proposed or I had posed as King, posed myself there. Ashes, ashes. All fall down!

In the third part—but it is the second section of the dream, for the Field and Its Dancers are two parts belonging to one section—I am shown a cavern underground. A throne room? There is a stone chair on a dais. Seeing it is the King's chair or, even, in some dreamings of this dream, finding myself a lonely King in that chair, there is no one rightly there. A wave of fear seizes me. All things have gone wrong and I am in the wrong. Great doors break from their bars and hinges, and, under pressure, a wall of water floods the cavern.

The open field, the dance and the presumption, the seeing the dark throne and the flooding of the underworld (the dream that my mother believed to be memory of a past life) seem now a prediction of what life will be, now a showing forth of some content of what life is, as in the Orphic mysteries the story of Persephone was shown in scenes. The restless dead, the impending past life, what had been cast away—a seed—sprouts and in the vital impulse would speak to us. The head of a giant woman rises from the ground.

"I have seen Kore," the initiate Heracles says: "What face more terrible? I am initiate, prepared for Hades." Wonder and terror seem to be signs of the rite. But in my life dream, I have not seen the Maiden, for I stand in her place or in her way.

Robert Duncan
RITES OF PARTICIPATION
Chapter 6 of Part I: *The H.D. Book*

The drama of our time is the coming of all men into one fate, "the dream of everyone, everywhere." The fate or dream is the fate of more than mankind. Our secret Adam is written now in the script of the primal cell. We have gone beyond the reality of the incomparable nation or race, the incomparable Jehovah in the shape of a man, the incomparable Book or Vision, the incomparable species, in which identity might hold & defend its boundaries against an alien territory. All things have come now into their comparisons. But these comparisons are the correspondences that haunted Paracelsus, who saw also that the key to man's nature was hidden in the larger nature.

In space this has meant the extension of our "where" into a world ecology. The O.E.D. gives 1873 as the earliest English use of the word in the translation of Haeckel's *History of Creation*—"*the great series of phenomena of comparative anatomy and ontogeny...oecology.*" The very form of man has no longer the isolation of a superior paradigm but is involved in its morphology in the cooperative design of all living things, in the life of everything, everywhere. We go now to the once-called primitive—to the bush man, the child, or the ape—not to read what we were but what we are. In the psychoanalysis of the outcast and vagabond, the neurotic and psychotic, we slowly discover the hidden features of our own emotional and mental processes. We hunt for the key to language itself in the dance of the bees or in the chemical code of the chromosomes.

The inspiration of Marx bringing economics into comparison and imagining a world commune, of Darwin bringing species into comparison and imagining a world family of the living in evolution, of Frazer bringing magic, rituals and gods into comparison and imagining a world cult—the inspiration growing in the nineteenth century of imperialist expansions was towards a larger communityof man. In time, this has meant our "when" involves and is involved in an empire that extends into the past and future beyond times and eras, beyond the demarcations of history. Not only the boundaries of states or civilizations but also the boundaries of historical periods are inadequate to define the vital figure in which we are involved. *"For the intense yearning which each of them has towards the other,"* Diotima tells Socrates in Plato's Symposium, *"does not appear to be the desire of lover's intercourse, but of something else which the soul of either evidently desires and cannot tell, and of which she has only a dark and doubtful presentiment."*

The Symposium of Plato was restricted to a community of Athenians, gathered in the common creation of an *areté*, an aristocracy of spirit, inspired by the homoEros, taking its stand against lower or foreign orders, not only of men but of nature itself. The intense yearning, the desire for something else, of which we too have only a dark and doubtful presentiment, remains, but our *areté*, our ideal of vital being, rises not in our identification in a hierarchy of higher forms but in our identification with the universe. To compose such a symposium of the whole, such a totality, all the old excluded orders must be included. The female, the proletariat, the foreign; the animal and vegetative; the unconscious and the unknown; the criminal and failure—all that has been outcast and vagabond must return to be admitted in the creation of what we consider we are.

The dissolving of boundaries of time, as in H. D.'s *Palimpsest,* so that Egyptian or Hellenistic ways invade the contemporary scene—The reorganization of identity to extend the burden of consciousness—this change of mind has been at work in many fields. The thought of primitives, dreamers, children, or the mad—once excluded by the provincial claims of common sense from the domain of the meaningful or significant—has been reclaimed by the comparative psychologies of William James, Freud, Levy-Bruhl, Piaget, by the comparative linguistics of Sapir or Whorf, brought into the community of a new epistomology.

"Past the danger point, past the point of any logic and of any meaning, and everything has meaning," H.D. writes in *Bid Me To Live:* *"Start superimposing, you get odd composites, nation on nation,"* So, Malraux in his *Psychology of Art* hears *"a furtive colloquy in progress between the statuary of the Royal Portals of Chartres and the great fetishes"* beginning in museums of the mind where all the arts of man have been brought into the complex of a new idea of Art and Man in their being superimposed. *"Our art world is one,"* he writes in *The Metamorphosis of the Gods,* *"in which a Romanesque crucifix and an Egyptian statue of a dead man can both be living presences." "In our imaginary museum the great art of Europe is but one great art among others, just as the history of Europe has come to mean one history among others." "Each civilization had its 'high places',"* he concludes in the Introduction: *"All mankind is now discovering its own. And these are not (as the nineteenth century took for granted) regarded as successive landmarks of art's long pilgrimage through time. Just as Cezanne did not see Poussin as Tintoretto's successor, Chartres does not mark an 'advance' on Angkor, or Borobudur, or the Aztec temples, any more than its Kings are an 'advance' in the Kwannon at Nara, on the Plumed Serpents, or on Pheidias' Horsemen."*

If, as Pound began to see in *The Spirit of Romance,* *"all ages are contemporaneous,"* our time has always been, and the statement that the great drama of our time is the coming of all men into one fate is the statement of a crisis we may see as ever-present in Man wherever and whenever a man has awakened to the desire for wholeness in being. *"The continuous present,"* Gertrude Stein called this sense of time and history, and she saw the great drama as man's engagement in a composition of the contemporary. Man is always in the process of this composition. *"The composition is the thing seen by every one living in the living they are doing,"* she writes in *Composition as Explanation:* *"they are the composing of the composition that at the time they are living is the composition of the time in which they are living. It is that that makes living a thing they are doing."*

"Nothing changes from generation to generation," she writes later in her lecture *Portraits and Repetition,* *"except the composition in which we live and the*

composition in which we live makes the art which we see and hear." "Once started expressing this thing, expressing any thing there can be no repetition because the essence of that expression is insistence." "Each civilization insisted in its own way before it went away." To enter *"our time,"* she saw as *"a thing that is very troublesome,"* for life itself was a disturbance of all composition—*"a fear a doubt and a judgment and a conviction,"* troubling the waters toward some needed *"quality of distribution and equilibration."*

*

The first person plural—the "we," "our," "us"—is a communal consciousness in which the "I" has entered into the company of imagined like minds, a dramatic voice in which the readers and the man writing are gathered into one composition, in which we may find kindred thought and feeling, an insistence, in Plutarch or Dante, Plato or D. H. Lawrence, closer to our inner insistence than the thought and feeling of parents or neighbors. The discovery of self, time and world, is an entering into or tuning to possibilities of self, time and world, that are given.

"The single experience lodges in an individual consciousness and is, strictly speaking, incommunicable," Sapir writes in *Language: "To be communicated it needs to be referred to a class which is tacitly accepted by the community as an identity. Thus, the single impression which I have of a particular house must be identified with all my other impressions of it. Further, my generalized memory or my 'notion' of this house must be merged with the notions that all other individuals who have seen this house have formed of it. The particular experience that we started with has now been widened so as to embrace all possible impressions or images that sentient beings have formed or may form of the house in question. In other words, the speech element 'house' is the symbol, first and foremost, not of a single perception, nor even of the notion of a particular object but of a 'concept,' in other words, of a convenient capsule of thought that embraces thousands of distant experiences and that is ready to take in thousands more. If the single significant elements of speech are the symbols of concepts, the actual flow of speech may be interpreted as a record of the setting of these concepts into mutual relations."*

There is no isolate experience of anything then, for to come into "house" or "dog," "bread," or "wine," is to come into a company. Eros and Logos are inextricably mixed, daemons of an initiation in each of our lives into a new being. Every baby is surrounded by elders of a mystery. The first words, the "da-da" and "ma-ma," are keys given in a repeated ritual by parental priest and priestess to a locus for the child in his chaotic babbling, whereby from the oceanic and elemental psychic medium—warmth and cold, calm and storm, the moodiness previous to being—persons, Daddy and Mama, appear. But these very persons are not individual personalities but communal fictions of the family cultus, vicars of Father and Mother, as the Pope is a Vicar of Christ. The Child, the word "child," is himself such a persona, inaccessible to the personality of the individual, as the language of adult personal affairs is inaccessible to the child. To have a child is always a threat to the would-be autonomous personality, for the parent must take leave of himself in order to enter an other impersonatiom, evoking the powers of Fatherhood or Motherhood, so that the infant may be brought up from the dark of his individuality into a new light, into his Childhood. For the transition to be made at all, to come into the life of the spirit, in which this Kindergarten is a re-created stage set of the mythic Garden, means a poetry then, the making up of an imaginary realm in which the individual parents and infant participate in a community that exists in a time larger than any individual life-time, in a language. For "Father," "Mother," "Child," are living words, deriving their meaning from thousands of distinct experiences, and the actual flow of family life, like the actual flow of speech, "may be interpreted as the setting of these concepts into mutual relations." The toys of the nursery are not trivia but first given instruments of an extension in consciousness, our creative life. There is a travesty made of sacred objects when the building blocks that are also alphabet blocks, the animal and human dolls, the picture books, are rendered cute or babyish.

"*The maturity of man—*" Nietzsche writes in *Beyond Good and Evil:* "*that means, to have reacquired the seriousness that one had as a child at play.*" In *The Zohar* of Moses of Leon, God Himself appears as *Child-Creator-of-the-World:* "*When the Holy One, blessed be He, was about to make the world, all the letters of the Alphabet were still embryonic, and for two thousand years the Holy One, blessed be He, had contemplated them and toyed with them. When He came to create the world, all the letters presented themselves before Him in reversed order. The letter Tau advanced in front and pleaded: May it please Thee, O Lord of the world, to place me first in the creation of the world, seeing that I am the concluding letter of EMeTh (Truth) which is engraved upon Thy seal.*" One by one the letters present themselves. At the last "*the Beth then entered and said: O Lord of the world, may it please Thee to put me first in the creation of the world, since I represent the benedictions (Berakhoth) offered to Thee on high and below. The Holy One, blessed be He, said to her: Assuredly, with thee I will create the world, and thou shalt form the beginning in the creation of the world. The letter Aleph remained in her place without presenting herself. Said the Holy One, blessed be His name: Aleph, Aleph, wherefore comest thou not before Me like the rest of the letters? She answered: Because I saw all the other letters leaving Thy presence without any success. What, then, could I achieve there? And further, since Thou hast already bestowed on the letter Beth this great gift, it is not meet for the Supreme King to take away the gift which He has made to His servant and give it to another. The Lord said to her: Aleph, Aleph, although I will begin the creation of the world with the beth, thou wilt remain the first of letters. My unity shall not be expressed except through thee, on thee shall be based all calculations and operation of the world, and unity shall not be expressed save by the letter Aleph. Then the Holy One, blessed be His name, made higher-world letters of a large pattern and lower-world letters of a small pattern. It is therefore that we have here two words beginning with beth (Bereshith bara)* "in-the-beginning He-created" *and then two words beginning with aleph (Elohim eth)* 'God the'."

In this primal scene, before the beginning of the world that is also here before the beginning of writing, the Self contemplates and toys in a rite of play until the letters present themselves and speak; as in another primal scene, in a drama or play of the family, the child contemplates and plays with the sounds of a language in order to enter a world in which Father and Mother present themselves and speak. So too in the fullness of the imagination, blocks and even made-up playmates present themselves. The teddy bear was once in the shaman world of the great northern forests Grandfather or Folk-Father. The figures we play with, the members of our play world, given as they are, like the Katchina dolls of the Zuni child, are spirit figures. *"My unity shall not be expressed except through thee,"* the Child-Creator promises. It is the first promise of love. *"on thee shall be based all calculations and operations of the world."*

These powers, the ambience in which all things of our world speak to us and in which we in turn answer, the secret allegiances of the world of play, the psychic depth of time transformed into eternity in which the conceptual persons of Father and Mother, Child and Play-Thing, exist—these are pre-rational. Brother and Sister have such an existence in the unreal that, where actual brother and sister do not exist or are unwilling to play the part, imaginary brother and sister may appear.

For men who declare themselves partisans of the rational mind at war with all other possibilities of being, the pre-rational or the irrational appears as an enemy within. It was not only the Poet, but Mother and Father also, that Plato would exclude from his Republic. In the extreme of the rationalist presumption, the nursery is not the nursery of an eternal child but of a grown-up, a rational man. Common sense and good sense exist in an armed citadel surrounded by the threatening countryside of phantasy, childishness, madness, irrationality, irresponsibility—an exile and despised humanity. In that city where Reason has preserved itself by retreating from the totality of the self, infants must play not with the things of the imagination nor entertain the lies of the poets but play house, government, business, philosophy or war. Before the guardians of this state the voices and persons of the Child-Creator stand condemned as auditory and visual hallucinations, a dangerous non-sense.

In the world of the Zohar, dolls were not permitted. The Child plays with the letters of an alphabet and Logos is the creator of the world. Man is to take his reality from, to express his unity in, the letter. But his letter is, like the doll, alive in the mind. *Tau* presents herself and speaks, just as the bear in our nursery does. To the extent that once for us too alphabet blocks were animate, all future architectures and worlds are populated, and we are prepared to understand the world-experience of the Kabbalist.

In this world-experience rationality does not exist apart from the whole, but the understanding searches ever to picture the self in the ununderstandable. The human spirit draws its life from a tree larger and more various than knowing, and reason stands in need of a gift, *"the gift of the queen to them that wander with her in exile.''*

There is a return in the imagination to the real, an ascent of the soul to its *"root"*, that Hayyim Vital describes in his life work, *The Tree of Life:* *"The imaginative faculty will turn a man's thoughts to imagine and picture as if it ascended in the higher worlds up to the roots of his soul...until the imagined image reaches its highest source and there the images of the supernal lights are imprinted on his mind as if he imagined and saw them in the same way in which his imaginative faculty normally pictures in his mind mental contents deriving from the world.''* We seem to be in the description of the process of a poem, for here too the mind imagines, but then enters a real it had not imagined, where the image becomes informed, from above or below, and takes over as an entity in itself, a messenger from a higher real. In his ascent the mystic is irradiated by the light of the tree and in his descent the light finds a medium through which to flow back into the daily world: *"The thought of the prophet expands and rises from one level to another...until he arrives at the point where the root of his soul is. Next he concentrates on raising the light of the sefirah to* En Sof *and from there he draws the light down, from on high down to his rational soul and from there, by means of the imaginative faculty, down to his animal soul, and there all things are pictured either by the inner senses of the imaginative faculty or by the outer senses.''*

Returning from *En Sof,* the unknowable, unimaginable God, from beyond sense, the imaginer, no longer imagining but realizing, carries a light from station to station, sefiroth to sefiroth, irradiating the imagined with reality, transforming the sense of the divine — the articulated Tree of Life — the cosmos, the rational soul and the animal soul, in light of a source that is a numinous non-sense or beyond sense.

This Tree, too, we saw each year, for at the birthday of the Child-Christos, we were as children presented with a tree from which or under which gifts appeared — wishes made real. This Christmas tree came, we know, from the tree-cults of the German tribes, ancestral spirits — a burning tree. But it is also a tree of lights, and where, in the time of Jacob Boehme, in the early seventeenth century, the Jewish and the Germanic mystery ways are wedded in one, the Christmas trees may have also been the Divine Tree of the Zohar, lit with the lights of the sefirah.

In this ritual of the imagination of Hayyim Vital, there is not only the ascent by pretending, the *"as if"* of his text, the pretension then, but the mystic is pretender to a throne, a *"source"* or *"root"* in the Divine. In the descent a magic is worked and all the pretended way of the ascent is rendered *"greater than Reality.''* Not only the deep dream but the day dream enlightens or enlivens. *"Occasionally,''* Werblowsky relates from Vital, *"the imaginative faculty may even externalize or project the effects of this 'light' so that the experience becomes one of external sense impressions such as of the apparition of angelic messengers, the hearer of voices.''*

This Tree of Life is also the tree of generations, for its branches that are also roots are male and female, and the light or life is a mystery of the Shekinah, the ultimate Spirit-Mother of Israel as well as God's Glory. The root or seed is a ultimate Spirit-Mother of Israel as well as God's Glory. The root or seed is a quickening source in the immortal or eternal womb, wherein each man is immortal.

*

In his study of Australian tribal rites, the psychoanalyst Geza Roheim draws another configuration of source, dream, and transformation of reality, that may cast further light on our way towards a picture of what is involved in poetry when the images and personae of a dream greater than reality appear as active forces in the poet's world:

"Strehlow, who as a missionary living for decades among the Aranda was certainly an authority on their language, tells us that he cannot explain the meaning of the word *altjira*, but it seems that the natives connect it to the concept of something that has no beginning—*erina itja arbmanakala*, him none made. Spencer and Gillen, however, have given another interpretation of the word. In their glossary we find '*altjerina*: name applied by the Arunta, Kaitish, and Unmatjera tribes to the far past or dream times in which their mythical ancestors lived. The word *altjeri* means dream.' Strehlow denies this; he says the word for dream is *altjirerama*, and gives the following etymology: *altjira*(god) *rama*(to see).

For one thing, it is clear that *altjira* means dreams and not god or ancestor (as Strehlow indicates) for I found that a folktale, a narrative with a happy end, is also called *altjira*.

It is evident that Strehlow, from his preoccupation with *Altjira* (God) of the Aranda Bible, managed to miss the real meaning of the word. *Altjira*=dream, *altjireramaa*=to dream; *altjirerinja*=dreaming. This is as near as I could get to Spencer and Gillen's *altjeringa*. Moses thought it must be a mistake for either *altirerindja* or *altjiranga*. There was no name for any mythical period. The time when the ancestors wandered on earth was called *altjiranga nakala*, i.e. 'ancestor was', like *ljata nama*, i.e. 'now is'. Other expressions were noted as equivalents of *altjiranga nakala*; these were *imanka nakala*, 'long time ago was' or *kutata nakala*, 'eternally was'. This led us to the explanation and etymology of the word *altjiranga mitjina*. Mitjina is equivalent to *kutata*, 'eternal'; *nga* is the ablative suffix *from*; therefore *altjiranga mitjina*='the eternal ones from the dream' or 'the eternal people who come in dreams.' This is not my explanation, but that of the old men, Moses, Renana, and Jirramba. Another Aranda word for dream, ancestor, and story, is *tnankara*. It is not often used, and as far as I could see it means exactly the same as *altjira*."

In story and tribal rite, the Australian native seeks to convert time and space into an expression of his unity, to create a language of acts and things, of the world about him come into one body. *"In an emu myth of the Aranda, Marakuja (Hands Bad), the old man emu, takes his bones out and transforms them into a cave...The kangaroo men take the mucus from their noses; it becomes a stone, still visible now. The rocks become black where they urinate."* Here the *altjiranga mitjina,* the ones living in a dream of time more real than the mortality of the time past, invade the immediate scene. For the Australians as for Heraclitus, *"Immortal mortals, mortal immortals, their being dead is the other's life."* The things lost in time return and are kept in the features of the place. *"Environment is regarded as if it were derived from human beings,"* Roheim observes.

In repeated acts—bleeding, pissing, casting mucus, spitting into the ground, or in turn, eating the totemic food and drinking the blood of the fathers—the boy is initiated into the real life of the tribe. *"An old man sits beside him and whispers into his ear the totemic name. The boy then calls out the esoteric name as he swallows the food. The emphasis on the place name in myth and ritual can only mean one thing, that both myth and ritual are an attempt to cathect environment with libido...The knowledge of the esoteric name 'aggregates' unites the boy to the place or to the animal species or to anything that was strange before."*

The "beast, anus, semen, urine, leg, foot" in the Australian song, chant or enchantment, that is also hill, hole, sea, stream, tree or rock, where *"in the Toara ceremony the men dance around the ring shouting the names of male and female genital organs, shady trees, hills and some of the totems of their tribe,"* are most familiar to the Freudian convert Roheim. He sees with a sympathy that rises from the analytic cult in which Freud has revived in our time a psychic universe in which dream has given a language where, by a "sexual obsession" (as Jung calls it), the body of man and the body of creation are united.

The "blood" of the Aranda, the "libido" of the Freudian, may also be the "light" of our Kabbalist text. "En Sof", Gershom Scholem tells us in *Major Trends in Jewish Mysticism: "is not only the hidden Root of all Roots*

> it is also the sap of the tree; every branch representing an attribute, exists not only by itself but by virtue of *En Sof,* the hidden God. And this tree of God is also, as it were, the skeleton of the universe; it grows throughout the whole of creation and spreads branches through all its ramifications. All mundane and created things exist only because something of the power of the Sefiroth lives and acts in them.
>
> The simile of man is as often used as that of the Tree. The Biblical word that man was created in the image of God means two things to the Kabbalist: first, that the power of the Sefiroth, the paradigm of divine life, exists and is active also in man. Secondly, that the world of the Sefiroth, that is to say the world of God the Creator, is capable of being visualized under the image of man the created. From this it follows that the limbs of the human body are nothing but images of a certain spiritual mode of existence which manifests itself in the symbolic figure of *Adam*

Kadmon, the primordial man. The Divine Being Himself cannot be expressed. All that can be expressed are His symbols. The relation between *En Sof* and its mystical qualities, the Sefiroth, is comparable to that between the soul and the body, but with the difference that the human body and soul differ in nature, one being material and the other spiritual, while in the organic whole of God all spheres are substantially the same."

"The world of the Sefiroth is the hidden world of language," Scholem continues, *"the world of divine names."* *"Totemic names,"* Roheim calls the whispered pass-words of the Australian rite. *"The creative names which God called into the world,"* Scholem calls the Sefiroth, *"the names which He gave to Himself."* It is the alphabet of letters revealed to the initiate as at once the alphabet of what he is and what the universe is and the alphabet of eternal persons.

As Scholem hints, *"the conception of the Sefiroth as parts or limbs of the mystical anthropos leads to an anatomical symbolism which does not shrink from the most extravagant conclusions."* Man's "secret parts" are secret names or hidden keys to the whole figure of man, charged with magic in their being reserved. In the communal image, the human figure is male and female. Ass-hole, penis, cunt, navel, were not only taboo but sacred, words to be revealed in initiations of the soul to the divine body, as at Eleusis the cunt of a woman in the throws of birth was shown. In what we call carnal knowledge, in the sexual union of male and female nakedness, God and His creation, the visible and invisible, the above and the below are also united.

Ham, who sees the nakedness of his father, is the prototype of the Egyptian who in an alien or heretic religion knows the secrets of God. To steal a look, like the theft of fire, is a sin, for the individual seeks to know without entering the common language in which things must be seen and not seen.

"At the initiation ceremony the point is to displace libido from the mother to the group of fathers," Roheim writes. In the contemporaneity of our human experience with all it imagines, there may not be a displacement but an extension of libido: the revelation of the mother remains, the revelation of the male body is added. *"Some old men stand in the ring and catching hold of their genitals tell the boys to raise their eyes and take particular notice of those parts. The old men next elevate their arms above their heads and the boys are directed to look at their armpits. Their navels are exhibited in the same way. The men then put their fingers on each side of their mouths and draw their lips outward as wide as possible, lolling out their tongues and inviting the special attention of the novices. They next turn their backs, and, stooping down, ask the novices to take particular notice of their posterior parts."*

For Roheim, the images and the magic of Australian story and rite are one with the images and magic of all dreams:

> After having withdrawn cathexis from environment, we fall asleep. But when the cathexis is concentrated in our own bodies we send it out

again and form a new world, in our dreams. If we compare dream mechanisms with the narratives of dream-times we find an essential similarity between the two. The endless repetitions of rituals and wanderings and hunting are indeed very different from a dream; but when we probe deeper we find that they are overlaid by ceremony and perhaps also by history. The essential point in the narratives as in the ritual is that man makes the world — as he does in sleep.

These natives do not wander because they like to...Man is naturally attached to the country where he was born because it, more than anything else, is a symbol of his mother. All natives will refer to their 'place' as a 'great place'; as they say 'I was incarnated there' or 'born there.' Economic necessity, however, compels him time and time again to leave his familiar haunts and go in search of food elsewhere. Against this compulsion to repeat *separation*, we have the fantasy embodied in myth and ritual in which he himself creates the world.

Where the nursing woman and the countryside itself are both "Mother", and where in turn the men of the tribe may initiate and reveal maleness as an other Mother, "Mother" means unity, what Gertrude Stein called the Composition. What we experience in dreaming is not a content of ourselves but the track of an inner composition of ourselves. We are in-formed by dreams, as in daily life we experience that which we are able to grasp as information. We see, hear, taste, smell, feel, what can be drawn into a formal relation; to sense at all involves attention and composition: *"It is very interesting that nothing inside in them, that is when you consider the very long history of how every one ever acted or has felt, it is very interesting that nothing inside in them in all of them makes it connectedly different,"* Stein writes in Composition As Explanation: *"The only thing that is different from one time to another is what is seen and what is seen depends upon how everybody is doing everything. This makes the thing we are looking at very different and this makes what those who describe make of it, it makes a composition, it confuses, it shows, it is, it looks, it likes it as it is, and this makes what is seen as it is seen."* The endless repetitions of rituals and wanderings and hunting as the pattern of life for the Australian is a living inside the Composition; and in their exhibiting the secrets of the male body to the boy, the men of the tribe are making a composition where what is seen depends upon how everybody is doing everything. In the ritual, song, parts of the body, parts of the landscape, man and nature, male and female, are united in a secret composite of magic names.

"One of the main sources of male creative power," Roheim tell us, *"is the incantation itself."*

When I asked old Wapiti and the other chiefs what makes the animals grow? the spirits? the ancestors? O, no, they said: *jelindja wara*, the words only. The form of the incantation is an endless, monotonous flow of words, and actually the men urinate very frequently while performing the ceremonies. This parallelism between the words and the fluid is brought out in a description by Lloyd Warner: 'The blood runs slowly and the rhythm of the song is conducted with equal slowness. In a second or two the blood spurts and runs in a rapid stream. The beat of the song sung by the old men increases to follow the rhythm of the blood.'

We may begin to see, given Stein's concept of insistence that informs composition, and then thinking of the pulse of the living egg-cell itself, that beat, rhythm, underlies every figure of our experience. Life itself is an endless, monotonous flow, wherever the individual cannot enter into it as revealed in dance and melody to give rhythmic pattern; the world about goes inert and dead. The power of the painter in landscape is his revelation of such movement and rhythm in seeing, information, in what otherwise would have been taken for granted.

Gertrude Stein, reflecting upon permanence and change in the artist's vision, sees that *"the only thing that is different from one time to another is what is seen and what is seen depends upon how everybody is doing everything."* Close to the Cubist Movement in Paris, she had experienced how painting or writing in a new way had revealed coordinations of what was seen and heard towards an otherwise hidden unborn experience of the world, so that one saw and heard with a profound difference. *"A new cadence means a new idea,"* H.D. and Richard Aldington, writing in the Preface to the *Imagist Anthology* of 1916, declared. Here too, cadence is how it is done; to make clear the meaning of cadence they referred to the choral line of Greek poetry that was also the movement of the choral dance, strophe and antistrophe. So too, Roheim, initiate of Freudianism, as Stein was initiate of Cubism, or H.D. of Imagism, sees in the narratives of his Australian informants how *"in all of them environment is made out of man's activity,"* for he had himself experienced a conversion in which a new environment for man had been made out of analytic activity. The *"manmade world"* in which *"environment is regarded as if it were derived from human beings,"* is the narrative itself; the unity of things in how the story is told.

Parts and operations of the human body, but also parts and operations of the cosmos, are related in a new ground, a story or picture or play, in which feeling and idea of a larger whole may emerge. The flow of sound from the throat and the flow of urine from the bladder, the flow of energy from the dancing feet, the flow of forms in the landscape, the flow of water and of air felt, translated in a rhythmic identity disclose to the would-be initiate what man is but also what the world is—both other and more than he is himself, than the world itself is.

Cezanne working at his vision of Mont Sainte-Victoire or Dali at his paranoic vision of the Catalonian landscape not only draw but are drawn by what they draw. From body and from world towards an other body and other world, man derives meaning in a third element, the *created*—the rite, the dance, the narrative; the painting, the poem, the book. And in this new medium, in a new light, "man" and "environment" both are made up.

The power of the poet is to translate experience from daily time where the world and ourselves pass away as we go on into the future, from the journalistic record, into a melodic coherence in which words—sounds, meanings, images, voices—do not pass away or exist by themselves but are kept by rime to exist everywhere in the consciousness of the poem. The art of the poem, like the mechanism of the dream or the intent of the trivial myth and dromena, is a cathexis: to keep present and immediate a variety of times and places, persons and events. In the melody we make, the possibility of eternal life is hidden, and experience we thought lost returns to us.

*

"The eternal ones of the dream," Roheim writes, *"are those who have no mothers;"* they originated of themselves. Their immortality is a denial of the separation anxiety. Separation from the mother is painful; the child is represented in myth as fully formed, even before it enters the mother. The tjurunga from which it is born is both a phallic and maternal symbol.

The tjurunga, like the cartouche that encircles the Pharaoh's name as the course of the sun encircles the created world, is a drawing of the spirit being, an enclosure in which we see the primal identity of the person. But all primal identities are Adamic, containing male and female, man and animal, in one. We are each separated from what we feel ourselves to be, from what we essentially *are* but also from the other we *must be*. Wherever we are we are creatures of other places; whenever we are, creatures of other times; whatever our experience, we are creatures of other imagined experiences. Not only the experience of unity but the experience of separation is the mother of man. The very feeling of melody at all depends upon our articulation of the separate parts involved. The movement is experienced as it arises from a constant disequilibrium and ceases when it is integrated.

"Composition is not there, it is going to be there, and we are here," Stein writes. Between *there* and *here* or *then* and *now*, the flame of life, our spirit leaps. A troubled flame: *"The time in composition is a thing that is very troublesome,"* Stein tells us—*"If the time in the composition is very troublesome it is because there must be even if there is no time at all in the composition there must be time in the composition which is in its quality of distribution and equilibrium."*

An anxious flame: *"In totemic magic the destroyed mother is re-animated and in the totemic sacrament, eternal union of the mother and child is effected,"* Roheim tells us. But the eternal separation of the mother and child is also celebrated therein. *"As a religion it represents the genitalization of the separation period and the restitution that follows destructive trends."* War, Heraclitus called the flame, or *Strife*.

"All men are bringing to birth in their bodies and in their souls," who here speaks as an Eternal One of the Mother, says to Socrates.

> There is a poetry, which, as you know, is complex and manifold. All creation or passage of non-being into being is poetry or making, and the processes of all arts are creative; and the masters of all arts are poets or

makers...What are they doing who show all this eagerness and heat which is called love?...The object which they have in view is birth in beauty.

Beyond beauty—birth in the eternal and universal.

"According to the natives of the Andjamatana tribe," Roheim tells us, *"children originate in two mythical women known as maudlangami. They live in a place in the sky. Their long hair almost covers them and on their pendulum breasts are swarms of spirit children who gather their sustenance therefrom. These women are the source of all life, each within her tribe producing spirit children of her own moiety."* But these women, we realize, are not first sources; they have their origin in turn in the telling of their story. In the communication of the story the narrator and the listeners have their source and all life has its source and draws eternal nourishment.

"Each Aranda or Juritja native has an immortal part or spirit double, whose immortality consists in eternally rejoining the Mother in the sacred totemic cave. From time to time they reidentify themselves with the eternal in them." It seems to Roheim that in the story *"they deny their great dependence upon Mother Nature and play the role of Mothers themselves."* But Mother Nature in the eternal bond with Man is Herself, as He is, the member of a cast in a drama. In the rites that Roheim sees as denials of dependence, we see the dancers reviving the human reality in all that is disturbing to union, involving themselves in, insisting upon, and taking their identity in, the loss of their identity, keeping the rime of their separation alive in the sound of their unity, rehearsing their exile in the place where they are. The flame springs up in a confusion of elements, times, places.

For the Freudian, it all rests in a *"psychical survival of the biologic unity with environment."* *"This 'oceanic feeling'* (Freud) *or 'dual unity situation'"*, Roheim argues, *"is something we all experience in our own lives; it is the bond that unites mother and child."* *"By taking the tjurunga along on his wanderings the native never gives up the original bond of dual unity which ties infant to his mother."*

From the unity once known between Mother and Child, the boy is initiated in a rite in which things once unified in feeling are shown as separated—this is the anatomization of the Australian scene, where parts of the body are exhibited as independent entities; but it is also the anatomization practices in which the poet is born, where words once unified in the flow of speech—the Mother tongue which in turn had been articulated from the flow of sounds in the child's earlier initiation—are shown as articulated—separated into particular sounds, syllables, meanings—in order to be reorganized in an other unity in which the reality of separation is kept as a conscious factor. The "Mother" is now the World, and the "Child" is the Self. The World is revealed as a "Creation" or "Poetry" or "Stage", and the Self, as "Creator" or "Poet". The man or the hero begins his life that demands something of him, a wandering quest of something known in the unknown. Taking with him the quest itself as his Mother, as the Australian takes the tjurunga or the devout Kabbalist the Shekina, he is to be most at home in his exile.

*

Roheim telling about his Australian natives does not mean to initiate us into the Aranda but through his creation of the Aranda in our minds to initiate us into the psychoanalytic fiction. The old men prancing, bleeding themselves and showing their private parts; the emu ancestors, the eternal ones who come in the dream, the primordial Mother and Child, are people not of the Australian bush but of a creative book, haunted by *"the wanderings of human beings from the cradle to the grave in a web of daydream,"* as the author of this mankind himself wanders in a web of psychoanalytic reverie. *"In the eternal ones of the dream it is we who deny decay and aggression and object-loss, and who guard eternal youth and reunion with the mother,"* Roheim writes in his coda:

> The old and decrepit men of the tribe become young and glorious once more. Covered with birds' down, the life symbol, they are identified with the eternally youthful ancestors. Mankind, the eternal child, *splendide mendax*, rises above reality...The path is Eros, the force that delays disintegration; and hence the promise held forth in the daydream and in its dramatization is no illusion after all. The *tjurunga* which symbolises both the male and female genital organ, the primal scene and combined parent concept, the father and the mother, separation and reunion...represents both the path and the goal."

This *tjurunga* we begin to see not as the secret identity of the Aranda initiate but as our own Freudian identity, the conglomerate consciousness of the mind we share with Roheim. "Above and below, left and right," the Kabbalist would have added in drawing his figure of the primordial man. The whole story is "daydream", a "web", and we are not sure that because the path is Eros, the promise may be "no illusion after all". The hero is the eternal child, but he is also *splendide mendax*, a glorious maker of fictions, in which all the conglomerate of what Man is might be contained. The simple *tjurunga* now appears to be no longer simple but the complex mobile, that Giedion on *Mechanization Takes Command* saw as most embodying our contemporary experience: *"the whole construction is aerial and hovering as the nest of an insect"*—a suspended system, so contrived that *"a draft of air or push of a hand will change the state of equilibrium and the interrelations of suspended elements...forming predictable, ever-changing constellations and so imparting to them the aspect of space-time."*

If, as in Malraux's *Psychology of Art*, we see painting and sculpture not only as discrete works but also as participants in a drama of forms playing throughout the time of man, so that what were once thought of as masterpieces of their time and place are now seen anew as moving expressions of—but more than expressions, creations and creators of—spiritual life, as acts of drama of what Man is that has not come to its completion, but which we imagine as a changing totality called Art; so poems too begin to appear as members of a hovering system called Poetry. The draft of air or the touch of a hand reappears now as the inspiration or impulse of mind that will change states and interrelations— *"time in the composition comes now,"* Gertude Stein puts it, *"and this what is troubling everyone the time in the composition is now a part of distribution and equilibration"* — *"past the danger point"* —throughout the history of Man. History itself, no longer kept within the boundaries of periods or nations, appears as a mobile structure in which events may move in time in ever-changing constellations. The effort of Toynbee's *Study of History*, beyond Spengler's comparison of civilizations, is towards an interpenetration of what before seemed discrete even alien areas of the life of man. Present, past, future, may then appear anywhere in changing constellations, giving life and depth to time. The Eternal Return, no longer conceived of as bound to revolutions of a wheel—the mandala of a Ptolemaic universe or of a Jungian Self—beyond the "organic" concept Toynbee derives from Vico's life cycles, we begin to see now as an insistence of figure in an expanding universe of many relations. The Composition is there, we are here. But now the Composition and we too are never finished, centered, perfected. We are in motion and our meaning lies not in some last or lasting judgment, in some evolution or dialectic toward a higher force or consciousness, but in the content of the whole of us as Adam—the totality of mankind's experience in which our moment, this vision of a universal possibility, plays its part; and beyond, the totality of life experience in which Man plays His part, not central, but in every living moment creating a new crisis in the equilibration of the whole. The whole seen as a mobile is a passionate impermanence in which Time and Eternity are revealed as One.

Elie Faure in *The Spirit of Forms* (from which, as from Spengler's *The Decline of the West*, Malraux's thought, we take it, develops) writes:

> We have reached a critical point in history when it becomes impossible for us to think profoundly—or to create, I imagine—if we isolate ourselves in the adventure of our race, if we refuse to demand a confirmation of our own presentiments from the expression in words or in the arts that other races have given themselves…One of the miracles of this time is that an increasing number of spirits should become capable not only of tasting the delicate or violent savor of these reputedly contradictory works and finding them equally intoxicating

(he speaks here of those fetishes and cathedral statues that Malraux in his work is to find "sinister" in their colloquy) but

> even more than that, they can grasp, in the seemingly opposed characters, the inner accords that lead us back to man and show him to us everywhere animated by analogous passions, as witnessed by all the idols, for all of them are marked by the accent of these passions…The critical spirit has become a universal poet. It is necessary to enlarge inordinately, and unceasingly, the circle of its horizon.

This "we" was "an increasing number," but it was also, Faure saw, a few, an élite—a cult, then, of *"the mobility of the spirit, favored by the exigencies of environment and the mixture of the species,"* projecting *"a limitless visible field of emotion and activity,"* towards a cathexis of all that was known of man and the word, in terms of an open and expanding consciousness, as our Aranda initiates project their field of emotion and activity in terms of a tribal consciousness as an enclosure of time and space. For the Australian, the hardness of Nature herself drives him out from his home-place. The Aranda is a man of an actual wasteland where he is again and again forced to wander in times of drought and famine when a man in want of water often opens a vein in his arm to drink the blood, and the brotherhood of the tribe must be kept in a constant imagination against the hunger in which men eat each other. Here the "we" is a term of survival itself. The creative fiction—the tribal narrative, the eternal ones of the dream, the spirit doubles, and the immortal sky-mothers—has its intensity of realization in the traumatic experience of the actual environment.

The esoteric tradition in Jewish mysticism again had its intensity in the loss of the home-land and in the long wandering in exile as children of a spirit-Mother, the Shekinah. She was the Glory, but She was also the Queen or Mother or Lady, and She might appear, as She does in The Zohar, as a great bird under whose celestial wings the immortal spirit-children of Israel nestled. The Jews, like the Aranda, lived in a threatening environment that called forth, if they were to survive, an insistent creation, the tenacity of a daydream to outlast the reality principle.

For the Imagists in London in 1912 there had already been exile. Pound, Eliot, and H.D., had sought a new spiritual home among eternal ones of the European dream, among Troubadors or the Melic poets, in refuge from the squalor and stupidity of the American mercantile, industrial and capitalist world—"the American dream", it was called. Joyce had chosen a voluntary exile from Ireland, "dear dirty Dublin"; and Lawrence had fled from his environment in the industrial working class village to wander in exile in search of his own Kingdom of the Sun.

It was the World War that provided the traumatic crisis—it was the very face of the civilization showing through at last, the triumph of squalor and stupidity where the cult of profits and the cult of empire combined to exact their tribute, and the other cult-world of the poetic vision was challenged as a reality. Only in the imagination would beauty survive. *"I would bid them live,"* Pound sings in his Envoi to *Mauberley* in 1919—

> As roses might, in magic amber laid,
> Red overwrought with orange and all made
> One substance and one colour
> Braving time...

He addresses in the Envoi a "her," whose *"graces give/Life to the moment"*—a Lady *"that sang me once that song of Lawes,"* but also a Mother that the Imagist poets had taken—Beauty. To survive in spirit men must be reborn in Beauty's magic amber, for the rest were revealed by War where

> Died some pro patria, non dulce non et decor
> walked eye-deep in hell
> believing old men's lies, then unbelieving
> came home, home to a lie
> home to many deceits,
> home to old lies and new infamy...

"Wrong from the start—" Pound describes himself: *"No,"*—

> ...hardly, but, seeing he had been born
> In a half savage country, out of date...

Richard Grossinger

ALCHEMY: PRE-EGYPTIAN LEGACY, MILLENNIAL PROMISE

I. Definitions

Alchemy is a form that comes to us from most ancient times. Its survival bespeaks numerous redefinitions and rebirths, many of them known to us from texts (Egyptian, Greek, Roman, Christian European, Islamic, Hindu, Taoist), but an equally large number no doubt occurring in preliterate times or among unknown peoples. There is no *single* alchemy, or there is only an intrinsic natural event transmitted in symbols across time and space.

Today alchemy survives in two different contexts. It is discarded as the primitive predecessor of chemistry and, as such, is a frozen landscape of museum pieces and quaint terminology with only archaeological or decorative usefulness. It is also honored in the underground and other millenary circles as a spiritual-magical science of great profundity and a source of creative energies. We can speak about the alchemists, but, for the most part, we cannot speak *for* them. Those who did alchemy beneath other blue skies on other green and brown earths are gone forever from this condition, and with them is gone a direct knowledge of what the work was.

I finally accept alchemy as a riddle, a riddle larger than our time. I can do little to resolve the contradictory claims of alchemists from different centuries and continents, except to suggest that they shared a process that was also larger than their times.

Despite all the ambiguities it is possible to summarize the basic components of a definition of alchemy. Some of them stand in contradiction and none of them are required in any given alchemical instance, but together they mark the ground from which alchemy arises:

1. A theory of nature as made up of primary elements (four in Greek alchemy, five in Chinese alchemy).
2. A belief in the gradual evolution and transformation of substance.
3. A system for inducing transmutation.
4. The imitation of nature by a gentle technology.
5. The faith that one's inner being is changed by participation in external chemical experiments.
6. A general system of synchronistic correspondences between planets, herbs, minerals, species of animals, signs and symbols, parts of the body, etc., known as the Doctrine of Signatures.
7. Gold as the completed and perfected form of the metals, in specific, and substance in general. (Alchemy is the attempt to transmute other substance into gold, however that attempt is understood and carried out.)
8. The existence of a paradoxical form of matter, sometimes called The Philosophers' Stone (the *lapis*), which can be used in making gold or in brewing elixirs and medicines that have universal curative properties.

9. A method of symbolism working on the simultaneity of a series of complementary pairs: Sun/Moon, Gold/Silver, Sulphur/Mercury, King/Queen, Male/Female, Husband/Bride, and Christ/Man.

10. The search for magical texts that come from a time when the human race was closer to the source of things or are handed down from higher intelligences, extraterrestrials, aliens, guardians, or their immediate familiars during some Golden Age (in Greece, Egypt, Atlantis, or before). These texts deal with the creation or synthesis of matter and are a blueprint for physical experimentation in a cosmic context (as well as for personal development). They have been reinterpreted in terms of the Earth's different epochs and nationalities.

11. In the Occident, alchemy is early inductive experimental science and is closely allied with metallurgy, pharmacy, industrial chemistry, and coinage.

12. In the Orient, alchemy is a system of meditation in which one's body is understood as elementally and harmonically equivalent to the field of creation.

(Between East and West, the body may be thought of as a microcosm of nature, with its own deposits of seeds, elixirs, and mineral substances.)

13. Alchemy is joined to astrology in a set of meanings that arise from the correspondences of planets, metals, and parts of the body, and the overall belief in a cosmic timing that permeates nature.

Writes Kenneth Rexroth in his preface to the works of Thomas Vaughn: "Alchemy as a subject is not just mystifying, it is intrinsically improbable. It is as though a textbook of chemistry, another of mining engineering, another of geology and mineralogy, another of physiology, several sex manuals, and many treatises of transcendental mysticism had been torn to pieces and not just mixed up together, but fused into a totally new chemical compound of thought."[1]

Alchemy is fundamentally involved with a mystery; and, though it is not identified so simply as saying it is the mystery of life itself, and man in this place of creation, it is almost that mystery. It *is* that mystery not in the abstract but as an ongoing series of exercises man must carry out in order to fulfill a destiny his mere existence, his "magical emergence" from sperm and egg in uterus, already fulfills.

II. History
A - Ethnogeology

The only artifacts that survive from the first societies three million years ago are stone tools, and though we have no grounds on which to claim a specifically magical use of stone, we know from existing native societies that stone, rock, crystal, and gem are powerful images and sigils. In systems we have record of, stones are related to higher consciousness, the heavens, and seeds of original matter. The Earth itself is a big stone, the stars are ethereal gems. Meteoric iron in the North American Arctic is a fiery celestial visitor from the land of lights.

Quartz is assigned special powers in Aboriginal Australian shamanism, as a window into the astral zone. There are the holy stones of Islam and Greek Christianity; Ka'aba, Petra; the Lapis of the Romans and Europeans; the fabulous stones of the East: the gems and rubies of India and China, seeds of inner consciousness. Precious stones have also been found in the charred corpses of the great masters, at the chakras from the internalization of the spirit. The early shaman-smiths went into caves and brought out telluric iron, a dark matricial stone containing all future technology even as it sustained a chthonian mystery. The Egyptians were still practicing this magic and medicine at the dawn of civilization. They had inherited the black earth, the medicinal powders, the hieroglyphs, the potions, from some older time. Eliade reminds us that this is the origin of alchemy, and that gold was a relative latecomer:

> "If, therefore, alchemy could not be born from the desire to counterfeit gold (gold assay had been known for at least twelve centuries), nor from a Greek scientific technique (we have...seen the alchemists' lack of interest in physico-chemical phenomena as such), we are compelled to look elsewhere for the origins of this discipline *sui generis*. Much more than the philosophic theory of the unity of matter, it was probably the old conception of the Earth-Mother, bearer of embryo-ores, which crystallized faith in artificial transmutation (that is, operated in a laboratory). It was the encounter with the symbolisms, myths and techniques of the miners, smelter and smiths which probably gave rise to the first alchemical operations. But above all it was the experimental discovery of the *living* Substance, such as it was felt by the artisans, which must have played the decisive role. Indeed, it is the conception of a *complex and dramatic Life of Matter* which constitutes the originality of alchemy as opposed to classical Greek science. One is entitled to suppose that the *experience of dramatic life* was made possible by the knowledge of Graeco-oriental mysteries."[2]

Harran, a town on the Syrian Euphrates, retained elements of Sumerian, Hittite, and Babylonian practice, as well as later Persian and Egyptian rites, well into the middle ages. Ancient metallurgical traditions could be observed in practice there long after they had passed elsewhere. Lindsay writes:

> "The temple of Kronos had an image of the god in Lead; the associated colour was Black, the geometrical structure of the temple was hexagonal, and the number of steps to the image's throne was Nine. The corresponding systems of the other six deities were as follows: Zeus, Tin, Green, Triangular, Eight; Ares, Iron, Red, Oblong, Seven; the Sun, Gold (hung with Pearls), Square, Six; Aphrodite, Copper, Blue, Triangle (with one side longer than the other two), Five; Hermes, an Alloy of all the metals (with Mercury in the hollow interior), Brown, Hexagonal (with square interior), Four (circular); the Moon, Silver, White, Pentagonal, Three. At the Wednesday service in the temple of

Hermes a Brown Youth, who was a good scribe, was killed and quartered; the quarters were separately burned and the ashes thrown in the image's face."[3]

Geological alchemy led to metallurgy, but it also led to shamanism, the great-grandsire of hermeticism. The metallurgical craft-fraternities were mystery cults with long traditions. They worshipped the living stone as a heavenly force lodged in the earth. To the Aborigines of Australia, giant rocks have remained oscillations of another time and space immersed in this one as they sit in the desert changing color in the degrees of day and night. Inanimate anchors in the current epoch, they are living bodies in the Dream Time. Eliade reviews the residue of this consciousness:

"Mining rites persisted in Europe up to the end of the Middle Ages; every sinking of a new mine was accompanied by religious ceremonies. But we must look elsewhere in order to estimate the antiquity and complexity of these traditions. For the expression of these rites, their purpose, their underlying ideology, vary at different cultural levels. In the first instance, one notes the desire to appease the spirits guarding or inhabiting the mine. 'The Malayan miner,' writes A. Hale, 'has peculiar ideas about tin and its properties. Above all, he believes that tin is under the orders and protection of certain spirits which he finds it necessary to appease. Likewise he believes that tin is alive and possesses many of the properties of living matter. It can, by itself, move from one spot to another; it can reproduce itself and it has special sympathies, perhaps affinities, for certain people and things, and vice-versa. And so it is urged that the ore of tin be treated with a certain respect, that note be taken of its special qualities and, what is perhaps still more curious, that the exploitation of the mine be directed in such a way that the tin ore may be extracted without its knowledge.' "[4]

The power images of alchemy (the stone, the sword, the forge, the sudden fire, the burst of gold) have a patriarchal and archaic ring; they rise, metahistorically, from Palaeolithic hunting bands whose rough metal-work the smith sodalities of later tribal communities inherited. But, like all things arising through human consciousness, this heavy metal cast a shadow, and from the shadow rose its Other in psyche. There is then the alchemy of yielding, transmuting forms; the waters, the extremely low fire, the medicinal healing, the mercurial agent, the marriage of opposites. These are matrilocal, civilizational; they are no doubt informed by the mysteries of plant and animal worlds.

Although the actual process was no doubt more complicated, we can argue that there is first an alchemy of stone, followed by an alchemy of herb. There is an alchemy of weapon and tool (iron, then bronze), and there is, later, an alchemy of athanor and alembic. Fire was melter and binder of tough ores, but it was also the subtle and incomprehensible heat of sexual union. Like the plants of the cultivated garden, stones were considered fertile too, though in their own way and on their own scale. There seemed no reason why the partitive clonal sexuality of flower, root, and vine should not extend to minerals, with their even more invisible seeds. The metals, in particular, had become sterile from their long abode in large underground deposits; they required a slow gestation and nourishing for awakening. Alchemical writings of all ages recall the famous garden of the stones:

> "The farmer knows the differing conditions by which plants may be made to multiply, and the alchemist likewise must know what treatment the metals demand from nature to give forth their special and characteristic result, and the virtues of the right metal needed to produce the Philosophers' Stone.
>
> "...metals have a life of their own, equal to animals and vegetables... This fact is not immediately obvious owing to the shortness of human life compared to the long stretches of time necessary for minerals to gestate and develop imperceptibly those changes in nature whilst they are in the earth."[5]
>
> "What Nature did in the beginning we can do equally well by following Nature's processes. What perhaps Nature is still doing, assisted by the time of centuries, in her subterranean solitudes, we can make her accomplish in a single moment, by helping her and placing her in more congenial circumstance. As we make bread, so we will make metals. Without us, the harvest would not ripen in the fields; without our millstones the corn would not turn to flour; nor the flour to bread by stirring and baking. Let us then co-operate with nature in its agricultural labours, and treasures will be opened to all."[6]
>
> "Not only among palm trees do male and female exist: they exist among all vegetable species, and likewise among minerals do we find the natural division between male and female."[7]
>
> "Furthermore, in the union of mercury and sulphur with the ore, the sulphur behaves like the male seed and the mercury like the female seed in the conception and birth of a child."[8]

B - Planet Science

The most conventional alchemical images arise in Egypt, but they alone do not explain the different versions of alchemy spread throughout ancient Europe and Asia. Apparently alchemy arises again and again archetypally from the human soul. Some alchemical techniques and philosophies pass between cultures, but they become part of the continuous interplay of technology, symbols, and imaginal desire as archetypes and sciences sequentially absorb each other.

In this sense alchemy belongs, with astrology, healing, music, and mathematics, to the collegium of planet sciences that survive civilizations. The identification of these sciences as "Atlantean" gives a sense of their simultaneous legendary and futurist character. Although present from the dawn of our species, they regularly herald the "new age" of each civilization.

Planet sciences not only transcend civilizations, they reflect civilizational changes. Since they are larger than any one aeon they tend to absorb and neutralize the work of that aeon, projecting outward as necessary attention the work that is undone. Alchemy could never be a testable science like physics, for it would always contain insoluble even unknown elements; in other words, its development is synchronistic and rhythmic not linear and progressive.

Although we can point to distinct historical appearances, the arts and sciences have no specific places or times of origin. As man intuits qualities implicit in the created world he must simultaneously develop the categories that go with them. External events become indistinguishable from the symbols for which they were the inspiration or confirming visions. Working with stone at the dawn of time (later with metals) was an initiation into the mysteries of stellar and disembodied spirits, for shapes and specters arose from the forge and the cave without precedent or explanation. Once man had embarked on the journey into consciousness the spiritual recalled the metallurgical and the metallurgical recalled the spiritual. The proto-alchemist was already empowered by the transmission of ancient formulas.

Claude Lévi-Strauss the anthropologist and Carl Jung the psychologist both hold that there is an ongoing correspondence between the structures of our minds (which originate in human nature) and nature itself (which is the matrix of human nature). While Jung assigns meanings derived from archetypes to these patterns of thought, Lévi-Strauss interprets them on a case by case basis according to single discrete intersections of environment and cultural history (the anatomy of the nervous system is presumed as the universal ground of all environments). It is no small difference; all of Darwinian thought lies between them. Jung locates human activities at the intersection of psyche and cosmos, both of which occur outside of conventional time and space, whereas Lévi-Strauss explains all cultural phenomena in terms of physiology, geography, and sociology, and rejects philosophical dualism in contemporary phenomenological fashion:

> "Ideal and real, abstract and concrete...can no longer be opposed to each other. What is immediately 'given' to us is neither the one nor the other, but something which lies betwixt and between, that is, already encoded by the sense organs as well as by the brain, *a text* which, like any text, must be first decoded to translate it into the language of other texts. Furthermore, the physico-chemical processes according to which this original text was primitively encoded are not substantially different from the analytical procedures which the mind uses in order to decode it...It is not being mentalist or idealist to acknowledge that the mind is only able to understand the world around us because the mind, when trying to understand it, only applies operations which do not differ in kind from those going on in the natural world itself." ("Structuralism and Ecology.")[9]

> "...even when raised to that human level which alone can make them

intelligible, man's relations with his natural environment remain objects of thought: man never perceives them passively; having reduced them to concepts, he compounds them in order to arrive at a system which is never determined in advance: the same situation can be systematized in various ways. The mistake of Mannhardt and the Naturalist School was to think that natural phenonmena are *what* myths seek to explain, when they are rather the *medium through which* myths try to explain facts which are themselves not of a natural but a logical order." (*The Savage Mind*)[10]

This structuralist tradition leaves us sitting rather uncomfortably inside the brain. That is, Lévi-Strauss has traced all matter back into the mind, but he has derived mind entirely from matter by Darwinian evolution. In the alchemical sense he has not combined the material and the spiritual paths; instead, by following the material path alone he has entered a psychospiritual realm only at the end of all possible space.

There is however an alchemical aspect to this grail, for the alchemists sought their own original document—the instructions from the Masters of their Order who, in a certain sense, were inside Nature herself, the primordial repository of signs and signatures. All cosmologies thus originate in "the savage mind," the mind of the wild prehuman spirits, even as all languages emerge from the deep structure of the nervous system behind speech.

Only later do we come upon specific philosophy-science, named "alchemy" as a Greek-Arabic business looking back into Egypt. *Kemia*, with an eta instead of an epsilon, is an old Greek form for the native name of Egypt (land of *Khem*, from the hieroglyph, *Khmi*, 'black earth,' in contrast to desert sand); this was later confused with the Greek *chymeia*, 'pouring,' 'infusion,' from the verb *che-ein*[11] 'to pour,' with an epsilon instead of an eta—both of these derived from *chymos*, 'juice,' 'sap.' Alchemy was considered an ancient Egyptian art in the transmutation of gold and silver, and its name was taken on gradually, perhaps unconsciously, by the participants themselves in a numinous event.

C - Egyptian, Greek, and Christian Alchemy

Egyptian alchemy was primarily a chemical-magical system which overlapped with the technologies of dyeing, brewing, gilding, baking, perfume-making, metallurgy, and embalming. All Egyptian technology in fact was engaged in mediation between the supernatural realm described in the *Egyptian Book of the Dead* and the properties of natural substance. Mummies were bodies frozen as souls; the oil on their flesh and the gold on their fingernails bound them to Osiris and Horus. The Babylonian inheritance of amalgamating metals became a series of spiritual initiations.

We do not know much about the actual alchemy of the Egyptians, but we intuit that, if it existed at all as a discrete thing, it was an invocation of phenomena rather than an inquiry into spirit and matter. Yet because Egyptian civilization was in the process of developing technology alchemy became the cutting edge of the new science, a position it has held in the West until (perhaps) relatively recent times.

The Greeks inherited one level of their alchemy from the Egyptians, possibly by way of Arabia after it had been transformed in Persia and the vast Eurasian border zone. The magical aspects of this foreign chemistry were no doubt influenced by Aegean mythology and shamanism, and the scientific parts were taken into a nascent Western psychology and physics. The pre-Socratic philosophers wanted to know of what matter was composed, how the invisible generated the visible, why motion was sustained, and where mind lay in the formation of things. Between the ancient Cronian forces of Olympus and the visible world of matter lay a zone of differential qualities. Earth, air, fire and water were born here as atomic principles of the inside of creation. They informed Paracelsus' Salt, Sulphur, and Mercury, and all future alchemical thought.

European alchemy retained these ancient meanings in the context of its own local cults and ethnosciences. Druid totems and star-alphabets derived from Stonehenge and other Mesolithic shrines participated in a revised system of elemental meanings. Over the centuries, the West has added gnostic, qabbalistic, and protoscientific levels, while Egyptian and Persian aspects (as well as Sumerian and Babylonian ones) have been absorbed deeper and more obscurely into the "planet science." Alchemy is never modern; it may "forget" a reference, but it cannot cast off its overgrowth like newborn biologies and astrophysics. It continues to echo what it no longer explicitly contains.

For the Medieval Christian, chemical and theological inquiry inevitably entwined. The formation of the Stone was an act of piety and devotion, for the alchemist with his jars and alembics was re-enacting (through matter itself) the Resurrection. Christ was perceived as a living seed within substance, a God who could be liberated from matter by chemistry. Paracelsus brings His Voice into a physical recipe:

> "Go away, ye cursed, into everlasting fire, prepared from eternity for Satan and the devils. For I was hungry and you did not feed Me; I was thirsty and you gave Me no drink; I was sick, and a prisoner, and naked, but you did not visit Me, did not set Me free, did not clothe Me."

But the alchemist was not fooled by the Church; he fed, he clothed, he exalted.

> "For I was hungry and you gave Me food; I was thirsty and you gave Me to drink; I was a stranger and you received Me; I was naked and you clothed Me; I was sick and you visited Me; I was in prison and you came to Me. So will I receive you also into My Father's house, in which are the many mansions of the saints."[12]

According to Carl Jung, Christianity had become sterile and authoritarian even by the Middle Ages. It had lost the unconscious meaning of its own rituals. Alchemy thus becomes the compensation for the Church's secular kingdom. "The point is that alchemy is rather like an undercurrent to the Christianity that ruled on the surface. It is to this surface as dream is to consciousness, and just as the dream compensates the conflicts of the conscious mind, so alchemy endeavors to fill in the gaps left by the Christian tension of opposites."[13] The alchemist then reclaimed the pagan sources of the Christian mystery, but even as he became the shaman-priest, he foreshadowed the chemist who would also become cut off from the roots of his ritual. Pagan restoration is ever the millennial task of alchemy:

"Whereas in the Church the increasing differentiation of ritual and dogma alienated consciousness from its natural roots in the unconsciousness, alchemy and astrology were ceaselessly engaged in preserving the bridge to nature, *i.e.*, to the unconscious psyche, from decay...

"...while the dogmas of the Church offered analogies to the alchemical process, these analogies, in strict contrast to alchemy, had become detached from the world of nature through their connection with the historical figure of the Redeemer. The alchemical four in one, the philosophical gold, the *lapis angularis*, the *aqua divina*, became, in the Church, the four-armed cross on which the Only-Begotten had sacrificed himself once in history and at the same time for all eternity. The alchemists ran counter to the Church in preferring to seek through knowledge rather than to find through faith, though as medieval people they never thought of themselves as anything but good Christians."[14]

Laboratory alchemy is not a parallel of the Mass; it is the authentic event of which the Mass has become an empty symbol. The alchemist is engaged in actual redemption of matter; the clergyman is left with the legitimization of doctrine.

"By pronouncing the consecrating words that bring about the transformation, the priest redeems the bread and wine from their elemental imperfection as created things. This idea is quite unchristian; it is alchemical. Whereas Catholicism emphasizes the effectual presence of Christ, alchemy is interested in the fate and manifest redemption of substances, for in them the divine soul lies captive and awaits the redemption that is granted to it at the moment of release...For the alchemist, the one primarily in need of redemption is not man, but the deity who is lost and sleeping in matter."[15]

Jung reports that even in current times "regressive development faithfully retreads the path of history to reach the pre-Christian level." So two dreams demonstrate the pagan landscape into which Christianity falls as soon as spiritual doubt punctures it. The first is the "dream of a clergyman who has a rather problematical attitude to his faith; *Coming into his church at night, he finds that the whole wall of the choir has collapsed. The altar and ruins are overgrown with vines hanging full of grapes, and the moon is shining through the gap.*

"Again, a man who was much occupied with religious problems had the following dream: *An immense Gothic cathedral, almost completely dark. High Mass is being celebrated. Suddenly the whole wall of the aisle collapses. Blinding sunlight bursts into the interior together with a large herd of bulls and cows."*[16]

Modernism was never quite able to remove Christianity from alchemy, but it forced it in so deep that spiritual being fused with the perception of physical substance, and God became an experiment in matter. It is with Christianity that European alchemy unmistakeably takes on its criterion of personal evolution for scientific success. The alchemist must be the moral equivalent of the creative force of nature, or fail. This warning hangs in abeyance yet.

D - Gold

The making of gold was the stereotyped standard for the alchemists even by the Renaissance (as uninformed parodies show), but it is a misleading concretization of a series of transformations. The alchemical process is a mode of exploring nature and transforming inner being; it is not a formula for precious metals. Leading to gold or failing gold, the experiment has an underlying authenticity.

In fact, the gold of the alchemists has changed from civilization to civilization. Aurification of other metals was a suitable "transmutation" in Egypt, and it remained so in ancient Europe. The Egyptian alchemist was satisfied with gold coatings and gold-colored alloys. Later there were respectable formulas for turning 24-carat gold into 19- or 10-carat gold. Objects containing some gold could be made more golden by treatment with sulphuric and hydrochloric acids on the surface or by gilding with a gum and some "lesser" metal (such as lead) which was then melted off by oxidation. Crafted gold and spiritual gold have been locked in an alchemical paradox for aeons, but it is likely that the vocational lineage of gold-craftsmen preceded spiritual alchemy by at least centuries and, through the ascension of technological culture, has exacted its regular due in gems, weaponry, and coins.

According to historian Jack Lindsay alchemists "used four main methods in gold-making; they produced yellow alloys of base metals like brass; they prepared debased gold; they superficially coloured metals or alloys; they tried a set of complicated processes in which distilled liquids were used or in which metals were subjected to the action of vapours...

"The brass-like alloys (including some of the alloys of copper, tin, zinc), which have been made in modern times under names like ormolu or mannheim-gold, were known to the alchemists. They prepared them by smelting mixtures of copper, tin, etc. with *kadmia* (a mixture of metallic oxides with a variable proportion of zinc, found in the flues of the furnaces)...As for brass alloys, the alchemists seem to have prepared a number of them with copper as the main ingredient, plus tin, lead, zinc, iron, silver, mercury, or some of these. Doublings of gold, so-called, probably often involved copper and silver. Silver gives gold a greenish, copper a reddish tinge; the admixture of both copper and silver hardly altered the hue...

"Superficial colouring was probably understood for what it was, at least to some extent; it is called tinging, not making of gold. Then as now, three main methods were used. The metal was coated with a tinted lacquer of gums; solutions were laid on to form a layer of sulphides; the base metal in debased gold was removed from the surface by corrosive substances so that a layer of fairly pure gold was left showing. (The corrosive would be something like sulphur trioxide got by calcining sulphates of iron and copper.)"[17]

Nowadays nuclear physicists can also make gold. In fact, a little-discussed coincidence is that mercury follows gold in the periodic table of the elements (79 for gold, 80 for mercury), which means that gold can be produced, in small amounts, by the nuclear bombardment of mercury. The physicists Sherr, Bainbridge, and Anderson did exactly this in 1941; they transmuted a radioactive isotope of mercury into gold. The quality and quantity of gold produced by such a method would hardly satisfy either the Egyptian gilder or the Christian magician, but then many of the gilded golds of the alchemists would have as little use for modern metallurgists or even spiritual alchemists. The minerals change semantically even as they do chemically.

One aspect of gold that gave it particular resonance in the European psyche was its basis of currency. Although his predecessors were also minters, the Mediaeval alchemist dramatized the fantasy of striking it rich by making currency for himself and his patrons. As Europe's access to real gold and the means of coinage dwindled after the fall of Rome and the Muslim conquests, the fantasy of gold increased, giving birth to the alchemical materialization. The historian Marc Bloch writes:

> "If anyone had ever wanted to see great masses of gold in 9th- and 10th-century Europe, anywhere outside Byzantium, he could probably only have done so in Scandinavia. 'Piracy,' so Adam of Bremen informs us, had caused precious metals to be heaped up in the island of Zealand; it glistened from the prows of Cnut the Great's vessels, as it still gleams nowadays in the museum showcases of Stockholm and Copenhagen, whose treasures recall the heroic age. But it was precisely these countries who were at that period ignorant of the art of minting. Gold was used for ornament; and if it was sometimes used for the payment of wages, it was only in the form of gold bracelets which the chiefs 'broke' and then distributed to their followers."[18]

As the Crusades showed too, Europe often reached back into tribal mythologies, confusing its socioeconomic plight with another equally unresolved spiritual crisis. This is the gap gold actively bridged.

E - Alchemy, Astrology, and Chemistry

Alchemy and astrology are not parallels. They are both aspects of the planetary science of cosmic-elemental origins, and they have different relationships to secular sciences. Traditional alchemy was susceptible to the type of partial solution chemistry offered. The microscope marked the end of traditional alchemy and the herbal medicine and Doctrine of Signatures that were its allies. With the microscope came a new way of looking into substance, and we have not yet recovered from our curiosity about infrastructure to seek the real center anew. Astrology continues in its traditional form because there is no equivalent tool for viewing the infra-structure of time and rhythm (the telescope is merely a specialized adaptation of the microscope, conferring no new dimensions). As chemistry is to alchemy, astronomy is *not* to astrology. Astrology remains the science of pure time and correspondence in the largest field of correlatable events, while alchemy's kingdom has been divided among a number of sciences and possible sciences, including chemistry, including psychology (as Jung has shown), and also, of course, including modern astronomy and astrophysics.

Historically, astrology seems to come from a fusion of ancient calendric systems, which were both practical and predictive in nature, and a general theory of celestial influence is almost universally disregarded in scientific circles, with some notable exceptions in the fields of parapsychology and astro-biology which study the influence of celestial rhythms on terrestrial life in certain contexts.

Astronomy is a geography and geology of outer space, and it does not cross with basic astrology. The pattern of stars and planets, as an event is too remote and obscure to have any other meaning or use, and the internal correspondences of personalities and predispositions belong to the psychology of types. Astrophysics is simply the field chemistry of heavenly objects, so it is clearly in alchemy's genealogy, not astrology's. In astrology then, internal and external events are inseparable, conceptually and as a system of language; there is no science which picks this up.

Astrology continues to be practiced today. Its relationship to society has changed, but essentially the same lines of cosmic-terrestrial synchronicity are drawn. Where, then, is alchemy? Certainly it does not merit columns in the daily paper or whole publishing companies devoted to its ongoing work.

Alchemy did not have to be transformed in order to become chemistry. It was always involved in matter and nature. Physics and chemistry are the literal realizations. Obvious alchemical techniques, as boiling to hasten, sealing to retain, burning to reduce, trapping the distillate with an alembic, gilding by quicksilver, in general, imitating and hastening nature, have all become part of modern scientific ideology and practice. Basil Valentine prepared hydrochloric acid from marine salt and oil of vitriol (sulphuric acid), extracted copper from its pyrites, first making copper sulphate, then soaking iron in the solvent; he got brandy from the distillation of wine and beer using carbonate of potassium.

Physics and chemistry uncouple from alchemy as they become obsessed with inanimate matter devoid of spiritual virtues. "The metallurgist's outlook on metals differs greatly from the alchemist's view. The latter looks upon metals as living things.....still unmade into some permanent form."[19]

No doubt, in the laboratories of the early scientists, alchemical experiments became chemical experiments without the participant even being aware he was crossing a boundary history would then fix. He still noted the color of the flame and the changing properties of the broth. His predecessors heeded spirits and divine waters, and his descendants would know only the laws of conservation of matter and energy and the elemental chart. At the turning point the alchemist was overwhelmed by the success of early (seventeenth- and eighteenth- century) physics and innovative technology. So wondrous were the demonstrations and uses of matter that he assumed these were the gifts of the old ones, the magi of his art. If he failed (at a certain moment of distraction) to assign the inner meaning, it is because he had come to take the internality of substance for granted. Physics were assumed to be spiritual also; for Isaac Newton, gravity was the demonstration of God. Who can tell spiritual from physical properties if both are known, alchemically, by their behavior as elemental ingredients? The reason alchemy ceased as a laboratory art is *exactly because it didn't*. The emphasis changed to purely external characteristics which had uses in society and on which mankind became dependent. The economic stratification of (ultimately) global industry arose in the laboratory of the sorcerors, and the technology maintains its fiefdom as jealously as any lord. The vitalistic phase of alchemy ended when we entrusted our survival to the secular aspect of matter: steel, plastic, and oil. But certain demons of alchemy prevailed. Could anyone doubt that looking out over New York City today? What other spirits would have given us telephones and satellites, laser beams and hydrogen bombs? Alchemy has taken place. The movement of the trucks, the enormous lit buildings, the planes shooting fire from their jets all prove it. Not only does this chemistry have an inside, but it is an inside which reflects the exact experiments we have done.

Seven long centuries ago—Archibald Cockren reminds us—the English alchemist Roger Bacon foresaw our transchemical situation: "He maintained that vessels might be constructed which would be capable of navigation without rowers, and which, under the direction of a single man, could travel through the water at a speed hitherto undreamt of. He also predicted that it would be equally possible to construct cars which 'might be set in motion with marvellous rapidity, independently of horses and other animals,' and flying machines which would beat the air with artificial wings."[20]

Mircea Eliade refuses the inevitability; to him it is the curse of alchemy corrupted:

> "The survival of the alchemist's ideology does not become immediately evident just when alchemy disappears from the pages of history and all its valid chemical knowledge is being integrated into chemistry. The new science of chemistry makes use only of those empirical discoveries which do not represent—however numerous and important one may suppose them to be—the true spirit of alchemy. We must not believe that the triumph of experimental science reduced to nought the dreams and ideals of the alchemist. On the contrary, the ideology of the new epoch, crystallized around the myth of infinite progress of industrializa-

tion which dominated and inspired the whole of the nineteenth century, takes up and carries forward—despite its radical secularization—the millenary dream of the alchemist. It is in the specific dogma of the nineteenth century, according to which man's true mission is to transform and improve upon Nature and become her master, that we must look for the authentic continuation of the alchemist's dream. The visionary's myth of the continuation of the perfection, or more accurately, of the redemption of Nature, survives in camouflaged form, in the pathetic programme of the industrial societies whose aim is the total transmutation of Nature, its transformation into 'energy.' It is in this nineteenth century, dominated by physico-chemical sciences and the upsurge of industry, that man succeeds in supplanting Time. His desire to accelerate the natural tempo of things by an ever more rapid and efficient exploitation of mines, coal-fields, and petrol deposits begins to come true. Organic chemistry, fully mobilized to wrest the secrets of the mineral basis of life, now opens the way to innumerable 'synthetic' products. And one cannot help noticing that these synthetic products demonstrate for the first time the possibility of eliminating Time and preparing, in factory and laboratory, substances which it would have taken Nature thousands and thousands of years to produce. And we know full well to what extent the 'synthetic preparation of life,' even in the modest form of a few cells of protoplasm, was the supreme dream of science throughout the whole second half of the nineteenth century and the beginning of the twentieth. Thus was the alchemist's dream too—the dream of creating the homunculus.''[21]

F - Rosicrucian Alchemy

Just before it was severed into exclusive scientific and occult traditions alchemy embodied both in a curious transitional technology which speaks directly still to the failed science of its daylight half. At its birth analytical method was subsumed in divination, and together they formed numbers and shapes that were simultaneously empirical and numerological. Astrology and physics, going different ways, crossed in the night. This "new alchemy" claimed an Egyptian lineage, with Oriental and Hebrew branches, but it most likely invented its own symbols and experiments and projected them back into an imaginary golden age. This is the alchemy of Robert Fludd, John Dee, Michael Maier, and the Rosicrucian Brotherhood of the Seventeenth Century. It is also the unconscious face of Robert Boyle and Isaac Newton, the occult face from which the "new physics" of the scholastic and industrial revolution turned away. But it is as fundamental to the history of atomic physics as it is to the history of modern magic. One alchemy goes toward occult societies, the other toward scientific academies. From the occult tradition follow the Masons, the theosophists, Aleister Crowley and the Golden Dawn, the later Rosicrucian sects, and the Builders of the Adytum. From the scientific tradition follow physics, astronomy, chemistry, geology, biology, and higher mathematics. Both have an alchemical origin at exactly that point where the qualities and quantities of matter merge.

The historian Frances Yates has written at length on this transmission. Her book *The Rosicrucian Enlightenment* discusses the relationship of an enlightened alchemical-scientific tradition to a conservative Catholic hierarchy at the onset of the Thirty Years War. At this moment in history (Western Europe, 1618) the distinction between magic and science is a narrow one in certain elite philosophical/political circles. Both are united as experimental progressive movements against a mystical dogma supported by the Church. Mediaeval alchemy, Paracelsist chemistry, and hermetic medicine are partially discarded by the new tradition which is anxious to develop the most modern "technology" possible and to use it to bring peace and prosperity to a Europe torn by political and religious warfare.

Yates describes this "new, or rather new-old, philosophy," as "primarily alchemical and related to medicine and healing, but also concerned with number and geometry and with the production of mechanical marvels. It represents, not only an advancement of learning, but above all an illumination of a religious and spiritual nature. This new philosophy is about to be revealed to the world and will bring about a general reformation."[22]

She calls it "Rosicrucian alchemy," saying, "By this I mean alchemy as revised and reformed by John Dee and of which his 'monas hieroglyphia' was the mysterious epitome. This alchemy included an intensive revival of the old alchemical tradition, but in some way added to the basic alchemical concepts, notions and practices deriving from the Cabala, the whole having a mathematical formulation. The adept who had mastered these formulae could move up and down the ladder of creation, from terrestrial matter, through the heavens, to the angels and God. This most ancient conception was in some manner brought alive in a new way through integration with Cabalistic and mathematical procedures."[23]

Whereas the full global technology of physics was withheld for three centuries, the Rosicrucian city seemed, by magical interpolation, to be at hand:

> "The plan of Christianopolis is based on the square and the circle. All its houses are built in squares, the largest external square enclosing a smaller one, which in turn encloses a smaller one, until the central square is reached which is dominated by a round temple. Officials of the city often have angel names, Uriel, Gabriel, and so on, and a Cabalistic and Hermetic harmony of macrocosm and microcosm, of the universe and man, is expressed through its symbolic plan. The description of the city is a fascinating mixture of the mystical and the practical. For example, the city is very well lighted; and this good lighting is of civic importance since it discourages crime and all evils which walk by night. It also has a mystical meaning, for this is a city which dwells in the light of God's presence."[24]

Even during its materialistic phases, alchemy has been primarily committed to a qualitative vision of matter: each substance is unique and has active properties that cannot be assayed from pure quanitative analysis. They can be modes of form like roundness, squareness, yellowness, twoness, or they can be molecular aspects: airness, wateriness, earthness, fireness. Either way, they suggest a componential vitalism because, even when they are partible and combinatory, they are so not in any numerical or regular way.

Lindsay discusses this in his book *The Origins of Alchemy in Graeco-Roman Egypt*:

> "[The Greeks] avoided all problems of mechanical causation...Instead, they asked what the nature of substance or identity was, and what were the links between the forms taken by substance. Relations thus became of extreme importance—*but relations regarded under the aspect of the powers or capacities of action residing inside the subject.* 'Relations were assumed to have the status of attributes securely anchored in the independently existing substance' (Cornford)."[25]

The single important "theory" was the conviction of the inner property of substance, which was rooted in its atomistic origin. It is the "quality" of sulphur, the "quality" of mercury that are used in alchemy, not the measurable substance of them. Substances were recognizable as things at all because they had indelible characteristics and behavior; they had the rudiments of "mind." The early Greeks were concerned with the underlying structure behind these characteristics, and their transmutability within a latent grid. Such a philosophy must contain a paradox: that unity is always involved in change, and change expresses unity. The qualitative reality of something, such as its yellowness or roundness, or its association with the Moon and silver, finally cannot be expressed quantatively and cannot be reduced to material categories, so it cannot evolve outside the maze.

It is no wonder that there are formulas, like Ostanes, for "the right testicle of an ass taken in wine or a bit of it worn as an amulet on a bracelet; or the foam of an ass after copulation, collected in a red cloth, and enclosed in silver." The homoeopaths were to gather dog's milk and pus of gonorrhea for similar reasons. Lindsay continues:

> "What the alchemists took over from classical Greek thought was the concrete sense of the object, the concentration on its qualities; but they attempted at the same time to break through the limitations of this attitude, not by ignoring qualities and concerning themselves solely with the quantitative mechanics and dynamics of objects in interrelation, but by putting the objects into interaction with one another as units composed of qualities. Their problem was that they could not effectively explore and extend this method without quantitative systems to provide a secure basis for their experimentations; the only way historically open for the creation of those systems lay through Philoponos and Galileo. Men were not able, as they are still not able, to deal simultaneously with

the... world of quantities and the... world of qualities.

"The alchemist sought to work outwards from the isolated bundle of qualities into the grasp of processes where objects remained whole and yet fused with one another into new unities. He failed in his objectives, because he tried to do too much with too little in hand; and with all his vast hopes he had far too limited a view of what the problems of material transformation involved. With his newly-found faith in the possibilities of transformation he had no sense at all of the stabilities or symmetries of organized matter, of the depths to which he must penetrate before he could touch the levels and the systems of transformation, of the minute and fugitive complexity of those systems. Despite the many tributes paid to Demokritos, no attempt was made to consider transformation at the atomic level. With the poor means of measurement at the disposal of scientists in ancient days we could not indeed expect any attempts to define elements at that level..."[26]

An occult symmetry returns to science a couple of millennia later, after quantification and measurement have permeated matter and claimed every nook and cranny of space and time. This suggests an oscillation throughout Western culture between two opposing insights (qualitative and quantitative) that seem to regenerate each other from within the insoluble riddle of psyche and matter. Post-quantitative qualitative thought is, of course, quite different from original elementalism. The alchemists were not yet capable of precise atomic measurement or analysis, but the analysis they did has a direct kinship with the later experiments of nuclear physics, as Werner Heisenberg was to recognize:

"The systematic thought of the Greek natural philosophers from Thales to Democritus had finally led to the problem of the smallest parts of matter. In place of the Parmenidean antithesis of being and non-being, with its termination in paradox, Democritus had postulated the antithesis between the full and the empty, *i.e.*, between atoms and empty space. The existent, according to Democritus, is present an infinite number of times, in the form of a minute, unchangeable and indivisible constituent of matter. The diversity of what happens in the world is attributed to the varying arrangement and motion of atoms in the void. Just as tragedy and comedy can be written out in the same letters, so the most diverse happenings, in Democritus' view, can be actualized by means of the same atoms. But as to the nature of the atoms, and why they are just so and not otherwise, there is no further inquiry. The atoms are the ultimate given; they are indivisible and unchangeable, that which truly exists, from which everything is to be explained but which is itself in no need of further explanation.

"Plato also took over significant elements of the atomic theory. To the four elements—earth, water, air, and fire—for him, correspond four kinds of smallest particle. In Plato's view, these elementary particles are basic mathematical structures of high symmetry. The smallest particles of the element earth are conceived as cubes, those of the element water as icosahedra, those of the element air as octahedra and finally those of the element fire as tetrahedra. But for Plato these elementary particles are not indivisible. They can be broken down into triangles and again be built up out of triangles. From two elementary particles of air and one of fire, for example, an elementary particle of water can be constructed. The triangles themselves are not matter but still simply mathematical forms. Thus for Plato the elementary particle is not the ultimate given, unchangeable and indivisible; a further explanation is needed, and the why and wherefore of these elementary particles is referred by Plato to mathematics. The elementary particles have the form Plato ascribes to them because mathematically it is the simplest and most beautiful. The ultimate root of appearances is therefore not matter but mathematical law, symmetry, mathematical form. Contention about the primacy of the form, the image, the Idea, on the one hand, over matter, the materially existent, on the other—or conversely, that of matter over the image—in short, the quarrel between idealism and materialism, has repeatedly agitated the thoughts of men throughout the history of philosophy. To the scientist, the difference between the two conceptions may often appear to be of no great importance. But Plato himself felt the conflict to be so profound that he is said to have expressed the wish that the books of Democritus be burned.

"But what does Planck's discovery have to do with this ancient question? For nineteenth-century chemistry, atoms were given as the smallest parts of the chemical elements. They were no longer themselves an object of investigation. The element of discontinuity or unsteadiness, which had manifested itself in the atomic structure of matter at first had to be accepted without explanation. But Planck's discovery made it obvious that this same element of unsteadiness also appears elsewhere, namely in thermal radiation, where it certainly cannot be regarded simply as a consequence of the atomic structure of matter. In other words, Planck's discovery made it easy to suppose that this feature of unsteadiness in natural occurrences, which finds independent expression in the existence of atoms and in thermal radiation, would have to be understood as the consequence of a far more general law of nature. At this point, therefore, Plato's notion makes a renewed entry into science, to the effect that a mathematical law, a mathematical symmetry, ultimately underlies the atomic structure of matter. The existence of atoms or elementary particles as the expression of a mathematical structure was the new possibility that Planck opened up by his discovery, and here he is touching upon basic problems of philosophy."[27]

Planck and Heisenberg are not talking about the same kind of vibration as the alchemists, so the connection between modern physics and ancient elemental theory is at best archetypal. Pre-atomic symmetry recurs not because the old solution fits the contemporary riddle but because psychic patterns oscillate within evolving knowledge. The alchemist performs a task the chemist and physicist do not. *They* may sustain the mechanism of civilization and trace a visible rule of nature, but they do not address the shadow that mankind casts through the stars. Alchemists draw their figures from an inner Earth in impenetrable darkness, so their conceits are often nonsensical in the civilizational glare. Without these figures, however, science is stuck in a vacuum trying to complete a multi-dimensional puzzle with pieces on only one plane. Alchemy, on the other hand, deals incompletely with concrete details but produces symbols of unknown and unconscious forces. The planet sciences thus always outlive the industrial sciences. Alchemists may someday raise substances to their astral form and fly ships between galaxies, but they will not be called alchemists (even as they were not called alchemists in the Old Stone Age or when employed as chemists developing rocket fuels).

Nowadays, the physical issues raised by the alchemy of the Egyptians and Greeks are handled well enough in the laboratory, well enough at least to satisfy the ancient curiosity. It is the inside of being that we horrendously lack, the meaning and essence of us and of matter, so it is the thing we ask alchemy to bring back for us. Our alchemy is spiritual in its quest, though planet alchemy remains as allied with the cyclotron as it is with meditation.

This is not to pretend that alchemy is everything. It is not. It is specifically planet physics, elemental science, the methodology of transformation. In any given epoch, alchemy will attempt to transform that which is most difficult to budge, be it mind, matter, or metal. It will always (not just now) seem to contain the unresolved problems of the current epoch while making the obsessions of previous alchemies seem obsolete. It will always suggest the unknowable past. It will contain the cuttings of technology from the immediately precedent era while suggesting their realization in the next. And it now contains the seeds of a parapsychological and spiritual inquiry we seem about to embark upon, foreshadowing a new Rosicrucian science in concert with biodynamic agriculture, solar energy, and homoeopathy, all of which share alchemy's ancestry.

Lindsay, whose prejudice is decidedly anti-spiritual but decidely humanist, is most eloquent when he struggles to some sort of conclusion about what alchemy was, is, and what it says about who *we* are, and what we are in danger of losing when we deny or trivialize it:

> "The alchemist accepts nature for what it is, in order to change it into what it might be; accepts himself for what he is, in order to change himself into what he might be. The lonely struggle with substances in still or alembic becomes the struggle of all men to free themselves from existing fetters and to advance into a qualitatively new sphere of experience, a new social union. Zosimos in announcing the indissoluble link of theory and practice has brought something quite new into culture; and it

is this more than anything else that sounds the doom of the ancient world with its bias towards contemplation and its sense of the active sphere (apart from war and government) as servile.

"In the last resort it is this unity of craft-process with theoretical thought which is the great revolutionary mark of alchemy and which explains why it could find no accepted place in the systems of the ancient world. When in the 17th century an assured scientific method was at last established with a mixture of the particular and the general, with an appeal to experimental method, this was not the same as the alchemic unity; for the concept of nature in perpetual qualitative change was omitted and in its place was put the concept of perceptual quantitative movement. Therefore the question of directions and of values was not present. For the exponents of post-Galilean science this lack has seemed a proof of virtue and objectivity. The alchemist would reply that if you exclude humanity (the concrete object of qualities), you exclude reality in any consequential sense and your results have a limited and ultimately anti-human bias. This book is not the place to argue such problems out; but I should be failing in my love and respect for the alchemists if I did not add that in this matter I am on their side. That is, I consider a true and complete science to be one which includes the alchemic viewpoints, but with the addition of the various methodological precisions which are the great achievement of post-Galilean developments. The complete science I visualize would then be one capable of dealing with more than symmetries in nature, the stable states which quantitative analysis can compass; it would know how to grasp and define at the same time all crucial points of change, in which new qualities emerge; and it would vitally link its inquiries into natural process with the needs of a humanity that knew where it was going."[28]

H - Alchemical Consciousness

The alchemical belief that one is changed by his (or her) interaction with substance (and works to the end of being so changed) survives in various artforms and psychotherapies. Ancient peoples wrote in metals, and danced in waters and fires, and painted in minerals and caves. Projective and radically disjunctive syntaxes in music, poetry, painting, dance, and film have an alchemical heritage: awakening of form in matter, hidden intelligence in nature, inner transformation of the artist, and the experiment which makes its own meaning. In addition, the shadow of the old alchemical experiment continues to haunt contemporary chemistry and physics. The techniques of the laboratory still generate psychic qualities of substances, and these persist as unexplored images in all the chemical and scientific experiments of our time, even for the most relentlessly puritanical recorders. These phenomena are transferred to an unconscious plane, where they will remain, until their unexamined equations are someday put into a larger planetary perspective. As Whitehead implied, we lie in the background of our experiment, and our real name is the one we don't utter.

Certainly his projections do not disappear when a contemporary chemist applies himself to pure science, but his emphases do not encourage him to note or report such events or to develop a framework for incorporating them in his work. Interestingly, chemical riddles *have* been solved in hermetic dreams. In 1865, Friedrich Kekulé had a closed-eye vision before a fireplace of a snake seizing hold of its own tail (the ouroboros); it was made of oxygen, hydrogen, and carbon, and it spelled a clue to the riddle of the benzene ring. James Watson notes that his dream of Hedy Lamar in the movie "Ecstasy" gave him insight into the DNA double helix.

We have generally applied this rule the other way around: i.e., the existence of psychological properties does not undermine or eliminate objective physical proof. But all that exists has a psychic basis. The material effects of our minds surround us. That we live with our evocations is an alchemical prophecy. That Hitler was mad does not nullify World War II; nor do the awesome consequences of his acts prevent his inclusion with the other paranoid fascists in the asylum. This is very much the crux of the alchemical problem in the modern world. What is lost through the attempt to make science purely objective and concrete, returns, of necessity, in other forms. Ecological philosophy and ethics begin to make us conscious of this anew, as they look back, simultaneously into nature and man's mind, to see the inescapable relationship between biology, consciousness, and history. This is from a scientific, not an alchemical perspective, but the laws are universal, and are the same laws, whether they come as Buddhism, structural linguistics or mystic Christianity. The unknown characteristics of the materials of the world still carry their ancient message, whether we can read it or not.

The growth of psychology and linguistics, meanwhile, has changed alchemy in other ways. Certain issues which were projected into matter and posed in explicit alchemical language are re-posed as issues about us. The scientific-philosophic cartel has integrated this psycho-linguistic perspective so thoroughly that there is no science which does not have some of what Owen Barfield calls "beta-thinking" ("...we can think about the *nature* of collective representations as such, and...about their relation to our minds.").[29] Quantum theory is certainly a child of this new speculation, as physics is forced once more to go through the hermetic wedding. Heisenberg quotes his associate Pauli:

> "For I suspect that the alchemistical attempt at a unitary psycho-physical language miscarried only because it was related to a visible concrete reality. But in physics today we have an invisible reality (of atomic objects) in which the observer intervenes with a certain freedom (and is thereby confronted with the alternatives of 'choice and sacrifice'); in the psychology of the unconscious we have processes which cannot always be unambiguously ascribed to a particular subject. The attempt at a pychophysical monism seems to me now essentially more promising, given that the relevant unitary language (unknown as yet,

and neutral in regard to psychophysical antithesis) would relate to a deeper invisible reality."[30]

I am not sure I would trade alchemy for Pauli's new psychophysical inquiry, but I agree that it is the "invisible reality" in nature with which we are concerned, and it is that same invisible reality in ourselves, first as we are the apprehenders of nature within the puzzle and hence a special case of knowledge, and second as we are the products of this exact nature, folded in on itself; the subtleties, paradoxes, and invisible realities that we contain, as we look outward, *or* inward, are of the same order as the invisible realities in objective nature at large.

I - Alchemy and Ecology

The Thirty Years War put an end to the Rosicrucian city, and the history of science has universally discarded it beyond the battlefield. But the prejudice that this hermetic science was purely fanciful has undergone recent revision, notably in the context of parapsychology, which allows unorthodox relationships of mind and matter.

The ecological distribution of the Earth by the victorious technology has given new meaning to a science in harmony with the spirits and the forces of nature. Is it possible that all experimentation that does not require the personal development of the scientist leads to upheaval and cosmic reprisals against our species?

An aspect of alchemical consciousness is expressed in the nonmanipulative technology and general aesthetics of alternative-energy systems. One of the most radical organizations developing self-renewing systems from sun, wind, gravity, plants, and animals is the New Alchemy Institute in Falmouth, Massachusetts, and on Prince Edward Island in the Maritime Provinces of Canada. The founder, John Todd, named it spontaneously one day in San Diego exactly in recognition of that impossible Rosicrucian city—his sole connection to alchemy was a few articles by Frances Yates that he had read. The New Alchemists are predominately scientists, mostly botanists and marine biologists, and they do not use magic in the usual sense, but they have studied the alchemical and geomantic texts of both the West and China in search of lost agricultural and scientific techniques. They practice what Todd calls a kind of alchemical meditation:

> "The internal alchemy is really directly related to the kind and quality of dialogue that one can have with external nature. This is an old saying, but internal alchemy is fired by a passionate interaction with all things sacred. What actually goes on is less important than how the behavior of the individual changes and whether that individual is capable of applying those elements which infuse him or her. Alchemy is also the practice of Earth stewardship. Here I am not talking so much about practicing a piano as practicing in a Buddhist sense. Maybe the mysteries are less what we should be worried about or think much about. To search for an explanation for the internal alchemy or the dialogue between sacred

things is really not as important as the fundamental attitude and the work that one does. Restoring a hillside is itself the alchemical act. What happens there is a mystery, a sense of the divine, the fullest that it can become. One doesn't need to look for a revelation in space. There won't be one anymore. The extraordinary thing is simply wherever you are."[31]

The New Alchemists collect and employ the movements of cycles of natural forces: streams, tides, evaporation, excretion, decomposition, embryogenesis, membrane-formation, digestion, run-off, geodesic domes, and so on. Like the "old alchemists" they recreate the Earth in microcosm. Their systems "breathe" as the planet does; their oceans are ponds, and their atmosphere is a gas trapped between transparent membranes of the domes; they share the Sun. In Todd's terms the physics is the falling of the stream; the dynamic is the radiant energy coming in; the biophysics is the relationship between wind and rates of transpiration; the biology is the the food resources and their relation to the overall ecology; the sociology is the people and their commitments and responsibilities; the sacred is the relationship of everything to everything else within that.

J - Alchemy in Asia and India

Oriental alchemy inherited its own Paleolithic traditions of shamanism and hermetic chemistry. We shall never know whether it is Egyptian alchemy transformed (or for that matter whether Egyptian alchemy originated in Asia). No doubt an underground trade and migration continued to marry continents that were otherwise isolated enough to be known to each other only in legend and tall tale.

Famously, Eastern alchemy takes place in the laboratory of the self, but there was also a considerable practical science. According to Rexroth, "Chinese lists of metals and inorganic substances with typical alchemical parallels or synonyms and correlations with parts of the body and the constellations date back to at least the fifth century, possibly to Tso Yuan in the fourth century B.C. and include quite sophisticated substances—arsenic, sulfide, sulfur, arsenious acid, mercuric sulfide, mercury, sal ammoniac, alum, diamonds, lodestones and other metals and their compounds. Mineral acids are described by the earliest Chinese travellers to India...

> "By the early Sung period Chinese alchemy was very highly developed on both fronts. Yogic practices, that is autonomic nevous system gymnastics, sexual techniques and methods of achieving several kinds of trance, were as advanced as any in India...At the same time alchemy by the twelfth century was busy with chemical phenomena that European science would not begin to explore until the end of the eighteenth century. Not only had they developed a crude but comprehensive chemistry of the common acids, bases, metallic salts, sulfur, invented gunpowder and greek fire, burning glasses, artificial pearls, discovered the use of coal and petroleum (Peking man used coal), but they had occupied

themselves quite intelligently with various mysteries and intriguing phenomena: luminescence, magnetism, production of a vacuum and so on. Exactly as in Europe most of this literature is at least quasi-Hermetic, with mysterious and misleading terms of sulfur, magnetite, mercury, etc."[32]

Tan ching yao chueh, a tenth-century (or earlier) text by Sun Ssu-mo, contains recipes for the augmentation of brass and for artificial white jade, pearls, and malachite. Nathan Sivin, an M.I.T. historian of science, attempted one of Sun's practical recipes, entitled "Formula for Making Scarlet Snow and Flowing Pearl Elixir."[33] Although he did not complete it, his yield, up to the adding of rice, was metallic arsenic, which corroded his metal crucibles. He surmises that cooked rice would have served as a reducing agent, causing the elixir to contain crystalline or fibrous arsenic trioxide.

While some Chinese texts are explicitly pre-chemical and pre-pharmaceutical, others maintain, with Asian regional images, the occult language familiar in much of European material:

> "Above, cooking and distillation take place in the caldron; below, blazes the roaring flame. Afore goes the White Tiger leading the way; following comes the Grey Dragon. The fluttering Scarlet Bird flies the five colors. Encountering ensnaring nets, it is helplessly and immovably pressed down and cries with pathos like a child after its mother. Willy-nilly it is put into the cauldron of hot fluid to the detriment of its feathers. Before half of the time has passed, Dragons appear with rapidity and in great number. The five dazzling colors change incessantly. Turbulently boils the fluid in the ting (furnance). One after another they appear to form an array as irregular as a dog's teeth. Stalagmites which are like midwinter icicles, are spit out horizontally and vertically. Rocky heights of no apparent regularity, make their appearance, supporting one another. When Yin and Yang are properly matched, tranquility prevails."[34]

Both Chinese and Indian meditative alchemy, in somewhat different ways, replace athanor and alembic with the belly, chest cavity, and breath or blood. We might say that, if the Western formulas are "mental" in ultimate intention, they still differ, for by "mental" they mean an imagistically-guided psychospiritual initiation, and the Oriental alchemists intend a specific yogic discipline. Eliade, writing on *The Treatise on the Dragon and the Tiger,* states this very literally:

> "The 'pure' transcendental metals are identified with different parts of the body, and the alchemical processes, instead of being realized in the laboratory, take place in the body and in the consciousness of the experimenter."[35]

A fuller parallelism between East and West depends almost entirely on the degree to which one accepts that Western alchemy was primarily an internal discipline of images and exercises held together by an external system of ritual chemistry. Or, seen from the other side, it might also rest on the degree to which one allows that all external transformation of matter that can be made in the laboratory can be done within the body by an enlightened magus. This is a bigger bite to swallow, but those who swallow it see Eastern alchemy as simply a streamlined version of "human" metallurgy.

In traditional internal alchemy the practitioner obtains the raw material within his body-mind and transmutes it internally into higher "metals." The mercury spirit-seed is charged in the athanor and the alembic of the self. The method, as described in *The Secret of the Golden Flower*, a seventeenth-century A.D. Taoist alchemical handbook, was one of Jung's guides to the internality of alchemy:

First, mental static is drained off, emotional entanglements dropped (they can be picked up later if one desires). As the dross of extraneous thinking drifts away, "The Gathering of the Light" begins. One sits with eyelids half closed, staring at the tip of the nose. Light streams in, the last thoughts evaporate, the image is worked to the Center, a place both near and far, both enormous and miniscule, but still located in one's attention, often at the end of a subtle humming sound. This is the dwelling place of the spirit-seed. It must be contained, nurtured, expanded, then circulated as light through one's whole being.

Each stage of this process corresponds to a step in laboratory alchemy, or perhaps each step in the laboratory is a concretization of inner phenomena. The two, in any case, converge. Calcination followed by coagulation, distillation, and projection is either a physical or a mental operation.

Very ancient systems have merged under Taoist influence—one a technique of breath and focus originating in yoga and the other a mythocosmology of metals from the tribal Neolithic smith:

> "Incorporation into the complex of Taoist arts has preserved alchemy intact, like a mummy...Alchemy was welcomed into Taoism in part for the light it threw on natural process—the *Tao*—but rather more, one suspects, because of its promise of immortality."[36]

Lu K'uan Yü, in his book, *Taoist Yoga: Alchemy and Immortality*, describes the sexually imaginal version of the process:

> "The heart is the house of fire. When the heart is stirred the penis stands erect in spite of the absence of thoughts. This is real fire in its house, which arouses the gential organ, and although thoughts are absent, this fire is not the genuine one which vibrates at the living hour of *tsu* (between 11 p.m. and 1 a.m.) when the penis erects. If you gather the alchemical agent at this unsuitable moment it is too young because vitality is not full and can scatter easily; hence the agent should not be gathered... but if you wait until this moment has passed to pick up the agent, the latter has grown old (and is useless) because vitality has scattered after the passing of fire in its own house..."[37]

> "At puberty when (a youth has not indulged in sexual pleasures and his) body is still unimpaired, it will suffice to hold the vital force in the lower *tan t'ien* cavity (under the navel) and to concentrate on it for about

ten months until its light manifests which is the moment for the macrocosmic alchemical agent's breakthrough to realize immortality..."[38]

"Therefore, alchemy consists first in controlling the heart (the seat of fire) so that it cannot be stirred by the seven emotions (pleasure, anger, sorrow, joy, love, hate and desire) and upset by the five thieves; the six sense organs are immobilised and the generative force cannot easily be aroused..."[39]

"When a golden light appears in the eyes, the back of the head vibrates audibly, the dragon's hum is heard in the right and the tiger's roar in the left ear, fire blazes in the lower *tan t'ien* centre, bubbles rise in the body, spasms shake the nose, and the genital organ draws in. These are the signs that the immortal seed is complete."[40]

The witholding of sperm apparently reverses the more qabbalistic sexuality of the European alchemist, who preferred a male-female union with full orgasm and even procreation. The Chinese Emperor, mythologically, chose beautiful women for *coitus interruptus* only — in order to fertlize *his* seed not theirs (the latter would have drained his vitality and alchemical potential). Holding back his sperm, he climbed the ladder of breath and feeling to the point of orgasm, then drove the seed back into the brain from the belly, stirring up the fields of cinnabar (*tan t'ien*) in both places. Controlling his breath and muscular spasm, and using the woman as a crucible, he achieved both precious metals and immortality. He did not have to concern himself, in the Western manner, with making a medicine out of the seed, for the seed was already inside him.

Rexroth writes:

"Not only were the sexual techniques of alchemy assumed to develop internal processes which paralleled operations leading to the production of gold, the philosopher's stone or the drug of immortality, but they were also thought to stimulate the growth of precious metals, cinnabar and sulfur in the wombs of the uprising mountains. This idea can be found in Proclus of the West and continues to dominate Medieval ideas until the translation of Avicenna's *Treatise against Alchemy*. The hieros gamos literally fecundates the earth. At the same time it achieves salvation for the soul."[41]

As a rule, Chinese alchemy yields a higher percentage of medicinal formulas than European alchemy, preferring these to the business of gold-making. Sivin cites dozens of elixirs in the *Tan ching yao chueh*, including: Eightfold Luminosity Elixir, Congealed Frost and Deep Snow Elixir, Elixir of Meteors' Halting at the Moon, Seven Luminary Supernatural Realization Elixir, Dark Pearl Elixir of the Emperor of the North, Elixir of Fright at the Falling of the Moon, Liquid Gold and Jade Flower Elixir, White Snow Elixir of Master Mao, Roseate Cloud Elixir of the Grand Immortal, Grand Concord Dragon Womb Elixir, Scarlet Brilliance Elixir, Red Luminosity Elixir, Elixir of Ascent into the Roseate Clouds, Seven Stars Evil-Alerting Elixir, and Supernatural Flight Elixir of

Grandee Chang.[42]

Jade (and sometimes other stones) also have a special priority in the East, rivalling the fame of gold. Sun's formula for the Grand Unity Jade Powder Elixir includes: cinnabar, realgar, jade powder, powdered magnetite, amethyst, quartz, silver powder, nodular malachite, and calomel. After much mixing, pounding, drying in the sun, bedding down in salt, and a gentle nine-day flame, one opens the cooled vessel: "Examine the product, which will be suffused with brightness and will resemble cool frost or virgin snow, or will be of the shape of stalactites or tassels of grain. Every color will be there; no simile is adequate to it."[43]

Alchemical substance is no ordinary substance. It is "hot" elemental stuff. Inner spirit gives it a delicacy and beauty. Gold is golden; iridescence penetrates the striations of matter; white powder shines as if moonlit.

Chinese alchemy uses a prehistoric five-element system. Each element has a set of associations, including: seasons, directions, viscera, colors, musical notes, numbers, flavors, odors, sounds, emotions, orifices of the body, animals, cereal grains, planets of the zodiac, bowels, and tissues. The distribution vis a vis organs is: kidneys/water, stomach/earth, liver/wood, heart/fire, lungs/metal (or gold).[44]

Chinese alchemy is also integrated in a Confucian philosophy of the lineage of just Emperors. The Palace is a holy place, a cultural laboratory; alchemy is then a science of diplomacy and jurisprudence. In elemental theory no one aspect of an energy can be separated from another. Fire can be a disease or a musical note, and it can appear as certainly in a flower or a bird as in a flame. Take away ethics, diplomacy, and justice, and you disturb the waters in every laboratory and every human vessel in the land. The holy work and the civil are combined, the King as officiating magus.

In t'ai chi ch'uan Taoist yoga is combined with martial postures. A ball of energy is formed in the electrical and "chi" field of the palms, and then its intensity is increased in a series of operations initiated by the waist and translated along the spine into the rest of the body; the ball is rolled through planes parallel and perpendicular to the upright body. As it moves along the planes, it activates the meridians, which are the energy-active remnants of the formation of the body (they continue to link embryogenic reservoirs). The ritualized language of this sequence is a subset of alchemical code: Grasp Sparrow's Tail, White Crane Spreads its Wings, Play Lute, Embrace Tiger and Return to the Mountain, Step Back Like a Monkey, Cloudy Hands, Pat Horse High, Needle at Sea Bottom, Spread Arms like a Fan, Point to the Seven Stars of the Dipper, Snake Creeps Down, Shoot Tiger, Kick like a Lotus, Fair Maiden Works the Shuttles.

According to some authors, breath alchemy in the Indus Valley began over five millennia ago and was not imported into China until the last millennium before the Christian era of the West. The emphasis in India is also on body discipline and the vegetative system, but the goal is ecstatic transcendence of the corporeal level, which Hindu ethics consider an illusion. Matter itself is unreal; the unconscious and primordial manifestations only support the apparent (prakriti), which is as illusory and vitiating as it is inexhaustible and indefatigable. Gold is merely another shell, a display of temporary and local stage magic. The higher medicinal gold can be attained by a skilled yogi penetrating the levels of consciousness, to which it corresponds. He can manifest these as spiritual gold, elixirs and medicines, black stones from his belly and mouth, or "milk" and oil from his palms. On an elemental level his body corresponds to the cosmos:

> "The atom of oxygen is like a sponge that holds a certain amount of etheric force or electricity (the Quintessence), each atom enclosing within itself a charge of vital energy. The human body is a chemical laboratory and the so-called atoms of oxygen, hydrogen, nitrogen, etc., contain within themselves charges of Vital Energy. The Yogi, in describing his breathing exercises, speaks of a certain vital principle of energy which he calls 'Prana,' which is in actual fact another instance of the manifestation of the Quintessence. In his system of breathing, the mind is so centered on the act of breathing that this Quintessence of the air is consciously taken in for the revitalization of every part of his body...
>
> "The alchemist, by his laboratory process, is taking this Quintessence or Vital Energy from metals, since he has found in his experience that it is obtained from minerals and metals in a more perfect form than from plant life, the minerals being of the first manifestation."[45]

Eliade discusses the relation of ores and Indian yoga:

> "To reduce the fluidity of mercury is equivalent to the paradoxical transmutation of the psycho-mental flow in a 'static consciousness,' without any modification and hence without the limit of time. In alchemical terms, to 'fix' or to 'kill' mercury is tantamount to attaining to the *cittavrittinirodha* (suppression of conscious states), which is the ultimate aim of yoga." He adds later:
>
> "To work actively on ores and metals was to touch *prakriti*, to modify its forms, to intervene in its processes. Now, in the ideological universe in which the alchemist works, and which is that of tantrism, *prakriti* is not only the cosmological principle of classical Sāṅkhya and yoga; *prakriti* is the primordial mode of the Goddess, of the Shakti. Thanks to the symbolism and techniques elaborated by tantrism, *prakriti* becomes accessible to immediate experience; for the tantric, every naked woman incarnates *prakriti* and reveals it... Operations on mineral substances were not, and *could not be,* simple chemical experiments. On the contrary, they involved (the alchemist's) karmic situation; in other words, they had decisive spiritual consequences. It is only when mineral substances have been emptied of their cosmological virtues and have become inanimate objects that chemical science proper becomes possible."[46]

III - Symbols and Meaning
A - Material Alchemy and Spiritual Alchemy

The split in modern alchemy has not been solely between believers and debunkers. There is a contention which cuts across them on another axis: *i.e.*, there are those who take alchemy as a concrete physical science (whether accurate or erroneous), and those who take it as a system of inner being using concrete imagery. Almost all such discussions have concluded in compromises which repeat the initial difficulty in some way.

On one extreme is chemical alchemy. The assumption that the alchemists were engaged in exclusively physical-scientific operations is espoused both by those who limit alchemy to a sterile fruitless procedure, a dead-end discarded by progressive science, and by those who accept it as a productive elemental laboratory. Neither camp would deny that the alchemical terminology is a code, but in the scientific prejudice it is a superstition in the absence of experimental precision, whereas for modern alchemists the surface imagery is an attempt to imagine extremely complex and synchronistic phenomena while hiding dangerous operations from the uninitiated.

The opposite extreme is to take the laboratory processes of alchemy as a screen, either consciously chosen or unconsciously developed, the real purpose of which is a psycho-spiritual awakening. The laboratory then may function as a mnemonic device for recording and confirming the stages of inner being, but not as the arena of "real" alchemy. Within this camp, there is an oft-waged and confusing battle over whether the alchemical imagery is unconscious and inevitable, a result of underlying archetypal energy, or whether it is an intentional refined system for attaining higher consciousness. Classically, passive and unconscious alchemy is a Jungian interpretation, and inner spiritual alchemy is Islamic and Oriental.

The result of these different positions is four polar interpretations of alchemy with various compromises between them. The physical bias either consigns alchemy to the history of chemistry denying present usefulness or imagines a whole shadow tradition of untested scientific modes; nowadays the latter most conventionally falls under paraphysics. The pyschospiritual pole generates more subtly diverging positions: Psychologists and anthropologists take alchemy as instinctual and unconscious; therefore they tend to accept physical chemistry as the historical outcome of operations understood as transmutation only to their practitioners (anthropologists regularly propose that material culture arises out of accidental symbols). The spiritualists on the other hand share with the paraphysicists the belief that alchemical transmutation can change matter; however, they see material change as arising from inner yogic change and personal development. The paraphysicists differ from the pure spiritualists in their assumption of a priority of physical energy waves and their premise that meditation inevitably is a "cover story" for telekinesis.

However, the problems with defining alchemy go well beyond these initial dichotomies and include virtually all levels of human activity. The alchemical symbols disguise (and reveal) not only scientific, religious, paraphysical, psychological, economic, and artistic traditions but political movements and revolutions as well. At the level of planet science it is in fact virtually impossible to distinguish the spiritual and scientific from the political. The *New Testament* has plagued the West with this dilemma so profoundly that politics and prophecy have become inseparable in the Holy Land, and Atlantis has come to stand simultaneously for the pure experiment in global geomancy (including travel to other dimensions) and the pacifist matriarchal utopia, each of which we have lost by betraying the other. A. E. Waite writes:

> "It is an open secret that the First Matter is called by many names and that all are veils, the *Secretum Artis*, as we have seen, having been declared by none. There is one point more: supposing for a moment an array of textual evidence against metallic transmutation as the real end in view, it does not follow that the alchemical concern was spiritual. Spiritual intimations—if any—discerned throughout the literature may be assuredly another veil. If William Shakespeare did not write the plays which pass under his name, the fact does not signify that of necessity they were the work of Francis Bacon. So also, if Alchemy is not that which it claims, a mystery of the mineral kingdom, the sole alternative is not that it is a mystery of the human soul. Its records may be cryptic manifestoes of some Secret Order which from time immemorial has prepared for a political transformation of the world. They may have told those who knew how it was faring with the scheme at one and another time, among these and those persons, and in that or this place and country of the world."[47]

The novelist Sol Yurick imbeds the alchemical-qabbalistic revolution (which extends across millennia) within the twentieth-century spy consortiums in such a way that agents and magicians disguise each other, and the mind-altering effects of modern drugs and brain surgery engage the ancient transmissions in occult language. Different secret orders battle for global power both within and outside the East-West axis:

"Mr. Kelley also took back with him a report provided by Mr. Helphand on the Aquilino family, their history and mode of operation. It was Richard Aquilino's father's interest in Cabala, coupled with the sudden disappearance of the family, the past possible intelligence background—that had alerted him to an ancient enemy. The Cabalists, like the Taoists, had been an invisible trading empire and intelligence operation that concealed itself behind mystic practices. He shook his head in admiration and despair. The Aquilinos were of the darkness battling Parvus, the merchants of light. As young people they had joined the Bolsheviks, and participated in the Revolution. Later they had been sent out of the Soviet Union. The mother, Lizaveta, and the father, Samael Samelovich, had both been assigned to work abroad between the period of 1925 and 1936, going from country to country, setting up networks. She was an activist, had trained operatives in crash courses of agitation, sabotage, assassination, setting up networks of sleepers. The father had originally been a linguist, a Cabalist, descended from a long line of mystic scholars tracing their ancestry back to the rabbis of Italy and Spain of the twelfth century. They were a people used to cover, concealment, the ambiguous statement and the recursive riddle...

"Yes. It was clear. In intelligence jargon, Richard Aquilino was a sleeper. In Cabalistic terms, a *golem* waiting to be woken up to its task. But what *was* his task?...The long history of his family, its flights from country to country, what was that all about? A briefing as a family saga that wound through different countries through the ages?"[48]

B - Texts, Origins, and Initiations

There is an aspect of alchemical practice that is sheer etymological deciphering and archaeology. Adepts scour the libraries, rare bookstores, and fragments of ancient languages and texts for more authentic transmissions of the riddle. The more modern the text (usually), the greater the corruption—unless a vision has cut through the ages.

At the sources seems to lie Hermes, or Moses. But these too are ceremonial names. In many cases authors take their identities from earlier alchemists, forming a chain of masters, from Hermes to Hermes to pseudo-Hermes, none of them authentic but none of them false. Even Geber, a recognizable historical personage, an Arabic alchemist, has been assigned generations of texts he could not have written; in Europe, where he becomes Jabir, he continues writing apocrypha long after his death, creating such confusion his name is synonymous for it (gibberish). Ostanes was perhaps a Medean-Persian alchemist, the actual teacher of Bolos-Bemokritos, but some of his writings come from Egypt, some from Asia Minor. His name finally becomes a traditional Persian honorific for a magus. No doubt pseudo-Dionysius would have been surprised to have been taken as a source, the only explanation for *his* "alias" being that he was not the god for whom he spoke.

But antiquarians may also fail to understand that the text is not only archaic; it is reborn each instant as vision. Alchemy is being made by those who are alive. Robert Kelly's "Alchemical Journal" is not hopelessly late or derivative; it continues to add to our sense of the unknown original: with its carp, its binary numbers, its North American city on the edge of a disc of living planets. The original text, after all, is not only a Paleolithic concordance of glyphs; it lies as much in the future with magi who have long since departed this place. It is a text we must be writing and living to be discovering; otherwise, we are left deciphering against the edges of crumbling parchment. There is good reason for "the experiment" in living matter, for Robert Fludd's vision of the naked human torso as cosmic calendar. Or Vico: "This then is an instance of an ideal eternal history traversed in time by the histories of all nations."[49]

The alchemist is, in a sense, looking for the places at which the divine voice within nature has been captured by a human agency. He hopes to find the literal medicine bundles of a lost civilization. Nicholas Flamel recounts his experience:

> "I acquired for two florins a very old, large, and finely gilded book. It was neither of paper nor of parchment as are other books, but seemed to me to be made of the smoothed-out bark of young trees. Its binding was of beaten copper and it was engraved with strange letters and figures—I think they were Greek letters or letters of some similar ancient language. At any rate I could not read them, but I know they were not Latin or Gallic letters... The book contained thrice-seven pages, for they were fastened together in sections in this way, and the seventh page was always without writing. On the first seventh page, instead of writing, there was a picture of a staff, aroung which two serpents were entwined. On the second seventh page was represented a desert, in the middle of which several beautiful fountains played, out of which serpents sprang in all directions."[50]

This is the kind of book one hardly comes across anymore. We are perhaps reminded of "The Greater Trumps," the pack of tarot cards in the Charles Williams novel of that name: card by card they come alive and turn into the elements, the substances and forces of nature. Flamel's tale does not stop with the text, for the discoverer now needs a translator. He must hunt through the slums of the Old World cities where the remnants of the hermetic orders remain secreted but intact.

The great Chinese chemist Sun Ssu-mo was not so lucky. His true Elixir was held on the Islands of the Immortals, somewhere in the South China Sea—islands which protected themselves by a wind which drove boats away:

> "I have read in succession the lore books of ancient times; they agree that, without exception, cases of men's bodies sprouting feathered wings and rising weightlessly in flight were due to the taking of elixirs. Never did I read of these things without feeling an ardent longing in my heart. My sole regret was that the divine Way is so remote, the pathway through the clouds so inaccessible. I gazed in vain at azure heaven, not knowing how to ascend it. I began to practice the techniques of preparing elixirs by cyclical transformation and of fixing substances in the fire, and the formulas for making potable jade and liquid gold. But they are obscure and difficult to fathom, abstruse and unpredictable. How can one without occult virtue comprehend them?"[51]

Another adventure is told in an Arab manuscript, *The Twelve Chapters by Ostanes the Philosopher on the Philosopher's Stone*. His grail is a remote and paradoxical substance:

> "Know, seekers, that it is a white water which is found buried in the earth of India, a black water which is found buried in the land of Chadjer, a red brilliant water which is found buried in Andalusia.
>
> "It is a liquid that bursts in flame at contact with wood into a violent fire; a fire that lights itself at stones in the countries of Persia; a tree that grows on the peaks of mountains; a young man born in Egypt; a prince

come from Andalusia who desires the torture of the seekers. He has killed their chiefs and made of some of them the runners of princes. The wise men are powerless to fight him. I see no arms against him but resignation, no other steed than science, no other shield but intelligence."

The adventure continues in *The Book of Thirty Chapters*, where the dangers of the translation itself are recounted:

"While I was examining the part I hadn't managed to decipher in this plaque, I heard a strong voice crying out to me, 'Man, get away from here before all the Gates are shut; for the moment of closure is come.'

"Trembling all over and afraid it was too late to leave, I went out. When I had passed through all the gates, I met an old man of unparalleled beauty. 'Approach,' he told me, 'man whose heart is thirsty for this science. I am going to make you understand many things that have seemed obscure to you, and explain what remains hidden.' "

As the unveiling continues, he meets "the three-bodied animal, whose parts devoured one another." It cries out to him:

"All the science can be perfected only by me, and it is in me that is found the key of the science. He who wants to accomplish the work in its perfection, let him recognize my true power and he will lack nothing of what the philosophers have said about the work.'

"Hearing these words, the old man said to me, 'Man, go and find that animal, give him an intelligence in place of yours, a vital spirit in place of yours, a life in place of yours; then he'll submit to you and give you all you need.' "

This work which is both science and magic, now hangs in the balance, historically and personally, for the seeker:

"As I wondered how I could give anyone an intelligence in place of mine, a vital spirit in place of mine, an existence in place of mine, the old man said, 'Take the body that is like your own, take from it what I have just told you, and hand it over to him.'

"I did as the old man bade me, and I acquired then the whole science, as complete as that described by Hermes.' "[52]

The alchemical magi murmur on all dimensions and in the forms of living men and women. Their message *must be* universal and transhistorical if not archetypal and interstellar, for it persists in new symbols and metaphors by the thousands even after the old ones and their cultures and meanings have become dehydrated and blown away. As the Persian message is hardened in stone and occult dogma, a North American hermetica arises from unknown sources. Even the popular breakthrough of the sixties had an alchemical metaphor: to see inside nature by ingesting hallucinogens, to transmute one's self by rare earths and laboratory chemicals. Paracelsus was "reborn" in another Swiss pharmacist named Hofmann. Mediaeval and Renaissance symbols of alchemy were resurrected to embroider this head-trip, revived as multicolored mandalas on drug posters, rock music ads, and other "visionary" paraphernalia. For a moment everything seemed to change, and an archaic dream became a millennial prophecy. This is fair enough given that alchemy's first message has always been: the mutability of substance (and man and woman are substance). However, the pretension of early drug culture to "Whole Alchemy" was naive.

The magi have also come in dreams and visions, like *The Chymical Wedding of Christian Rosenkreutz*, credited after the fact to Johann Valentin Andreae, but to this day the author and meaning remain unknown. Jung describes his own interest in alchemy as arising from a dream of a library filled with pigskin volumes of sixteenth-century texts (shades of Flamel). It took him fifteen years to assemble in his own house the library of the dream. He did not seek a translator, for his generation had come to understand that all men and women carry the text in their cells. Their projections reveal a quest, a Stone, a philosophical Arbor, a fountain of fountains, a golden flower, an eternally ascending staircase, a spirit named Mercurius—something they inherit as bare species memory, something they no longer practice. So Jung's patients became his teachers—a fully alchemical reversal, the mage searching once again in primal Earth and among common and despised things for the *prima materia*. Through the alchemical transference the doctor evoked, the patients began to heal themselves, to individuate, even as alchemists had healed their cultures with the same paradoxical symbols. Jung found the primal black earth in psyche long after the raw materials of the alchemists had been sterilized and placed into test tubes, their atomic numbers assigned and their synthetic identities frozen millennially.

Christian Rosenkreutz received, as they say now, an invitation he could not refuse:

> "As soon as I had read this Letter, I was presently like to have fainted away, all my Hair stood on end, and a cold Sweat trickled down my whole Body. For although I well perceived that this was the appointed *Wedding*, whereof seven Years before I was acquainted in a *bodily Vision*, and which now so long time I had with great earnestness awaited, and which lastly, but the account and calculation of the *Plannets*, I had most diligently observed, I found so to be, yet could I never fore-see it must happen under so grievous and perilous conditions."

It is eternally dangerous as it is simple:

> "...to be a well-come and acceptable Guest, I needed only to be ready to appear at the Wedding."[53]

While living in Oakland and working on the prior version of this essay in 1979, I had a dream that a friend who was a homeopath, Dana Ullman, was pulling bars of molten gold from a furnace. The substance was brilliant and glowing but did not burn him; the bars were like shards of pure golden light. The next afternoon Dana called me, and I told him about the dream, suggesting that the bars might have been homoeopathic essences. He said that a very strange thing had happened to him the previous day: he had been called out of the blue by a woman who said she was an alchemist and told him she had a laboratory in her apartment for making gold. He didn't take it seriously, or choose to explore the matter but she had seemed sincere, so he gave me her name and phone number as follow-up to the dream—a classically alchemical name: Elisabeth Kelley.

When I called her, she sounded young and flirtatious. She said: "I have just finished preparing the elixir. Can I offer you a drink?"

I was determined to follow through the sequence initiated by the essay and dream, so I set out to find her. I had expected fairly funky circumstances, but the directions led to a section of palatial houses a little way up toward the Oakland hills. I came finally to a gate enclosing a beautiful garden in which there were cages with colorful tropical birds. Her entrance was to an apartment on the side of a large house. She came downstairs to the ring of the doorbell. She looked nothing like an alchemist but was small and beautiful in a manner suggestive of a late fifties teen-age rock queen: dark, wide-eyed, and yet piercing. She wore tight stylish clothes, gold pants, a light blue blouse. "Come upstairs," she said, and I followed her up around a narrow staircase. Her apartment was a couple of rooms, very modern, and her laboratory was the electric stove with pots and coffee cisterns. She took a jar of auburn liquid from the shelf above the stove and set it on the coffee table as she sat down on the couch. She explained that it was the elixir and that she had worked on it for many months. "It comes out of me," she said, pointing to her navel. She then poured a small glass and offered me one also, but I was afraid. She looked at me quizzically as though to ask why I came. I felt simultaneously compelled by her and terribly anxious to leave. She spoke about a Circle of Gold she belonged to and how she had made great sums of money from it. "There is wealth enough for everyone, but it comes from our hearts. All gold can be made into more gold, but we must be open."

I told her about the series of alchemy books I was doing, and she laughed. "Come here," she said, leading me to the side of the livingroom. After a moment I realized that she was pointing to a small patch of sun on the rug; it was rich and textured in the late afternoon. She lay down putting her head in half of the spot. "Here," she said. "Put your head in the sun." There was nothing to do but follow. I lay down and put my head in the sun almost touching hers. Then she handed me a strand of her hair. "This is gold," she said. I held it. It was crusted on the tips with clumps of small stones, light brown and not particularly shiny so that they were not apparent at a distance. "I have been turning my hair into gold," she told me. "Feel it." As I held her hair, she said, "This is what I would tell you for your alchemy book. Gold is God. It is love, light, life, Lilith, Elisabeth. We are lying in gold. Gold comes from our hearts; now let us rest quietly in this dream." We lay on the floor in the sun for several minutes; then the visit ended, and I left.

Flamel bought a book; Ostanes entered the gates; Zosimos climbed a staircase in dream; Christian Rosenkreutz was invited to a wedding which was a bloody murder followed by a resurrection; Fulcanelli read the Gothic cathedrals as alchemical diagrams, their rose windows and gargoyles; Jung assembled a library from a dream; and Robert Kelly: "I detected on a bookshelf a tantric text I didn't know," which turns out to be the body of the female chauffeur of the vehicle. He has stumbled into the body of matter itself. His literacy cannot match its literality, which reads as silence. He is forced to fondle her, stroke and pinch her, but she gives no recognition of him. The frustration and shame in alchemy comes, as in all else, with the sense that one's sentience is not matched because one is not sentient enough—that however much we want, our intelligence is dumb before the divine intelligences that sweep through the atmosphere of this planet and our minds, hurricanes and electric storms. "The car was still moving. I grabbed the intercom & shouted I'm sorry, please forgive me, please forgive me. What have you done that merits forgiveness? She asked."[54]

It is no surprise that the *Edward* Kelly texts, for all their al-chymistry and divine symbolism, end up in sexual experiments involving the wives of Kelly and John Dee, or that the alchemist is always in a questionable moral circumstance for the unChristian fervor with which he pursues a corporeal object.

The downtown New York City showing of Harry Smith's *Heaven and Earth Magic Feature* was attended by hundreds who had heard that the alchemical secrets would be unveiled in the course of an evening. There were no psychedelics. A simple series of alchemical transformations were portrayed on the screen; they went on for hours, and hours, the result of years of painstaking animation. But the audience was dropping like flies. They fled the theater until, at the transmutation, it was almost empty.

"Perhaps they found their way into the neighboring theaters," Robert Kelly suggested, an allusion to the porn houses also on 42nd Street. If the symbols of alchemy had become dead for them, then they should in fact, return to the bloody source of male and female torn asunder and reunited in flame. Alchemy forever hangs between trite, no longer usable symbols and living forms from which new symbols will come. Kelly speaks of "The Alchemist" whose gown is sewn thick with suns and moons and planets and the signs for such operations but who no longer knows that these are living bodies, hot and cold, populated, gestating, "brown breath, brown blood."[55]

We continue to search for authentic documents, but we are also drowned in information on all channels. The various esoteric traditions have been researched and traced to historical events; their texts are in libraries and bibliographies. The collective unconscious and its contents have been catalogued so thoroughly by the Jungians that we go to *their* alchemical writings now for the sources of hermetic wisdom. The structure of the elements and the matrix of time and space have been probed and revealed. We look only to extraterrestrials and Oriental gurus for information from outside our entire dominating system. Or we find ourselves in contact with their archetypes: flying saucers piloted by evasive but immortal creatures, and spirits who lecture us from another dimension through their priestess-mediums. Yet the origin of hermetic wisdom is no more in India or the Pleiades than it was once in Africa or Atlantis. Alchemy stays alive by hiding not only itself but its tracks. The ones we expose reveal only us, certainly not "them."

C - Matter and Spirit

Alchemy occupies the middle ground between matter and spirit, avoiding false distinctions between the two. Likewise alchemy does not dichotomize "mental" and "physical" or "internal" and "external;" it is always both and so defines a predualistic system of thought.

In a seminar I taught with Charles Stein,[56] he objected to my occasional tendency to impose a spirit/matter split on alchemy, arguing that alchemical thought can neither address nor resolve dualism because it originates outside the Western dichotomy and its various epochal resolutions (including the modern versions of relativity, psychosomatics, and the Tao). Stein says:

"I became interested in alchemy in that Mediaeval period where exactly that question of—is it a spiritual process or is it a material process?—can't be asked. There has got to be a sense in which it is both. And the area of attention that alchemy seems to occupy is exactly that middle ground of a way of thinking about the world and ourselves (another two which sounds like body and spirit), in which two can't be posed because there's a central middle medial term, the alchemical stuff, which is also in some sense alive. Life and death are only another such pair. It is exactly where the ambiguity and imbeddedness of the two poles in each other take center stage that, there, the alchemical stuff exists. Thinkers and artists and writers again and again have been involved in ways of overcoming what seems to be the main problem in Western civilization, which is exactly the creating of those splits. You have mind on one side, body on the other, spirit and matter, then spiritualism and materialism.

"When you say that alchemy is spiritual now because the physical sciences are materialistic, the other concern still remains: we are throwing ourselves back into believing in issues which constellate themselves in those pairs. What if alchemy were to occupy the middle ground and say: no spirit and matter, no body and mind, no self and world—but what? what? I know that there have been many different approaches to articulating that middle ground in this century, and it is notable that those approaches tend to be appropriated by the two sides. You'll have a doctrine like Whitehead's 'process and reality,' which attempts to be a rational philosophy in which you don't have mind and matter but you have *the first term*—not atoms, not cosmic mind. The first term is an actual entity; it is in the middle of both. Yes, it is organic. Yes, physical matter partakes of it. Inorganic complex molecules partake of it. Human life also. Thought, yes. Artistic creation. Visionary experience. All are seen as different varieties of a central term, an actual entity. But look what happens to Whitehead. He immediately gets appropriated by the spiritualists and roped into something that appears to justify a spiritual position."

I suggested to Stein that perhaps this was because it is the spiritual position which is presently lacking proof, while materialism sees no reason to compromise, being presently in the driver's seat. Since Whitehead *appears* to compromise with pure materialism, he is taken as a spiritualist. Stein responded:

"Why is that so? Why doesn't materialism have to compromise? Material positions try to generate images of the world that are not dualistic. The Wittgensteinian position, or even later, the structural position, are attempts on the part of materialism to overcome the duality between mind on the one hand and matter on the other without submitting to an old concept of matter. Heisenberg too. Every position is compromised. The materialist position is as much compromised.

"And the spiritualists are no more able to agree on a pure position. Look at the two versions of God in Western thought. On the one hand, there's this God that's ultimately remote, that represents the changeless eternal transcendent structure, the logic of the universe as fixed once and for all, a logic that determines absolutely the magic, the magic that then is the working out of the logic in time and space. And the other is this transcendent person who does things in the world and whose relationship to the world is active. Both are transcendent and mixed up in the world, and theology is always wavering between what qualities it wants to represent.

"The opposition between dead stuff and living stuff is a metaphysical duality that science itself is finally not concerned with. It's a previous bias of an earlier phase of science that would argue life-stuff itself is finally dead, and that we, as generated by possibilities of matter, are reducible to the same. But energy and matter are no more than abstractions from two kinds of observations of things."

D - Jungian Alchemy

The alchemists whose writings we have inherited describe a physical/chemical method for liberating and containing the vital spirit within matter. The chemical procedure is precise and rigorous, requiring not only a sequence of operations but a responsiveness to signs and changes within the solutions being worked upon and a timing of stages to achieve a synchronization with cosmic rhythms. In other words, alchemy could not simply be reduced to a metaphor for psychological and philosophical processes; it was always an extremely sophisticated laboratory science.

What Carl Jung recognized was that the stages of the alchemists *also* corresponded to a process of psychological individuation. The psychic stages were as precise and rigorous as the chemical ones by which they became imaginal. Furthermore, they generated a physical and even quantitative terminology for an undiagnosed tension of opposites in the human psyche arising from male and female archetypes, a struggle they sought to resolve by the creative unity of the chemicals in the Stone. Jung realized that this dilemma was stated almost axiomatically by the oft-quoted legendary alchemist Maria Prophetissa: "Therefore the Hebrew prophetess cried without restraint: 'One becomes two, two becomes three, and out of the third comes the One as the fourth.' "[57]

Alchemy is thus a form of chemical research into which unresolved psychic elements were projected. The alchemical *nigredo*, the initial phase of the operation which produces "black blacker than black," is also an internal experience of melancholia, an encounter with the shadow. Yet in the laboratory it is not just a hopeless chaos; it is the "black, magically fecund earth that Adam took with him from Paradise, also called antimony" in which the seed of the gold and the *lapis* is sown.[58]

The *lapis* is "not just a stone," Jung reminds us, "since it is expressly stated to be composed *'de re animali, vegetabili et minerali,'* and to consist of body, soul, and spirit."[59] The *lapis* is a living creature, a guide and ally; it is the self which has been lost, a hermaphrodite/Christ buried within. It is also a numinous symbol for unity expressed in pseudochemical language, bringing together man and woman, personality and society, and unconscious and conscious in a *hieros gamos*, a 'chymical marriage.'

The *circulatio*, often represented as a revolving wheel or zodiac, is a state of wholeness the unconscious mind is trying to force into objectivity. It may contain four mountains or eight petals of a flower; an asymetric snake or lightning bolt may penetrate its protective circularity—the force of awakening. The Wheel is also the planet itself spinning Yang and Yin into matter and light; the evolution of mind is the global serpent.

The alchemical King cries out from the unconscious; he is the Spirit trapped in Matter, the entombed Gold; he has become inanimate and his lands are barren. But he is also the *prima materia*, the bisexual serpent, the sun-beetle; he swallows the *lapis*, which is reborn through the alchemical stages as the *coniunctio*, the Marriage of Sun and Moon. The fragmentation of the personality becomes a unity again through individuation. The Philosophical Gold, the Golden Flower grows in black pagan dirt—sometimes it is "the sapphire blue flower of the hermaphrodite."[60]

Jung proposes that the alchemists from antiquity through the Renaissance were only ostensibly and secondarily involved in a chemico-physical process. The real psychic purpose of their operation was to project unconsciously-experienced archetypes into the world. The chemistry was the necessary vehicle for the projection; the chemicals and their stages of transformation corresponded to entities of the psychic deep. If the alchemist denied them in order to idealize his philosophical goal, then he had no material for his projection.

> "The prerequisite for this [work], of course, is that the artifex should not identify himself with the figures in the work, but should leave them in their objective, impersonal state. So long as the alchemist was working in his laboratory he was in a favourable position, psychologically speaking, for he had no opportunity to identify himself with the arche-

types as they appeared, since they were all projected immediately into the chemical substances. The disadvantage of this situation was that the alchemist was forced to represent the incorruptible substance as a chemical product—an impossible undertaking which led to the downfall of alchemy, its place in the laboratory being taken by chemistry."[61]

Jung leaves alchemy in a curious dilemma: a psychotherapeutic process of great depth and clarity but a sterile science. In fact, it is only after the development of chemistry that we are able to see the psychological basis of alchemy, for scientific chemistry exposes that alchemy was essentially a symbolic process appropriating laboratory substances for its representations:

"Since the process never led to the desired goal and since the individual parts of it were never carried out in any standardized manner, the change in the classification of its stages cannot be due to extraneous reasons but rather to the symbolical significance of the quaternity and the trinity; in other words it is due to inner psychological reasons."[62]

Hence, alchemy's authenticity lies almost one hundred per cent in its capacity to generate archetypes. Modern-day physics and chemistry may likewise be reinterpreted by some future era in terms of unresolved conflicts of which we were not aware and so thrust into science. The cyclotron and the computer are psychic relics even as they are prodigious physical manifestations. The fundamental correspondences between mind and matter have assured that the alchemical symbols will not die; they have become scientific symbols and pharmaceutical symbols even in the devaluation of their animate properties. Thus science can never quite throw off the etymology of its alchemical past even as it cannot prevent psychic projections which will become the alchemy of the future. Jung examines the psychophysical paradox in great depth:

"The real mystery does not act mysteriously or secretively; it speaks a secret language, it suggests itself by a variety of images which all indicate its true nature. I am not speaking of a secret personally guarded by someone, with a content known to its possessor, but of a mystery, a matter or circumstance which is 'secret,' i.e., known only through vague hints but essentially unknown. The real nature of matter was unknown to the alchemist. He knew it only in hints. Inasmuch as he tried to explore it he projected the unconscious into the darkness of matter in order to illuminate it. In order to explain the mystery of matter he projected yet another mystery—namely his own unknown psychic background—into what was to be explained: *Obscurum per obscurius, ignotum per ignotius!* This procedure was not, of course, intentional; it was an involuntary occurrence.

"Strictly speaking, projection is never made; it happens, it is simply there. In the darkness of anything external to me I find, without recognizing it as such, an interior or psychic life that is my own. It would therefore be a mistake in my opinion to explain the formula 'tam ethice quam physice' by the theory of correspondences, and to say that this is its 'cause.' On the contrary, this theory is more likely to be a rationalization of the experience of projection. The alchemist does not practice his art because he believes on theoretical grounds in correspondence; the point is that he has a theory of correspondence because he experiences the presence of the idea, or of spirit in physical matter. I am therefore inclined to assume that the real root of alchemy is to be sought less in philosophical doctrines than in the projections experienced by individual investigators. I mean by this that while working on his chemical experiments the operator had certain psychic experiences which appeared to him as the particular behavior of the chemical process. Since it was a question of projection, he was naturally unconscious of the fact that the experience had nothing to do with matter itself (that is, with matter as we know it today). He experienced his projection as a property of matter; but what he was in reality experiencing was his own unconscious. In this way he recapitulated the history of man's knowledge of nature. As we all know, science began with the stars, and mankind discovered in them the dominants of the unconscious, the 'gods' as well as the curious qualities of the zodiac: a complete projected theory of human character. Astrology is a primordial experience similar to alchemy. Such projections repeat themselves wherever man tries to explore an empty darkness and involuntarily fills it with living form."[63]

For Jung all planet sciences are archetypal: involuntary and inevitable, having little to do "with matter as we know it today," except insofar as the trinity and quaternity lie at the psychological basis of mathematics, physics, and chemistry, and thus define our primordial intuition of substance. The alchemists project these archetypes directly out of their intellects into the undefined chaos of their materials. What they see is their own imagination, which they mistake for the ascendence of matter. The gold they sought, whose origin was in dung and decomposed minerals, was the unshaped and oft-spurned contents of their unconscious selves.

The unconscious mind thus provides the shapes and images of alchemy and astrology as compensation for the conscious mind's repression of its essentiality. It finds gods in minerals and stars, and when these are redefined as electrons, protons, and nuclear forces in general, the gods abandon these inanimate bodies and find new representations. Their symbols may die, but they are immortal.

Jung's position is often misunderstood; he is damned by spiritual alchemists for "blasphemies" he never committed; on the other hand, he is a "new age" source for a spiritual exaltation of alchemy he strictly avoided throughout his writings. His position is radical psychologically in that he traces the lineages of cosmic shapes that transcend yet generate individual psyches, but he is absolutely conventional in his acceptance of scientific evolution and his assumption of the primitivity of ethnoscience:

"From the point of view of our modern knowledge of chemistry [alchemy] tells us little or nothing, and if we turn to the texts with their hundred and one procedures and recipes left behind by the Middle Ages and antiquity, we shall find relatively few among them with any meaning for the chemist. He would probably find most of them nonsensical, and furthermore it is certain beyond all doubt that no real tincture or artificial gold was ever produced during the many centuries of earnest endeavour. What then, we may fairly ask, induced the old alchemists to go on labouring—or, as they said, 'operating'—so steadfastly and to write all those treatises on the 'divine' art if their whole undertaking was so portentously futile? To do them justice we must add that all knowledge of the nature of chemistry and its limitations was still completely closed to them, so that they were as much entitled to hope as those who dreamed of flying and whose successors made the dream come true after all. Nor should we underestimate the sense of satisfaction born of the enterprise, the adventure, the *quaerere* (seeking) and the *invenire* (finding). This always lasts as long as the methods employed seem sensible. There was nothing at that time to convince the alchemist of the senselessness of his chemical operations: what is more, he could look back on a long tradition which contained not a few testimonies of such as had achieved the marvellous result. Finally the matter was not entirely without promise, since a number of useful discoveries did occasionally emerge as by-products of his labours in the laboratory. As the forerunner of chemistry alchemy had a sufficient *raison d'être*. Hence, even if alchemy had consisted in—if you like—an unending series of futile and barren chemical experiments, it would be no more astonishing than the venturesome endeavours of medieval medicine and pharmacology."[64]

(Jung adds with amazement in a footnote, that people in the twentieth century still "believe[d] in the possibility of the alchemical method." If anything, this belief has increased since the time Jung wrote *Psychology and Alchemy,* and includes, as well, exactly those "venturesome endeavours of medieval medicine and pharmacology," revived as homoeopathy, anthroposophical medicine, naturopathy, etc.)[65]

E - The Limits of Jungian Alchemy

Jung did not intend to demean alchemy by making it "only psychology;" after all, the archetypes are the *mind* of creation, the highest possible consciousness. Through his work the alchemist is linked to the heart of nature as well as to the divine. But Jung could never satisfactorily resolve the physical and spiritual aspects of alchemy except by recourse to an archetypal level on which the physical body was the manifestation of forces resembling mind and the mind was the imaginal force of unconsciousness penetrating matter. At at few points in his alchemical writings he explores this treacherous territory:

"The *imaginatio*, or the act of imagining, is thus a physical activity that can be fitted into the cycle of material changes, that brings these about and is brought about by them in its turn. In this way the alchemist related himself not only to the unconscious but directly to the very substance which he hoped to transform through the power of imagination. The singular expression 'astrum' (star) is a Paracelsian term, which in this context means something like 'quintessence.' Imagination is therefore a concentrated extract of the life forces, both physical and psychic. So the demand that the artist must have a sound physical constitution is quite intelligible, since he works with and through his own quintessence and is himself the indispensable condition of his own experiment. But, just because of this intermingling of the physical and the psychic, it always remains an obscure point whether the ultimate transformations in the alchemical process are to be sought more in the material or more in the spiritual realm. Actually, however, the question is wrongly put: there was no 'either-or' for that age, but there did exist an intermediate realm between mind and matter, *i.e.*, a psychic realm of subtle bodies whose characteristic it is to manifest themselves in a mental as well as a material form. This is the only view that makes sense of alchemistic ways of thought, which must otherwise appear nonsensical."[66]

Spiritualists and paraphysicists both attack Jung on this point—the former because they take alchemy as an art of higher consciousness and the latter because they accept at face value the physical transmutations described by the alchemists. We can summarize these objections around three overlapping issues:

First, Jung cannot claim the one correct interpretation of alchemy. His version, like all the rest, must take its place in planet history, to be deconstructed over time. Unquestionably Jungian alchemy is part of the alchemical tradition, but its actual position cannot be assured by our own psychoanalytic prejudices.

Secondly, Jung appears to take a dimmer view of alchemy than the other spiritual sciences. For instance, he accepts causation outside of time and space in his theory of synchronicity, and he strongly suggests his own belief in reincarnation in his writings on *The Tibetan Book of the Dead*. Given his parapsychological leanings elsewhere, we might guess that Jung was so heavily swayed by the mid-twentieth-century renaissance in the physical sciences that he participated in a general cultural devaluation of the physical aspects of the mediaeval Western sciences. Synchronicity was immune to this, being drawn in part from physics, and the Oriental sciences were also excluded because Jung took them to be a wholly different and (in many ways) more advanced system.

Thirdly, Jung identifies spiritual alchemy wholly with the unconscious mind, which is passive and beneath consciousness and thus can have only a subliminal import upon individual development. Various occultists (most vocally Titus Burckhardt) honor alchemy as a superconscious work requiring rigorous initiation and discipline—an intentional system of training with ritual images (not unintended projections).

A more general problem is raised by practitioners of yoga, meditation, and t'ai chi ch'uan: Jung appears to be concerned only with the visual, image-forming, and hallucinatory (visionary) projections of the alchemists and alchemical consciousness in general—dreams, symbols, colors, mandalas, mythical narrations, signets. But the Taoist alchemist is involved in other somatic and physiological experiences which are prior to the images and generate them secondarily. This may also have been the case in Western alchemy. The whole run of symbols and archetypal representations would then be a description of states of alchemical yoga that could be experienced only through actual experiments. The alchemical texts would have been, all along, a vision-quest (much like *The Tibetan Book of the Dead*).

Burckhardt sets himself up as the champion of those opposed to Jung's version of alchemy:

> "One must make a distinction between, on the one hand, a more or less darksome layer of consciousness lying beneath everyday consciousness (which layer in any case cannot be completely unconscious in that it somehow does enter consciousness) and, on the other hand, the true, purely passive, and thus in itself unformed, ground of the soul. The darksome layer referred to (which resembles a sort of dusk, with a downward tendency toward darkness, rather than a completely dark night) is filled with the sediments of psychic impressions and behavioral modes. The true ground of the soul, on the other hand, is in itself neither dark nor light; nor is it a brooding volcano of irrational eruptions. On the contrary, when it is not completely veiled, and so apparently dark, it is the faithful mirror of its complementary pole, the Universal Spirit, and thus of all truths, which, when the latent force of imagination approaches the pure condition of *materia prima*, occasionally express themselves in the form of symbols...Not the least of the dangers of modern 'depth psychology' is that it hopelessly confuses true symbols with their distortions. This happens, for example, when Far-Eastern *mandalas* are placed on the same level as the concentric paintings of the mentally ill... The 'suprarational' must never be confused with the 'irrational.' "[67]

Continuing in this vein, he completely overshoots Jung:

> "From the 'inward' point of view, the 'reduction of metals to their primary substance' has nothing to do with a somnambulistic immersion of consciousness in the 'unconscious.' The 'reduction' occurs only after arduous combat against the conflicting tendencies of the soul, whereby all irrational 'knots' or 'complexes' must from the first be dissolved. The alchemical work is not a treatment for mental illness."[68]

While attacking Jung where he is vulnerable on the verity of alchemy as spiritual practice, Burckhardt trivializes the unconscious and underestimates the power as well as the peril of its contents. He does not realize that the journey into the realm of the shadow is often a far more substantial spiritual quest than a mimicking of exotic exercises in a cult situation. Stumbling in the dark, when honest and heartfelt, can be more substantial and true to the self than blindly fol-following a master without internal change. Thus Burckhardt mistakes individuation, a process of soul-making in which all humans are engaged by the fact of their incarnations, for some sort of visualization therapy practiced only on psychotics. Furthermore, Burckhardt's alchemy is only "spiritual;" it excludes paraphysical metallurgy far more definitively than even Jung does. The base metal, notably lead, corresponds to the "chaotic soul on the mineral plane." The soul is freed "from its coagulation and paralysis" by the dissolution of this *materia* out of the "crude and one-sided combination." It is then "coagulated" anew in the form of a perfect crystal. The alchemical gold has only "an inward reality." On the chemical process, he comments:

"...the true alchemists were never ensnared in any wish-fulfilling dream of making gold, and... they did not pursue their goal like sleep-walkers or by means of passive 'projections' of the unconscious contents of their souls! On the contrary, they followed a deliberate method, of which the metallurgical expression—the art of transmuting base metals into silver or gold—has admittedly misled many uninitiated enquirers..."[69]

F - Spiritual Alchemy

In our seminar[70] Charles Stein and I explored the problems of physical and spiritual alchemy and their relationship to both images and archetypes. The transcript of this section is presented in full:

Stein says: "I would like to get to that actual transformation through alchemy. What happens if you actually do these things, if you put together the laboratory?"

I respond: "I don't think that's so simple. When I first started thinking about it, as you can see in the original *Alchemy Issue*, I simply collected some texts I liked around Kelly's *Alchemical Journal*, and presented the whole gold problem in a silly wishful way. As if it would all go away by my belief in it. And parapsychology always gives you an out. You read about experiments in which mind directly or indirectly changes matter. If anyone says, 'It can't be done; you can't make these materials into gold,' you say: 'Well, people have projected pictures out of their head onto film, they lift dishes with their mind, they locate water underground with dowsing rods, they see the future; is making gold so much more difficult?' That's, of course, on the level of government sponsorship. The traditional situation is a little more tricky."

Stein: "How quickly we're willing to acknowledge authority when they come up with stuff like that."

I continue: "Sure. The next step would be obviously to ask who's done the actual experiments and what are their results. There was the one guy in Minnesota I corresponded with. But he turned out to be a debunker. At the time I thought he had promise because he was a chemist. Now I see it differently. There's no way this pedant, with his limited spiritual background and perspective, could have come close to the actual experiments, no matter how hard he tried to follow the recipes. It would be like expecting a dancer, because of her strong legs, to become an immediate master of t'ai chi. But I think one reason no one does the experiments is that no one is clear on what the experiments are. That became clear to me after the third edition of the *Alchemy Issue* when I began to feel we hadn't dealt with real alchemy at all, only the metaphors, the Jungian symbols. I realized that in order to know what the experiments were, you had to understand their language and be able to reproduce them on all the levels tha language described, all the inner images and experiences and initiations, and all the outer choices of materials, temperatures, vessels, sequences, and so on. You *at least* had to know something as basic as: what is alchemical mercury? Is it the metal mercury? Is it the metal in a special state? Is it another substance that is astrologically mercury? Now, lately, I have read in three different texts by people who say they have alchemical laboratories currently operating that mercury is simply a code word for something we know as antimony. That is, Lapidus, William Leo, and Frater Albertus, which themselves are code names for that matter. But I'm still not clear. Is it pure antimony? Is it antimony in solution with something else, say iron? Because even if you identified it as antimony, you'd have to know what it meant to be calling it mercury. Mercury's a big word, like Sulphur, or Salt. When Paracelsus uses these names, he's referring to atomic and elemental principles, not something you can isolate in the environment. But there still are Sulphur, Salt, Mercury, and they have some relationship to the elemental principle. Since you need something to work with, maybe antimony is a better source for elemental Mercury than the metal mercury. I don't know. Maybe antimony is the name of a stage within a process of occult chemistry. Is it the seed? Or is it the solution to which another seed is added? Is the green lion which it becomes during the initial phase of the alchemical process really copper, or is copper a code name for the color green?

Stein: "So the distribution of the nouns themselves, that stand for the substances, is a problem?"

"Yes. Even well before you get into deeper philosophical and syntactic problems. For instance, how does living chemistry coincide with inorganic chemistry? It would seem to coincide exactly, so then where does it diverge? I remember in my interview with Carl Sagan he said that a molecule of iron is a molecule of iron, wherever it is found, anywhere in the universe. It doesn't matter where the matter of your body comes from or that it's alive; which star furnaces cooked you up and which other living beings on this planet or others used your materials in ages past; you contain no remnant, only a molecule of iron, a molecule of potassium, and so on. Yet here we are talking about a chemistry which proposes going deeper, which proposes there being a deeper to go."

Stein: "You've really got to ask: how does *that* concept of iron come into being, when clearly the alchemical concept of iron was not that. Notice where the modern definition of iron comes from. You have an exact application of scientific criteria in establishing a system in which consistent properties will be assignable to consistently-behaving substances.

"The principles would be consistent no matter what kinds of observational material was derived. The molecule viewed at any scale is intelligibly translatable into any other scale. Through an electron microscope, as part of a chemical substance, as part of life: all those things are inter-intelligible, you could relate them to each other. Now before that system was derived, there was another way of dividing up the phenomena that were apparent in nature—not just perceptually, in terms of immediate perceptual experience, but intelligibly. Because it's very clear that the dividing up of natural objects into ninety, a hundred odd elements is not something that's immediately apparent to the senses. That's where the Jungian thing comes in, and what it means that Jung says the alchemists were projecting images from a collective unconscious. Because in any circumstances, when the world is being described in any other way than the scientific way, the very possibility of discovering pattens, of dividing up the material world into different categories and patterns, will be determined scientifically. Jung claims that there are scientifically determinable patterns that the psyche will project onto matter, and that's what was really happening with the alchemists, that you had a prescientific process, experience, thought, way of relating to the *experience* of matter. Its order and intelligibility were determined by patterns which were psychogenic, psychologically originated; they were ultimate patterns in the unconscious. But, and this is a big *but,* those patterns themselves, mysteriously, or not so mysteriously, correspond to certain basic patterns that exist objectively in nature and which, on another level, appear as being the actual morphology of the chemicals themselves. So that the basic constituent of the material world, the organic world, in post-alchemical times, turns out to be carbon, and the molecular structure of carbon is that it has four valences, and that number four, again and again and again, in psychological material, comes to represent the material basis of organic life.

The whole thing flips around. On the one hand, it looks like Jung is putting down alchemy by saying that this was really psychological projection they were unaware of; on the other hand, he's saying that those psychological projections are, in an intimate internal sense, in touch with the real internal structure of the material world. So that the revelations the alchemists have to give are of universal validity, not in the sense that they yield a practicable chemistry, but in the sense that the actual images of something much more profound, in human terms, are delineated."

I add: "Then, on some level, internally and unconsciously, the intensity of the real chemistry is felt, and expressed, through being, *as* being, as the psyche of being."

Stein: "Or in some way determines it.

"Our whole going on includes realms that are beyond any possible scale of perception out of which, nonetheless, all of our possible experience is, in some sense, constituted. Since we are also, even in the scientific view, physical beings, we have some primary intuition of that, we feel a connection. When you read about microphysics or astronomical spaces or periods of time calculated in billions of years, that produces a specific reaction in you, that is imaginary in one sense, but is on the other hand, *precisely imaginary*. The world of fantasy that is awakened in you when you think ten billion years is different in a precise way from the world of imagination that's produced in you when you think six thousand years. That has something to do with the actual physical structure of the universe and our relationship to it, as any kind of real data. Subjective fantasy isn't something that has to be, in an ultimate sense, severed and separated off as a process from the process of natural investigation. The actual investigation of one's own subjective experiences in relationship to matter is of primary interest in itself because the content of the fantasies you have will be true of the physical universe as such. They are ways of revealing structures of the particular way in which our constitution exists in relationship to the rest of the world. Which is objective, even though it's subjective.

"The scientific view of wanting to separate, radically, the fantasy from the data for the purpose of establishing general universal external structures, is itself a phase in a process, which has to be reunited. And in apparently our time, although no one has really found out how to do that. We are in the middle of a whole series of efforts to plug it back together in some way."

At this point I object that Stein has minimized alchemy; his response is that no one is presently practicing alchemy in mediaeval terms. Though I feel that there are probably alchemists still carrying out the old science, I acknowledge that my own interest is in the power of the imagery, the uniqueness of the alchemical phenomenology:

"The peacock's colored tail, the sudden startling appearance of the green lion: that's what captures my attention, not the theory, not the terms of this discussion—the feeling of something being purified, distilled, made essential in the alembic, the depths of blackness in the decomposition in the flask, like a black bog deeper than that of Beowulf but in a minute space, the shining citron of the yellow water, the goldness that is not alive yet radiates from the precipice of the sun in someone's room, *can* be touched, is alive like but unlike crystal. I enjoy the arguments, but they are not alchemy. So why don't we turn it over to Chinese alchemy, which has many of the same images, but as an expressly internal imagery, and not directly related to scientific solutions. The lungs become metal; the breath is fire; the semen or the blood is seed; the process of gold ascends from the slow furnace in the belly to the final brilliance behind the eyes and in the mind. This is another way of saying that the archetypal principle the metals represent is present in the body."

Stein: "Tell me if you don't share this. In reading the alchemical texts of China, as they've been translated, there's a peculiar thing. First of all, what is only implicit and what one has to dig out of Western alchemy seems completely explicit in Chinese alchemy. The fact that by the seed they mean an internal experience of light that is directed, and that the alchemical process as a whole is assimilatable as some kind of meditating concentrating process: this is completely explicit. To find anything like that in Western alchemy must be an act of your own work with it.

"Second of all, it doesn't seem to be so much a system with an ideology. Alchemy is transmittable through the various t'ai ch'i ch'uan exercises and teachings that are now floating around the country, but they don't require that one submit to a vocabulary, or to any system of mythical belief at all. However, what happens, eventually, is that one is initiated into the exact process, the exact bodily process, and the terms that made no sense at all at the outset begin to make more and more sense. They become the natural words, associated with the new conditions of experience that are generated in the course of doing the exercises. One isn't first learning a language and then being involved in a system of experiences that language conditions, unless one includes in the language *the entirety of the somatic process*. The word 'chi,' for instance, which is in 'The Yellow Emperor': they translate it as atmosphere; they talk of the organs having different atmospheres. But the word 'chi' starts out meaning nothing when you first do the exercises; then you begin to think, 'Oh, this has something to do with what the Indians mean by "prana".' Then you realize, 'Oh, gee, if what I'm beginning to experience doing this is "chi," it's a little different from "prana".' When you experience prana in yoga, it's involved in a different system of attention.

"And it gets more and more refined, and one's curiosity gets more explicit. The terms get distributed around very very specific concrete objective things that go on. But they don't make the slightest bit of sense divorced from the totality of the experiencing of the body. It's not abstract at all. And that reprograms the question about Western alchemy, since there was some sort of magical meditative practice that went along with it. And that's where the criticism of the Jungian position opens up again. If *that's* what's going on, then it's nonsense to say that it's a projection. It's something much more specific."

I pick up: "So that the difference is that, in the alchemical discipline, the symbols are part of training yourself in a specific mode of perception, and, in the Jungian system, the symbols are what you get inertially, for free, simply by existing?"

Stein: "The symbols are the process. For Jung, it would be as if he were to say (and this is where his language describing Chinese alchemy becomes very silly), it really didn't matter what actually happened; the part that was really powerful was the symbols that got generated to explain it. The Jungian system is really a Western system in that deep sense that Western systems again and again think that the serious action is the action of symbolic identification. The way that the Catholic theology rescues itself from the onslaught of the modern world is to say the Mass is symbolic action, that what the Church is here for is not as a model of behavior, not to encourage people to be good in the world in some moral sense, but to be the authoritative vehicle for a symbolic action. What faith means is that you participate within the symbolic structure. That's a heavy position, but it's a typically Western position. What matters then is the symbols which are operative, and which you identify with, and that you are the victims of and the experience of. That's where your true soul life is. Soul is something that's created in the process of symbolic identifications. Not material processes.

"But the Chinese is very materialistic. What's happening in your psyche in relation to doing t'ai chi ch'uan is *always what's in your way*. The more symbolic, the more in the way. It's exactly the thing that you're constantly being required to let go of—the part of you that is giving it a meaning, that is interpreting it in any way whatsoever. Any thought that arises in relation to the thing you're doing is exactly what has to be dropped. The system is a system of constantly dropping one's symbolizations, one's conceptualizations.

"I may be overstating it to say that what the process has to do with is dropping symbols—until what? It certainly is like that for a Westerner, who constantly asks, 'What does this mean? How should I understand this?' They say, 'Lift your arms,' and you say, 'Well, *lift* means this,' and they say, 'No, not like that. You're doing too much. Don't do anything!' You say, 'What do you mean?' And you keep trying to do the ridiculous thing that they tell you to do until something happens, and you say, 'Oh. That clearly is not doing something. There's a difference between what I thought doing and not-doing was and what *they* meant. It didn't mean going limp, and it didn't mean just doing.'

"There's something else that happens. And the system is to make that something else happen and *not* to make you have a clear idea about it. If you're anything like me or Richard, your motivation to understand it and think it out beforehand is crucial. In the West it is crucial. Because in Western religion, what matters is what you believe. In Western terms, certainly up until ten years ago, to be interested in alchemy at all was putting you in dangerous terms in the culture. You were immediately suspect unless you had had Jungian analysis."

G - Alchemical Dreams

Jung's alchemy is a system of imagery that arises spontaneously in particular psychic constellations (one of which, of course, was chemical alchemy, an imaginal system with concrete physical application). Archetypal alchemy does not require a chemical experiment and readily occurs in prescientific cultures (or in the dreams and mental states of ordinary people in all cultures). The sacrifice to achieve fertility, the pure whiteness that can come suddenly from blackness, and the medicine liberated from dung are just a few instances of universal alchemical imagery. As aspects of archetypes, these are indelible notions and produce their own phenomenology. Jung discovered repeated occurrences of the quaternity and the battle between intrinsic "threeness" and "fourness" in the sand-paintings of the Navaho Indians, Hindu and Buddhist mandalas, and myths and dreams from widely divergent cultures and epochs. The circle guarding its unconscious center, i.e., the princess in the castle, the serpent coiled about the egg, the spider whose web is encircled by the ouroboros are instances of spontaneous alchemical phenomenology. We might say that chemistry is the particular case in which imaginal alchemy rediscovers its own quantitative basis through a projection back onto matter. Science progresses through the epochs only because the elements are destined to find themselves again through psyche. Archetypal Sulphur reveals common sulphur even as Fire and Water lead historically to hydrogen and nuclear fission.

We tend to treat the alchemical images of common (or even mythic) consciousness as if they were symbolically connected to the work of traditional alchemy. This is more or less what Jung does when he finds alchemical modes of transformation and self-realization in fairy tales, myths, and dreams. But archetypal alchemy is not tied to the themes of traditional alchemy. Alchemical images are themselves the spontaneous by-product of individuation. They are not the passive residue of becoming conscious; they are the active means whereby the self creates the grounds of its own existence, the precise psychochemistry of that occurrence.

My own present experience is that alchemical dreams mediate important transitions of consciousness. Whenever my sense of my own nature is changing I have a series of cosmic dreams, usually over several nights. These involve distant planets, shifts of stars, articulate animals, and profound intimations of life-span and mortality. There is also an alchemical element which invariably grounds the numinous phenomena in mysteriously animated chunks of matter. Traditional alchemy likewise allowed the cosmic magician to perform as a chemist who could handle and order ordinary substance.

In the oldest dream I remember[71] (from about age seven) I am playing with the sorceror's bottles at a long laboratory table. I knock one of them over, and as it begins to break I hurriedly remove it from the table and rush to the bathroom to pour its leaking contents into the toilet bowl. While I am running I spill the fluid and it burns my legs. I am afraid it is poisonous and I am going to die.

At the time, a psychiatrist interpreted this as a dream of wetting my pants; I accepted the interpretation for thirty years until Charles Poncé pointed out an additional (not an alternative) meaning of the image: the spilled chemicals might be the burning mercurial waters the alchemists experienced on a concrete level. These waters belonged to the sorceror; coming from the underworld, they were imprinted with life and death. For a time I handled and experienced them, but most of the fire of waters spilled back or remained in the unconscious. The dream initially led to a child's initiation: when it was interpreted psychiatrically I learned that the daily self I had become familiar with was simply representational and that there was a deeper being within quite capable of speaking through me. Even though the analysis of the burning waters was limited to their role as urine, the revelation of their "secret" taught me very early that most of the real world was hidden. The problem of "keeping dry" is also an alchemical matter insofar as "toilet training" requires bringing consciousness to the autonomic realms of the body.

The old dream was brought to mind by a current one that occurred in 1981 after the alchemical dream cycle described below: I am returning to the dark brownstone in Greenwich Village where the original psychiatrist practiced (he had been dead twenty-four years). I have to pee very badly, and I stumble into a bathroom so dark I cannot see the toilet. As the urine hits the "water," I smell sulphur and then I hear hydrochloric acid bubbling in the bowl. I rationalize that it is not my pee but a substance in the toilet, and in any case, it stops. Then, as I am leaving the room I hear the bubbling sound again, like sizzling rice soup, and I realize my upper lip is burning from having touched it. I am wondering why there is a burning element in my urine, and I think that I must tell this dream to Poncé. The result is a reinterpretation of the childhood dream. But no doubt these waters come to the surface periodically for different reasons.

An important alchemical dream followed my taking of homoeopathic phosphorus for a digestive ailment in Vermont in 1976. In a fever that night I dreamed (or half-awake saw) my body stretched out before me on the bed as on a doctor's examination table. Thin tubes flowed down from my left and right eyes, meandering somewhat and crossing each other in the area of my diaphragm, ultimately connecting to the testicle opposite the eye from which they began. In the left eye's tube flowed silver liquid, and the symbol for the moon hung like an aura below my right testicle, and in the right eye's tube a golden liquid was running (although at times it seemed red), and the symbol for the sun shone below my left testicle. These were perhaps partial representations of the *Ida* and *Pingala,* the psychic nerves running down the left and right sides of the Kundalini subtle body. At the time of the "vision" I felt strong but also dizzy, and I understood that I would be sick for a long time while the medicine was working. In fact I was sick for almost two months in the time approaching my thirty-first birthday, but the illness also led to my meeting Edward Whitmont, a doctor involved in the alchemical tradition, and, quite separately, to a crucial secret of my ancestry.

Four years later I had a similar though less intense ailment, and on its final night, after a day in heavy surf on the beach in San Diego, I dreamed that I was carrying my own dead body out of a prison and solemnly burying it in the ebb tide under the Moon. The horror that it was my own body was countered by my amazement that I was still alive to do this. Unknown to me then, two months later this dream would bring me to a year of work in the alchemical mysteries with Charles Poncé. A particular theme made its first explicit appearance during a dream cycle in January of 1981:

There is a mound, maybe a dead body. I am supposed to fertilize it. Coming down from the sky in a column and passing directly through me are the letters of the Hebrew alphabet, one by one and moving very fast like insects. They are tiny and imprinted in black. The shaft seems to form diagonally out in front of me in the distance, but it enters the top of my head. I sense that these are seeds, and I am going to fertilize the mound with them. I will split it open with the force from my penis. I feel an electrical buzz pass into me suddenly with the letters, and I cannot move. I see *lamed.* I wake up.

Falling back asleep I am standing in an unknown place something like the colored fountain in Flint, Michigan. Huge chunks of wood are piled up in the basin of the fountain, a disorganized heap whose clutter extends like a tower with the lower boards supporting a platform high in the heavens. The wood is very very old. It has been undisturbed since before man came to the New World, and even long before that. It has almost no weight left in it, no gravity. A row of people has formed in front of the fountain, and one by one men and women are stepping into the wood and bathing. I am in line and being pushed forward. I try to escape because it looks dark and cold, but I cannot get out of line, and I find myself in the water, which is very thick. I am struggling to hang onto these light boards and pull myself up. I turn back and shout for others to retreat because the boards are falling and are too insubstantial to climb. But the person ahead of me says that I should just climb, that I cannot sink. "Don't you realize that this water has been undisturbed for hundreds of thousands of years," says a voice. "It has nothing left. You cannot possibly drown." Since there is no way out, I start pulling myself up rapidly like a lemur through gravityless space, springing from plank to plank. At the same time I seem to be going down into the water, or pulling myself up into new water. It is heavy stuff, and I don't want to be contaminated by it. I sink down through the quality of the wood and the water, but I do not drown. I seem to emerge on the top plaza.

It is no wonder I am afraid. First I am asked to fertilize the absolutely mute mound which has not yet been touched by consciousness, and I am given the magic of the stream of original language with which to do it. Then I am asked to bathe in the raw waters and materia of which I am myself made. Six nights later the mound reappears in an altered condition.

I am on an airplane flight across the country, but it is also like a bus and the passengers are able to talk to the pilot. It only becomes clear we are in the air when we pass over the scene of an old accident—far off to the right behind a wooded hill and close to the ocean. It is less like a crash, on closer inspection, than like an earth mound heaped up and shaped like a plane with part of its right wing missing. Later in the dream the pilot recalls the ancient crash that this mound of dirt now marks. No one lost their life, but there are people walking around with no brains or minds from it, and it is considered a great tragedy. Although the pilot can remember it, the accident happened so long ago that the site has fossilized.

The next night I am in a deep and dark forest with Benjamin Lo, the t'ai chi master. We are headed toward the lake, and I am tossing aside large branches of trees that have fallen. I am wishing I had a chain-saw to cut them into firewood. But Ben is involved in what seems to be a piece of wood and then turns out to be a living wormlike entity, also a fish, a frozen fish still alive. It is gradated pink and white with cartilage in the center. It has an obvious fish exterior with scales. I ask him what it is, and he holds it toward me, saying, "This weighs more than a skid of books." He cuts it into three pieces across its length, as though such a division were natural. I want to feel how heavy it is, but I am not empty enough. It is of neutron star density, and he is able to hold it because of his mastery of chi. I look at it in his hands. It is solid, rich, and complex; yet it is alive and dead both, wood and worm. It is shaped like the mound. I sense the darkness all around us. It has just rained, and soft pink salamanders have come out; like glow-worms, are the only light. This is a hopeful moment, for a dream ally, one not fluent in English, has come to share the burden with me, to divide it and expose some of its nature.

A month later I dream of being in the same forest, only alone. It is even blacker than before, and I sense that I am standing in the night of the creation, the night behind the night—above me certainly but also beneath me as my feet sink into unknown dense substance with every step. I sense omniscience everywhere. I try to find the cottage from which I wandered. I suddenly see new moons appearing around a planet; there is a meteor shower rushing me through the stars, and they are searching for me. I hide in the grass, but slowly a few of them break ranks; UFOs, giant faces leap out at me until I cannot look at them anymore and awake.

One night after the dream of Ben Lo in the forest I dream of being back at our house from years ago in Maine. We have returned to repair something. Yet it is indistinguishable from our present house in California. The work must be done under the house in a very cramped space. It has something to do with making the soil more fertile. Vegetables have grown in the winter, but they look more like precious stones than living things. It is snowing, and the plants stand out brightly in the ice. The forest seems to be growing under the house making the space dark and dense. It is cluttered with cartons of books. I am working with a hoe when I uncover a huge chunk of apple, a slab about 2½ feet long, a foot and a half across, and six inches thick. It is pure juicy apple shaped like a prism. I think this should be broken up, and I remember that there are instructions for this. I begin hacking at it with the hoe, but this has no effect. I am about to abandon it when I get the idea of cutting a groove into its surface. I work with a sharp tool, and the apple crumbles fairly easily leaving a slot. Then I strike it very hard with the hoe in order to split its long surface; instead it splits beneath the surface so that I have two long thinner slabs of apple which I place in the soil under the house. I think it is a waste to fertilize ground out of the sun, but apparently the apple was meant for there. Now I look out from under the house and see that it is a garage or barn, and there is a real house across the field. A very tiny white rabbit has gotten loose where I am working, and it is running toward the house carrying children's underpants in its mouth.

The dense object has become softer and tastier, and it has given rise to a gemlike winter garden. It splits only along its own nature, not by the nature I would assign it. A living thing arises and carries out a prank, something mercurial and joyful. The following night the dense object has become a medicine. I go to bed with a bellyache and dream of having homoeopathic Nux prescribed for me. It has formed not in the usual little white balls but as cubed chunks with smaller cubes coming out of the faces of mother cubes in all directions. There is a hidden spiral motif so that it resembles the crystals of galena lead but is still white and crumbly. I put the medicine in my mouth, and it tastes thick and insoluble. I am not sure I ever swallow it, but my symptoms diminish instantly. I am now translating the density inward as sensation.

That same night I dream of visiting a woman with whom I used to do work on breathing. During our dream session she gives birth. I must help the infant out, and in the process I become merged with the birth waters, become the baby, and kiss her on the lips. I return to my body, and the baby squirts out and slides around on the bed until both of us, using our arms, corral it. Then she picks it up and talks to it in a sweet hoarse babble. Something has finally been born—not a symbol, but actual material out of unconscious thought.

Two nights later I am at a vacation place in Florida. I am standing on the beach when a gigantic flat boat comes by. It is not a boat so much as a huge piece of rough unfinished wood with masses of people standing on it. I am with my family, and we are told that we can ride on it and be taken around the peninsula out into the southern sea. We stand on this big flat piece of wood rushing through the waves as through the sky. The shore moves in the distance. This is the first time anyone has seen these jungle lands; they are a new unexplored continent. The water comes in great rushes and waves upon the beach and fills it with tiny animals. Everything now is swarming with life.

IV - The Alchemical Process
A - Stars and Metals

Practical alchemy is based on the supposition of the natural (though slow) gestation of the metals in the Earth. Gradually, over the aeons, lead turns to copper, copper to iron, iron to tin, tin to mercury, mercury to silver, and finally silver to gold. The Earth is a loom in which the planets weave their vibrations. Each metal is the thread of a planet sown over the aeons of the evolution of the cosmos. The vibrations may be thought of as musical notes that become concretized in the loom; transmutation is thus a changing of the planetary note. In nature it occurs very slowly:

> "Natural cyclically transformed elixir is formed when mercury embracing lead becomes gravid. Wherever there is cinnabar there also are lead and silver. In four thousand three hundred and twenty years the elixir is formed."[72]

The planetary natures differ, so their metals have unique qualities and congeal at different levels of the Earth. Lead is formed deep in the underground by the planet Saturn; it is slow, heavy, and inanimate. At the other extreme gold is the residue of the Sun and the state of matter toward which the other metals are evolving. The alchemist is an active participant in this cosmic drama.

Jung paraphrases an idea from Michael Maier: "The sun, by its many millions of revolutions, spins the gold into the earth. Little by little the sun has imprinted its image on the earth, and that image is the gold. The sun is the image of God, the heart is the sun's image in man, just as gold is the sun's image in the earth..."[73]

This idea is revived hundreds of times, but memorably in the recent writings of Pierre Teilhard de Chardin,[74] for whom this Sun/Gold is the ethereal bioplasm out of which human consciousness is spun. In true twentieth-century fashion, it is the intelligence which apprehends and assays a goldenness that is truly psychic and not a metal at all. The evolution of consciousness was always the goal of the alchemists, and Teilhard portrays it on a global scale. He is a priest who has taken two pagan visions—the one of a living metal, the other of the evolution of species—and merged them into a Christian paradigm of anointed man.

Paracelsus was the astrological alchemist supreme:

> "The metals which come from the upper regions derive their origin from the seven planets. But these planets are manifold. There are many suns, many moons, many Marses, Mercuries, Jupiters, and Saturns."[75]

Alchemy is the inside body of astrology.

> "...stars...cast forth from themselves gems, granates, and other forms of stones...There are many stars which consist of ruby Sulphur, many of sapphire Salt, and many which are powerful in emerald Mercury."[76]

> "...fire destroys wood, leaves, grass. Whatever is left in the field decaying and passing into rottenness is consumed by the sun and the movement of the galaxy, so that it is no more left on the earth..."[77]

The Golden Treatise of Hermes states simply:

> "The matter which comes out of the center is imagined by the stars, operated by the elements, and formed by the earth."[78]

Just as the Sun is the harmonic realization of the planets and moons and meteors, comets, and asteroids singing together, so is Gold the harmony of metals, minerals, and substance. It is the celestial heart of the Earth. Paracelsus asks and answers the alchemical questions of his time:

> "Q. How many species of gold are distinguished by the Philosophers?
>
> "A. Three sorts:—Astral Gold, Elementary Gold, and Vulgar Gold.
>
> "Q. What is astral gold?
>
> "A. Astral Gold has its centre in the sun, which communicates it by its rays to all inferior beings. It is an igneous substance, which receives a continual emanation of solar corpuscles that penetrate all things sentient, vegetable, and mineral.
>
> "Q. What do you refer to under the term Elementary Gold?
>
> "A. This is the most pure and fixed portion of the elements, and of all that is composed of them. All sublunary beings included in the three kingdoms contain in their inmost centre a precious grain of this elementary gold.
>
> "Q. Give me some description of Vulgar Gold?
>
> "A. It is the most beautiful metal of our acquaintance, the best that Nature can produce, as perfect as it is unalterable in itself."[79]

B - Fire

Albertus writes that "alchemy is above all the art of fire." The skill of controlling the flame is inherited from the ancient metallurgical and shamanic forerunners of the alchemists.

"When my father felt that his movements were being impeded by the apprentices crowding round, he would silently motion them to stand back. Neither he nor anyone else would utter a word. No one dared to speak, and even the minstrel was silent. The stillness was broken only by the wheezing of the bellows and the low hissing of the gold. But though my father said not a word, I knew that he spoke inwardly; I could see that from his lips which moved silently as he stirred the gold and the charcoal with a stick—which, as it caught fire, he had to keep replacing. 'What could he be saying inwardly?' I cannot say for sure, as he never told me. Yet what could it be but an invocation? Did he now invoke the spirit of the fire and of the gold, of the fire and of the wind—the wind which blew through the bellows, of the fire that was born of the wind, and of the gold that was wedded to the fire? Assuredly he summoned their help and entreated their friendship and communion; assuredly he invoked these spirits which are amongst the most important, and whose aid indeed is necessary for smelting."[80]

The alchemist was working with far subtler minerals and oils, and he sought to understand and master the different degrees of natural and artificial heat. Artephius writes:

"We have properly three fires, without which our art cannot be perfected; and whosoever works without them takes a great deal of labour in vain. The first fire is that of the lamp, which is continuous, humid, vaporous, spiritous, and found out by art. This lamp ought to be proportioned to the enclosure; wherein you must use great judgement... For if this fire of the lamp be not measured...you will not see the expected signs, in their limited times, whereby you will lose your hopes...by a too long delay; or else, by reason of too much heat, you will burn the 'flores auri,' the golden flowers...

"The second fire is ignis cinerum, an ash heat, in which the vessel hermetically sealed is recluded, or buried; or rather it is that most sweet and gentle heat, which, proceeding from the temperate vapours of the lamp, does not equally surround your vessel. This fire is not violent or forcing, except it be too much excited or stirred up; it is a fire digestive; alterative, and taken from another body than the matter...

"The third fire, is the natural fire of water... This fire is mineral, equal, and participates of sulphur; it overturns or destroys, congeals, dissolves, and calcines; it is penetrating, subtile, incombustible and not burning, and is the fountain of living water, wherein the king and queen bathe themselves..."[81]

For Paracelsus, fire is a religion, recalling pagan ancient Europe and Christian Mediaeval Europe, reaching back to Heraclitus even as it reaches forward to Blake:

> "Know, then, that the ultimate and also the primal matter of everything is fire... It is this which makes manifest whatever is hidden in anything."[82]
>
> "No philosopher will deny that the sun generates a sun like itself; but it is not every one who will acknowledge that this foetus exists in the centre: least of all will those disciples of the philosophers who have no other knowledge of the Actnaean fire than that which comes from the fleshy eye, just like rustics in this respect. This terrene sun of the lower, or elementary, machinery is kindled by the fire of the higher sun. Just in the same way the centre of our matter is kindled by the centre of our world, or athanor, which is a fire, discharging after a manner the function of the natural sun.
>
> "Who does not see—I ask you, my brethren—that the form of the whole created universe has the similitude of a furnace, or, to speak more respectfully, the form of that which contains the matrix of a womb—the elements, that is to say, in which the seeds of the sun and the moon, cast down by the stars in their different influxes, are decayed, concocted, and finally digested for the generation of all things?"[83]

Burckhardt describes the psychospiritual aspect of the alchemist's oven:

> " 'Athanor,' from the Arabic *at-tannûr* ('oven'), is the word used by the alchemists to designate the oven in which the elixir is prepared. In alchemical manuscripts it is usually prepared in the form of a small tower surmounted by a dome. It contains the glass vessel (usually egg-shaped) which lies in a sand-bath or ash-pit situated immediately above the fire. All of this has both a literal and a symbolical meaning, for although it is certain that ovens of this shape were in fact used for all sorts of chemical and metallurgical operations, the real athanor—as far as the 'Great Work' was concerned—was none other than the human body, and thus also a simplified image of the cosmos.
>
> "That the oven of the alchemists is reminiscent of the human body has already been noted by other modern writers on alchemy. It is misleading, however, to try to establish this likeness on an anatomical basis, as, from the 'methodic' viewpoint of alchemy, the 'body' does not mean the visible and tangible body, but a tissue of powers of the soul which have the body as their support, and which are accessible *via* bodily consciousness. When it is said that love dwells in the heart, this assumes a relationship between soul and body similar to the one which, in a much more subtly graduated manner, lies at the basis of the alchemical symbol of the athanor.
>
> "The most important element in the oven is the fire. The alchemists

stress that the heat which transmutes the *materia* contained in the glass must be threefold, namely, the open heat of the fire, the evenly distributed heat of the ash- or sand-bath (in a trough of which the glass vessel sits like an egg in the nest), and finally the latent heat that is actualized in the substance itself, a heat which thereafter becomes active in its own right...

"The fire clearly corresponds to the generative power, which is first aroused and then tamed in order to serve inward contemplation. From this it can at once be understood why the alchemists have always warned against a violent or unsteady fire. A violent flame might well consume the 'flowers of gold.' The indirect warmth of the ash-pit, on the other hand—which must be 'mild, enveloping, and penetrating'—signifies the concentration of the soul, which is indirectly brought about and maintained by the 'open' fire. Ash is burned living material which can no longer be set on fire—that is to say, which is no longer attainable by the passions...

"The fire is invigorated both by a current of air which enters through the air holes in the oven, and by the use of bellows. This is an indication that, in spiritual concentration as practiced by the alchemists, the regulation of the breath played a part just as in yoga."[84]

C - The Twelve Stages

The twelve stages, as stated in the literature, are usefully divided into three sequences of four. The first sequence appears to describe the creation of a black brew and the extraction of spiritualized substance; it includes: calcination, dissolution, separation, and conjunction. The second sequence is conceivably a series of signs and operations occurring during the first; it may also include some repetition. It is uncertain whether it adds any new information, but, however defective it is as a linear sequence, it is clearly important in its emphases: putrefaction, congealation, cibation, and sublimation. The third sequence involves only what happens after the powder or liquid known as the Philosophers' Stone has been made; then fermentation, exaltation, multiplication, and projection are employed in the transformation of substance. The twelve stages can also be understood as two basic cycles, one corresponding to the reduction of physical matter and the other involving its spiritualization or sublimation. The cycles oscillate throughout the process in alternating reductive and reconstitutive phases.

The number "twelve" probably is a standard adaptation of various formulas to fit the traditional numerology of the zodiac. Some stages are clearly defined and require active intervention whereas others are merely observation points. Jung takes these aberrations as an expression of not chemical but psychological realities:

"The arrangement of the stages in individual authors depends primarily on their conception of the goal: sometimes this is the white or red tincture *(aqua permanens)*; sometimes the philosophers' stone, which, as hermaphrodite, contains both; or again it is the panacea *(aurum potabile, elixir vitae)*, philosophical gold, golden glass *(vitrum aureum)*, malleable glass *(vitrum malleabile)*. The conceptions of the goal are as vague and various as the individual processes. The *lapis philosophorum,* for instance, is often the *prima materia,* or the means of producing the gold; or again it is an altogether mystical being that is sometimes called *Deus terrestris, salvator,* or *filius macrocosmi...*

"Side by side with the idea of the *prima materia,* that of water *(aqua permanens)* and that of fire *(ignis noster)* play an important part. Although these two elements are antagonistic and even constitute a typical pair of opposites, they are yet one and the same according to the testimony of the authors. Like the *prima materia* the water has a thousand names; it is even said to be the original material of the stone. In spite of this we are on the other hand assured that the water is extracted from the stone or *prima materia* as its life-giving soul *(anima).*"[85]

Any given author may also purposely or unintentionally confuse the order of the steps. Alchemists tend to understand and correct for each other, either in matters of symbolism or sequence, or at least they think they do. The "emblems of our magistery" are peacocks, spotted dragons, heads of ravens, flying vultures, and creeping toads. Sometimes these can be visualized as chemical events (the colors of the peacock's tail, or the distillate-vulture that rises while the toad sinks to the bottom). Yet, even then, they are not unambiguous.

Black, white, yellow, and red are the color signs, but they are rarely in perfect sequence and are often replaced by other important colors, such as blue and green. Yellow is frequently missed.

The serious alchemist must make continuous decisions about which events to disregard and by which to measure his progress. Since any wrong decision can ruin a many-year experiment, it is little wonder that twenty, thirty, and forty years are spent on the completion of a single formula.

D - Sulphur, Salt, and Mercury

The first practical difficulty is in the choice of materials with which to work. Alchemy proposes a universal quality to matter, so, theoretically, anything is a possible candidate, *if* the experimenter knows how to extract from it what he needs. Some substances, however, are preferable, and the alchemical riddle tends to hover between the accurate identification of those substances and a means of extraction which would be applicable to a variety of substances.

We can start with the division of substance itself into three categories: Sulphur, Salt, and Mercury. These are not rock sulphur, sea salt, and metallic quicksilver; they are three principles of indestructible prime matter. In that sense, they correspond to the four elements: Earth, Air, Fire, and Water, of which they are the purest possible mineral realizations. The nineteenth-century philosopher of science, Albert Poisson, offered a conversion chart for elements and principles. Sulphur was to be taken as the fixed principle, Earth when solid, Fire when subtle; Mercury was the volatile principle, Water when liquid, Air when gaseous, Salt was neither fixed nor volatile and was comparable to Quintessence, or Ether.

Alchemy consists of the extraction of pure Sulphur, Mercury, and Salt from raw material; the fusing of these materials into a new and unknown substance called The Philosophers' Stone; and the merging of material from this "Stone" with some other material, classically lead, to produce gold. These essences may be extracted from other metals or organic substances depending on astrological or other sympathetic correspondences. It is important to remember that the spirit is not the already-formed body of the element.

According to William Leo, "In all cases the true Spirit of Sulphur is an incombustible oil, and it sends out a vapor described by the alchemists as 'penetrating.' Minerals said to be high in sulphur are gold, silver, copper, iron, vitriol, and verdigris."[86]

Paracelsus is unambiguous about the difference between mineral and spirit:

"Sulphur, one of the three primals, is the first matter of gold. If Alchemists could find and obtain this Sulphur, such as it is in the auriferous tree at its roots in the mountains, it would certainly be the cause of effusive joy on their part. This is the Sulphur of the Philosophers, from which gold is produced, not that other Sulphur from which comes iron, copper, etc."[87]

Every metal contains Sulphur as principle: it gives silver its whiteness, copper its ability to attract lightning, iron its strength in steel, mercury its malleability.

Mercury is considered the most elusive of the primals, the one that exerts the most unexpected and profound power on the materials. If Sulphur conveys pure matter, Mercury is the matrix of pure energy—and Salt combines them. One aspect of Mercury is an elemental component of all the metals; it can be extracted from lead, or, for that matter, from gold itself. But triumphant Mercury is a spirit, Mercurius, the divine winged Hermes, caducei in his arms, the Sun on his right, the Moon on his left. He is also Hermes-Thoth, the god or mortal who invented alchemy, the distinguishing name for a lineage of elite alchemists. According to Jung, he is "world-creating spirit concealed or imprisoned in matter," for which Ouroboros, the tail-eating dragon, stands, the "oldest pictorial symbol in alchemy." For Mercurius "stands at the beginning and end of the work: he is the *prima materia,* the *caput corvi,* the *nigredo;* as dragon he devours himself and as dragon he dies, to rise again as the *lapis.* He is the play of colours in the *cauda pavonis* and the division into four elements. He is the hermaphrodite that was in the beginning, that splits into the traditional brother-sister duality and is reunited in the *coniunctio,* to appear once again at the end in the radiant form of the *lumen novum,* the stone. He is metallic yet liquid, matter yet spirit, cold yet fiery, poison and yet healing draught—a symbol uniting all opposites."[88]

Mercurius is the strangest and most charismatic figure in alchemy, and he stands in the center of the work. Sometimes he talks as a man; sometimes he talks as a metal; mostly he does a mute regenerative dance at the root of nature, a dance modern physicists have come to describe as the imponderable quantum states of atoms, unpredictable fluctuations through which particles form and vanish in waves of gravity and electricity. He also sits at the center of this terrestrial solar system harboring the volatile potentiations of all the planets, and the essence of sun-ness and moon-ness, male-ness and female-ness, opposites enclosing a unity which keeps the celestial and sublunary spheres composed and in motion. As a liquid, he is highly volatile, colored either ruby, clear, or golden. As a planet, he is closest to the Sun itself. As a god, he is the messenger among all the gods, meaning messenger between planets and between metals.

One of the more famous alchemical errors is the notion that common mercury, with its wet glitter, is Spirit of Mercury. Apparently there could be few worse choices, and a mistake can lead to poisoning and death. Mercury of lead is less deadly, easily extractable, but cold and quickly lost to volatility. In more recent times both alchemists and scholars agree that antimony is the best source for not only Mercury but all three principles. Lapidus summarizes this position:

"...the main reason for the failure in finding the true road to success has been the ignorance of true mercury, which is nothing else than the metallic vapour of Antimony purified by iron, with which everything is done, and without which nothing will be achieved. Although it is well known to the modern metallurgist that ordinary mercury or quicksilver (or argent vive, as the alchemists called it) will mix with most metals, and reduce them to a liquid condition even at room temperature, many experimenters of old failed, as they never gave up experimenting with this metal. But mercury will separate from any metal with which it has been amalgamated if it is heated. As soon as a correct heat is applied, it separates and as the alchemist's work was to produce a fixed metal that would not do this, ordinary mercury was not the answer."[89]

References in the literature support both that the prime matter could not have been mercury and that it might have been a spirit of antimony. Lapidus quotes from *Bacstrom's Alchemical Anthology:*

"The mercury of the philosophers is not found in the earth, but must be prepared by art, by joining the sulphur (of Mars) to the mercury (of antimony)...

"This saturnine antimony agrees with gold and contains in itself argentum vivum, in which no metal is swallowed up except gold; and gold is truly swallowed up...for this is friendly and agrees with the metals...

"Let the two heroes saturn (antimony) and mars (iron) fight together. Though the former is peaceably inclined, let them have three or four violent assaults. After this they will be reconciled and as a token thereof they will erect a glorious banner resembling a star."[90]

Lapidus adds:

"...common mercury is silvery and opaque, and the philosophers' mercury is not a metal, and is clear; as clear as the tears of the eyes, a beautifully clear, brilliant, and shining water..."[91]

Behmen: "There is nothing in nature capable of qualifying matter to be harmonized, but one mineral spirit, the ore of which is equal in attraction and repulsion, and the pure metal in a star-like circle of irradiated circulation. Antimony, purified by iron and pounded fine, might be circulated, that is, digested to a perfect harmony of the principles...

"The prime matter is antimony purified by iron, and finely pounded. The invisible mercury is the spiritual air of antimony which combines with vegetable or animal fluids, and the solids in its spiritual or watery form, and from thence, combines with metals and stones...The gas will not unite easily with metals or minerals, until it is embodied for that purpose. This may be done either with the thick red or white mercuries, which are the oil or water of antimony...By circulating, that is, digesting the impregnated liquid two months, the gas floats as an oil on weak liquids, or is united with the strong, subduing their corrosion."[92]

In the seventeenth century, Boerhaave:

"...antimony dissolves metals with as much ease as fire thaws ice... there is no method yet known of recovering metals with which antimony has once been fused...This is certain, that nothing is better suited to alter the nature of metals than antimony."[93]

The most common source of Salt, as has already been implied by the association of Red Mars with the Green Antimony Lion, is Iron, but it was also classically Arsenic, whose very name means Salt. Robert Kelly reminds us that for the Martian alchemist green Earth would be the planet of antimony, to be mixed with the local red sand.[94] At the distance of Sol the Green and Red Lions merge, and their elemental nature is Azoth. Artephius writes:

"Now this our second and living water is called 'Azoth,' the water washing the laton, *viz.* the body compounded of sol and luna by our first water; it is also called the soul of the dissolved bodies, which souls we have even now tied together, for the use of the wise philosopher...It is the royal fountain in which the king and queen bathe themselves; and the mother must be put into and sealed up within the belly of her infant; and that is sol himself, who proceeded from her, and whom she brought forth and therefore they have loved one another as mother and son, and are conjoined together, because they come from one and the same root..."[95]

But the *prima materia* also remains a riddle, ubiquitous and commonplace, yet unique and rare. Gather what is cheap, despised, and common is an alchemical motto—"the sodden, moist, fat, and muddy earth of Adam, materia prima, from which this large world, we ourselves, and our powerful stone were created," says Heinrich Kunrath in *Theatrum Sapientiae Aeternae*.[96]

"I know well your secret Quicksilver," says Fra Marcantionio in *The Light which Proceeds from Darkness*. "It is nothing other than a living, omnipresent and innate spirit which, in the form of an aery haze...it continually descends to earth in order to fill earth's porous body...it takes on the form of primordial humidity."[97]

And Thomas Vaughan: "The earth...being the subsidence or remains of that primitive mass which God formed out of darkness, must needs be a feculent, impure body; for the extractions which the Divine Spirit made were pure, oleous, ethereal substances, but the crude, phlegmatic, indigested humours settled like lees toward the centre. The earth is spongy, porous and magnetical, of composition loose, the better to take in the several influences of heat, rains and dews for the nurture and conservation of her products."[98]

And Ripley:

> "The philosophers tell the inquirer that birds and fishes bring us the lapis, every man has it, it is in every place, in you, in me, in everything, in time and space. It offers itself in lowly form. From it there springs our eternal water (*aqua permanens*)."[99]

Perhaps the most remarkable documented experiment of contemporary alchemy is Armand Barbault's thirteen-year making of the exilir. For this work, which apparently produced a substance unknown to science, Barbault chose the simplest and most available *prima materia:*

> "What *is* this First Matter hidden several centimetres under the turf? Is it not—at least as far as the layman is concerned—plain ordinary earth? For the initiated person it is something quite different: it is *living* earth, seized from the ground by a very special process belonging to the sphere of High Magic, which allows the adept assigned to the task to gain possession of an entire collection of physical and metaphysical principles. It is indeed physically earth, but charged with the forces of life which would instantly be returned to the ground if someone unaware of the necessary preparation sought to imitate our actions."[100]

Barbault was gathering material from the zodiacal cycle as well as the earth, so the exact time of collection was crucial. The matter had to be celestial as well as terrestrial:

> "...the operation had to be supported by a long lasting cycle like that of Saturn and Pluto, beginning that very day with the conjunction of the two planets. It was known that the work would be very lengthy and could not reach its first perfection until the moment Saturn had completed one half of its revolution, i.e., had reached Aquarius...
>
> "...allowance had also to be made for the combinations of subsequent

cycles, particularly the grand conjunction of Uranus and Pluto in opposition to Saturn, occurring in 1965-6, which was also to mark an important stage in the work.

"That's why the *decision* was taken on Sunday, August 3rd, 1947. The following week saw intensification of the currents while the sun passed successively through conjunction with Saturn and Pluto. February 15th, 1948, night of the new moon in Aquarius, was fixed as the date of *acquisition;* the time was to be soon after midnight, at the moment when the sun passed to the depths of the sky under the feet of the seeker. This was so that the charge, the germ, might be gathered with the portion of black soil taken from the earth."[101]

The site of collection was chosen by a woman guide, in touch, in Barbault's words, "with a higher spiritual plane." Synchronously, she picked a pregnant zone of earth, and, at the moment of perception, planted, by her awareness, the germ of the experiment. "Through the power of the Word, the Guide perceived the living colors which, in the form of globes, were fixed under her feet for the duration of the first magical ceremony, devised for that very end. *In this way the birth of the germ of the Germ, or pre-matter, is brought about.*"[102]

Returning to the site between the time of selection and the time of gathering, she perceived an enlarging circle of green crossed by two strong currents. She drew a first and then a second magical circle, each of which protected the egg, which had become delicious prey to invading forces. She later saw two astral stars "casting thousands of rays on the metallic foetus which, after passing through all the colours of the rainbow, finally became a vivid red." A day later she was forced to do dream battle with prehistoric animals who surrounded the egg. The battle lasted for three days, and on the fourth day, she saw a spectrum of the "most beautiful colors in the world" coming directly from the sun and fertlizing the stone.[103]

Barbault does not go into details about the collection of the material, except to indicate that the most minute and subtle ritual cleansings took place and that no implement was used: the Philosopher's Peat was dug by hand. His description continues:

"We were lucky enough that year to have an early spring. So, soon after acquiring the Matter, we were able to start collecting the first few drops of dew each morning. We moistened the Earth with this, impregnating it with the required vital forces. We moistened and dried alternately and as frequently as possible until we could begin collecting the first plants and herbs with which to nourish it."[104]

After the mixture has been washed, dried, and pulverized small plants and buds are added to it. "It is important to use very young plants, full of sap and dew. This mixture is left to steep slowly at a low temperature until a deposit is formed. The mixture is then gently heated in an especially prepared alembic, ensuring that the temperature never rises above 40 degrees centigrade...

"Any sort of plant may be picked, but we looked above all for the truly beautiful, those which grew at random in wild areas, in the forests or the mountains and in those areas not over-populated and hence free of chemical additives...

"At the same time, when the weather was fine and still, we set about collecting mountain dew...what we did was to choose a field of green, yet fairly stiff corn and then slide a very fine yet porous canvas up and down the rows. The canvas became saturated with dew drops which formed at the tips of the plants and every twenty metres or so we would stop and squeeze the canvas over a vessel, gaining several glasses of dew each time. The method shown in the *Mutus Liber* (lengths of canvas spread out on the grass) is definitely preferable, the dew so gathered being of purer, more etheric composition."[105]

As vegetable matter was continually added, the solution grew blacker, first as a result of the humus formed (the first degree of blackness), then as a result of the dew itself becoming black water (the second degree), and finally an absolute black (the third degree). Barbault says that it took him three years to achieve the first degree, another two or three to reach the second degree, and apparently another three years to complete the corruption. He summarizes the meaning of this long stage:

"The phenomenon of corruption has the following effect on the matter: it brings about the separation of the mixtures, allowing the life forces to become fixed in the salts formed from incineration. In this way the life forces are made assimilable by the human body..."[106]

Since metals are not used, his Blood of the Green Lion is the concentrated force of the sap and dew. The Red Lion is the ripening of the fruit under Leo, which marks the passage to the second degree, at which point the mixture smells and tastes like raspberry.[107]

Barbault's method is traditional in many of its aspects; he refers to Basil Valentine, John Dee, *Mutus Liber*, Paracelsus, Raymond Lully, Fulcanelli, Cyliani, etc., for clues and help—but he emphasizes that he must make his own way, and that there are no quantitative measures for any stage, nor specific instructions as to heat or exact sequence. The alchemist must intuit the work as he proceeds.

D - The Destruction and Reconstitution of Matter

Calcination (or reduction) is the first stage. The original materials are reduced to a raw pulp. They are dissolved in liquid, crushed, stirred. Some sources describe an ash, but there is no flame; natural heat comes from within; the "fire" may literally be time.

Paracelsus departs from a strict definition of the first stage, explaining that some materials are prepared for etheric isolation by reduction while others are prepared by different means.[108] Homoeopathic pharmacists also grind and crush some materials and dissolve others in alcohol as the first stage in the spiritualization of the substance.

Dissolution (also called solution or digestion) follows calcination, and appears to be the natural consequence of bringing materials together. Most descriptions of calcination lead right into dissolution. The following is from Philalethes:

> "Calcination is the first purgation of the stone, the drying up of its humours, through its natural heat, which is stirred into vital action by the eternal heat of water, whereby the compound is converted into a black powder, which is yet unctuous and retains its radical humour. This calcination is performed for the purpose of rendering the substance viscous, spongy, and more especially penetratable; for gold in itself is highly fixed, and difficult of solution even in water, but through this calcination, it becomes soft and white, and we observe it in its two natures, the fixed and the volatile, which we liken to two serpents...
>
> "When the substances are first mixed, they are at enmity with each other, by reason of their contrary qualities, for there is the heat and dryness of the sulphur fiercely contending with the cold and moisture of the mercury. They can only be reconciled in a medium which partakes of both natures, and the medium in which heat and cold are reconciled is dryness which can co-exist in both. Thus cold and heat are brought to dwell peaceably together in the dryness of the earth, and the dryness and the moisture in the coldness of the water.
>
> "Its sufficient cause is the action of the inward heat upon the moisture, whereby everything that resists it is converted into a very fine powder; the moving and instrumental cause is the fire contrary to nature, which being hidden in our solvent water, battles with its moisture, and digests it into a viscous or unctuous powder.
>
> "Calcination then is the beginning of the work, and without it there can be neither peaceable commixtion, nor proper union. The first dealbation reduces the substance to its two principles, sulphur and mercury; the first of which is fixed, while the other is volatile. They are compared to two serpents, the fixed substance to a serpent without wings, and the volatile substance to a serpent with wings. One serpent holds in his mouth the tail of the other, to show that they are indissolubly conjoined by community of birth and destiny, and that our art is accomplished by the joint working of this mercurial sulphur, and the sulphureous mercury."[109]

Artephius discusses dissolution, but apparently jumps ahead to sublimation:

> "This composition is not a mechanical thing, or a work of the hands, but, as I said, a changing of natures; and a wonderful connexion of their cold with hot, and the moist with the dry...by such a dissolution and sublimation, the spirit is converted into a body and the body into a spirit...

"Wherefore, let our body remain in the water till it is dissolved into a subtle powder in the bottom of the vessel and the water, which is called the black ashes... in them is the royal diadem, and the black and unclean argent vive, which ought to be cleansed from its blackness by a continual digestion in our water, till it be elevated above in a white colour, which is called the gander, and the bird of Hermes."[110]

The Golden Treatise of Hermes has the following description:

"Take the flying bird and drown it flying, and divide it and separate it from its pollutions. Draw it forth and repel it from itself."[111]

Separation of the light parts from the heavy is the next specific sign or stage. For metal Paracelsus recommends reducing them to a state of flux. "When this has been done, throw in for every pound of the metal one ounce of the most perfectly sublimated and refined sulphur. It will there be burnt, and in the course of that operation it will attract to itself, on the surface, one metal, the lightest, whilst it will leave the heavier on the bottom." For gold and silver, he recommends *Mercurius vivus*, and for vegetables, nuts, roots, etc., a combination of pressing and heating.[112]

Conjunction is the result of the collective processes preceding it in the traditional sequence. William Leo, a contemporary alchemist, gives a full version of his method:

"Once you've found your *prima materia*, your first job is to calcine it, to reduce it to a fine powder or salt. This is done by placing the material in a well-sealed flask over a gentle heat, maintaining the fire at a steady temperature until you do in fact have a fine black powder resting on the bottom of the glass. When this is done, take the glass from the fire and allow it to cool. Remember to save the dregs of the metal; you'll need them later.

"Next take the cooled powder and combine it with the aqua regia (nitric acid) until a solution is formed. You can watch the nitric acid 'devour' your powder; this process is represented in alchemical literature as 'the Green Lion devouring the sun.' When the solution is complete, put it in one of your ceramic or earthenware containers, attach a still to the top, and attach a receiver to the arm of the still. Into the still head you should pour vinegar which itself has been distilled up to seven times. Place the distilling apparatus over a slow fire (the ash-furnace should do nicely) and heat it until all the vinegar is driven off into the receiver. Then pour the vinegar back in and repeat the process. Keep repeating the process until all the vinegar is either absorbed or evaporated, at which point you should have a fine white powder clinging to the sides and bottom of the container.

"...now your powder must be separated into two parts; one an incombustible oil and the other a clear, volatile water. The oil represents the Spirit of Sulphur, the water the Spirit of Mercury. This separation is performed by means of gentle heat (use the ash fire), and by repeating calcination and distillation of the end product. If you are following Cockren, you may wish to add a solution containing nitric acid and the salts of gold. When the operation is complete, you should have either a deep golden liquid or two distinct liquids; one clear and watery, the other a red oil. Either of these results is acceptable, for the golden liquid can be separated into the clear and the red, while these latter two can be recombined to produce the original gold...

"Now put your two principles in separate containers, seal them tightly (wax is best), and store them for awhile in a cool, dry place; having found the two essential spirits, you can let them rest for a time while you go after the Spirit of Salt. For this you must use the dregs left behind by your first calcination. Using mild heat, reduce these dregs to a white salt; you'll then have the Three Spirits well in hand."

Conjunction follows only after a suitably long period.

"When the Spirits are mixed in proper proportion and subjected to long, mild heat a black earth or powder should form on the bottom of the flask. This black earth should be cooled and refined up to seven times, or until it is absolutely dry. You've now reached the stage which the medieval alchemists called 'The Sign of the Crow.'

"Place this powder in a sealed flask and set the flask over a gentle fire...after a time the matter should begin to turn color. Maintain the heat and you'll see the powder proceed through all the spectral colors until it reaches a state of perfect whiteness."[113]

The early twentieth-century alchemist Fulcanelli writes:

"The operation is the more important because it leads to the acquisition of philosophic mercury, a living, vital substance issuing from pure sulphur wholly fused with primeval, celestial water... The two methods of the Work need different means of vitalising the original mercury. The first is for the short way, and consists of a single operation, by which the solid part is moistened gradually—for all dry matter drinks its humidity avidly—until the reiterated fusion of the volatile with the solid makes the mixture swell and turns it into a pasty or syrupy mass as the case may be. The second method consists in diluting the whole of the sulphur with three or four times its weight of water. Pour off the solution into a bottle, then dry out the residue, and begin again with a proportionate amount of fresh mercury. When dissolution is complete, separate any sediment there may be, and collect the liquids in an open vessel to undergo slow distillation. Any superfluous liquid will thus be eliminated, leaving the mercury at the desired consistency, without the loss of any of its virtue, and ready to undergo hermetic coction."[114]

"It is necessary to cook the celestial salt, which is the philosopher's mercury, with some terrestrial metallic body, in a crucible and over an open fire, for four days."[115]

In his book, *The Secret of Alchemy,* Stanislas Klossowski de Rola describes the stages following the preparation of the *prima materia:*

"The resulting 'compost' is then enclosed in a hermetically sealed vessel or Philosophic Egg, which is placed in the Athanor, the furnace of the Philosophers.

"This Athanor is devised in such a way as to be able to keep the Egg at a constant temperature for long periods of time. The outward fire stimulates the action of the inner fire, and must therefore be restrained; otherwise, even if the vessel does not break, the whole work will be lost. In the initial stage the heat is compared to that of a hen sitting in her eggs...

"In the Egg the two principles with the *Materia Prima* — one solar, hot and male, known as sulphur, the other, lunar, cold and female, known as mercury — interact...

"Thus death, which is separation, is followed by a long process of decay which lasts until all is purified and the opposites dissolved in the liquid *nigredo*. This darker than darkness, this 'black of blacks' is the first sure sign that one is on the right path...

"The *nigredo* phase ends with the appearance on the surface of a starry aspect, which is likened to the night sky which told shepherds and kings that a child was born in Bethlehem. And so the first work, the first degree of perfection, nears completion when, from the mutual destruction of conjoint opposites, there appears the metallic, volatile humidity which is the Mercury of the Wise.

"The volatile principle of mercury flies through the alchemical air, within the microcosm of the Philosophical Egg, 'in the belly of the wind,' receiving the celestial and purifying influences above. It falls again, sublimated, on the New Earth which must eventually emerge. As the outer fire is very slowly intensified, the moist yields to the dry until the coagulation and desiccation of the emerging continent is complete. While this is happening, a great number of beautiful colours appear, corresponding to a stage known as the Peacock's Tail.

"The end of the 'second work' comes with the appearance of the Whiteness, *albedo*. Once the Whiteness is reached, our subject is said to have acquired sufficient strength to resist the ardours of fire, and it is only one step more until the Red King of Sulphur of the Wise appears out of the womb of his mother and sister, Isis or mercury, *Rosa Alba*, the White Rose."[116]

In the color sequence, blackness corresponds to the original destruction of matter (the melanosis or nigredo). The following phase (leukosis or albedo) consists of a shining whiteness sometimes called white gold, or *terra alba foliata*, and is lunar and female in imagery. The Peacock's Tail is part of the leukosis. The colors are absolutely magnificent; the observers' accounts of the vapors are metaphysical hymns in the spirit of Donne and Marvell. We have not yet reached the age in which chemistry is seen as a mere mechanical interaction of molecules. The gods are still present in matter:

> "When the regimen of the fire is moderated, the matter is by degrees moved to blackness. Afterwards, when the dryness begins to act upon the humidity, various flowers of different colours simultaneously rise in the glass, just as they appear in the tail of the peacock, and such as no one has ever seen before. Sometimes, too, the glass looks as though it were entirely covered with gold. When this is perceived, it is a certain indicaion that the seed of the man is operating upon the seed of the woman, is ruling it and fixing it...Afterwards, when the humidity has died out before the process of drying, those colours disappear, and the matter at length begins to grow white, and continues to do so until it attains the supreme grade of whiteness."[117]

E - Putrefaction through Sublimation

Putrefaction is a natural decay from internal heat. Congealation, also called coagulation, is a succeeding solidification of some of the matter in solution. By cibation, it is wetted down again. Barbault's description of adding dew is instructive.

Of putrefaction, Philalethes writes:

> "The body of old must be dissolved, destroyed, putrefied and deprived of all its powers and this the beginning of the work, assumes first a dark, and later a perfectly black colour called the Raven's Head. This takes place in about forty days. During this blackness the anima of gold is extracted and separated, and is carried aloft and totally separated from the body, the body remaining for some time without life, and like ashes at the bottom of the vessel."[118]

Cyliani describes the darkness in *Hermes Unveiled*:

> "...the mixture seems at times to be quite dry, and at others it boils like melted pitch—which is a terrible thing to see...It is no ordinary blackness that is seen here, but is of so tremendous a depth that by the very fact of being black it appears shining and resplendent. And if at any time you see the matter thickening to a paste in the bottom of the vessel, rejoice for this tells you that a quickening spirit is at work..."[119]

Artephius also writes of these stages:

> "The whole secret lies in our knowing how to extract non-buring Quicksilver from the body of Magnesia, that is to say, one must extract a

living and incombustible water and then coagulate it with the perfect body of the sun, which dissolves this water into a white creamy substance, until everything is white. At first, however, the sun will lose its splendor, be extinguished, and become black, as a result of the putrefaction and dissolution which it undergoes in this water."[120]

Sublimation, the eighth stage, specifically denotes the extraction of material from solution by forced evaporation (distillation). Historically, it may be the oldest and most fundamental stage of laboratory alchemy. Lindsay puts this into context:

"The alchemists seem to have been the first investigators of distillation. At times some sort of sublimation of liquids had been attempted, e.g. seawater had been heated in a covered cauldron, then the drops condensed on the lid were shaken off and used as drinking water. Also oil-of-pitch was made by heating pitch and condensing vapour on fleeces; and mercury was produced by heating cinnabar on an iron saucer in a pan covered by a pot called *ambix*, on which the mercury vapour condensed. But none of these crude devices was truly a still or an alembic, which consists of three parts: the vessel in which the material is heated, a cool part for condensing the vapour, a receiver. Maria (the Jewess) describes the still and seems to have invented it. The *balneum Mariae* or *baine-marie* seems first used as a name by Arnald of Villanova in the 14th century."[121]

F - The Alchemical State of Matter

The primal elements and the Stone itself *look* like different states of matter. They are *amazing* substances: radiant, simultaneously liquid and dry, extremely active. They do not at all resemble a simple distillate or alloy. In the Renaissance they were described as radiant stones, nowadays they sound like radiations, suggesting Gurdjieff's octaves of crucial materiality at which matter turns into energy, energy into consciousness, and consciousness into soul.

In a curious novel by a Frater Albertus, called *The Alchemist of the Rocky Mountains*, by implication at least, non-fictional, a magus who has been busy making and stockpiling gold somewhere in Utah invites naive but spiritually receptive guests from Los Angeles, and he gives them a tour of his laboratory in the desert. He is a traditional alchemist, but, at one point he explains that "our stone is not exactly identical with the one of the alchemists of the middle ages. Theirs was a crude yellow colored mineral that, when added to molten metal, was absorbed and brought about the transmutation. Ours, by comparison, is a glass-like crystal that radiates light; and any metal coming in the field of its rays will be transmuted into the next higher specimen, such as copper into silver and silver into gold."[122]

Later, he shows them his Stone, which turns out to be a mirror into which he suddenly disappears. The scene continues:

> "No one was looking into the mirror anymore. All five had penetrated the glass and were part of another sphere of existence. In fact, none of them were in the alchemist's laboratory at that time. The sensation each experienced separately from one another was nevertheless a joined experience. All four, in their own frame of mind, saw the alchemist in a high mountainous place covered from its icy peaks to the lower slopes with eternal snow. It was not as lush a place as James Hilton described in his book, *Lost Horizon*,...but there was a similarity, especially in a stately rock-built mansion-like structure nestled in a volcanic valley. From on top of the surrounding mountains, one could not see very much because warm air rising from the crater lake and its few companion geysers left a cloud blanket over the valley.
>
> "At first it appeared that the constant blanket of clouds would not let the bright sun shining above it penetrate to the large valley below. But a gentle air caused by the turbulent mixture of warm and cold air caused continuous pockets of clear sky, allowing the blue sky to be seen in all its bright and clear brilliance."[123]

The alchemist explains that a fluctuation in polarity allows simultaneous mental and physical changes; the alchemical transformation is more than just the fissioning of visible gold; it is tuning the landscape to its lushest and most vibrant aspect.

At least we know that the alchemical state of matter cannot be confused with conventional chemistry. When chemistry emerged from alchemy it took certain aspects with it forever, but it did not touch the production of spiritualized matter—and this remains of interest to twentieth-century alchemists as a real thing not a metaphor, *even if it does not exist*.

> Stephanos: "For these melted and metallic bodies, when reduced to ashes, are joined to the fire and again made spirits; for the fire gives freely its spirit to them. As they manifestly take it from the air that makes all things, just as it also makes men and all things, thence is given to them a vital spirit and soul. So also the fusible bodies, reduced to ashes with the metallic bodies, recover their soul by a certain method, as if becoming akin to the fire. And likewise all the elements have creations, destructions, changes, and restorations from one to another."[124]

On the one hand, this would seem to be a clear statement of change by heat and chemical reduction; on the other hand, the heat is associated with a vitality that it does not have as fire alone. The fire has a "spirit."

> Kleopatra: "The waters, when they come, awake the bodies and the spirits that are imprisoned and weak. For they again undergo oppression and are enclosed in Hades, and yet in a little while they grow and rise up and put on various glorious colors like the flowers in spring and the spring itself rejoices and is glad at the beauty they wear.

"For I tell this to you who are wise. When you take plants, elements, and stones from their places, they appear to you to be mature. But then are not mature till the fire has tested them. When they are clad in the glory from the fire and the shining colour of it, then rather will appear their hidden glory, their sought-for beauty, being transformed to the divine state of fusion. For they are nourished in the fire and the embryo grows little by little nourished in its mother's womb; and when the appointed month comes near is not held back from coming out. Such is the procedure of this worthy art. The waves and surges one after another in Hades wound them in the tomb where they lie. When the tomb is opened they come out from Hades as the babe from the womb."[125]

Alchemy is at once a paraphysical science and an art; it involves a way of life, a continuous vision of the living stone, the animate sun, the source within fire, the frustrated perfection of metals and gems, the delicate flower-like crystals of quartz and campylite, the rose and sunflower as gold, the wild spurge as copper. Even if the Stone is never actually achieved or experienced directly, it can be honored as a spirit within all nature, an ongoing aspect of creation itself. It *is* experienced in the energy of the atmosphere, the flow of life-substance through the fields, and the throb of breath and blood in one's own alembic. The Stone is a numinous object, like a flying saucer, but it occurs mostly in daylight and as an inward aspect of cosmic solar light. The alchemical waters, as in the fairy tale of "Rumplestiltskin," do truly hang between straw and molten lava.

A few months after finishing the previous version of this essay I was travelling across the country with my family, and we stopped in Salt Lake City to visit relatives. I decided to try to find Frater Albertus. An address in the phone book took me to an ordinary residential street by a highway, and I arrived with a carload of kids (my own and their cousins). I told them that the real magical center of Salt Lake was not the Mormon Temple but this undistinguished looking house. A woman let us in and briefly showed us around. We saw a modern laboratory hung with beautiful qabbalistic paintings, tarot cards, and classical alchemical scenes of the bloody king and his court. The effect was powerful—that the mystery should be present in the heart of our suburban tracts.

We were then directed to the unincorporated outskirts of the city, and after driving some fifteen miles through a mixture of fields and small industrial developments, we came to a barren clump of houses set in a flat treeless area—a few warehouses and homes, and the headquarters of the Paracelsus Laboratories. The waiting room was vaguely like a veterinary office; after fifteen minutes our whole group was ushered into Albertus' office for a brief visit. He sat at his desk, a small elegant mixture of a pharmacist and a priest, perhaps in his sixties. Either his presence was invocatory, or I myself had summoned the gods of alchemy by my desire. Despite the nuclear-apocalypse preaching I had heard on the car radio on the way out and the arid Utah land around us, I felt calm and slowly experienced a vision—that I stood in the Solar System in cosmic time and had been summoned to this meeting among the planets. Perhaps it was just a science-fiction high. "There *is* a collegium," I thought. I remember (otherwise) little of the perfunctory greetings that were exchanged: my promise to send him a copy of my book when it was published, his invitation to study with him, and my own response that it was not the right time in my life now. My answer surprised me, for I found myself responding precisely to his dignity. "I am raising my family now," I said, "but I will remember you." Even as I said it I realized for the first time that it was true, and also that I was speaking not to him but the magi themselves, that my promise was to them.

Two years later Elisabeth Kelley called me for the first time since our meeting to tell me that Frater Albertus was speaking that Saturday afternoon at the Oakland Airport. I was astonished and disappointed at the the site, but I met her and another student of alchemy in the convention room of the airport motel where Albertus was advertised. He arrived a little late on the plane from Salt Lake (he took the return flight after his talk). He spoke of the rebirth of alchemy, the significance of his medical discoveries, and then he turned the meeting over to his marketing manager, a Texan with a cowboy hat and a drawl.

The scenario was anomalous: a room filled mostly with well-dressed middle-aged black people wearing lots of jewelry; a spread of Sanka, coffee, and sugary pastries supplied by the motel; and an Austrian alchemist considered by some the reincarnation of Paracelsus, arriving from the Mormon capital and returning on the same flight; and finally a salesman diagramming on a blackboard how to make great amounts of money from buying and reselling distributorships in alchemical medicine, naming the different "alls" (oils) and giving their virtues in standard American advertising language, a mixture of superlatives upon superlatives with quotes from the ancients. But alchemy is, remember, an occult science; it will come in many guises, and it has a characteristic of looking always like exactly what it is not. Again and again the nature of our own society is revealed and alchemy remains millennial. I have no discrete opinion of Paracelsus/Albertus; I simply present my own brief glimpse of his presence on the Earth.

G-King and Queen

Alchemy contains a male-female mystery and, because it does, it suggests a sexual application of the alchemical process: the King and Queen who mate in the generation of the Stone become the alchemist and his woman; or in Chinese yoga the alchemist-King uses the Queen as the vessel for his experiment. The circulating fires of orgasm, withheld or not, are also the alchemical fires. The Red Man and his White Wife are married within the flask, and in the palace of the Rosy Cross, as Christian Rosenkreutz learned.

Iron is married to antimony, famously; when both turn red and single, they must be married again, to mercury. When mercury digests them they are married as one to red gold. The alchemist portrays this orgy in his flask: the naked King and Queen, wearing only their crowns, wingèd, bob in solution, he inside of her, copulating. Sol sits above his body, Luna in the water beneath hers. They are substances reacting, but they are creatures too. The sperm and egg of the human being contain the Sulphur and Mercury as iron and antimony. Men and women are flasks, and their offspring arise from fertilization of their minerals (as the spirit somehow penetrates matter). Alchemy implicitly accepts that the union of man and woman falls within its realm. In the words of Thomas Vaughan, "Marriage is a comment on life, a mere hieroglyphic or outward representation of our inward vital composition. For life is nothing else but a union of male and female principles, and he that perfectly knows this secret knows the mysteries of marriage—both spiritual and natural..."[126]

As John Dee proposed, the alchemist can experience the sacrament from within (himself the seed) or without as master of the forge. So he and Edward Kelly went from the laboratory to weird sexual experiments. And Rexroth reminds us:

"Thomas Vaughan and his wife, his soror mystica, wrapped in entranced embrace at the Pinner of Wakefield were, it is true, blundering into a region of revelation which they little understood and which, it would seem, eventually destroyed both of them."[127]

Nicholas Flamel apparently exercised greater wisdom. According to legend, he and his wife worked until they had enough gold to last several lifetimes, enough of the elixir to insure eternal life. Then they placed logs in their clothing and burned them, leaving behind fake corpses, and repaired to India where they continued the experiment of love and metals. It is a science-fiction story now; Nicholas and Perrenelle are the characters. They are alive today; they are alive in the first colony on the moons of Jupiter; and they are alive eighty centuries from now in another solar system. They are carrying their work back into the limitless cosmos from which it comes:

"The first time I made the projection, I applied it to quicksilver, and transmuted about one and a half pounds of it into pure silver, which was better than that from the mine...This took place on the 17th January 1382, a Monday, toward midday, in my house, in the presence of Perrenelle alone. Later, following my book word for word, I accomplished the work with the red stone on a similar quantity of quicksilver, again in the sole company of Perrenelle, in the same house, on the 25th day of April of the same year, at five o'clock in the evening, when I truly transmuted the quicksilver into almost the same amount of gold, which was clearly better than ordinary gold, in that it was softer and more malleable."[128]

Thomas Vaughan again: "The sun and moon are two magical principles—the one active, the other passive; this masculine, that feminine. As they move, so move the wheels of corruption and generation."[129]

Bernard of Treviso writes of a strange country, small enough that we can hold it in our hands, so large it encompasses the whole of creation:

"The Hagacestaur unites a pure and beautiful maiden with a hale and vigorous old man. The maiden and the old man are cleansed and purified. Then the man offers his hand to the girl, who takes it in hers, and they are conducted to one of these apartments. The door is then sealed with the same material as that of which the whole edifice is built. They will remain enclosed there together for nine full months, during which time they make all the splendid furnishings I had been shown (a large room hung with damask tapestries all covered with gold lace and edged with a fringe of the same...the material was iridescent green and gold, picked out with very delicate silver threads, the whole veiled in white gauze). At the end of that period they come out and are found to have been merged into a single body; and, having also a single soul they are now one and indivisible."[130]

Chemistry or sex; a woman or a metal: how is Rosenkreutz to know?

"Herewith I espied a rich Bed ready made, hung about with curious Curtains, one of which he drew, where I saw the Lady *Venus stark-naked* for he heaved up the coverlets too, lying there in such Beauty, and a fashion so surprizing, that I was almost besides my self, neither do I yet know whether it was a piece thus carved, or a humane Corps that lay dead there; for she was altogether immoveable, and yet I durst not touch her."[131]

Sexual alchemy provides a lesson: desire must be built up, contained in the athanor of self, and then transformed in the union with another. If the desire is given sloppy expression, is not contained and transformed, then no true union will occur. Burckhardt writes:

"Man and woman, who in natural fashion incarnate the two poles of the alchemical work (Sulphur and Quicksilver), can by their mutual love—when this is spiritually heightened and interiorized—develop that cosmic power, or power of the soul, which operates the alchemical dissolution and coagulation (*solve et coagula*)."[132]

H - Fermentation through Projection

The powder (or substance) made during the first eight stages is strengthened and put to use in the final phase. Fermentation involves sowing the substance with a metal (antimony, iron, gold, or silver) in order to increase its capacity for transmutation:

"And therefore when the lion doth thirst/Make him drink till his belly burst."[133]

Exaltation, which follows, is a purer sublimation. Then comes multiplication, which increases the quantity (and perhaps the quality) of the concentrate. Philalethes explains:

"To the multiplication of the Stone, is required no labour, save only that thou take the stone, being perfect, and join it with three parts or at the most four parts of mercury of our first work, and govern it with a due fire, in a vessel well closed, that all the regimens pass with infinite pleasure, and thou shalt have the whole increased a thousand fold beyond what it was before the multiplication of it."[134]

The homoeopaths were also to increase the virtue of their remedies by diluting them in regular phases—not simply a multiplication but a series of harmonic transmutations. At a certain point no actual molecules of substance remained, but as long as the spiritual essence had been captured, it continued to increase through successive dilutions. The alchemical medicine is the forerunner of the homoeopathic potency. Lapidus says:

"The augmentation or multiplication of the Stone can be performed in two ways. (1) By repeated s lution and coagulation. This coagulation increases the Stone in virtue, (2) By fermentation, which added, then increases the Stone in quantity."[135]

Philalethes: "When the perfect powder, white or red, is taken out of the philosophical egg, it appears like the most impalpable powder, whose atoms appear more minute if possible than those in the sun's light, and yet it is very ponderous, like burnished gold. But when united to or mixed with a perfect body of its own kind, it appears like white or red glass...The philosophers advise us to project by gradation till projection ceases; that is to project one part of the tincture on ten parts and again one part of the latter on ten until after the last projection pure gold or silver comes from the fire."[136]

Projection, then, is the last stage, in which the material prepared in the previous eleven is used to raise the virtue of some other metal to silver or gold.

Yellow and red are the main colors of culmination. The red is the rubedo or iosis, the melting of the gold itself, the heat of sunrise and Sol's purest and most intense fire. According to the *Turba Philosophorum*, it is during iosis that the sun swallows the moon, and the king is reborn. This is not only the manufacture of Gold; it is an old European rite both J.R.R. Tolkein and C.S. Lewis remembered in their tales: Gandalf the magician and Aslan the lion return from their deaths with greater powers than before.

The cinitritas (xanthosis) is less clear. It may correspond to ripening ears of barley springing up in the flask, clouded on the glass, or Lully's "fixed salt of Urine," but despite its yellow color, it is not gold itself.

Barbault's alchemy (up to 1969) has been more medicinal than metallic, more inventive than traditional, so his stages do not correspond to these except in their general meaning. His work is also far from complete fruition, though he did follow an important side-experiment to its conclusion in 1960. He extracted from his ashes the first drops of a potion called potable gold (made by adding powdered gold and dew to his ashes, and heating with a bellows on a flame at regular intervals). The result was a greenish colored alkaline liquid with a pH of between 11 and 12. When he put this into a bath of dew for several hours, it took on a gold color. He then subjected the "liquor of vegetable gold" to laboratory tests, and no gold showed up. The solvent powder contained sodium, silicon, iron, aluminum, copper, magnesium, and boron, whereas iron, aluminum, copper, and magnesium dropped from the liquor. German pharmaceutical tests indicated a wide range of medicinal uses, especially in disorders of the heart and kidneys, but, for a reason not stated, the liquid defied analysis and was considered unreproducible.[137]

Barbault adds that a tincture can be made from any of the metals, and he recommends silver and antimony highly, the former especially for digestive maladies and poor circulation, and the latter for psychosomatic conditions, caused or worsened by materialistic living. There is no reason, he continues, why the full range of astrological-alchemical medicines described by Paracelsus should not be possible to repeat with such vegetabalized metals: mercury for nervous system disorders, copper for the glands, iron for the gall-bladder, tin for the liver, lead for the spleen and skeleton.[138] This is also the work of Frater Albertus.

Of the whole Great Work, Barbault contends, medicine-making is a mere epochal stopping point en route to the Stone. It is perhaps the greater complication and materialism of our civilization that requires such a long and subtle gestation. Our distance from the Stone has increased, so another scale of work is needed to bring it about. The mother solution continues to age and enrich itself, and, after twenty-two years, Barbault feels he is approaching—but has not yet reached—the second degree of perfection in the quest.

> "This year 1969, the sap is not very plentiful nor sufficiently rich, because two eclipses of Aries and the conjunction of the new moon with Saturn coincided with a frost that damaged plants on which we had been relying. It is therefore not certain that I shall succeed in bringing the substance to the second degree of perfection this year. At the same time, I discovered to my surprise that part of my Stone which I was able to preserve promised well—it was a dark mass, its surface covered with little crystals, and within the mass were quantities of stellate specks. Tradition leads me to believe that this means that there is mercury ready to emerge from its matrix."[139]

I - The Powder

A transmutative powder made the rounds of Europe during the sixteenth and seventeenth centuries, causing confusion and wonder. The modern verdict is trickery, substitution of gold for base metal by sleight of hand, the same verdict debunkers use for telekinesis and key-bending. Clearly the scientific and magical paradigms wrestled with each other throughout those centuries, and it is impossible to know through whose eyes we are looking at any one moment, even in the accounts of the same person. Newton, after all, was an alchemist too.

Edward Kelly received the powder quite by accident while staying at an out-of-the-way inn in Wales. The landlord of the inn had an old manuscript and two little balls that he had stolen from a Catholic bishop's grave. He had hoped that his learned visitor might be able to read the strange language. Kelly purchased the manuscript and balls for one pound sterling. The balls turned out to contain red and white powder, respectively, and the manuscript was of such technical alchemy that Kelly could not understand it. He contacted that famous hermetic and scientific scholar John Dee, and the two of them engaged in a series of magical adventures in the late sixteenth century. In the course of these episiodes Kelly made repeated public transmutations of other metals into gold. In one case, he transmuted a piece of metal which he cut out of a warming-pan, and then sent both gold and pan to Queen Elizabeth as homage and verification.

Their activities eventually drew the greedy and antagonistic forces of the time against them. After the powder was exhausted, they were locked in a laboratory by Maximilian II of Germany, and asked to make more of it. But they were unable, and Maximilian would not set them free. Eventually Kelly killed one of his guards and was imprisoned in a fortress. He fell when a rope he made of bedclothes snapped as he tried to escape, and he died of the injuries in 1597. Dee, meanwhile, returned to England, where his library, the best secular one in England, and laboratory, were burned by an angry mob accusing him of sorcery and necromancy.[140]

E. J. Holmyard has a description of Alexander Seton's transmutation with a powder of his own making:

> "Seton ordered a fire to be lit, the lead to be placed in the crucible together with the sulphur, and the crucible to be covered with its lid. The lid was raised from time to time so that the mass within could be stirred. Seton himself touched none of the materials or apparatus, but chatted with the others while the heating was in progress. At the end of fifteen minutes, he said, 'Throw this scrap of paper into the melted lead, well in the middle, and do not let any of it fall into the fire.' In the paper was a fairly heavy powder of a lemon-yellow colour, but so little of it that it could scarcely be distinguished... After further heating for a quarter of an hour, Seton ordered the miner to quench the crucible with water; which when he had done there was left a mass of gold equal in weight to the original lead. The jeweller attested to its purity, which excelled that of Hungarian and Arabian gold, and Seton said mockingly, 'Now where are you with your pedantries? You can see the truth by the fact, which is more cogent than anything else, even your sophistries.'"[141]

The Belgian scientist Jean-Baptiste Van Helmont participated in a transmutation of gold under very unusual circumstances. He was visited in his laboratory by a stranger who baited him into a denial of the merit of alchemy. Having planned this moment, the stranger offered to share with him a bit of the Stone itself. Van Helmont agreed to test it as long as the stranger was not present and he himself devised the experiment. The stranger was satisfied, and left, never to return. He required nothing, he said; Van Helmont's conversion would be sufficient.

So Van Helmont had his laboratory assistants melt eight ounces of mercury into a crucible. To this he added the powder; then he closed it with a lid. After fifteen minutes, he threw water over it, cracked it open, and found a lump of gold. He was shocked. He wrote in *The Garden of Medicine*:

> "I saw and handled the Philosopher's Stone. It was saffron-coloured powder, very heavy, and it glittered like splinters of glass."[142]

In 1666, another scientist, Helvetius, was visited in his home by a similar stranger who, after complimenting him on his latest book (which condemned alchemy), took out of his breast pocket a small ivory box which he opened to show a suspicious sulphur-colored powder. Helvetius expressed an interest in testing it, and the stranger said he required permission from his master and would return. But Helvetius had stolen a few grains in his fingernail, and he tested these on melted lead. They burned and stuck to the lead without changing it.

When the stranger returned, Helvetius admitted his theft and then reported the results. Nonplussed, his visitor attributed it to his failure to wrap the powder in paper or wax. Adding that he had no time to stop right then, he left for good, promising, however, to return the next day to help in the experiment. Although he was inclined to forget the whole thing, Helvetius was convinced by his wife to test the powder in wax. He found a piece of old lead piping, had a fire made, melted it, and placed the powder on it. Bubbling and hissing followed, and when the turmoil ceased, he had a lump of gold for which a nearby goldsmith offered fifty florins an ounce.

Elated and dismayed, he had it tested by the Dutch Office of Assay; the inspector said it was gold of the highest standard he had ever seen. Next he took it to the impeccable goldsmith Brechtel, who shredded some, dissolved it in nitric acid, and mixed in some silver. Then he melted the mixture down and separated it back into gold and silver. Not only did the gold not lose weight; it had increased, for some of the silver had apparently been transmuted by contact with hermetic gold.[143]

There are innumerable other stories, from the sixteenth through the eighteenth centuries, of alchemists, or the beneficiaries of alchemists, taking from their pockets little boxes containing things that look like "tiny splinters of fiery red glass" and using them to transform matter into gold. Then that tradition ends, and, on the other side of the bridge, we come to Cockren, Fulcanelli, Barbault, Albertus.

These stories have the ring of myth cycles, but to this day we can hardly say what alchemy is. If we had perfected our world by other means and were sure of our future, we might be able to cast out the ghosts and discard the failed arts and sciences. But we are not even close. Even as we will require the bugs and fish and weeds whose habitats we destroy, so we even now require the shadow-dancers and bumbling magicians of our global dream times. They too are becoming extinct at an increasingly hastened pace.

I am left with the feeling that alchemy will survive until its work has been done.

And the gifts of alchemy will be delivered, if not to our species then to creatures whose shapes rise spontaneously in the castle: sentient sea mammals and octopi and tarsiers. Yet I suspect that we will be the alchemists yet, for all the unresolved pairs and numinous beasts and five-pointed stars are ours. They arose from us, and we keep them with us even during a secular time.

When not abused, alchemy has a benevolence sensed by anyone who has come into contact with it—winged mermaids bear snakes in chalices and drowned lions lions surface as spirit suns. Even the King whose flesh is razed and whose very skeleton is dismembered and bleached returns with a doubly radiant crown. The lovers merge and become more than either of them alone. It is not a synthetic modern benevolence that overlooks who we really are and turns nasty when challenged. Alchemy is well-appraised of modern warfare and poverty and comes again and again from the darkness with hope and good spirits. It is mature enough to be mellow.

Alchemy is one thing that cannot be resolved until we are resolved. Until then the bird will fly about the alembic, the lion will arise to swallow the sun, the King and Queen will bubble up through distant star plasma, and, ever again, as long as we have no real sense of what it denotes in us, "one will become two, two three, and out of the third will come the one again as the fourth."

NOTES

Parts of this essay were written in the winter of 1972-1973 and published in the third edition of the *Alchemy Issue* (*Io*/4, enlarged), 1973, under the title "A Discussion of Alchemical Matter." It was rewritten and enlarged in the fall of 1976 and distributed in xerox form. A second essay was drafted in the spring of 1977, and the two essays were merged in summer-fall, 1978, to form the first draft of this essay which appeared in *Alchemy: pre-Egyptian Legacy, Millennial Promise* (*Io*/26), North Atlantic Books, 1979. The essay was then rewritten and enlarged again in the spring of 1983 to form the present version.

1 Rexroth, Kenneth, "A Foreword to the Works of Thomas Vaughan," in *The Works of Thomas Vaughan, Mystic and Alchemist*, edited by A. E. Waite, first published in 1919, reprinted by University Books, 1968; page 3.
2 Eliade, Mircea, *The Forge and the Crucible, The Origins and Structures of Alchemy*, translated by Stephen Corrin, Harper and Row, New York, 1971; pages 148-9.
3 Lindsay, Jack, *The Origins of Alchemy in Graeco-Roman Egypt*, Barnes and Noble, New York, 1970; pages 314-5.
4 Eliade, *op cit.*; page 54.
5 Lapidus, *In Pursuit of Gold, Alchemy Today in Theory and Practice*, Samuel Weiser, New York, 1976; page 18.
6 Reynand, Jean, quoted in Eliade, *op. cit.*; page 47.
7 Asher, Bahya Ben, quoted in *Alchemy Issue*, enlarged edition, Plainfield, Vermont, 1973; page 177.
8 Fribergius, Colbus, *op. cit.*; page 178.
9 Lévi-Strauss, Claude, "Structuralism and Ecology," Commencement Address given at Barnard College, New York, 1972.
10 Lévi-Strauss, Claude, *The Savage Mind*, anonymous translation, University of Chicago Press, Chicago, 1966; page 95.
11 Lindsay, *op. cit.*; page 75.
12 Paracelsus, *The Hermetic and Alchemical Writings of Paracelsus*, edited by A. E. White, first published in 1894, reprinted by Shambhala, Berkeley, 1976; Volume 1, page 170.
13 Jung, Carl, *Psychology and Alchemy*, translated by R.F.C. Hull, Pantheon-Bollingen Foundation, New York, 1953; page 22.
14 *ibid.*; page 35.
15 *ibid.*; page 299.
16 *ibid.*; page 135.
17 Lindsay, *op. cit.*; pages 217-8.
18 Bloch, Marc, "The Problem of Gold in the Middle Ages," in *Land and Work in Mediaeval Europe*, Harper and Row, New York, 1969; page 195.

19 Lapidus, *op. cit.*; page 18.
20 Cockren, Archibald, *Alchemy Rediscovered and Restored*, David McKay, Philadelphia, no date; page 61.
21 Eliade, *op. cit.*; pages 172-3.
22 Yates, Frances A., *The Rosicrucian Enlightenment*, Routledge & Kegan Paul, London and Boston, 1972; pages 44-5.
23 *ibid.*; page 198.
24 *ibid.*; page 147.
25 Lindsay, *op. cit.*; page 4.
26 *ibid.*; pages 387-398.
27 Heisenberg, Werner, "Planck's Discovery and the Philosophical Problems of Atomic Theory," in *Across the Frontiers*, translated by Peter Heath, Harper and Row, 1971; pages 10-12.
28 Lindsay, *op. cit.*; pages 391-2.
29 Barfield, Owen, *Saving the Appearances, A Study in Idolatry*, Harcourt, Brace, & World, New York, no date; page 25.
30 Heisenberg, Werner, "Wolfgang Pauli's Philosophical Outlook," in *Across the Frontiers*; pages 35-6.
31 Todd, John, "An Interview Conducted by Richard Grossinger and Lindy Hough," November, 1982 (the bulk of the interview, not including this section, will appear in a future issue of *Omni*, New York).
32 Rexroth, *op. cit.*; page 7.
33 Sivin, Nathan, *Chinese Alchemy: Preliminary Studies*, Harvard University Press, Cambridge, Massachusetts, 1968; page 182.
34 Ts'an T'ung Ch'i, quoted in *Alchemy Issue*, enlarged edition, pages 189-90.
35 Eliade, *op. cit.*; page 120.
36 Sivin, *op. cit.*; page 52.
37 Lu K'uan Yü, *Taoist Yoga, Alchemy and Immortality*, a translation of *The Secrets of Cultivating Essential Nature and Eternal Life* by Chao Pi Ch'en (born 1860), Samuel Weiser New York, 1970; page 54.
38 *ibid.*; page 11.
39 *ibid.*; page 28.
40 *ibid.*; page 131.
41 Rexroth, *op. cit.*; pages 9-10.
42 Sivin, *op. cit.*; pages 152-60.
43 *ibid.*
44 *Huang Ti Nei Ching Su Wên*, translated by Ilza Veith as *The Yellow Emperor's Classic of Internal Medicine*, University of California Press, Berkeley, 1966.
45 Cockren, *op. cit.*; pages 107-8.
46 Eliade, *op. cit.*; page 133.
47 Waite, A. E. *The Secret Tradition in Alchemy*, first published in 1926, reprinted by Samuel Weiser, New York, 1969; footnote on page 3.

48 Yurick, Sol, *Richard A.*, Avon Books, New York, 1983; pages 261-2.
49 Bergin, Thomas Goddard and Fisch, Max Harold, *The New Science of Giambattista Vico*, Cornell University Press, Ithaca, New York, 1970.
50 Flamel, Nicholas, quoted in Burckhardt, Titus, *Alchemy, Science of the Cosmos, Science of the Soul*, translated by William Stoddart, Penguin Books, Baltimore, Maryland, 1971; page 143.
51 Ssu-mo, Sun, quoted in Sivin, *op. cit.*; pages 147-149.
52 Ostanes, quoted in Lindsay, *op. cit.*; page 143.
53 *The Chymical Wedding of Christian Rosenkreutz*, translated by E. Foxcroft, reprinted in *A Christian Rosenkreutz Anthology*, compiled and edited by Paul M. Allen, Steiner Books, Blauvelt, New York, 1968; pages 69-70.
54 Kelly, Robert, *The Alchemist to Mercury*, North Atlantic Books, Richmond, California, 1981; page 81.
55 *ibid.*; page 3.
56 The Stein seminar was conducted at Goddard College, Plainfield, Vermont, May 1977.
57 Jung, *op. cit.*; page 152.
58 *ibid.*; page 313.
59 *ibid.*; page 170.
60 *ibid.*; page 77.
61 *ibid.*; page 37.
62 *ibid.*; page 219.
63 *ibid.*; pages 233-4.
64 *ibid.*; pages 228-30.
65 *ibid.*; footnote on page 230.
66 *ibid.*; page 246.
67 Burckhardt, *op. cit.*; pages 99-100.
68 *ibid.*; page 101.
69 *ibid.*; page 9.
70 See note 56.
71 Grossinger, Richard, "A History of Dream," in *Dreams (Io/8)*, second edition, Plainfield, Vermont, 1974; page 14.
72 Ssu-mo, Sun, quoted in Sivin, *op. cit.*; pages 38-9.
73 Jung, *op. cit.*; page 330.
74 Teilhard de Chardin, Pierre, *The Phenomenon of Man*, translated by Bernard Wall, Harper and Row, 1961.
75 Paracelsus, *op. cit.*; Volume I, page 222.
76 *ibid.*; page 224.
77 *ibid.*; page 229.
78 *The Golden Treatise of Hermes*, quoted in *Alchemy* by William Leo, Sherbourne Press, Los Angeles, 1972; page 124.
79 Paracelsus, *op. cit.*; Volume I, page 301.
80 Laye, Camera, *L'Enfant Noir*, quoted in *Alchemy Issue*, enlarged edi-

tion; page 198.
81 Artephius, *op. cit.*; page 56.
82 Paracelsus, *op. cit.*; page 90.
83 *ibid.*; page 284.
84 Burckhardt, *op. cit,;* page 130.
85 Jung, *op. cit.;* pages 134-5.
86 Leo, *op. cit.*; pages 134-5.
86 Leo, *op. cit.*; pages 134-5.
87 Paracelsus, *op. cit.*; page 249.
88 Jung, *op. cit.*; pages 280-2.
89 Lapidus, *op. cit.*; pages 133.
90 Hamilton-Jones, J. W., *Bacstrom's Alchemical Anthology*, quoted in Lapidus, *op. cit.*; page 81.
91 Lapidus, *op. cit.*; page 81.
92 Behmen, Jacob, *Primal Matter or First Principles*, quoted in Lapidus, *op. cit.*; pages 72-3.
93 Boerhaave, Hermann, quoted in Lapidus, *op. cit.*; pages 72-73.
94 Kelly, *op. cit.*; page 69.
95 Artephius, *The Secret Book*, quoted in Lapidus, *op. cit.*; pages 47-8.
96 Kunrath, Henrich, *Theatrum Sapientiae Aeternae*, quoted in *Alchemy Issue*, enlarged edition; page 199.
97 Marcantonio, Fra, *The Light Which Proceeds from Darkness*, quoted in *Alchemy Issue*, enlarged edition; page 199.
98 Vaughan, Thomas, "Anthroposophica Theomagia," in *The Works of Thomas Vaughan, Mystic and Alchemist*; page 23.
99 Ripley, Sir George, quoted in Jung, *op. cit.*; page 311.
100 Barbault, Armand, *Gold of A Thousand Mornings*, translated by Robin Campbell, Neville Spearman, London, 1975; page 39.
101 *ibid.*; pages 38-8.
102 *ibid.*; page 43.
103 *ibid.*; page 50.
104 *ibid.*; pages 52-3.
105 *ibid.*; pages 55-6.
106 *ibid.*; page 73.
107 *ibid.*; page 124.
108 Paracelsus, *op. cit.*; page 151.
109 Philalethes, Eirenaeus, *A Brief Guide to the Celestial Ruby*, quoted in Lapidus, *op. cit.*; pages 24-5.
110 Artephius, *op. cit.*; pages 63-4.
111 *The Golden Treatise of Hermes, op. cit.*; page 124.
112 Paracelsus, *op. cit.*; page 164.
113 Leo, *op. cit.*; pages 139-41.
114 Fulcanelli, quoted in *Alchemists and Gold* by Jacques Sadoul, translated by Olga Sieveking, Neville Spearman, London, 1972; page 241.

115 *ibid.*; page 255.
116 Klossowski De Rola, Stanislas, *The Secret Art of Alchemy*, Bounty Books, New York, 1973; pages 11-12.
117 Paracelsus, *op. cit.*; page 83.
118 Philaethes, *op. cit.*; page 148.
119 Cyliani, *Hermes Unveiled*, quoted in Sadoul, *op. cit.*; page 250.
120 Artephius, *op. cit.*; page 42.
121 Lindsay, *op. cit.*; page 244.
122 Albertus, Frater, *The Alchemist of the Rocky Mountains*, Paracelsus Research Society, Salt Lake City, 1976; page 118.
123 *ibid.*; pages 146-7.
124 Stephanos of Byzantium, quoted in Lindsay, *op. cit.*; page 319.
125 Kleopatra, quoted in Lindsay, *op. cit.*; pages 254-5.
126 Vaughan, *op. cit.*; page 34.
127 Rexroth, *op. cit.*; page 10.
128 Flamel, *op. cit.*; pages 180-1.
129 Vaughan, *op. cit.*; page 29.
130 Bernard of Treviso, *Allegory of the Fountain,* quoted in Sadoul, *op cit.;* page 94.
131 *The Chymical Wedding, op. cit.;* page 130.
132 Burckhardt, *op. cit.*; page 130.
133 Ripley, *op. cit.*; page 151.
135 Lapidus, *op. cit.*; page 146.
136 Philalethes, *op. cit.*; page 149.
137 Barbault, *op. cit.*; page 101.
138 *ibid.*; pages 113-4.
139 *ibid.*; page 125.
140 Holmyard, E. J., *Alchemy*, Penguin Books, Baltimore, Maryland, 1957; pages 204-9.
141 *ibid.*; page 125.
142 Sadoul, *op cit.;* pages 138-9.
143 *ibid.;* pages 140-4.